Political Electricity

POLITICAL ELECTRICITY

What future for nuclear energy?

TERENCE PRICE

Oxford   New York
Oxford University Press
1990

Oxford University Press, Walton Street, Oxford OX2 6DP

Oxford New York Toronto
Delhi Bombay Calcutta Madras Karachi
Petaling Jaya Singapore Hong Kong Tokyo
Nairobi Dar es Salaam Cape Town
Melbourne Auckland
and associated companies in
Berlin Ibadan

Oxford is a trade mark of Oxford University Press

British Library Cataloguing in Publication Data
Price, Terence
Political electricity : what future for nuclear energy?
1. Nuclear power. Political aspects
I. Title
323.7924
ISBN 0–19–217780–X

Library of Congress Cataloging in Publication Data
Price, Terence.
Political electricity : what future for nuclear energy? / Terence Price
p. cm.
Includes bibliographical references and index.
1. Nuclear industry—Government policy. 2. Nuclear power plants—
Government policy. I. Title.
HD9698.A2P675' 1990 333.792'4—dc20 90–43708
ISBN 0–19–217780–X

Typeset by Pentacor PLC, High Wycombe, Bucks

Printed in Great Britain by
Biddles Ltd, Guildford and King's Lynn

Preface

This book, written from the safe haven of recent retirement, is a personal and—so far as possible—non-technical exploration of the political and policy issues that have influenced the development of nuclear power. Part One describes the successes, failures, horse-trading, and infighting that make up nuclear power's history, taking nine countries as examples. Part Two reviews the main problems that now confront us. I make no claim to be exhaustive: a definitive nuclear history of the past thirty to forty years would require a dozen volumes this size. In any case, like all contemporary accounts, the book is unavoidably incomplete, since history did not stop at my cut-off date, June 1990. By then, fortunately, it was possible to make provisional judgements about two very important recent influences: the political consequences of Chernobyl, and concerns about the greenhouse effect. The Iraqi invasion of Kuwait came too late for inclusion, though the instability of the Middle East, its restored dominance in oil production, the inroads nuclear power has made into the oil market, and its contribution to energy supply diversity are all recurring themes.

The story that emerges is of a nuclear industry that has rarely been guilty of dereliction of duty, though it was undeniably complacent in not addressing sooner the causes of the public's entirely reasonable anxieties. The anti-nuclear lobby has been skilled in debate, and sometimes extraordinarily percipient; but less than fair in failing to acknowledge the industry's achievements and its willingness to learn from past mistakes. As for the politicians, the book contains many examples that show how the flames of controversy can be deliberately fanned when there are votes to be gained. The story has few heroes, but within the industry fewer villains than the public has been led to believe. I hope that my anecdotal selection of events and issues may help readers to form their own judgements, and make it a little harder for glib assertions, from whatever quarter, to go unchallenged.

It was difficult to decide what to exclude because of the exigencies of space, and it was with considerable regret that I limited myself to only a passing reference to the USSR, and then only in the context of the Chernobyl disaster. While that country has had its share of nuclear problems, the interaction between technology and normal democratic politics, which is my central theme, has been absent until very recently. Chernobyl, when it came, had the major repercussions in the West which are described; but its consequences within the USSR were far more radical. It destroyed the myth of Communist Party omnicompetence even more surely than the recurring food crises. By drawing attention to the likely nature of nuclear war, it brought forward a new attitude to *détente* and disarmament. We know that the disaster has engendered a fierce nuclear debate within the USSR which mirrors that in the West. In time there should be a fascinating nuclear-political history of the Soviet Union to be written.

The book could not have been completed without the generous help provided by the many to whom I went for advice and comment. I particularly wish to thank my former colleagues Jan Murray, Mary Acland-Hood, Charu Jasani, Judy Sellers, Peter Bird, and Tony Hay for their unfailing courtesy in the face of frequent demands for information; Peter Agrell, Lewis Baker, Roger Beetham, Umberto Belelli, Fred Bonner, Jawahar Chakravatti, Vic Crocker, Barrie Dale, James Eggins, Denis Fakley, David Fischer, Peter Fischer, Lennart Fogelström, Claude Gaboreau, Bertrand Goldschmidt, Peter Hubbard, Harry Hara, Peter Jones, Barry Lloyd, Geoffrey Long, Tom McInerney, Nigel Monckton, Sebastian Pease, Michael Price, Geoffrey Roberts, Lewis Roberts, Carsten Salander, Donata Saluzzi, David Sowby, John Stather, Erik Svenke, Peter Vinter, Heinz Wagner, Philip Watts, Tom Wigley, Carl-Erik Wikdahl, and John Wright for reading earlier drafts; Reuben Clark, Warren Donnelly, John Gaunt, Loring Mills, and John Siegel for a mountain of advice on the American scene; and Tom Sawyer, Andrew Stirling, and members of the Natural Resources Defense Council for educating me about the anti-nuclear view. To all these, and the many others who made this book possible, my sincere thanks.

T.P.

Jordans, Buckinghamshire, England.
August 1990

Contents

NOTE ON REFERENCES

Figures in square brackets within the text refer to the numbered entries in the list of References.

PART ONE
POLITICAL HISTORIES

1   The Broad Issues

THE history of energy is the story of the human race itself. Man has always sought to supplement his puny muscles by whatever means he could find: horses, elephants, tides, wind, water-mills, slaves. The industrial revolution brought him steam power, and a huge leap in his ability to command nature. The widespread use of electricity and the internal-combustion engine followed. Once the fission of uranium had been discovered in January 1939, it was inevitable that attempts would be made to harness nuclear energy not only for military purposes in the war which immediately followed, but for civil use—the generation of electricity—as well. Having succeeded in creating a major new energy resource, it is not in man's nature to forgo such a prize.

But there is no concealing the difficulties: the accidents at Windscale, Three Mile Island, and Chernobyl have seen to that. There are widespread and deeply felt anxieties about radiation. No one can see or feel it. Few understand it. In sufficient intensity it can kill. It reinforces the anxiety we all feel about cancer. We fear genetic risk to our descendants. The public is sceptical about the feasibility of safely storing highly radioactive nuclear waste. There is anxiety about the problem of nuclear-weapons proliferation, stemming from an uneasy suspicion that a stronger connection may exist between civil nuclear energy and armaments than is willingly admitted. It is difficult to forget Hiroshima, even though many Japanese have come to terms with the atom. When even energy experts disagree over the economics of nuclear power, ordinary people not surprisingly wonder whether it is worth the bother of continuing.

The question comes twenty years too late. A quiet revolution has been taking place in the production of electricity. Nuclear power is already part of the everyday life of industrial society, and it would be squandering resources to return to a world which no longer relied on its contribution. France is already generating 74 per cent of her electricity by nuclear means, a remarkable increase over the 1977 figure[1] of only 8 per cent. Thirteen countries are above the 25 per cent mark (Table 1.1). In the Third World Taiwan and Korea are well up with the leaders. In the world as a whole nuclear power in 1988 produced[2] almost exactly as much electricity as was generated from all sources in 1957—both about 1800 terawatt-hours (one terawatt-hour is one thousand million kilowatt-hours).

Table 1.1 Nuclear electricity generation (end 1989)

	Operating nuclear capacity		Nuclear % of electricity production
	No. of units	GWe	
United States	110	98.3	19.1
France	55	52.6	74.6
USSR	46	34.2	12.3
Japan	39	29.3	27.8
Germany (FRG)	24	22.7	34.3
Canada	18	12.2	15.6
United Kingdom	39	11.2	21.7
Sweden	12	9.8	45.1
Spain	10	7.5	38.4
Korea, Rep. of	9	7.2	50.2
Belgium	7	5.5	60.8
Taiwan, China	6	4.9	35.2
Czechoslovakia	8	3.3	27.6
Switzerland	5	2.9	41.6
Bulgaria	5	2.6	32.9
Finland	4	2.3	35.4
Hungary	4	1.6	49.8
World TOTAL:			
operating	426	318	
in construction	96	79	

Notes: (1) One gigawatt electrical (GWe) is equal to one thousand megawatts (MWe), or one million kilowatts. It is a convenient unit in this context, since a large modern nuclear station produces about this amount of power. For comparison the total generating capacity of the USA in 1988 was 630 GWe. (2) Nuclear power is expected to supply 23.8 per cent of OECD electricity in 1990, and then decrease slightly to 22.7 per cent by 2000 as some older reactors are retired[3]. Total nuclear electricity production in 1989, worldwide, was 1,854 TWh—about 17 per cent of electricity from all sources.

Source: Reference 2.

The impact of nuclear electricity on the world economy is already substantial. Without counting the 44 GWe in Eastern Europe, the 260 GWe now installed in OECD are the energy equivalent of something like 500–600 million tonnes of coal per year, or around 8 million barrels of oil per day—40 per cent of the output of OPEC in mid-1988. While other factors contributed to the decline in the level of oil prices in real terms following the second oil price shock of 1979, the displacement of significant quantities of oil by nuclear energy has been acknowledged[4] by OAPEC, the Organization of Arab Petroleum Exporting Countries, to have had a major influence. It follows that the growth of nuclear electricity has helped to avoid further oil-induced inflation, and so materially safeguarded the living standards of the industrial world.

The policy objectives of leading industrial countries to save oil are quite explicit: Japan[5, 6] reduced her dependence on oil from 77 per cent of her primary energy in 1973 to 58 per cent in 1989. For electricity generation the change has been even more striking: in France, in 1973, the year of the first oil price shock, oil and gas accounted for 46 per cent of her electricity; by 1990 the figure[1] was planned to fall to 2 per cent.

Behind these statistical trends is a significant shift in favour of electricity as a preferred form of energy: electricity consumption is growing faster than other energy sectors in industrialized economies[7]. It is therefore doubly significant that the cost of nuclear electricity is insensitive to the cost of the raw material, uranium, which at the long-term prices ruling in the late 1980s contributed only 10 per cent to the cost of power. Given the nuclear industry's confidence in the adequacy of uranium supplies for at least the next four decades, it follows that any country with a large nuclear programme can count on electricity at costs which will remain relatively stable in constant-money terms for the foreseeable future—costs which in many countries are broadly competitive with other forms of electricity generation. Despite this, the official Swedish policy since 1987 has been to abandon nuclear power by 2010, starting in the mid-1990s, not for economic but for political reasons. It is doubtful whether this policy will survive, once the Swedish public has fully weighed the costs of changing over, and the potential economic risks of forgoing stable nuclear electricity prices.

What is striking about the impressive growth in installed nuclear generating capacity that has already taken place is how much it is at variance with the popular image. At the beginning of 1990 there were 426 electricity-producing reactors spread around the world, and another 96 under construction. Yet many believe that 'nuclear power is dead', particularly in the United States, which was its cradle—when in fact there are about the same number of reactors there as in the whole of Western Europe. Many Australians oppose the export of uranium on the grounds that it contributes to nuclear weapons proliferation, but remain in ignorance of the treaty measures, backed by international inspection, which have existed for many years to give warning if there is real danger of that happening. And the misleading view is widespread that no satisfactory solutions can ever exist to the technical problem of disposing of nuclear waste.

The explanation does not lie simply in public reactions to Chernobyl. These views were already heard well before that disaster took place at 1.23 a.m. on 26 April 1986. Behind this striking disparity between perception and reality lies a nexus of interwoven economic, political, and technological events which became mutually reinforcing almost by accident. Their interplay is our subject.

Early history

The engineering effort to extract energy from the fission of uranium began immediately after its discovery in January 1939. Fission— the breakup of a uranium atom—is accompanied by the production of heat, which can be used to raise steam to turn a turbine, and so power an electric generator. But the initial motivation was military: as a by-product of fission a new element, plutonium, is formed, which can be used as the explosive material in nuclear weapons (as we shall see later, it also has peaceful uses in nuclear reactors). In the early reactors about one gram of plutonium was produced for each megawatt-day of heat generated by the fission process. If a few kilograms were needed for a weapon, and if a few hundred weapons were required within a few years for an arsenal, then a major weapons state would clearly need several reactors all generating several hundred megawatts of heat.

In the early stages the effective use of the heat was immaterial— in fact it was something of a nuisance, because to keep a reactor operating safely without melting the heat had to be extracted continuously and reliably. But engineers have a professional horror of throwing away potentially useful energy, and it did not take long after the end of World War II for the next developments to take place. The years 1954–7 were a period of striking progress. The Calder Hall station was opened in the United Kingdom in October 1956. It was 'dual purpose' in the sense that the electricity it produced—50 MWe from each of four reactors—helped to reduce the cost of military plutonium production. Calder Hall became the prototype of the purely civil advanced gas-cooled family* of reactors (AGRs). In the Soviet Union a small demonstration reactor producing 5 MWe had been opened in 1954 at Obninsk, near Moscow. It became the progenitor of the RBMK reactor type which Chernobyl later made notorious. In the United States much of the running was made by the Navy engineers working under Admiral Rickover, who developed the pressurized-water reactor (PWR) which first powered the prototype nuclear submarine *Nautilus* in 1955. A scaled-up land-based version started producing electricity at Shippingport, Pennsylvania, at the end of 1957. The PWR has since become the most popular type of reactor; and the output per unit has grown enormously, to today's figure of around 1.3 GWe, equivalent to 1.7 million electrical horsepower.

Despite the public acclaim which surrounded the early steps towards harnessing the atom to make useful power, nuclear energy initially found it hard to compete with coal and oil for electricity production. In submarine propulsion the freedom from needing oxygen for combustion was giving nuclear boats an entirely new underwater capability, while in Russia nuclear-powered ice-breakers were able to carry out missions requiring quantities of fuel which conventional vessels could not possibly carry. But civil nuclear reactors do no more than produce electricity, identical in every respect to that produced from coal, gas, oil, hydropower, geo-thermal heat, wind, or solar cells. Competition from these other sources is clear and explicit. Moreover, except in a few exceptional cases, electrical utilities have no special commitment in favour of nuclear power. Indeed, they have a duty towards the public to be

---

* The non-technical reader may find it helpful to glance at the Technical Appendix, which describes the various reactor families and the relevant physical processes.

neutral, in the sense that they should not particularly care what technical means are used to discharge their obligation to produce electricity, provided they are safe, cheap, and reliable. So to make real progress nuclear power first had to be much closer to holding its own in these respects.

It was necessary to wait until 1965 before reactor orders reached a significant level. Western countries ordered only 1 GWe of nuclear generating capacity in the first half of the sixties, but over 23 GWe in the second. It was, however, a false dawn. Competition from generation from oil and natural gas grew, as the already low price of hydrocarbon fuel fell even further as the 1960s progressed. The nuclear programme was also held back by construction delays and steadily more stringent safety requirements, which added to the cost. But by 1970 confidence had been re-established, and orders began to grow again. In 1970 reactors totalling 25 GWe were ordered worldwide, 45 GWe in 1971, 65 GWe in 1972—all this, interestingly, before the dramatic events of 1973 led to the first oil-price shock[8].

That shock occurred after a period of rapidly rising oil consumption—up 70 per cent in the eight years to 1973. By then OPEC was producing half the world's oil. With supply dominance came political power. Against the turbulent background of the Middle East it could be only a matter of time before an upset occurred. When the first oil shock came following the Yom Kippur War in 1973 the immediate reaction was that the way was now open to the full exploitation of nuclear energy's potential. It seemed a natural conclusion. One quarter of OECD's electricity generation came from oil. As electricity consumption had been growing in all the industrial countries for many years at 6–7 per cent compound per year—doubling in a single decade—there was understandable anxiety about security of energy supplies.

The sharpest reaction occurred in France, which has little oil or coal, except low-grade lignite. That country had begun its nuclear programme with gas-cooled reactors similar to those developed in the United Kingdom; but in 1968–9 a switch had been made to pressurized-water reactors, initially of an American design. At first orders were at the modest rate of one or two PWRs per year; but everything changed with the oil shock, which brought home to France her special economic vulnerability. There was an astonishing acceleration in the pace of the nuclear programme. The result was that by 1987 there were 50 French reactors, with a combined output twice that of her entire national grid at the start of the programme. The whole of the base-load is now taken by nuclear power, and even part of the peak-load (where the economics are more demanding for high capital-cost nuclear installations because of only part-time use). No other country has matched her single-minded pursuit of an agreed national energy objective. Not every country has the political institutions which enable such an objective to be formulated!

Other countries did not fare so well. What was not immediately understood was the macro-economic effects of the huge increase in oil prices imposed by OPEC. The price rose from 3 dollars per barrel prior to the October 1973 war to nearly 12 dollars by Christmas of that year; and following the 1978 Iranian crisis prices rose further to over 30 dollars. This imposed what was in effect a massive tax on the industrial economies, created a major inflation, and halted economic growth for some years. By 1975 economic activity, far from continuing to grow as the pattern of nuclear ordering implicitly assumed, had already begun to decline. Even when growth resumed some years later it was at a much lower level. Consequently many of the nuclear power stations that had been ordered on the assumption that generating capacity would continue to double every ten years were suddenly found to be redundant, and large numbers were cancelled. Only in France and a few other countries was this demand constraint overridden by deliberate government-backed policies of changing to nuclear electricity generation to improve security of energy supplies.

It took time for the unpalatable economic reality to be recognized by the generating industry. With the long lead times for new plant construction there was understandable reluctance to cancel stations already started. But this slowness to react to changed economic circumstances only added to the problems, which were to dog the industry for nearly a decade and a half. The unwillingness even of governments to accept the prospect of reduced demand is illustrated by OECD's forecasts[9]. OECD's 1975 figures for anticipated nuclear electrical capacity for the year 1990—only fifteen years ahead—have since proved to be more than three times the true figure (the forecast for OECD countries was from 875 to 1002 GWe; compare with Table 1.1).

This general but unfounded over-optimism not only delayed the necessary corrective action, but led to a severe liquidity crisis in the American electrical generating industry which helped to prepare the ground for the subsequent spate of cancellations. After continuing for many years, these cancellations resulted by the mid-1980s in the widespread view that nuclear power, at least in the USA, was about to be abandoned. Few noticed that the whole generating industry had been affected. It was not that nuclear power-stations *per se* were not needed, but rather that for some time there was no immediate need for new power stations of any kind: no less than 70 coal-fired stations were also cancelled in the United States in the ten years from the mid-1970s. But the perception of nuclear failure, once formed, fed on itself and created a climate of public and commercial scepticism that has remained hard to dispel.

The special importance of the United States of America

No country occupies a more significant place in the history of nuclear power than the United States. None operates a greater number of reactors. It was the US Navy that promoted the first naval nuclear propulsion experiments which created the water-moderated technology that today dominates the world reactor market. But America was also the home of the environmental movement. Its beginning was signalled in 1962 with the publication of Rachel Carson's seminal book *Silent Spring*[10]. By 1970 the movement had received the accolade of President Nixon's unqualified support in his 'State of the Union' message, and had fired the imagination of the rest of the world. A United Nations Conference on the Human Environment was held in Stockholm in 1972.

Against that background the accident which took place at the Three Mile Island (TMI) power plant at Harrisburg, Pennsylvania on 28 March 1979 was of far more than local significance. Although half the reactor core was destroyed the ultimate safety barrier, the surrounding 'containment', functioned as intended and trapped the bulk of the toxic radioactive fission products. There was, however, great public anxiety, verging in places on panic in the hours and days immediately following the accident.

The absence of casualties—and indeed of adverse health effects of any consequence—did not protect the American industry from having to live with the consequences of TMI: reappraisal of safety requirements, many engineering modifications ('retrofitting') requiring reactors to be taken out of service, delays in licensing until higher safety standards were met, and inevitably a great strengthening of the anti-nuclear campaign. In the lawyer-dominated system of separated powers by which the USA is administered, which allows intervention by third-party objectors at local, state, and federal levels, those who were opposed to nuclear energy were able to mount a degree of opposition which greatly hampered further expansion.

The objectors were also assisted by other factors peculiar to the United States. One is a legal provision applying to most investor-owned utilities—not only those using nuclear reactors, and not only those concerned with electricity—which can prevent any revenue being earned until the test of 'used and useful' is satisfied. Unlike electrical utilities in most other countries, which can charge their customers for progress payments for investments in new plant as costs are incurred, many American utilities have been unable to charge a cent until the plant has actually gone on line. And that has had to wait for a final stage of pre-operational licensing, with the finished reactor standing idle, sometimes for years, while a further review of the design was undertaken. Following the second oil-price shock cash-hungry utilities found themselves having to borrow long-term at rates of 15 per cent or more. During the six or more years which even an efficiently managed construction programme could reasonably be expected to take—and because of extensive retrofitting and licensing problems few in fact met this timetable—interest charges could more than double the original capital cost of the station.

The result was that when many American nuclear stations were switched on, the rate charged to consumers necessarily moved significantly upwards, to allow recovery of the accumulated costs. The conclusion was easily, if wrongly, reached that nuclear electricity is intrinsically uneconomic. The truth about nuclear competitiveness lies elsewhere. Even tight site management and speedy construction—Florida Power and Light, like France, has trimmed construction times to six years or less—can be of no avail without a more rational approach to charging for the ongoing renewal of such a vital service, and without a less cumbersome licensing procedure. The licensing problem has now been recognized by the US Nuclear Regulatory Commission, which in 1989 published new rules which should minimize future licensing delays. There are further problems which particularly affect the USA. Whereas in other countries electrical supplies are provided by a few major organizations—sometimes by only one national entity—America has over 3,000 electrical utilities, mostly State- or municipally-owned. Even the 282 investor-owned utilities which provide three-quarters of the country's electricity are all small when set alongside Électricité de France, with correspondingly limited financial and technical resources. In 1988 no less than 53 were operating nuclear stations. Given this structure, the problems—the climate of protest, much retrofitting, the oft-delayed licensing hearings, and in some cases litigation—eventually had the effect of scaring many utilities away from any additional nuclear commitment. They were further discouraged by the introduction of 'prudency hearings', through which Public Utility Commissions—the bodies at state level which regulate the electricity prices of shareholder-owned utilities (though not publicly-owned undertakings)—could decide retrospectively whether past investment in nuclear facilities had been 'prudent', and therefore eligible for inclusion in the 'rate base' (i.e. the computations on which electricity charges are based). It may be argued that the Commissions were not necessarily wrong in taking this line, in the face of somewhat variable management standards in the American nuclear utility industry. But whatever the justification, the operational reality was that this kind of 'second-guessing' made utilities much more cautious when considering possible future nuclear investments.

There is yet another consequence of the fragmented nature of the US electrical supply industry: standardization of design becomes more difficult. Furthermore, standardization requires industrial collaboration, and that has been discouraged by US anti-trust law. Without standardization not only do construction costs go up—almost every reactor is a 'one-off' prototype—but climbing the learning curve, which is essential for safety, is also delayed. A beginning was made with standardization in the USA in the early 1970s, but all impetus was lost in the spate of cancellations following the oil-price shocks. In sharp contrast, the more smoothly-running French expansion programme, launched in 1973 in the wake of the oil crisis, opened the way to a policy of concentrating on successive 'campaigns' of reactor construction, all using a high degree of commonality, while progressively increasing reactor output to obtain the benefits of economy of scale.

While it has all become too much for most American utilities, it is worth noting that industrial fragmentation has not necessarily been a handicap elsewhere, nor even a problem in a different administrative context. A number of entirely successful nuclear programmes have been carried out by small utilities in Belgium, Finland, Korea, Switzerland, and Taiwan—countries where nuclear power continues to have the prestige which it once had in America. What is more important than size is competence—which depends on attracting and holding a highly professional work-force. After that come the considerable benefits of swimming with a national policy tide, not against it. Nuclear power is already sufficiently demanding without the further burden of having to surmount arbitrary political and bureaucratic hurdles.

Half a dozen special local factors have therefore contributed to the slow progress in recent years of nuclear power in the United States, compared with elsewhere: surplus generating capacity, Three Mile Island, the possibility of third-party intervention in the licensing process at a variety of levels, a regulatory regime that for too long was unhelpful, the fragmented structure of the electricity generating industry, the explicit withdrawal of political support during the Carter administration, and the indigenous hassle-free alternative of cheap coal. The reason for dealing so soon and in some detail with what might seem a purely national matter is that the slow pace of nuclear progress in the USA has been of worldwide importance. Its significance lay not only in the USA's position as the country with the largest stock of reactors (Table 1.1), but also in its seminal role in creating and exporting environmentally conscious activist organizations. These spread the message that the United States had abandoned nuclear energy, by implication inviting other countries to follow suit. A more correct statement would be that throughout the 1980s nuclear energy became entangled in quite complex ways with the peculiarly American institutional framework.

One reason for a degree of confusion is the difference between the fairly vocal nuclear-*construction* industry, which for many years has been short of new orders in the USA, and the less publicity-minded nuclear-*operating* industry, with which this book is more concerned. The historical accident, that massive reactor orders had been placed immediately before the Yom Kippur War halted demand growth and falsified previous planning assumptions, left the US nuclear-construction industry with little to do in the

.980s. It kept itself occupied with completing existing orders and retrofitting to meet developing safety requirements (the reactor construction industry elsewhere was a little more fortunate). Meanwhile, as reactors were brought into service, the USA's nuclear-operating industry was growing steadily if unspectacularly. Though the position is less extreme, there is an analogy with that of the British railway construction industry in the late nineteenth century. Construction was largely complete by 1875; the construction industry had little left to do; but the operating side of the railways was fully in business.

It was only at the beginning of the 1990s that an improvement in the outlook for the US nuclear construction industry could be discerned. The lessons of the Three Mile Island accident were beginning to bear fruit in improved safety and operating efficiency. There was more than a hope of speedier licensing. A drive had begun to create a new generation of reactors with a higher level of inherent safety. A realization was growing that other forms of electricity generation also had special environmental problems. And additional electrical capacity would soon be needed.

The problem areas

The nuclear debate which has been taking place in all developed countries in recent years has drawn attention to the issues of economy, reliability, and safety. The underlying scientific concepts are still so unfamiliar to most people, the solutions so esoteric, that it has not been difficult for those who, for whatever reason, wish to call a halt to nuclear development to convince a substantial proportion of their fellow citizens that nuclear energy 'threatens man's survival'. If that were true it would indeed be a compelling argument against proceeding. Meanwhile, the nuclear-power industry has been so involved in repelling assaults on a day-to-day basis that it has not found time to argue the broader issues effectively. The prosecution has therefore succeeded to a remarkable degree, in large part by default of the defence. In addition, in several countries, the industry has been abandoned by the political authorities.

And yet the nuclear industry does have a very reasonable case; and the alternative power sources are neither as simple nor as economic as is often suggested. Nor are the practical alternatives always safer, though the dangers are of a very different kind. Quite apart from the ordinary industrial risks of coal-mining and oil-rig operation, it now seems probable that the consequence of continuing to burn oil and coal, pumping carbon dioxide into the atmosphere in the process, will be to change the earth's climate. Carbon dioxide warms it by trapping more of the sun's heat, as in a greenhouse. The sea will expand a little, like mercury in a thermometer. Melting of the polar ice could make things worse. Present estimates are uncertain; but we face the possibility that by the second half of the twenty-first century the rise might be sufficient to cause serious problems for many cities, and for low-lying areas like Bangladesh, the Maldives, or Louisiana (see Chapter 13). That would be only a beginning: there is a global catastrophe potentially in the making. Nuclear power does not contribute to the greenhouse effect, except indirectly and to a minor extent during manufacture. This factor alone provides a compelling reason for reassessing the arguments, for and against.

There are four main strands in the anti-nuclear case: the dangers of radiation; the associated issue of operational safety in the mining of uranium, in the operation of reactors, and in the disposal of waste; the dangers of nuclear weapons proliferation; and economics—the extent to which nuclear power can compete with other ways of producing energy. These points are examined in more detail in Part Two of this book. On all of them there is more to be said in the industry's favour than is commonly brought up in argument. It is not true that an irresponsible nuclear priesthood forges ahead in ignorance of what it is doing. Given the resources and intellectual capital that have been expended since 1950, in forty years of unremitting effort, a serious lack of professional understanding would indeed be astonishing. But the problem of bridging the gap between nuclear engineers and the interested, fair and neutral members of the public remains difficult, because of the nature of the subject.

The public has no broad corpus of general knowledge regarding *protection against radiation* to draw on, not least because it cannot be detected by our senses—even though every human body since the beginning of time has itself been slightly radioactive. But there has been a long history of industrial and medical involvement with radiation. X-rays have been in common use for the best part of a century. Radiologists and health physicists have learned from what happened to early workers with radium—poorly-protected surgeons fighting cancer with radium needles, and factory workers using radium paint for illuminating instrument panels and watch-dials. Even the simplest precautions were lacking: workers pointed the brushes with their lips, making ingestion inevitable. In sharp contrast, atomic-energy workers have been rigorously monitored in their work environment for the past four decades. In many cases their medical records have been followed up systematically after leaving the industry. There are also the uniquely valuable, though infinitely regrettable, statistics of human casualties at Hiroshima and Nagasaki. The human race does not throw away such hard-won information. Independent national and international reassessments are regularly carried out. Any apparently new indication of danger is immediately followed up—like the incidence of small numbers of possibly radiation-connected childhood leukaemias. It is hard to think of another industry where so much attention is paid to occupational and public health.

The second field which self-evidently needs constant attention is *engineering safety design*, to provide operational safety not only in normal conditions, but even when something goes wrong, or if the operators are confused. After the Three Mile Island accident the fact that an unexpectedly small proportion of the toxic fission products escaped from the partially melted reactor led to experiments which successfully explained why the outer containment had been so efficient. The results created confidence that a high degree of assurance could be given about limiting the consequences of any future accident to the immediate vicinity of the reactor building. Seven years later Chernobyl provided a stark reminder of what can happen when safety is not taken seriously. Unlike TMI, the Chernobyl RBMK-type reactor did not have a surrounding pressure-vessel—it was 'uncontained'. Moreover, in a nuclear sense it was dangerously unstable. The instrumentation was out-dated (when the Finns bought a different kind of Russian reactor they insisted on fitting German instrumentation). The control gear was slow to take effect, and at the time of the accident was positioned largely outside the core, where it was virtually useless, in gross violation of local regulations. The operators, who in order to complete a special experiment broke the rules in at least five other significant respects[11], clearly had no idea of the hazards they were bringing on themselves. They were not only criminally disobedient; they were seriously deficient in understanding. In all these ways what happened at Chernobyl was far removed from the best modern practice.

None of this was denied in Academician Valerii Legasov's splendidly objective and intellectually honest presentation to the international post-mortem[12] held in Vienna in the summer of 1986. It was a great human tragedy when he took his own life two years and one day after the disaster. We now know from an article in *Pravda*[13] that he had been worried about the RBMK reactors long before the accident. But the question remains why there had been so little discussion internationally of its potentialities for failure. The reactor's characteristics had been published years previously. A British visiting team had privately expressed substantial reservations after returning from a technical visit. The RBMK had even been used as an example of a dangerously unstable reactor design in the nuclear-engineering course at Manchester University. Its problems should have been thoroughly discussed with the world nuclear-energy community. The fact that this did not happen demonstrates the need for more open and effective safety discussions, in a forum which is professional rather than political—one where mistakes can be admitted. Chernobyl provides the strongest argument for *glasnost*. It was the suffocating secrecy of the pre-Gorbachev regime that made normal peer-group debate with other countries impossible.

The magnitude of the Chernobyl disaster released political forces which overrode these constraints. Within three years a new international industry-level body, the World Association of Nuclear Operators, was formed with the full support of the Soviet Union to facilitate the exchange of operating experience. In addition, the bitter surprise of Chernobyl strengthened Gorbachev's call for *perestroika*, made only two months previously at the 27th Communist Party Congress. Direct experience of massive radiation fall-out induced a sharp change in Russian attitudes to nuclear warfare, and so to disarmament. History may judge that some good came from this wholly avoidable disaster.

Follow-up action at government level was centred on the International Atomic Energy Agency in Vienna, where in September 1986 two conventions were adopted—one on early notification of a nuclear accident which 'has resulted or may result in an international transboundary release' of radioactivity, the other on international assistance in case of a nuclear accident or radiological emergency. The Agency also gave greater emphasis to safety studies in its own programme of research.

The accident revealed clear inconsistencies between the regulations of the different European countries governing human consumption of food suspected of being slightly contaminated with radioactivity, and led to their revision. The inconsistencies were evident even within the boundaries of a single country like Germany, where permitted radioactivity levels in vegetables passed as fit for human consumption differed in some cases by as much as fiftyfold between adjacent administrative regions. Differences were just as marked between different countries. On opposite sides of the Rhine cattle were treated very differently: they were allowed to graze normally by the Swiss, who after a careful assessment had decided that sheltering was unnecessary, but taken indoors as a protection against radioactive fall-out on the German side. In such ways the accident provided valuable opportunities for reappraisal. But it also made clear to the public that much learning was unfortunately still necessary.

The problem of *nuclear-weapons proliferation* is nowadays addressed through an extensive armoury of political controls, which are constantly under scrutiny. As in everything else, there is a learning curve, and experience serves as a test for regulations and procedures. The situation today is far more tightly controlled than it was in 1974, when the Indians exploded a 'peaceful nuclear device', the explosive material for which had been obtained using a Canadian type of reactor and heavy water from the USA. The explosion in the Rajasthan desert was modest in the scale of nuclear weaponry, but sent political shock-waves round the world. The two supplier governments most closely concerned immediately set up much stiffer controls. Like-minded governments, including the USSR, took similar action. The battery of controls created in direct response to the Indian explosion, and others that have developed subsequently, are described in Chapter 7. They have become a permanent part of the daily life of the industry, which knows it will have an uncomfortable ride unless the public can be assured that further proliferation will be the most extreme rarity.

The Swedish physicist Hannes Alfvén's caustic comment that nuclear power and nuclear weapons are inseparable 'Siamese twins' is not easily forgotten. The full potential of the nuclear-energy resource is attainable only if large-scale extraction of plutonium becomes a routine industrial operation. But plutonium is the potential weapons material that was used for the Indian explosion, and before that at Nagasaki. It will take many years without further incident before the public will be ready to forget Alfvén's remark.

Fourthly there is the issue of *economics*. It goes without saying that nuclear power must be well managed, from start to finish. The question is basically whether it can remain competitive even after meeting the considerable cost of ensuring a level of safety that is acceptable to the public. The steady growth of installed nuclear-generating capacity is some kind of a positive answer, a collective affirmation of confidence on the part not only of many utilities themselves, but of their political masters as well. It is a judgement which looks as much to the circumstances of the next twenty-five to thirty years as to present conditions: how the relative cost of nuclear power will move relative to that of the possible alternatives, and also of energy conservation (which is certainly not cost-free). Since the cost structures of these various options are all different, reaching the best economic choice is far from straightforward. It is necessary to make assumptions about electricity demand growth, capital, fuel, and operating costs, discount rates, operating life-times, insurance, waste disposal, and decommissioning costs—and about whether the considerable and unavoidable overheads can be spread over time and over a multiplicity of units. That in turn depends on whether a country has a strategic political commitment to nuclear power for reasons of energy diversity, or whether the accounts must always be drawn on the pessimistic assumption of possible early termination for political reasons. The extraordinary escalation of nuclear prices which occurred in the course of the British electricity privatization in the autumn of 1989 is most easily understood as due to a sudden change in the accounting treatment of capital amortization and of overheads, once it was realized that government underwriting of nuclear financial risks throughout a station's lifetime could no longer be taken for granted. Yet at the time the UK was regularly importing substantial quantities of cheap nuclear electricity from France, made by pressurized-water reactors almost identical to the Sizewell B project, which had overnight come to be regarded on the north side of the English Channel as seriously uneconomic!

There are some factors which evade analysis, notably the future cost which will be visited on the world's population by the 'greenhouse effect', created by the alternative of fossil-fuel burning. On every economic point there are abundant opportunities for dissenting views, which are regularly aired and exhaustively reconsidered at nuclear planning inquiries. For instance, the 'softer' fuel prices of the mid- and late 1980s have sharply improved the competitive position of coal. But electrical utilities are unlikely to forget that if nuclear power did not exist the additional demands on coal markets would certainly lead to higher prices: softer short-term prices do not automatically provide a sound argument for wholesale nuclear abandonment, when the planning time horizon lies more than a quarter of a century ahead. Economic issues form the subject of Chapter 6.

Facing the public

These problems have provided ready-made grist for the anti-nuclear movement, which had its most active period in the mid-1970s. It is a moving expression of the humanity of the race, and of people's desires to limit the growth of the polluting Megalopolis in which so many perforce spend their lives. Nuclear power is not the only target; but it is newsworthy and mysterious, the ideal 'flag-ship' issue. And it is easily linked with nuclear weapons, the target for the world-wide campaign spearheaded by morally impeccable organizations like the Campaign for Nuclear Disarmament, which have yet to be convinced that it would be safe to depart from Alfvén's view.

The environmentalists have had notable successes, which no one should begrudge. But at times some of them have taken lines which concerned and reasonable people, having some knowledge of the facts, must consider absurd—like the attempt in the 1970s to breed suspicion of 'centralized power' by linking the technically essential centralization of the electricity grid with the ridiculous suggestion that it was in some way necessarily associated with a police-state mentality. They have accepted uncritically the Club of Rome's view that 'zero growth' should become public policy, and opposed plans for expanding electricity supplies. Mrs Dahl, then the Swedish energy minister and herself a leading environmentalist, admitted in London in 1988 that this stance had been unrealistic. The 'Greens' have made inadequate attempts to grapple seriously with the ineluctable conflicts and contradictions of resource policy. They mostly enjoy a freedom from responsibility which is denied to those in the world of action. When they say that nuclear power is unnecessary—because with due attention to energy conservation the growth in electricity demand which provides part of nuclear power's *raison d'être* would disappear—they omit to mention the social and economic costs of any sustained movement in that direction. In any case, electrical utilities cannot behave like coercive Utopians: they have to meet electricity demand as it is, not as it might be after a period of 'conservation engineering'. They are in no position to reshape cities to benefit from the undoubted conservation advantages of 'combined heat and power' (CHP)— i.e. using the waste heat from power-stations for district-heating rather than throwing it away. District heating is widely used in northern and central Europe; in the UK, with a different political approach (and a milder climate!), it hardly exists.

The media remain alert to sniff out any whiff of incompetence in nuclear matters. Scandal and disaster are the keys to maintaining circulation: for the media 'bad news is good news'. And as becomes very clear from the histories which follow, many politicians are ready to oppose nuclear power if running on an anti-nuclear ticket is likely to win votes.

So the nuclear industries have formidable critics. They are not helped in their task of justifying their position by the difficulties of presenting such a complex and unfamiliar subject to a lay public which, though it may be ready to see fair play, is rightly suspicious of anything smacking of propaganda. The public is seeking assurance and certainty in a field where the information does not come readily to hand; and where the proper use of caveats is an essential part of stating the truth, and indeed a test of the author's honesty. The nuclear industries—at least those in democratic countries—have no alternative to telling as much as they know of the whole story, with all the admissions of difficulty which this may entail, against opponents for whom sweeping generalizations have for years effectively carried the day. The industry cannot escape this discipline, because any suggestion of 'being economical with the truth' would quickly rebound.

The presentational problems are unfortunately most serious in the greatest force for mass education, television, with its sad tendency to encapsulate complex information in 20-second 'news bites'. When time is so short, the studio chairman is king: 'Do you agree that all radiation is damaging?' 'Yes; *but* . . . '. The case is lost in those first two words. Unfairly; for what the nuclear expert would go on to say is that a substantial case exists that in practice there is no cause for the general public to be alarmed. The underlying problem of quantification, which should be at the heart of the debate, is one of the most difficult to put across to a public for whom radiation units and levels of safety understandably mean very little. We all grasp the difference between taking one and five hundred aspirins. Few know the corresponding facts about the units of radiation measurement: sieverts, grays, roentgens, and becquerels.

The industry has been slow to respond with public information packages, closer contacts with the press, and site visits and exhibitions. Two major reactor accidents in a decade have eroded its authority to act as educator in its own field. Its difficulties are illustrated by the attacks that have been levelled during public inquiries even at some national regulatory bodies and distinguished expert assessors, on the grounds that because they know about nuclear matters they cannot be objective. That is carrying propaganda beyond the point of reason: one would not relish being operated on by an amateur surgeon.

The outcome is what we see today—a curious ambivalence in a still-growing industry which, while professionally self-confident, nevertheless knows itself to be beleaguered. For too long it hoped that by lying low and operating successfully these problems would disappear. TMI called that view into question; Chernobyl blew it away. The industry is at last applying itself with some energy and skill to the task of explaining what it does, and why.

The central issue is not one of *them* versus *us*. The extent to which nuclear energy will be a part of our future is not a matter of a Faustian bargain between scientists and profit-dominated corporate executives, at the expense of the mass of humanity. The question is one for every member of the community. At bottom, it is about the best way of safely delivering electrical energy in the huge quantities demanded by modern society, at reasonable cost, with a high degree of safety, and with benign environmental consequences. Nuclear power is certainly not the whole of the answer; nor can all energy uses be dealt with via the electricity grid; nor are fossil fuels the only important contributors to the 'greenhouse effect'. But nuclear power seems certain to remain an important element in any rational approach to energy policy, and suggesting otherwise simply misleads the public.

Once a country—and there are already several—makes something like half its electricity using the nuclear option there is no easy return path. Controls will need to continue, just as they must over other potentially dangerous but essential industries, such as chemicals, pharmaceuticals, or aviation. Nuclear safety will stay on the political agenda for the foreseeable future. The origins of nuclear power will ensure that its political sensitivity will never diminish: we shall always need nuclear non-proliferation safeguards. But what has already been done on the political front to prepare for the decades and possibly centuries of nuclear power which lie ahead deserves to be better known.

2 Introducing the Nuclear Industries

THIS book is mainly concerned with the *operating* nuclear industries—reactor operations and all the backup which makes them possible—which is where most of the political problems arise. The reactor-*construction* industry also has some political involvement, through safety requirements and export licences, but is much less in the day-to-day political firing-line. Our interest is in how political issues affect the work of the companies which handle the seven steps which make up the 'nuclear fuel cycle':

  (i) *mining* and *milling* of the uranium ore;
 (ii) *conversion* of the chemically concentrated uranium into gaseous uranium hexafluoride; which is needed for
(iii) *isotopic enrichment*, which artificially increases the proportion of the rarer 'fissile' form of uranium, U–235, which is the essential constituent of nuclear fuel;
 (iv) fuel-element *fabrication*;
  (v) *energy production in a reactor* for as long as the fuel elements can withstand the damaging effects of radiation;
 (vi) optional chemical *reprocessing*, after a period of storage, to recover from the spent fuel elements any residual uranium or by-product plutonium (see Technical Appendix), both of which are still useful sources of energy—and at the same time to separate and package the highly radioactive residues produced while the fuel was in the reactor; or alternatively *storage*, without chemical treatment, for up to fifty years to allow the radioactivity to diminish;
(vii) and finally *disposal* where, depending on the engineering of the disposal facility, the nuclear fuel may be recoverable if needed again, or else remain permanently irretrievable.

Steps (i) to (iv) are known colloquially as the 'front end' of the fuel cycle; 'back end' refers to what happens after the fuel comes out of the reactor, steps (vi) and (vii).

Although it is young this is already a substantial industry. World trade in the basic fuel, uranium, amounts annually (1989) to around $2 billion. As this represents 10 per cent, or a little less, of the total cost of producing nuclear electricity, the annual turnover of the whole nuclear electricity industry in the Western world is already of the order of $20 billion. In broad terms the whole 'operating' industry and its industrial support involves several hundred thousand jobs spread around the world. Phasing-out nuclear energy, as some wish, could not be a simple or minor operation.

The first stage: Uranium

Since it became a strategic military and energy commodity just as World War II was beginning uranium has had a fascinatingly chequered existence, never far from the politics of non-proliferation, energy supply, and trade policy. It is also interesting for the profound effect it has had on the history of this planet. The energy arising from its feeble radioactivity has helped to keep the earth warm over the 4.5 billion years since its formation; otherwise it would long ago have become a cold sphere like the moon. We pay a price for this benefice in the form of the vulcanism and earthquakes which are the visible manifestations of a planet which is molten except for a thin crust a few tens of miles thick. In this sense uranium may be held responsible for thousands of deaths per year—though of people who would never have lived had it not been one of nature's constituents!

In its pure form uranium is a metal, of very high density: nineteen times denser than water, compared with eleven times for lead or eight for iron. It also has the largest and most complex atomic structure to be found in nature, which under the conditions found in a nuclear reactor results in an instability—the fission process—which as explained in the Technical Appendix is the basis for the controlled production of energy.

Uranium is a fairly abundant element—there are around 10^{12} tonnes in the top kilometre of the earth's crust. It occurs in a variety of mineral forms, usually in concentrations too low to be commercially exploitable. It is often found in coal: in the UK the average content is just over one part per million[14]—which means that many tonnes are discharged from the smoke-stacks of conventional power stations in the course of a year.

For a uranium deposit to be commercially viable its concentration should be above (and in today's market preferably well above) 0.03 per cent by weight. At such a low figure it is necessary for both physical and economic reasons to mine on a prodigious scale, as at the Rössing mine in Namibia. Rössing can shift over 150,000 tonnes of ore per day. Alternatively, low-grade uranium deposits can be successfully mined if other minerals are also present to share the production costs—as in the very large South Australian deposit, Olympic Dam, which as well as being a major copper and gold ore-body also contains a million tonnes of uranium. A number of very much higher-grade major deposits have been found in recent years: e.g. 2.3 per cent in the world's largest mine (judged by output) at Key Lake in Northern Saskatchewan; and up to 14 per cent at Cigar Lake, also in Canada. At such grades the penetrating nuclear radiation from the ore-body creates novel safety problems for the mining engineers when drawing up the mining plan.

In a few places geological conditions allow uranium to be dissolved directly by pumping weak acid underground, bringing it back to the surface, and extracting the dissolved uranium. With this 'in-situ leach' there is almost no surface environmental disturbance. Indeed, cattle can be seen grazing in the fields directly above one US ore-body. In more conventional mines the uranium-bearing rock is scooped up, or brought to the surface if underground, crushed, and then treated in an on-site chemical plant, or 'mill', to extract and concentrate the uranium. As a first step it is converted into 'yellow-cake' (hydrated ammonium or sodium diuranate), which is the starting-point for further treatment.

It has been said that 'uranium is where you look for it', and the remark contains a germ of truth. Certainly it is the countries which are developed and politically stable, and where systematic explo-ration has therefore been possible, that have so far provided the bulk of uranium supplies. One-third of the Western world's production comes from Canada (Table 2.1); about a seventh from the USA; most of the rest from South Africa, Australia, and France. Of the developing world only Namibia, Niger, and Gabon make sizeable contributions. Uranium production in the Soviet Union and the countries of Eastern Europe has been regarded as highly confidential, and no reliable figures have been available. Very little Soviet and Eastern European uranium has been sold on the world market—though this could alter following the dramatic political

Table 2.1. Western World Uranium Production, 1988
(thousands of metric tonnes of contained uranium)

Canada	12.3
United States	5.2
South Africa	3.8
Australia	3.6
Namibia	3.5
France	3.4
Niger	3.0
Gabon	0.9
Others	0.8
Western World TOTAL	36.4

Notes: (1) This Table does not include production from the Soviet Union, Eastern Europe, and the People's Republic of China. (2) There are two ways, both in common use, of describing the quantity of uranium: one *metric tonne of uranium element* (abbreviated as tonne U) is contained in 1.3 *short tons* (2,000 pounds) *of uranium oxide*, U_3O_8. The latter is used in North American mining, the former more commonly elsewhere and in reactor applications—and in this book.

Source: Reference 15.

changes in Eastern Europe, and the post-Chernobyl scaling down of the Soviet nuclear programme.

Chinese uranium began to reach the western market in the 1980s. The first Chinese long-term contract with a US utility was signed in 1988, when China's export potential was believed to be 700–1,500 metric tonnes U per year. Most western utilities harboured doubts about the country's reliability as a long-term supplier, and the events of June 1989 in Tiananmen Square showed that the political stability they were looking for did not exist. However, some still took a pragmatic view, and were prepared to continue business if the price was right.

Of the countries shown in the Table only three—the United States, France, and Canada—have substantial nuclear power programmes of their own (South Africa's is just beginning). There are around twenty other significant user countries in the Western world; so international trade is a built-in feature of the nuclear-fuel market. This is even more evident when we consider that organizations in four countries (USA, France, UK, Canada) offer conversion services; several (in the USA, France, and the USSR, and the UK/Netherlands/West Germany Urenco consortium) carry out enrichment; a number manufacture fuel elements; and two (in France and the UK) offer commercial reprocessing services. A consumer can select almost any combination of these suppliers, and a batch of uranium can pass over several frontiers during its journey from the mine to the ultimate disposal site. Most of the primary producers and providers of fuel-cycle services take a close political interest in what happens downstream from their point in the fuel cycle. Inter-governmental treaties apply non-proliferation controls ('safeguards') to the material they produce, to ensure as far as possible that only what the suppliers regard as permissible takes place (see Chapter 7).

The history of uranium production

For a century and a half after its discovery in 1789 by the German chemist Martin Klaproth uranium was mined on a small scale in Bohemia mainly for its use in ceramic decoration: its compounds can be used to make a rich variety of orange, yellow, green, red, and black glazes. It was also used as an intensifier in photography. A new commercial interest was created by the discovery of its natural radioactivity, and from 1905 it was mined in Bohemia and in the USA, and later in Canada, as a source of the daughter-product radium, needed for the 'Curie' radiation therapy for cancer. However, the discovery in 1913 of far richer deposits in the Belgian Congo (now Zaïre) ended the US radium industry by 1925, though the Port Radium mine in the Canadian Arctic did not close until 1940. Uranium mining continued in the USA throughout the 1930s as a source of the associated mineral vanadium, used in special steels. The uranium remained unused in the spoil dumps until the discovery of nuclear fission in 1939, when they became a valuable raw-material source for the American wartime military programme. Production restarted at Port Radium in 1942, and the Congo provided additional supplies[16–18].

After the war the military still needed uranium, and until 1961 procurement was handled by the Combined Development Agency, a tripartite body set up by the US, Canadian, and British governments in 1944. The CDA assisted Canada and South Africa to develop their uranium production—in South Africa as a by-product of the gold industry—and also sponsored the first Australian mine, Rum Jungle. The industry boomed, and by 1959 production had reached over 33,000 tonnes U, a figure which was not equalled for nearly two decades; but then the military requirement changed. The US cut back heavily on purchases at a time when civil nuclear energy was still years away. Uranium mining in Canada, Australia, and South Africa was hard hit. All but two of the eleven integrated mines and mills in the Elliot Lake area of Ontario were closed, and Canadian production fell[8] from 12,000 tonnes U in 1959 to 3,000 tonnes in 1965. The Canadian government offered some support to the industry via a government stockpiling programme, which accumulated 7,000 tonnes by 1970. South African production was helped by the fact that uranium was a by-product of gold mining. But nineteen out of twenty-six of its uranium producers ceased production, and output fell from 6,000 tonnes in 1959 to 2,650 tonnes by 1965. In Australia only one mine remained in operation—Rum Jungle—and this finally closed in 1971. Partly for domestic political reasons, it was almost a decade before Australian production restarted; so the surge in demand which came at last in the 1970s operated on a correspondingly narrowed production base.

Even in the USA the mining industry did not escape some damage, despite active support from the government: its production fell by half between 1960 and 1966. Government support included a minimum production guarantee for each mine, the creation of stockpiles, and the Private Ownership of Special Nuclear Materials Act of 1964, which created an embargo on imports of uranium, which was not finally withdrawn until 1983.

This first recession of the industry lasted only a few years, until the middle of the 1960s. By then increased interest in nuclear energy was beginning to come to its rescue. New mines were opened and exploration expanded. But countervailing economic forces were also at work. Oil prices were very low, and this encouraged electrical utilities to expand on the basis of oil-fuelling; while reconsideration of reactor safety requirements did nothing to assist the emergent nuclear industry. The result was that this second boom quickly petered out.

At about this time political differences between France and Canada made their own contribution to the excess of uranium production. In 1965 negotiations between the two countries had failed owing to fundamental differences regarding the political conditions to be attached to a projected contract for several tens of thousands of tonnes of uranium which were still in the ground[8]. France took her exploration efforts elsewhere, and these bore fruit at about the same time as new high-grade ore-bodies in Saskatchewan started to add to the surplus of uranium in the early 1970s.

The end of the 1960s brought better times for the nuclear industry. Power-reactor technology was at last making progress, and this was reflected in a steady growth in reactor orders, and in some exceedingly optimistic OECD forecasts[9]. There were indeed grounds for optimism: one hundred nuclear power-plants had been ordered in the USA by the time of the 1973 oil crisis. In all, electrical utilities placed forward orders that year for an astonishing amount of uranium, equal to four times the western world's annual production.

The oil-price shock was the signal for all energy commodities to jump in price. Uranium was no exception. The spot price in current dollars leapt from $6 per pound of oxide in January 1973 to $40 by April 1976. This increase, although large, was not in fact out of line with the general run of even non-energy metal prices at this time. Zinc rose eightfold between 1971 and 1973, tin fivefold by 1978, gold tenfold by 1982. Of these increases a factor of nearly three can be attributed to world-wide inflation induced by the oil-price shock. But in the case of uranium there were other special factors at work, which substantially altered uranium's trading conditions.

One was the general though ill-founded perception in the electricity industry that the sudden price increases for hydrocarbon fuels were likely to provide a ready-made springboard for nuclear power: OECD had been optimistic about nuclear prospects even before the oil crisis. Unfortunately, as we saw in Chapter 1, such predictions overlooked the additional influence of OPEC's new 'tax' on the economies of the industrialized countries. The result of the inevitable stream of reactor cancellations was the unloading onto the spot market of large quantities of uranium which had already been ordered under firm delivery contracts. The spot market, which peaked at $43 in 1979, fell back abruptly; it drifted down to $14.25 in April 1985, and continued to slide to below $9 in 1989, before starting to recover in June 1990.

Another factor pushing the price upwards in the 1970s was a significant change in contract conditions for uranium enrichment.

The enrichment phase is an essential step in the preparation of nuclear fuel for almost all power reactors, and up till then the United States Atomic Energy Commission (USAEC) had enjoyed a virtual enrichment monopoly in the western world. But by 1973 other operators were about to enter the market—notably the French Eurodif project, which started up in 1978. The USAEC therefore announced, in its own interests, a new kind of contract, with the purpose of ensuring full capacity usage for the Commission's enrichment capacity. Reflecting the USAEC's monopolistic attitude, this contract was very inflexible, committing utilities to firm deliveries of enriched uranium many years in advance, and imposing heavy penalties for cancellation or deferral. The utilities therefore had to rush to match their commitments with appropriate purchases of uranium, and orders on the mines grew accordingly. The USAEC's inflexible enrichment terms undoubtedly helped to drive up the uranium price.

The Westinghouse affair

Another almost simultaneous influence was the market's reaction to the discovery that contracts entered into by the Westinghouse company, to supply uranium on a massive scale to electrical utilities, had not been covered by orders on the mines. Westinghouse was at that time the leading manufacturer in the world of nuclear reactors and their fuel elements. The company had taken orders for uranium supplies as part of a package approach to reactor sales, and in the normal course of events such orders should have been covered by physical procurement. But the uranium price was falling, and Westinghouse instead waited, presumably in the expectation (prior to the 1973 oil and subsequent economic crises) that uranium prices would continue to be stable at around $6.50 to $8 a pound of oxide, or fall. Westinghouse's average contracted selling price was about $10 a pound[19]. The utilities' orders were for a total of 33,000 tonnes U, or 40 per cent more than the Western world's annual production at that time. Only 6,000 tonnes U were covered by Westinghouse's orders on the mines. 'Going short' on such a heroic scale would play havoc with any commodity, even though the obligations were spread over a number of years. The price weakened steadily, and the foreign miners found themselves bidding against each other for supply contracts in a market already shrunk by the US import embargo. Eventually a defensive producers' association was formed to assist in market-sharing, and so maintain a floor-price which would enable the industry to survive. The existence of 'The Club'—whose activities, though blessed by the members' governments, were contrary to US anti-trust law—became known, with awkward consequences for the producers.

So began one of the most celebrated international cases of the decade. It and its offshoots lasted more than seven years. It led to a whole chain of extraordinary events: the serving of Letters Rogatory on a number of foreign organizations; the issue of a regulation by the Canadian government prohibiting the disclosure of relevant documents; in Britain an appeal for a ruling to the House of Lords, sitting in its judicial capacity; the taking of the American Fifth Amendment by a British Knight of the Garter during a hearing in the American Embassy in London; an attempt on the part of the American trial judge to extend US legal jurisdiction into British territory, by inviting the London branch of one of the USA's most distinguished law-firms to disregard the instructions of the British government concerning permissible 'discovery' of documents; and the subpoena of hundreds of 'privileged' documents held in Washington under client–attorney privilege by the same firm, which had been engaged by the London-based Uranium Institute—an industrial association of uranium producers *and consumers*—to ensure that its activities complied with US anti-trust law. The great irony of the whole affair was that The Club was hardly necessary: a revival in nuclear orders as a result of growing confidence in nuclear power, upwards pressure on the uranium price following changes in USAEC enrichment contracts, and the further encouragement provided by the second oil price shock, were all only a year or two away.

Westinghouse came under pressure from electric utilities to deliver against its uranium contracts, but had to admit that its storehouse was empty, apart from about 6,000 tonnes U. The extent of the shortfall only became clear from actions for specific performance started by seventeen utilities in 1975. With the uranium price increases that were then taking place with extra-ordinary speed—heading towards $40 and even beyond—Westing-house was technically on the verge of bankruptcy, like many others who had attempted to play the commodity markets. The company began its defence rather unconvincingly by pleading 'commercial impracticability', based on a provision in section 2–615 of the US Uniform Commercial Code; but it was rescued by an extraordinary turn of events. An environmental group stole a set of documents relating to The Club from the offices of a mining company in Australia. They were sent to the Attorney-General of California, and were immediately published. This opened the way to a quite different, extremely innovative, and brilliantly conducted defence-through-attack. Westinghouse sued the various producer companies in US courts for criminal conspiracy and treble damages totalling $6 billion. With a sum like that in play life in the industry remained difficult, until the lawsuits were finally settled years later.

Westinghouse's target, The Club, was no ordinary industrial cartel. It had been formed with encouragement from the governments of Canada, France, Australia, and South Africa. It established a private agreement aimed at setting a floor under the price of uranium, and so preserving the industry until nuclear power was better established. According to the stolen documents such a possibility was first explored in a meeting hosted under the auspices of the French government by the Commissariat à l'Énergie Atomique in February 1972. Soon afterwards, in Johannesburg, a price-structure was agreed, allowing (with slight variations) for a rise from the current level of around $4.50 to $5.75 per pound of oxide for delivery in the following year. The arrangement operated in secret; but eventually its existence became known. It was first publicly referred to in an article in *Forbes Magazine* in January 1975 ('It worked for the Arabs'). By the late summer of that year, for the reasons already mentioned, market conditions had become much more favourable for the producers, and The Club was no longer needed. According to a statement issued in 1976 by the Canadian government it ceased to function in October 1975.

This, however, did not protect the producers from Westinghouse, whose legal actions (and some others which were related) dragged on until 1983, creating an enormous additional burden for the managers of the uranium-mining industry. Throughout Westinghouse continued to assert that the price rise to over $40 came about primarily as a result of the producers' actions. While that was a strong attacking argument for trial purposes, it did not stand up to close examination. Indeed, John Shenefield, when Assistant Attorney-General of the United States, concluded after a lengthy inquiry[20] that possibly one dollar only, out of the total price rise of nearly $40, could be attributed to the actions of the producers. It is one of the ironies of the case that a much more significant influence forcing up the price had been the various self-interested decisions of the American government's own Atomic Energy Commission and its successors regarding enrichment contracts. It is a further irony that the supposed justification for the anti-trust law underlying the Westinghouse litigation was the need to avoid restrictions on free trade; but so far as non-US producers were concerned, the 1964 import embargo had cut their links with the American market.

Further American influences on the market

The surge in uranium prices was eventually halted by a combination of factors: many reactor cancellations; nuclear fuel orders at a much lower level than had been predicted by OECD in 1973 and 1975; new mines coming on stream as a result of successful exploration some years earlier; and, as time went on, resale of the unwanted nuclear fuel, often at distress prices, by electrical utilities which had cancelled their reactor orders. When a reactor is ordered it is usual for provision to be made also for the initial fuel charge and for the first reload core. For a 1 GWe pressurized water-reactor—a normal size today—each initial reactor core requires the purchase of nearly 400 tonnes U, and reloads at the rate of a further 150 tonnes U per year. Thus the cancellation of over fifty reactors world-wide, in the three years following the Three Mile Island accident in 1979, resulted in a surplus of uranium on a scale that was significant in comparison with the Western world's annual production, which at the time was running at around 38,000 tonnes U. A period of painful readjustment began for the producers.

The precipitous decline in the spot price started a fresh chain of politically significant events. The US civil requirements for uranium are the biggest in the world. Partly as a result of political representations, but perhaps more because of the needs of the growing American nuclear-electricity industry, the 1964 embargo was gradually withdrawn, starting in 1977. By 1982 60 per cent imports were permitted, and imports in 1985 in fact amounted to over half the US market. This re-entry of foreign uranium, on top of a sharply falling price, had the effect of driving out of production, between 1979 and 1986, about two-thirds of the American uranium industry, which had previously been the world leader. Its ore-bodies, though large in total volume, are mostly small and low-grade, and therefore unable to compete with the excellent grades and far larger ore-bodies found elsewhere. By 1982 only a few US producers were able to cover even marginal costs. This led once again to a demand for protection against the commercial strength of the newer Canadian and Australian mines, which enjoyed excellent ore-grades.

The means chosen was indirect: an attack in the courts on the US Department of Energy, challenging its policy of continuing to enrich foreign uranium for use in American reactors, allegedly in defiance of its obligation to ensure that the domestic mining industry remained 'viable'. The meaning of this conveniently elastic word had been extended outside its dictionary definition to become a legal term of art, meaning in effect national self-sufficiency. 'Non-viability', which would trigger protective measures, had been defined as being associated with a foreign share of the uranium market exceeding 37.5 per cent. The American producers' case reached the Supreme Court, which agreed that according to this definition the US uranium industry was certainly 'non-viable'. However, as foreign enrichment of foreign uranium was also available to US utilities, the issue was whether a restriction on US Department of Energy enrichment would have the effect of returning the domestic mining industry to viability. If no amount of restriction of US enrichment of foreign uranium would serve that goal, then DOE would not be violating the viability statute by declining to impose restrictions. The Supreme Court agreed with DOE that its responsibility to restrict enrichment was not proven, and in June 1988 returned the case to the lower court, which was invited to develop a factual analysis of the linkage between such US enrichment and mining viability.

But by then broader political interests had supervened: it was becoming clear that a Free Trade Agreement would be completed with Canada, virtually assuring US buyers that uranium from the world's leading producer would be free to enter the USA without import restrictions. The US producers saw little point in continuing, and withdrew the lawsuit. The US–Canada Free Trade Agreement came into effect at the beginning of 1989.

One other influence of US politics on the uranium industry

concerns South African uranium. (For as long as it was controlled by South Africa, Namibian uranium was treated on the same basis.) The Comprehensive Anti-apartheid Act of 1986 banned, from 31 December 1986, the import into the USA of uranium ore and uranium oxide from Southern Africa—with no 'grandfathering' of existing contracts—while apartheid in its present form continued. The ban applied even to South African ore and oxide intended for re-export. (The Act did not apply to uranium from Southern Africa imported into the USA in the form of natural or enriched uranium hexafluoride, presumably because this would have imposed sanctions on friendly non-South African suppliers of fuel-cycle services.) It is interesting to speculate how far this economic pressure contributed to increasing South African acceptance of the movement towards Namibian independence, given that the most significant economic unit in that large but underpopulated country is the Rössing uranium mine. With the holding of free elections in November 1989, the US government announced that constraints on Namibian uranium under the Anti-apartheid Act 'will be lifted automatically, without the need for further Congressional action, upon Namibian independence'. This was attained as agreed, in a ceremony attended by many world statesmen, on 21 March 1990.

Government pricing policies

Like the USA, governments of other uranium-producing countries face domestic political problems when the uranium price falls on world markets. Both Canada and Australia operate price support systems, directed towards securing the commercial viability of their own mining industries, and cushioning them from the adverse effects of market forces. Canada announced in December 1976 that there would be an escalating floor-price and an annual price negotiation based on the prevailing 'world market price'—which was not defined. The Australian government's policy has also been to underpin the general pursuit of price stability with a floor-price mechanism. The government justified this policy by the very large capital sums required to develop extensive deposits in remote areas: it was intended to provide a degree of 'bankability' for long-term contracts. Australia in particular did not find it easy to maintain its chosen floor-price in the face of a long-lasting buyers' market. If sales were to be made a good deal of flexibility and creative accounting was needed when interpreting the rules, in the face of a spot price which fell as low as $9 in early 1990.

Ensuring security of uranium supplies

Uranium mining is a highly political industry which has had a roller-coaster history ever since its creation, for reasons which have rarely if ever been under its own control. This is something which the consumers—the electrical utilities—have to take into account, if they are to safeguard their huge investments in reactor hardware. They know from experience how political decisions in other countries have, sometimes unintentionally, held up the supply of nuclear fuel or nuclear services. They remember the cessation of Australian production for several years while an inquiry, whose original motivation stemmed from domestic party politics, was held into the future of the uranium mining industry (Chapter 5). There were temporary difficulties with Canadian uranium throughout 1977, and over a period with the USA, for reasons connected with non-proliferation policy.

The electricity supply industries in all countries which do not have their own assured supplies of uranium or fuel-cycle services have therefore developed practices which, so far as possible, protect them against unforeseeable political disruptions at the hands of other countries. The greater the proportion of electricity production that nuclear energy provides, the more necessary these defences become. Attempts were made for several years in the 1980s to find political solutions to the problem of supply security via the International Atomic Energy Agency's Committee on Assurances of Supply, but to little avail; self-help on the part of the consumer has proved to be a better way forward. The electricity supply industries in all countries which do not have their own assured supplies of uranium or fuel-cycle services have therefore developed practices which, so far as possible, provide protection against unforeseeable disruptions of their foreign supplies.

Defensive practices aimed at ensuring security of supply vary from country to country, but there are three common features. One is stock-piling: it is easy to provide a two-year stock-pile for even a large national programme, in sharp contrast to coal or oil, where a few months stocks are all that can be provided. A second is diversification of supply sources. If a utility holding two years stocks buys its uranium from four sources, preferably all from politically and geographically independent suppliers, and if for any unforeseen reason one source becomes unavailable, there will be something like eight years in which to find an alternative, which should be ample. So strong is the desire for diversification that when an additional and politically independent source—Australia— returned to an already over-supplied market in the early 1980s, its mines were nevertheless able to acquire orders, for reasons which had at least as much to do with the need for diversification as with price.

A third element is a substantial degree of long-term contracting. Mining is an unusual industry in financial terms. Ore-bodies, though owned by the mining companies, are not always bankable assets, there being no cash value until the ore has been brought to the surface. But supply contracts *are* bankable. The result is that mining companies welcome long-term arrangements with major customers. Customers for their part look for stable relationships with reliable suppliers. In most countries outside the USA, therefore, long-term purchases account for more than half, some- times three-quarters or more, of total supplies; the rest is filled from the 'spot' market, which is characterized by smaller lot sizes and considerably more volatile prices.

Having very large indigenous uranium resources the USA has never felt as potentially vulnerable as European countries to supply disruptions. Even though its own uranium industry sharply contracted in the 1980s, the presence of Canada immediately to the north meant that anxieties about long-term security were hardly necessary. Furthermore, the large number of reactor cancellations from the mid-1970s to the mid-1980s have led in recent years to a surplus of uranium looking for a home, at very attractive prices to the purchaser. The result has been much greater use of the spot market, and American utilities have become used to trading on this basis. Moreover, the fifty state Public Utility Commissions, which regulate the electricity price charged to US consumers, have given the impression in their often retrospective 'prudency' hearings that they find it easier to accept published spot-price figures than the commercially confidential prices of longer-term contracts. The result is that many US utilities have fought shy of paying the somewhat higher prices asked in the late 1980s in return for long- term contractual security. Some US utilities run on uranium stocks which—given the uncertainties of life—their European equivalents would regard as being too low to guarantee security of reactor operation.

Conversion to hexafluoride; and 'flags on atoms'

After milling and the production of 'yellow-cake', the next stage of the fuel cycle is *conversion* to gaseous uranium hexafluoride, needed as feed to the subsequent enrichment stage. Transport is not a major contributor to total costs; so users are fairly free to buy services where they can, and in many cases the conversion stage takes place in a country different from that which mined the uranium. This, if it wishes, gives the second country also the right to impose its own conditions on downstream use.

At the conversion stage the 'nationality' of a uranium sample can change—for purposes of nuclear non-proliferation policing—for more than one reason. Chemically it is no longer traceable to a particular mine, having in the process of conversion lost the impurities which previously allowed identification of the source at the oxide (U_3O_8) stage. It may also have been 'commingled' in the conversion plant with material from other sources. For these reasons, if conversion is carried out in Europe, it has become industry practice for the European converters to organize the paperwork associated with political controls—import and export licences, shipping advice, notification to 'safeguards' authorities, etc.—and for their host governments to maintain oversight of safeguards during further downstream movement. Canada treats the conversion stage differently, and its documentation continues to identify a country of origin—which implies the acceptance of substitution, molecule for molecule, unless conversion is invariably and completely a batch process.

Keeping track of the nuclear fuel as it travels through the complexities of the nuclear fuel cycle, in the process acquiring 'flags on atoms', can involve quite complicated bookkeeping. However, South Africa has adopted a less bureaucratic procedure, overseen by the South African Atomic Energy Commission. The SAAEC requires assurance that its uranium will be delivered into a reactor; but where other supervisory authorities are available, it is prepared to relinquish responsibility to them. One is the Vienna-based International Atomic Energy Agency, which carries out 'safeguards' inspections on invitation by host governments. Another is Euratom, whose controls, operating within the area of the signatories to the Euratom Treaty, predated those of the IAEA.

It will be appreciated that the obligations imposed by supplier governments on consumers can be a complicating factor in international nuclear trade, at all stages of the nuclear fuel cycle. It might, for instance, become apparent that commercially desirable economies could be made on transport by swapping the title to a batch of uranium hexafluoride for that of an equivalent batch elsewhere. From the physical viewpoint there would be no problem: the atoms and molecules would be identical, as with any other fungible commodity. However, the obligations to which those batches were subject might not be the same, nor to the same governments, and a direct swap might not be permissible. To avoid such commercial inefficiencies wherever possible, administrative techniques have been developed which facilitate swaps of obligation at the same time as title swaps, subject to the regulations of the governments to whom the obligations are owed. The US government in particular keeps a close eye on such transactions, not only for non-proliferation reasons, but also to satisfy itself that they are not intended to by-pass the provisions of the Comprehensive Anti-apartheid Act for material of South African origin[21].

Enrichment and the remainder of the 'front end'

After conversion of uranium to gaseous hexafluoride the next stage is isotopic enrichment. The term 'isotope' describes the various naturally occurring forms of an element like uranium, which have identical chemical properties but often radically different nuclear properties. They also have slightly different atomic weights, which provides a physical basis for enhancing the concentration of the lighter and rarer isotope of uranium, U–235, which is needed for reactor operation. As explained in the Technical Appendix, without enrichment reactor design is very tightly constrained, because most good structural materials strongly absorb the neutrons which are the activators of the nuclear reaction; but with enrichment to about 3 per cent U–235 content—four times the naturally occurring con-centration—normal engineering materials can be used, and the design becomes much more flexible. Only Canada has successfully pursued a power reactor design—CANDU—which dispenses with the need for enrichment.

Enrichment services are provided by the USA, France, and the UK/Netherlands/West Germany consortium known as Urenco; also by the Soviet Union, which in the past has provided as much as 30 per cent of West Germany's enrichment; and on a small scale, since 1981, by China. The participation of the USSR came to public attention when the ship *Mont Louis*, taking hexafluoride containers to Russia, sank in shallow water off the Belgian coast after a collision in August 1984. The public anxiety which erupted was just one more example of the difficulty of explaining to a sceptical and unprepared public that the word 'radioactive' is not necessarily synonymous with hazardous, since it contains no quantitative indication of the strength of the radioactivity. The natural uranium contained in the drums of hexafluoride aboard the *Mont Louis* in fact constituted no significant radioactive hazard. The worst that could be said was that if a drum had been breached—none in fact were—there would have been a local *chemical* hazard to fish immediately around the wreck. Chapter 8 examines the question of radiation hazards.

There are two main forms of commercial enrichment plant: gaseous diffusion and the centrifuge process developed by Urenco and in the USSR. There is also a third process whose development is well advanced: AVLIS, or atomic vapour laser isotope separation[22, 23]. The earliest the US could take a decision to build an AVLIS production plant is 1993. Since the basic technologies for bomb-grade enrichment by any of these routes are essentially the same as those for lower-enrichment reactor material, the enrichment stage is clearly one of the 'sensitive' areas at the centre of non-proliferation policy.

From the enrichment plant the uranium goes to the fuel fabricators, to be made into solid fuel elements of a wide variety of types, depending on the particular design of reactor. They frequently use bundles of small-diameter metal tubes packed with ceramic uranium dioxide pellets, whose high-temperature resistance provides a first protection against accidental damage from over-heating. Fuel elements are manufactured commercially in many of the major industrial countries.

The 'back end' of the fuel cycle

The finished fuel elements stay in the nuclear reactor for a year or more, and during this time the nuclei of the U–235 atoms are broken up by encounters with neutrons. It is this process which releases the heat energy which can eventually be converted into electricity. At the same time, however, highly radioactive and toxic waste products are formed, necessitating remote handling of the fuel elements after they have been irradiated for the desired length of time. The waste products, once their concentration passes a certain level, begin to affect the mechanical properties of the fuel elements, which is why the fuel has to be taken out for reprocessing or storage. Its discharge typically occurs after twelve to twenty-four months in a reactor. At this point the spent fuel is still producing large quantities of heat, due to the energy of the highly radioactive waste products which it contains. The fuel is therefore stored for years, or even decades, to allow this radioactivity to fall to a level at which the intensity of the radiation and the heat generation are both much lower, to facilitate subsequent handling.

At this stage a choice, basically an economic one, presents itself. The fuel can either be stored for a further period, before being placed in a repository for final disposal; or it can be chemically reprocessed to extract the still-useful remaining uranium or by-product plutonium. As explained in the Technical Appendix, the plutonium is created during irradiation by the interaction of neutrons with the non-fissile isotope of uranium, U–238. It is a potentially useful secondary fuel, being itself fissile in a reactor, like U–235. But it is also a bomb material. Because of the possibility of direct use of plutonium in military weapons—something which is not possible with 3 per cent reactor-grade enriched uranium—the plutonium extraction phase, in which plutonium may be separated in pure form even for civil power purposes, is a further politically sensitive part of the fuel cycle.

By the 1970s the United States had become acutely aware of the proliferation dangers inseparable from the open disclosures of the Atoms for Peace policy that it had sponsored in the 1950s: the Indian explosion of 1974 had made the possibilities only too explicit. One political reaction was the US Nuclear Non-Proliferation Act (NNPA) of 1978, which sought to dictate certain basic aspects of nuclear energy policy to other countries, insofar as fuel reprocessing and plutonium figured in their plans—under threat of withholding US nuclear co-operation, on which at that time many depended. The Americans argued that uranium was abundant and reasonably priced, and that reprocessing and plutonium extraction were therefore unnecessary. Not only that, they were also dangerous to world peace. Other countries pointed out that one's view depends on where one sets the time-horizon; that at some stage in the future uranium will become more expensive, and recovery of the residual uranium still present in the fuel after irradiation, and of the by-product plutonium, will be necessary; that this can only be done if the technology is available, but that it will take many years to perfect; and that meanwhile the cost of reprocessing is the price we pay for this strategic insurance. This is a view widely held outside the USA.

Having reached their own conclusions regarding the best long-term nuclear energy strategy, other countries found it difficult to accept the US contention that their nuclear futures, a significant part of their national energy strategies, should be contingent on cumbersome case-by-case approvals at some future time by unknown officials in the USA—as required by the NNPA. Moreover, other countries besides the USA have laws determining what should happen at the back end of the fuel cycle. For instance, the Swedish 1977 Stipulation Act, which predated the NNPA, had already imposed on Swedish utilities a mandatory requirement to demonstrate in advance of reactor startup a safe way of disposing of the resulting radioactive wastes, reprocessing being one of the permitted options. This jurisdictional clash had nothing to do with any disagreement about the need for effective nuclear proliferation controls: it was entirely concerned with efficiency, predictability, and responsibility for Sweden's own energy policy. We shall meet the proliferation problem again in Chapter 7, and the political problems associated with managing radioactive waste in Chapter 10.

Long-term uranium availability

There is one final aspect of the fuel cycle which touches on energy strategy: the issue of availability in the very long term, which is becoming increasingly important now that nuclear power already provides 23 per cent of OECD's electricity. Long-term assurance is based on two arguments. First, even on the basis of present geological knowledge we can be quite sure that there is sufficient uranium to fuel existing designs of reactors for at least another forty years or so. Secondly, as explained in the Technical Appendix, the family of reactors collectively known as 'fast reactors'—the adjective refers to the unusually high average speed of the neutrons which propagate the chain reaction—has the potential for extracting up to fifty times more energy from a given weight of uranium than present-day reactors, thus enormously extending the world's nuclear energy resources. This factor derives from being able to exploit virtually all the uranium in a nuclear reactor, instead of being limited to the 2 per cent or so which is normal in an ordinary reactor.

It may be asked why, if the fast reactor has this almost magical capability, it is not yet the preferred option. The answer is partly technical, but mainly a straightforward matter of economics: the large inventory of fissile material needed to start up and run a fast reactor costs money. The economics of the fast reactor will not be established with certainty for many years; but it seems likely that its electricity generation cost could be as much as 30 per cent more than with conventional power reactors. For as long as the basic fuel—uranium—remains cheap enough it therefore makes good sense to continue with well-tried existing designs, while developing the fast reactor as a hedge against the time when uranium is less readily available than it is today.

Inexorably, as uranium resources become depleted the price will rise. But the raw uranium only contributes 10 per cent or less to the present cost of nuclear electricity; so, on the basis of the 30 per cent figure just quoted, the uranium price could rise even threefold in real terms before the fast reactor could be sure of breaking even. (It should be stressed that any current estimate of the cost of power produced by a fast reactor is still speculative, but this general line of argument shows what is likely to happen.) A threefold uranium price rise would have a significant effect in prolonging the availability of uranium for existing reactors. Metal commodity prices are affected by many factors, notably the balance of supply and demand; but this is only part of the story. A price rise, certainly one as substantial as this, would bring into the realm of economic mining other ore-bodies which had previously been regarded as commercially unexploitable. It would therefore have a direct effect on how much uranium could be considered as an economically minable 'reserve'. In addition a large price rise would trigger a wave of exploration, which would almost certainly be successful in finding even more ore-bodies, much of the world being still only sketchily explored. When prices are low exploration is reduced; when they rise the mining industry always takes it as an immediate call to boost its exploration activity.

It will be some decades before there is any serious risk of exhausting even the ore-bodies which are already known, without counting resources whose existence can safely be inferred. Even with a steady growth in demand it would be safe on present knowledge to think in terms of forty or fifty years of guaranteed supplies. For the reasons just given any substantial price increases would further extend the period of virtually guaranteed uranium availability.

Although it is impossible to be precise, the broad pattern of what will happen is clear enough. Reactors similar to existing types will continue to dominate the market until the rising price of uranium erodes their competitive advantage over the fast reactor, or until improved designs make the fast reactor substantially more economic. While there is little doubt that some time in the next century the fast reactor will need to take the lead—always assuming it has passed the tests of safety and operability—there is likely to be a period of inter-reactor competition which could last for up to half a century. By the time the fast reactor takes on the main burden the nuclear industry will be approaching, or even past, its centenary.

The factor of fifty would give us electrical energy production for a time measured in millenia, with the further bonus that enormous additional uranium resources are to be found in sea-water. The successful development of a fully commercial fast reactor would place nuclear power above coal, natural gas, and oil in terms of total long-term energy availability. The fast reactor's somewhat less favourable economics might of course imply stronger competition for a time from low-cost coal; though who is to know what the price of coal will be in a century's time, or whether by then 'greenhouse' considerations will have discouraged coal burning— or what technical improvements in reactor design will be possible? What is not in doubt is that nuclear power is a major long-term option.

3 Nuclear Power in a Context of Long-term Planning

ALL the countries taken as examples in this and the two following chapters have fine engineering traditions, but their sharply differing responses to the nuclear option show that this is only one factor amongst many. Nuclear development takes time, and teams need to be able to work unworried about future career prospects. Nuclear leadership can be exercised only where policy stability is to some extent guaranteed, and where governments are returned for sufficiently long, with sufficient power, and with sufficient foresight to maintain a systematic long-haul approach; or alternatively where some other kind of machinery exists for maintaining a national consensus on energy policy. Countries whose political and constitutional structures lead to policy U-turns at frequent intervals, or offer abundant opportunities for privately sponsored delaying tactics, are unlikely to be the standard-bearers for such a complex technology.

Nothing offers a greater contrast to the turbulent nuclear politics of so many other countries—including Germany, Great Britain, Italy, Sweden, Switzerland, and the United States—than the calm determination with which the French and Japanese governments have pursued the development of nuclear power. This is no accident. Both countries have a commitment to the explicit search for a long-term view which eludes many other democracies (the French call it 'prospective'). They seem to have solved the institutional problem of how to press forward steadily with developments extending far beyond the lifetime of a single parliament or president. They have market-orientated economies which nevertheless know when to avoid the weakness and fragmentation which can stem from a naïve pursuit of competition for quasi-theological reasons. Institutional 'flywheels' maintain momentum and ensure continuity despite periodical appeals to the ballot-box. Other countries may find it constitutionally difficult to follow their lead; but France in particular provides a standing demonstration of what a rational approach can make possible, and how much can be achieved in a mere twenty years.

France: the drive for independence

The roots of the spectacular French nuclear success go back to the end of World War II, when a national determination to rebuild the defeated country was reinforced, in the nuclear field, by a sudden and unexpected sense of being deserted by wartime friends. France had made what contribution she could to the Anglo-American-Canadian efforts to produce the bomb. She had supplied twenty-six casks of precious heavy water, which were shipped out of Bordeaux on 17 June 1940, on one of the last vessels to leave before the Germans arrived. With it came Halban and Kowarski, who in March 1939 had participated in the key experiment showing that a nuclear chain reaction should be possible. Bertrand Goldschmidt, a radio-chemist who had been one of Madame Curie's assistants in 1933–4, joined them in North America. There he worked at the Chicago laboratory, where Fermi made his first rudimentary demonstration of a nuclear reactor, and later became a leading member of the Montreal laboratory under Cockcroft.

So France's exclusion from the Anglo-American understanding reached at Hyde Park between Roosevelt and Churchill in September 1944, coupled with the terms of the 1943 Quebec agreement—by which the UK undertook not to communicate atomic information to a third party without American approval—was deeply wounding. The lesson was clear: if France was to develop either civil nuclear energy or nuclear weapons, it could only be through her own efforts. Having reached this conclusion, she was spared the humiliation subsequently experienced by Britain, when first the Hyde Park agreement and then the subsequent agreement between Truman and Attlee were so reinterpreted as to become pale shadows of the original intention (partly on the grounds that Britain had not made her links with France clear at the time of the Quebec agreement); and again shortly afterwards when the 1946 McMahon Act wrote America's determination to adopt a policy of nuclear isolation into the statute book[24].

The Commissariat à l'Énergie Atomique (CEA) began life on 18 October 1945. With the aid of some uranium which had been supplied to the Collège de France just before the war—it had lain hidden in Morocco since the Armistice—plus a wagon-load of Belgian origin which turned up fortuitously in the marshalling yards at Le Havre, work was started on basic reactor physics. At this time no decision had been taken to go down the military road, though it was certainly intended to keep the option open. In this respect France differs from the other nuclear weapons states, which started their nuclear programmes with military development as the highest priority. A low-power reactor, ZOE, was built, the Saclay research establishment started near Paris, and uranium mining begun in Metropolitan France, the first ore appearing in 1949.

A major step was taken in 1952, when the dynamic young Minister in charge of atomic energy matters, Félix Gaillard, piloted through the first five-year plan. It was his firm intention to provide France, a country with few natural energy resources, with a complete nuclear industry. The CEA developed an industrial wing. The Marcoule natural uranium-fuelled, graphite-moderated (see Technical Appendix) plutonium-producing reactors G1–G3 were started. As a promise of things to come they were fitted with heat exchangers giving useful amounts of electrical power: 38 MWe each from G2 and G3. These reactors also represented a crucial step towards acquiring a weapons capability.

The Prime Minister, Mendès-France, returned from the United Nations in 1954 after appealing unsuccessfully to the two superpowers to stop atmospheric testing, and on the day after Christmas took a decision to begin preliminary work on weapons, and on nuclear-propelled submarines. Despite government changes the instructions to the CEA hardened within two years into a firm directive to produce weapons (the trauma of the Suez crisis undoubtedly played a part). De Gaulle, who had returned to power in 1958, announced on 3 November 1959 the formation of a 'force de frappe'. Just over three months later, on 13 February 1960, the first weapons test was made at Reggan, 600 miles south of Algiers. Almost immediately French troops deployed in Germany as part of NATO were allowed to handle American tactical nuclear weapons, and continued to do so until France left the alliance in July 1966.

Meanwhile France's plans for nuclear electricity had begun to take shape. Joint studies with the nationalized utility, Électricité de France (EdF), began in 1955, and an influential advisory commission was formed jointly by government officials, EdF, CEA, and industry. It was known as PEON—production d'électricité d'origine nucléaire. The commission agreed on a plan which was not dissimilar to that which had been adopted a few months previously across the Channel: Pierre Ailleret, of EdF, commented[24] that 'one cannot do other than follow the line taken by the British'. A first EdF 70 MWe prototype would be based on the concepts pioneered at Marcoule; later stations would be more powerful; and three or four stations would be completed in the course of ten years. The programme was given parliamentary sanction a couple of years later, in the aftermath of the Suez crisis. In the event the next two stations were considerably larger than originally foreseen, at 200 MWe. They were in service in Chinon, on the Loire, by 1965.

Their construction was not without incident. The CEA had recommended pre-stressed concrete pressure-vessels. EdF, which by then had taken over responsibility for construction, favoured steel and had its way. But a serious rupture occurred in the course of construction, causing three years' delay. Concrete was adopted for the next station, Chinon A3 of 400 MWe.

In the wider European context 1957 saw the report of the European 'Three Wise Men'. The French representative, Louis Armand, former head of the French railways, was to be the first chairman of Euratom when it was formed in January 1958. (The British had opted out of the new Europe, leaving the French as clear leaders.) The Wise Men's report fell into the trap of over-optimism: it was hardly realistic at such an early stage to suggest that 15 GWe of the European Community's electricity production could be nuclear within ten years: in the event less than 10 per cent of this target was achieved. But their report gave a great push; and it was in this context that the first sales pressures were felt from the USA, to persuade European countries to abandon the gas-cooled graphite route, and instead adopt American light water-cooled technology. A USA-Euratom accord became effective in 1959.

It took a little time for Europe to realize that American light-water reactors (LWRs) were not the fully-proven designs they were held out to be. Meanwhile the American offer effectively killed off French hopes of interesting Europe in graphite gas-cooled reactors (GGCRs). If Britain had decided to be a founder-member of Euratom things might have been different: by now there might have been a safe and economic alternative to the pressurized- (PWR) and boiling-water (BWR) reactors. What actually happened was that in

1962 the Germans, who were the key to the European market, awarded their first order for a commercial-size reactor, a BWR, to the American company General Electric—in the process turning down a British graphite-moderated proposal.

In France graphite gas-cooling was still accepted policy, not least because it was possible to build such reactors with natural uranium, without the need for foreign enrichment. PEON proposed in 1964 that between 2.5 and 4 GWe of GGCRs should be built. But the low price of oil, coupled with high interest rates, made the relative economics of GGCRs less attractive. Nevertheless President de Gaulle took a hand in 1967, and decided on a still larger twin GGCR station at Fessenheim, on the Rhine near Mulhouse. One GGCR was sold to Spain, and operated very successfully.

Meanwhile France was not entirely devoid of access to water-cooled technology. On the military side there was the submarine programme. On land a small heavy-water reactor of 70 MWe had started up in 1967 at Brennelis in Brittany. And EdF was associated with the Belgians at Chooz in the French Ardennes, in a joint 240 MWe PWR project completed at about the same time. Gradually the view hardened that France should build a PWR. In April 1968 PEON agreed, after receiving assurances that France could herself supply the necessary enriched uranium, using technology developed for the Pierrelatte military enrichment plant. Just a year later de Gaulle, who had been the CEA's strongest supporter, retired after failing to win a major constitutional referendum, and Georges Pompidou took over as President.

Before 1969 was out the death-knell sounded for GGCRs, in bizarre circumstances. The official opening of the largest reactor of this family, of 480 MWe, took place at St Laurent-des-Eaux, on the Loire. The celebrations were somewhat dampened when the press were informed that the reactor could not compete with oil at its then current price, and that EdF now intended to turn to light-water reactors. That same night an operator's mistake led to the melting of a fuel element. The reactor was out of service for a year.

Pompidou had taken over as President in the middle of the economic troubles brought on by the 'événements'—student riots in the streets of Paris—in April and May 1968. Austerity was the economic watchword, the foreign exchange deficit being in the neighbourhood of a billion dollars. Import-saving technologies like nuclear power had a special importance as part of a national recovery and modernization programme. Pompidou gave his consent for the change in reactor policy, and his firm decision spared the French the traumatic uncertainties which were to plague the British during twenty years of vacillation.

The policy switch was made as a response to the force of circumstances, and without great enthusiasm. There was no general belief that the PWR was intrinsically safer than the French gas-cooled technology; and on economic grounds there was only a modest difference between the two systems. The PWR was ahead, but the 10 per cent margin was within the range of possible future developments in gas-cooling. The decision stemmed from a different consideration: a realization that unless a switch was made France would be cut off from the benefit of the operating experience which was being accumulated around the world, and in all probability from world markets for reactor exports.

The change of policy began slowly. A new company, Framatome, based at the steel town of Le Creusot, was designated the French monopoly nuclear constructor, and a Westinghouse licence was taken as a practical means of getting into the new technology with minimum delay. In the first year only a single order was placed, for a 900 MWe Westinghouse-licensed PWR to be built at Fessenheim (the better economics of PWRs had overtaken de Gaulle's decision regarding gas-cooling for this station). The PEON commission's recommendation had been built into the 6th Economic Plan for a programme of 8 GWe over five years (1971–5), and accordingly in the next couple of years three more orders were given. The tempo changed dramatically following the soaring energy prices caused by the 1973 Yom Kippur War. An extraordinary momentum developed—reminiscent of the expectations which had been held out sixteen years previously by the Three Wise Men. At the time of the crisis, oil, almost all imported, accounted for 66 per cent of French primary energy; it was much more significant than coal and gas, which together[25] made up only 26 per cent. Oil and gas accounted for 46 per cent of electricity production, coal 17 per cent, nuclear only 8 per cent. The government determined to free France from the oil cartel's bondage, and with it her dangerous dependence on imported energy. In March 1974, after a full parliamentary debate, it authorized a sharply increased annual rate of ordering of five or six nuclear stations per year, each of 900 MWe. There was still some residual interest in a boiling-water reactor for a new station to be built at Bugey, near Lyons; but Framatome's PWR proved cheaper.

The beginning of the great leap forward

So France was led by the force of events to the formula which provided the engine for her leap forward: one strong user and one strong supplier, operating in a buoyant market, and both with every incentive to exploit the benefits of standardization[26]. In retrospect this may seem like a typically *dirigiste* French solution. But it must not be forgotten that during the gas-cooled graphite period there had been nothing like this tidiness; indeed, EdF was criticized for going to the other extreme, and scattering orders around French industry, apparently without any obvious system in mind. The tidiness of the final arrangement sprang from reconsideration in the light of institutional pressures and external circumstances.

EdF took a further bold policy step in 1973 by announcing its intention to place no more orders for coal and oil stations. For the future the objective was that more than 60 per cent of French electricity should be nuclear by 1985. The figure actually achieved was 61 per cent—a remarkable tribute to the accuracy of EdF's forecasting. Apart from conversion of fifteen oil stations to coal, 3.5 GWe in total, the all-nuclear policy held for the next ten years. The sheer magnitude of the building programme gave rise to considerable financial anxieties at the outset; but the French commitment to consistency in economic planning was such that the general momentum of ordering did not flag. Forty nuclear reactors were ordered over the eight years 1974–81, about one every ten weeks.

The progress which such statistics represent had its effect on the CEA—inevitably, because its launching task was largely complete. What lay ahead when Pompidou became President was the further development of the fast reactor and parts of the fuel cycle, and a very active industrial programme, which would require major reorganization of the nuclear industry. As a beginning CEA and EdF were placed under the same minister, Xavier Ortoli. A report on the future of CEA was ready by April 1970. The general stance of the Commissariat was changed. It still occupied a central position through its shareholdings in other nuclear organizations, but it became more open—an expert adviser to the French nuclear industry, instead of the all-powerful and somewhat secretive élite of earlier years. By the time the first oil crisis arrived the nuclear industry was far better placed to deal with it.

In 1976 a CEA associated company COGEMA was created, to handle the various operations involved in the fuel cycle, from mining onwards. France has indigenous reserves of 100,000 tonnes of uranium ore, and close associations with mining companies in her former colonies Niger and Gabon. Most of Westinghouse's 45 per cent stake in Framatome was bought out, and the relationship between the two organizations became a more equal partnership. The Westinghouse licence lapsed in 1981, to be replaced by a co-operation agreement. The way was open for the manufacture and export of wholly French designs.

Pressurized-water reactors require enriched uranium as their fuel; so France, profiting from her dominant position in Euratom, proposed to her European neighbours that a large gaseous diffusion plant—Eurodif—should be built jointly. A site was selected at Tricastin, on the Rhône, and Belgium, Italy, and Spain joined France as shareholders. Production started in 1973.

The nuclear market saturates

Eventually the task of switching the basis of national electricity production began to approach completion. It had been accelerated by a progressive increase in reactor size—from 900 MWe for the early stations ordered in 1974 to 1,300 MWe, and finally (by 1984) to 1,400 MWe; and by an equally impressive improvement in plant availability[1, 27], from 62 per cent in 1980 to 79 per cent in 1984. (This excellent operating record was marred in 1989, when troubles occurred in the steam-generator tubing of several of the 1,300 MWe reactors, apparently as a result of oxidation of metallic grit left in the generators or piping during manufacture.) The slowdown in economic growth caused by the second OPEC-induced fuel-price shock in December 1979, following the Iranian crisis, also played a part in bringing about market saturation; as perhaps did a loss of business confidence and a period of slower growth following the defeat of President Giscard d'Estaing by Mitterrand, the first Socialist to head the Fifth Republic. His 1981 decision to cut back nuclear construction was more a reflection of the economic realities that had been increasingly evident since 1978, than a doctrinal swing away from nuclear power. His supporters had been looking for a complete nuclear embargo. They were disappointed: French commitment to the imperatives of managing an industrial economy goes across the political spectrum. What they got was a handful of medium-sized (600 MWe) coal stations.

From 1983 the nuclear station ordering rate fell sharply. Framatome suddenly found that so far as the home market was concerned its job was largely done. A trickle of orders, one per year, slowing to one every two years in the 1990s, was all that was possible from 1985 onwards—just enough to keep the organization and technology alive. The reactor export markets which might have been sought were largely dead, for the time being at least, during the long drawn-out period for reflection after the 1979 accident at Three Mile Island in the USA. But France had provided herself with a new energy source which by 1990 could claim not only to supply three-quarters of her electricity, but also to be the single biggest contributor to her primary energy supplies[25]—at 34 per cent slightly ahead of oil (30 per cent), and significantly more than coal and gas combined (27 per cent). Nor was a degree of over-provision a major worry: given France's geographical position it could be taken up by exports of the relatively cheap electricity which the size of the programme made possible. France exported 13 billion kwh in 1983, 42 billion in 1989, and is aiming eventually for nearly 50 billion. This export industry uses the equivalent of the output from half a dozen large reactors. Domestic consumers had little to complain about: prices had been kept constant in real terms—after allowing for inflation—since 1973.

The scale of the achievement is even more impressive if we look back a quarter of a century. French *nuclear* electricity production in 1990 is nearly three times larger than the *total* production of the whole French grid in 1965, when the nuclear programme was just getting under way[1]; and almost ten times greater than French electricity production in 1950. So perhaps the optimistic prognostications of the Three Wise Men were not so wide of the mark.

The financial burden

The cost was of course enormous, and is held out by EdF's detractors as evidence of the dangers of technocratic megalomania[28]. It is also said that by excessive investment in electricity generation EdF has starved other French industry of investment, and held back economic growth generally. The actual figures hardly justify such strictures. As a percentage of total French national investment EdF's share rose to just over 5 per cent in 1983; it had been at that level once before in 1958, during the big expansion of hydroelectricity and conventional power-stations, but had fallen back to less than 3 per cent by 1973, when the rapid nuclear buildup began. At the end of 1989 EdF's debt stood at 232 billion francs. This was 1.6 times the annual turnover, which is not beyond the bounds of financial management, particularly for a public monopoly with a captive market. The ratio had been nearer 3 : 1 in the period 1958–68, though interest rates were then lower and with them the annual financing charges. In Switzerland it reached 2.5 in 1986, without creating an outcry in that country of legendary financial prudence. Since 1982 EdF has had no direct support from public funds, financing being either from debt or from operating surpluses. A substantial part of the debt is in foreign currency— about 35 per cent at the end of 1988, down from the peak of 46 per cent in 1984. EdF was for a time the most important borrower in the US market, and when the dollar appreciated against the franc there were difficulties. The critics are right on one point: there was certainly substantial over-ordering, amounting to about 6 GWe in the late 1980s. However, the EdF management was always conscious that if its plans proved to be too ambitious exports could provide the necessary cushion. That commercial view, taken a decade ago, seems vindicated not only by the very satisfactory level of export sales already achieved, but also by the promise implicit in the moves towards a free market in electricity throughout the EEC after 1992.

EdF's financial management is interesting in other respects, notably the sophisticated way the utility has pioneered new uses for electricity: during the years of the rapid expansion electricity consumption rose 50 per cent faster than in the EEC as a whole. EdF's experience is that consumers are somewhat averse to innovation, and that if the utility wishes its clients to use electricity in new ways it must make it easy for them. So, for what are basically financial rather technical reasons, EdF has been active in promoting new industrial uses which, to be viable, depend on first finding ways of economizing in electricity consumption[27]. Critics claim that this programme has had only limited success, and that by far the greatest expansion has been for heating in the home—a 'peaky' demand, for which they say direct heating by coal or oil would make more economic sense, given the 70 per cent loss of energy inseparable from electricity production by PWRs, and the economic penalties of using nuclear power for peak-load. As with so many issues of public policy, what matters is where one sets the bounds of the problem: architectural preference and clean air in the crowded high-rise areas of Paris and Lyons deserve some weight.

French public opinion

Throughout this story the unseen observer has been the public. It would be mistaken to think that it has silently acquiesced in all the decisions of the technocrats. There was of course initial pride and indeed euphoria over the wonders of nuclear power; but this did not permanently insulate France from nuclear protests any more than elsewhere. The protesters were reinforced by those who genuinely believed that the pursuit of the 'force de frappe'—or 'force de dissuasion', to give it its later and more euphemistic title— was not in the country's long-term interests, and that power reactors in all probability had closer links with this military activity than was generally admitted. Despite the oil crisis of 1973, and the obvious need to reduce dependence on oil imports, the French nuclear programme went through a difficult period in the mid-1970s. The environmental and non-proliferation messages emanating from America had at least as strong an appeal as fears that the lights would go out. In 1975 just over half the population were in favour of nuclear power; but the situation deteriorated sharply, and for a time two years later two out of every three Frenchmen who ventured an opinion were opposed (there were also many 'don't knows'). This, it will be remembered, was the period of the most rapid expansion, when the changes which the programme was bringing about were at their most visible—but when it was virtually impossible to put the industrial machine into reverse. In 1976 there were anti-nuclear demonstrations in France which were dispersed with tear gas, and sympathetic manifestations in Switzerland. In July of the following year one person was killed and several severely injured at a well-organized demonstration against the fast reactor at Creys-Malville—though many of the 30,000 participants were foreigners rather than local inhabitants, using the reactor as a symbolic target. In the face of public opposition plans were abandoned for a new power-station at Plogoff in Brittany—cynics say this had something to do with a pre-election pledge by

Mitterrand—and for another in Languedoc. Yet by 1982, despite a steadily mounting reactor programme, despite the Three Mile Island accident, two-thirds of the population had swung behind the nuclear programme.

Sober reconsideration of the effects of the second oil shock in 1979 may have had something to do with the change of mood. The slow-down of the construction programme may also have helped. But the educational efforts of Électricité de France in all probability played a part. A deliberate choice was made in 1977 to carry the debate on to economic territory[29]. Safety was of course always important; but so far as public debate was concerned it was a subject on which it was almost impossible to reach agreed conclusions either way. Despite the complexities which will become evident from Chapter 6, economic arguments could be made more clear-cut. EdF started an advertising campaign in the press, which simply invited the public to write in for information if they were interested in nuclear power.

The response was extraordinary: for several years the daily mail-bag was 300 to 500 letters. The problem was how to answer them—both handling the volume, and deciding what the public most needed. A decision was taken not to write new brochures, but to identify 200 existing articles, graded according to difficulty of comprehension, and make them available to any who were interested. An office was set up to answer the daily torrent of mail, using appropriate brochures to answer specific questions. Where the query was less precise, an index of what was available was provided. Two million brochures and one million indexes were distributed in five years, always in response to letters received. EdF also accepted every invitation to take part in debates—several hundred a year—the only stipulation being that the chairman should be neutral. Visits to nuclear power plants were encouraged—a third of a million people paid visits in 1982, and public interest was still at about this level in 1988. And finally a consciously helpful policy was directed towards the news media: a roster system was organized so that questions could be answered whenever they arose.

This information was backed up in a number of other ways, including modifications to planning procedures. In the early days there had been few problems over siting, and it was enough to rely on the procedure known as an Inquiry into the Public Interest

(Enquête d'Utilité Publique). This is a very different type of inquiry from the quasi-judicial policy reviews which occur in Britain and the United States. The French process is more limited, and concerned with settling local compensation. But with the waves of discontent in the 1970s some changes had to be made, including appeals to local self-interest. A ministerial committee dealing with major construction sites agreed that priority should be given to the employment of local labour. In 1976 certification procedures were altered. Later local information commissions (commissions locales d'information) were set up for each reactor site, to provide elected representatives, mayors, and environmentalists with reliable information on the operation of the plant.

These procedural concessions, which to Anglo-Saxon eyes appear minor, were backed up for a time by financial inducements for the host communities in the shape of reduced electricity tariffs—'bribes' so far as the nuclear opposition was concerned. However, in 1985 the Conseil d'État ruled that this was contrary to the principle of equality amongst electricity consumers, as required by the Electricity Nationalization Act of 1946. For its part EdF did what it could to minimize environmental disquiet by sensitive planning of otherwise intrusive features. Where possible these were sunk in the ground, or hidden behind natural features such as the cliff edge at the coastal site of Flamanville, near Cherbourg. These measures must also have contributed to the easing of nuclear tensions.

By the time President Mitterrand took office and called for a 'great debate' on the issues of nuclear power, the public was either satisfied—two out of three people were in favour—or losing interest: there was virtually no response to his invitation. The opposition was fragmented, dispersed amongst the political parties. They knew they had in effect lost the strategic battle, defeated by the speed at which events had moved. What was left was the more limited and less exciting self-imposed task of maintaining a watching brief on operations such as the reprocessing plant at Cap de la Hague, opposing plans for waste disposal, and attempting to rebuild support for the anti-nuclear movement through books both scholarly and popular (e.g. reference 30).

Inevitably, the level of public support was dented by Chernobyl. Once the French housewife discovered that there were problems over buying that gastronomic essential, the green salad, protests were heard about undue secrecy over the exact level of fall-out. Chernobyl sensitized the public to other environmental issues—for instance, anxieties about possible effects on Parisian drinking-water supplies of a new nuclear station at Nogent, in the upper Seine valley. Three years after the disaster, in April 1989, only 36 per cent of the population were ready to agree unequivocally that 'the construction of nuclear plants has been a good thing for France', 43 per cent were generally in favour, 52 per cent felt that no further nuclear stations should be built, 25 per cent thought that existing plants should be phased out, and 20 per cent felt unhappy about safety enforcement.

Nuclear power is only one amongst a number of environmental issues that trouble the French public, and as the 1980s drew to a close it seemed to figure no more prominently in public debate than, for instance, oil pollution in Brittany. But the activists were still looking for opportunities to protest. Plans for making geological investigations of four candidate underground sites for the disposal of high-activity waste were disrupted, not for the first time, after a march by 15,000 people at Angers on 20 January 1990. Three days later the local Prefect suspended operations, and shortly afterwards the French Prime Minister, Michel Rocard, imposed a moratorium on further drilling for at least twelve months, to give time for a better public understanding of what was intended to develop.

It remains to be seen what effect the growing awareness of the dangers of the 'greenhouse effect' will have on nuclear power's public image. René Dumont, one of France's best known environmentalists, has pointed out that avoiding fossil-fuel combustion is henceforth an absolute priority. So far as electricity production is concerned, France in this respect is second only to Sweden in protecting the environment, thanks to nuclear electricity.

Other nuclear programmes

The EdF power programme is not the whole of the French nuclear story. Longer-term development work has continued on the fast breeder, first with Phénix at Marcoule in 1973, subsequently with the much larger (1.24 GWe) Super-Phénix at Creys-Malville, which was connected to the grid in January 1986. Unfortunately a component (outside the reactor core) developed a leak in March of the following year, and the reactor was shut down for nearly three years. A big effort has gone into the back end of the fuel cycle, both at the La Hague reprocessing plant on the Cherbourg peninsula, and in the development of the vitrification process for packaging radioactive waste in glass at Marcoule. French companies participate in uranium exploration and mining throughout the world. Some work also continues on non-nuclear renewable energy sources, not only for its own sake, but also as a useful defence against complaints of tunnel vision from the more cynical members of the nuclear opposition.

The lessons

Three points stand out from this recital of French nuclear political history. One is the organizational stability which the country has enjoyed at the policy level, which far from inducing rigidity has promoted flexibility. With the formation of the PEON commission in 1955 a forum was created where experience could be exchanged between the interested parties, conflicting views reconciled, and policy changes initiated. PEON proved to be flexible in its views. It underwrote the switch to light water reactors. It was still in existence when the accelerated programme was adopted. The twenty-seven years of its life—until 1982—provided a continuity of approach which contrasts sharply with the flailing around which, as we shall see, was what happened in the name of competition in Britain and in the United States. The French nuclear effort had the benefit of clear organization, one strong electrical utility which was also responsible as architect-engineer, direct access to the highest political levels, politicians who were prepared to do the job they were paid for—taking decisions instead of sheltering behind a parapet of quasi-judicial inquiries—support across the political spectrum from four very different presidents, a national system making for farsightedness in economic planning, and a highly-skilled and self-confident technical élite; plus perhaps a little luck, not least in the relative absence of direct competition from other indigenous energy resources, and in the success at the crucial period in carrying public opinion behind what was being achieved. That was no less than the realization of Félix Gaillard's early dream of a complete nuclear industry.

The criticism that other countries cannot avoid making is that France has put all her eggs in the nuclear basket, and moreover backed one family of designs. That places enormous responsibility on all concerned to get things right, and to continue to do so into the indefinite future; or, should things go wrong, as with the troubles over the 1300 MWe steam-generator tubes, to put them right quickly and efficiently. Few countries place such a high degree of confidence in their professional engineers. But the French have been brought up to have the highest regard for the products of their Grandes Écoles. That belief in professionalism—it is more than mere élitism—is one of the things that makes France such a profoundly 'different' country.

Japan: consistency and pragmatism

The Japanese interest in commercial nuclear power began with a public relations flourish in 1954, when Yasuhiro Nakasone, who was later to become Prime Minister, authorized the allocation of 235 million yen—a sum suggested by the isotopic weight of the fissile isotope of uranium! The Japanese Atomic Energy Basic Law, passed in December 1955, set out the main lines of a policy which was to be pursued in a spirit of 'transparency, democracy, and independence'—to quote from a government report which preceded the Act. Since then seven 'Long-term Programmes for Development and Utilization of Nuclear Power' have been published at intervals of four to six years. There have been progressive downwards revisions of targets, as difficulties were identified, but no abandonment of the nuclear option. Indeed, the 1987 plan makes clear that the intention remains one of providing a full range of fuel-cycle services by about the beginning of the next century, followed in time by a commercial fast reactor. Strategically the intention is to make Japan as nearly as possible independent, so far as this source of energy is concerned.

This is a deliberate policy reaction to the demands on energy created by the country's phenomenal economic growth. Throughout the 1960s growth ran at more than 10 per cent per year, which meant that energy demand doubled in less than a decade. But Japan's economy was vulnerable: seven-eighths of her energy was imported, and at the time of the first oil price shock in 1973 the oil sector accounted for 77 per cent of the total.

The crisis proved a turning point. Energy supplies were suddenly revealed as the Achilles' heel of the Japanese miracle. The government moved rapidly, introducing a comprehensive programme of energy conservation, promotion of greater use of coal, natural gas, geothermal, and hydropower, and an acceleration of the nuclear-power programme. The conservation programme was successful: energy consumption per unit of GNP declined by a quarter in the first seven years after the 1973 oil crisis, and even more—by 34 per cent—in the industrial sector. But eating into oil imports was bound to be a slow process, because economic growth was still proceeding in what for the rest of the world would be regarded as boom conditions, even though for Japan it was at a sharply reduced rate. By 1989 imported oil still accounted for 58 per cent of Japan's total primary energy.

Shortly after the first oil crisis, a target of 49 GWe was set[5] for the nuclear capacity to be installed by 1985. It was an oddly unrealistic figure—the actual figure when the time came was 24 GWe—and everyone knew it. But it did represent a political commitment to nuclear power on a massive scale.

The problem of reactor siting

The failure to meet the planned target was not due to any lack of need, nor to an inability to carry through the engineering at that speed. The problem lay in finding sites for the new stations. In the mid-1970s the country was already paying a price for its rapid economic expansion, in the form of unacceptably high levels of pollution, which stimulated a distrust of government and big enterprise, nuclear power not excepted. In addition, Japan's mountainous geography meant that coastal stations were preferred; but the local fishermen were claiming legal protection. Local inhabitants generally were also complaining about the disparity between their own living standards and those of the town-dwellers who used most of the electricity produced in their communities. Some reform of the system for regulating and supervising nuclear power was clearly needed, together with financial inducements to reduce the level of local opposition.

For all their familiarity with high technology, the Japanese were strongly ambivalent in their attitudes towards nuclear energy. They accepted its economic necessity, and set no exaggerated hopes on the renewable sources of energy. Between 1980 and 1984 the proportion of people believing that nuclear energy would be the main future source of electricity rose from 33 to 51 per cent, while the corresponding expectation for solar energy fell from 28 to 18 per cent. But the Japanese were also acutely aware, from their own history, of the problems of radioactivity. It was not only the traumatic experience of wartime bombing. There was also the explosion of the 15 megaton H-bomb at the Bikini test site on the first day of March 1954, when the fall-out contaminated twenty-three Japanese fishermen on board the inappropriately named *Lucky Dragon No. 5*; the wireless operator, Aikichi Kuboyama, died six months later.

The Three Mile Island accident in 1979 reawakened these anxieties. Two-thirds of those polled by *Asahi Shimbun* two months later anticipated that a similarly serious accident could happen in Japan in the long run. By 1984—five years after TMI—70 per cent of the population were still worried about nuclear plants, for a variety of reasons: ignorance of how they operate, how they differ from nuclear bombs, anxieties about nuclear waste disposal, the effects of radiation on health. These were the general responses to a poll question about what more they would like to know about nuclear energy. They are strikingly like those in other countries, even though as a nation the Japanese are unusually aware of economic imperatives. What finally determines public attitudes, and what in the end provides the government with the mandate to pursue its nuclear policies, is a degree of net perceived benefit.

The majority of those who are worried about nuclear power live far from power station sites. The problems posed for the fishermen and coastal inhabitants who have to make room for the new stations are of a more directly personal nature: displacement from their family homes; thermal pollution from the waste cooling water; and anxiety that the public might refuse to buy their catches for fear of radiation contamination. These are anxieties for which money can provide at least partial compensation.

Fishery compensation is used to cover the losses of fishermen whose catches might be reduced by the hot cooling water pumped into the sea from coastal power stations, or by the disappearance of fishing areas due to reclamation. It is paid by the electricity companies to fishermen's co-operatives. Secondly, under legislation passed in 1974 the central government can award *special grants* to the local authority where a nuclear power station or fuel cycle facility (e.g. an enrichment plant) is to be situated, and a smaller amount to the surrounding areas. The grants, which can be applied to social welfare or to public facilities and infrastructure, are scaled according to the power of the station. A similar scheme applies to fossil-fuel plants, but at roughly half the rate per unit of output. This has the interesting result that it is more profitable to a local authority to accept a nuclear plant in its locality than a conventional plant. The revenue needed to fund the grant is collected from a tax on electricity production, authorized by Three Acts for the Development of Electric Power Resources (1974). One of the Acts deals specifically with areas adjacent to generating plants. Some grants based on the Three Acts can be paid in the form of a deduction from electricity bills, thus providing a direct link in the public's mind. Finally, as a good-neighbourly though non-statutory gesture, some utilities make voluntary contributions to the cost of regional development[31].

Given that nuclear stations are built whenever possible in regions remote from major population centres, the sums obtainable from these grants provide the local population and the local authorities with revenues which in their own terms are highly significant. This is more true the smaller the local population. The improvements which can be put in hand help to make the locality more attractive, and in some cases stem the exodus from areas of declining population. But while these various subsidies have improved relations with local inhabitants, they have not entirely removed all opposition. In 1984 1,400 riot police had to be mobilized in the town of Ohi-cho, on the coast north of Osaka, because thousands of demonstrators were protesting against a proposal to build two more reactors in the area. This, however, did not stop their construction.

The acceptance of anti-proliferation safeguards

Besides these domestic concerns there were also external political problems to be considered. From the moment of the 1973 oil crisis, decreasing dependence on energy imports became a cardinal principle of Japanese politics. Because of its low import content— at least for a manufacturing nation like Japan—nuclear power behaves in economic terms almost like an indigenous energy source. For Japan only uranium posed a potential problem in the long term. The breeder reactor therefore took its place in the nuclear strategy, originally being planned as a development for the 1990s, with a commercial model available a decade or so later. The date followed logically from a perception in the mid-1970s that uranium supplies might by then be coming under strain. This is not now thought likely before about 2030, and accordingly the commercial Japanese breeder programme has since been put back until the beginning of the second quarter of the next century. As part of a 'belt and braces' policy Japan also participates in uranium mining ventures around the world.

A major Japanese interest, in the period immediately after the negotiation of the 1968 Nuclear Non-Proliferation Treaty (NPT), was to ensure that acceptance of 'safeguards' (i.e. international inspection of their nuclear installations by inspectors from the International Atomic Energy Agency) did not interfere unduly with their long-term energy plans. The Japanese wished for no restrictions to be placed on their freedom in research and development, and on their choice of nuclear fuel-cycle options, including enrichment and reprocessing. Before accepting the NPT, therefore, they carefully monitored the safeguards negotiations between the IAEA and Euratom, which ended successfully in April 1973, as a check that the corresponding Japanese safeguards agreement was not unequal or disadvantageous. The Japanese negotiation with the IAEA was successfully concluded in February 1975, and a Bill for ratification of the NPT was introduced shortly afterwards. As a result of this cautious approach Japan was the ninety-sixth nation to ratify the Treaty. Similar anxieties were expressed over the guidelines of the Nuclear Suppliers' Group which, following a demonstration nuclear explosion by the Indians in 1974, set up informal but strict controls over the supply of sensitive nuclear materials and equipment.

In 1977–8 this caution was reinforced when the Japanese strategy of working towards nuclear self-sufficiency came into conflict with the nuclear policies of President Carter's administration. Relations with the United States, although extremely close, had already gone through more than one difficult period in the post-war years, the domestic political consequences of the Bikini bomb being a conspicuous example. Now the International Nuclear Fuel Cycle Evaluation, which the US President had launched, appeared likely to have the effect of calling into question Japan's chosen strategy of fuel-cycle self-sufficiency. It also provided Japanese anti-nuclear groups with ammunition, in the form of the doubts expressed in the Evaluation's report about the world's ability to erect reliable safeguards against further nuclear proliferation. Furthermore, the

1978 US Nuclear Non-Proliferation Act (NNPA, discussed in Chapter 7) reinforced the Carter policy of strongly discouraging reprocessing and plutonium utilization, which are both necessary if the fast reactor is ever to become a reality. Coincidentally, at almost the same time a politically induced year-long interruption (January 1977 to January 1978) to uranium supplies from Canada occurred, as Canada sought to revise its bilateral agreements around the world in order to reinforce their safeguards provisions. Australia took a similar stance in May 1977, and for this and other reasons it was 1982 before Australian uranium became available. All of this, in Japanese eyes, underlined the need for caution regarding constraints on nuclear fuel supplies.

Subsequently the Carter administration's view that uranium was really more abundant than seemed possible in the light of the high uranium prices of 1978 has proved to be right. But as Japan is determined to pursue the 'back end' of the fuel-cycle, the introduction of some flexibility into the highly bureaucratic rules established under the NNPA has helped US–Japanese relations. By 1988 these had improved to a point at which a revision and thirty-year extension to the US–Japanese agreement on nuclear co-operation removed some of the constraints on fuel-cycle commercial operations that Japan had found so irksome. Clumsy case-by-case decisions were replaced by long-term 'programmatic' consents for reprocessing material which had been enriched in the USA—and which were therefore subject to US non-proliferation controls.

The outlook following Chernobyl

Chernobyl, when it came in 1986, might well have placed the slightly grudging acceptance of nuclear energy by the Japanese people in immediate jeopardy; but this did not happen. One important factor was distance. No fall-out was observed in Japan until 3 May, a week after the accident, which gave the government ample time to make preparations; and when it did arrive it was at a very low level. The incident was handled firmly and effectively. To avoid the confusion which had been so evident in Europe all communications were co-ordinated by the Prime Minister's office. Meetings were immediately held between government representatives and inhabitants living near power-stations. The people as a whole received the news calmly; though four months later an *Asahi Shimbun* poll found for the first time that more people were against continuing with the nuclear programme than those in favour—41 per cent against 34 per cent. This was a much more pronounced reaction than had been noticed at the time of Three Mile Island. However, by the autumn of 1987 the number believing that the use of nuclear power should be increased had grown to 57 per cent—bearing out the Swedish experience that short-run reactions should not be taken as necessarily typical of the views the populace will hold after time for mature reflection.

Nevertheless, a degree of ambivalence has persisted, and the anti-nuclear movement has been successful in recruiting large numbers of Japanese women to their cause. It has also become more innovative. Small parcels of land have been bought at likely sites for future stations, to block construction. In Hokkaido, protesters collected nearly a million signatures in an unsuccessful attempt to prevent the operation of the Tomari–1 reactor. Radiation-monitoring equipment has been used to identify trucks carrying nuclear fuel, as a prelude to harassment. A horrifying poster has been published of a small child in a gas mask to 'illustrate' the effects of a nuclear emergency. There was agitation against a load-following test in 1987–8 at the Ikata reactor because it was mistakenly thought to be similar to the one that brought on the Chernobyl disaster. A campaign has been planned to collect ten million signatures in favour of a denuclearization law. It is hardly surprising that a poll (NHK) in January 1989 found that two out of three who were interviewed believed nuclear energy to be somewhat dangerous. On the other hand the poll provided a further demonstration of the public's ambivalence that is so often evident on nuclear issues: 60 per cent said that further nuclear expansion should continue.

The most recent long-term plan for nuclear power (1987) brushes aside such doubts, and like its predecessors plots the course needed to lead Japan towards nuclear self-sufficiency. With the low borrowing rates and easy access to capital which Japan enjoys the high cost of nuclear power is far less of an economic deterrent than in the West, and its generating costs come out about 20 per cent cheaper than coal, and 30 per cent ahead of hydropower. Nuclear power is already the largest single component of Japanese electricity supplies, making more than twice the contribution of coal. By 1989 nuclear power was providing 27 per cent of Japan's electricity, and the figure is planned to rise to 34 per cent by the end of the century, corresponding to 13 per cent of total primary energy. As with France, the growth in electricity demand holds down the percentage figure, and masks the magnitude of what is being achieved. The future installation programme may slip, as it has done in the past; but the policy is likely to remain one of consistency of purpose on the part of the government. Despite the increasingly vocal opposition, particularly amongst Japanese women (dealt with more fully in Chapter 11), enough of a consensus regarding objectives has been maintained to ensure a smooth path for nuclear power. Barring another major accident, this seems likely to demonstrate, over the years, that a sensible non-zero-sum strategy is possible, where both environmentalists and industrialists can gain[31]. That will mean going out to meet and explain nuclear energy to the people—which, on its own admission, the Japanese nuclear industry has so far failed to do effectively.

4   Nuclear Power and Political Sensitivity

THE constancy of purpose shown by France and Japan in the face of the challenges posed by the nuclear debate is a rarity. Nor is this surprising. Nuclear energy has all the ingredients needed to qualify as a permanent political issue, forever ready to be exploited when there are no more pressing matters to keep the pot boiling: a whiff of danger, rumoured genetic effects, links with the morally explosive issue of nuclear disarmament, a technical élite—above all an arcane mystery, where the arguments for and against are so complicated that even the 'pros' take care to qualify their claims, while the 'antis' know that rebuttal will take so long that the audience may depart before the job is finished. In such circumstances half-truths flourish, and unless a government has clear vision, determination, and parliamentary strength, tactical voting too easily becomes the test of what is considered to be 'right'. Strength is lacking where, for historic or constitutional reasons, coalition or devolved government is the order of the day.

The thumb-nail case-histories which follow[32] describe events in recent years in Sweden, Italy, Germany, and Switzerland—all countries where circumstances give political activists unusual opportunities for influencing nuclear policy, and where the volume of public clamour on nuclear issues owes at least as much to the chances of being heard at the political level as to the intrinsic merits of the nuclear debate. In such a context a degree of political opportunism is only to be expected. One may regret that one of the greatest intellectual and engineering triumphs of the human race has become a political whipping-horse. But party politics is a fact of public life; the first duty of a politician is to win and retain power; and if attacking nuclear energy offers a convenient stepping-stone to high office that is what will happen. The best hope for the nuclear industries in coalition-government countries is to try to outlast the present difficult period, which is largely the result of errors by their professional colleagues at Three Mile Island and

Chernobyl. Once politicians again believe they can secure credit by making favourable reference to nuclear power they will do so readily enough—as in the fifties and sixties. The industry's task is not to wring its hands, but to provide politicians with the opportunity of revising their views in due course, in the light of growing 'greenhouse' concerns, by maintaining an immaculate operating record.

The Swedish decision to phase out nuclear power

The Swedish nuclear industry has a particularly distinguished record—whether judged by technology, reactor availability, organization, economics, safety, or the low exposure of its operating staff to radiation. Its waste-management system is probably the best in the world. Nevertheless, the industry has laboured for nearly two decades against difficulties which have more to do with the country's political structure than with any objective appraisal.

For many decades five political parties have been represented in the Swedish parliament: the Centre Party (once known as the Peasants' Party), Conservatives, Liberals, Communists, and Social Democrats. The last two have formed a left-wing bloc, and the others a loose non-socialist grouping. From the 1930s until 1976 the Social Democrats ruled continuously, either alone or with the support of the Peasants' Party (in the 1950s) or some passive acquiescence from the Communists.

Nuclear power was not always controversial. In the 1950s and 1960s there was a consensus in its favour. The first Swedish experimental reactor was built in 1954, the first commercial reactor in 1972 at Oskarshamn. By 1973 eleven reactors had been licensed for construction. But voices led by the Centre Party leader, Terbjörn Fälldin, and by the physicist Hannes Alfvén—who had earlier been a strong nuclear supporter—were heard opposing further nuclear expansion. Almost immediately the oil crisis occurred, and fuel costs soared, making the economic advantages of nuclear power clear to all. In 1975 the Swedish parliament voted for an expanded programme of thirteen reactors, supported by both Social Democrats and Conservatives. The Liberals were marginally less enthusiastic, but were prepared to settle for eleven. The programme included a strong commitment to energy conservation.

However, at the general election of 1976 Fälldin strongly opposed nuclear power. He issued an ultimatum that the phase-out of nuclear power was a condition for his participation in a non-Socialist government; and by so doing he succeeded in bringing the long rule of the Social Democrats to an end. On this occasion those who were in favour of nuclear energy did not oppose him, because their overriding purpose was to get rid of the Social Democrats; so the Conservatives, Liberals, and industrialists remained silent. The Centre Party did unusually well, with 24 per cent of the votes, and formed a coalition with support from outside its own ranks. But the new government was uneasily divided over the nuclear energy issue, and to restore the national consensus a commission on energy was appointed. Unfortunately it reached no clear conclusion, being split over policy for nuclear waste. A 'Stipulation Act' was passed in the spring of 1977, requiring power companies to demonstrate a 'completely safe method' of finally disposing of used nuclear fuel before permission could be given to load fuel into new nuclear reactors. The five completed reactors were unaffected. The sixth, Barsebäck–2, which was almost on the point of starting up, was dealt with by a special provision requiring that it could only continue to operate if an acceptable reprocessing contract could be negotiated for its spent fuel.

The Fälldin government believed that the Stipulation Act would have the effect of imposing a partial *de facto* nuclear moratorium; but the actual result was to stimulate the nuclear industry to heroic efforts to meet the new requirements. Reprocessing contracts were arranged with France, and proposals prepared for two highly engineered underground repositories. The latter received strong support from the twenty-five foreign experts and laboratories which the government unexpectedly approached for their opinion. This produced a schism in the ranks of the governing coalition, between the Fälldin supporters who felt that the terms of the Stipulation Act had not been met—particularly on account of reliance on a foreign organization for reprocessing—and those who regarded the industry's response as adequately discharging their legal obligations.

Fälldin found himself in an untenable position, and his government resigned in October 1978. The short-lived Liberal government that succeeded him, backed by the Social Democrats, proposed that there should be twelve reactors. This number was eventually completed. But the anti-nuclear movement was collecting both its strength and signatures in favour of a referendum. The stage was set for a strong reaction to the Three Mile Island accident when it occurred in 1979, one day after the Swedish Nuclear Power Inspectorate had approved a site for the disposal of nuclear waste, after a thirteen-hour meeting held in the full glare of media publicity. From that point the nuclear industry's plans for waste-storage facilities progressed steadily[33]. A waste organization was in place by 1982; a first storage facility (CLAB) was completed in 1985; a disposal facility (SFR) in 1988. All proved to be models of their kind.

Reactor safety took the place of the waste issue at the head of the political agenda. The Social Democrats—under their leader, Olof Palme, who had been Prime Minister three years earlier—broke away from the Liberals and supported the proposal for a referendum. At that point the proposal commanded broad political support. Given this consensus on how the issue was to be resolved, nuclear power ceased to be a major problem in the general election of September 1979, which brought Fälldin back to power, though with a majority of only one.

The referendum, which was held in March 1980, was only the fourth time in the country's history that this method had been used to resolve an awkward political problem[34]. As with the previous issues (prohibition; right- or left-hand traffic; and pensions) this course was adopted because in some important respects public opinion did not divide on normal party lines. The Conservatives did not want to throw away what had already been achieved, and put forward Option 1 (see Table 4.1), which was basically to continue cautiously with the planned programme. The Social Democrats, needing for political reasons to put forward a line of their own, added a gloss regarding nationalization (Option 2). The Centre and Communist parties were against nuclear energy, and supported Option 3. The three options were carefully described in a statement of guidance to the electorate. Even immigrants were not overlooked, and received information in their own languages. Despite this, there may have been some confusion in the public mind, judging by the remark of a lady on Swedish TV on the day of the referendum: 'I still don't understand why we want nuclear power, when I've got electricity in my house already.'

A majority proved to be in favour of proceeding with the nuclear

Table 4.1 Options Presented to the Swedish Electorate in the Referendum of March 1980

1. Retain six reactors in service; commission the four already completed; complete two under construction; no more thereafter (Conservatives).
   - Voting: 18.9 per cent.

2. As Option 1, but coupled with nationalization measures (Social Democrats and Liberals).
   - Voting: 39.1 per cent.

3. Phase out the six already operating reactors over 10 years; remainder of programme to be abandoned (Centre and Communists).
   - Voting: 38.7 per cent.

   Note: 3.3 per cent of the papers were blank or spoiled.

programme; but there was a substantial minority—nearly 39 per cent—which supported the 'anti' line of Option 3. The voting was more anti-nuclear than the results of the previous year's general election had seemed to indicate, suggesting that it had been astute of Palme to support the idea of a referendum.

The voting pattern gave everyone the feeling of having to some extent won. Politically the immediate result was to establish a consensus that the planned programme of twelve reactors should be completed. However, no doubt because of the substantial anti-nuclear minority vote, and as a political sop to take the issue out of politics altogether for the foreseeable future, parliament some months later decided that nuclear power should be 'phased out' by the year 2010—a date then comfortably over the political horizon, particularly in a country whose parliaments have a fixed duration of three years. This effectively removed the contention surrounding nuclear power. But outside government there was widespread scepticism about the realism of such a policy, which was regarded as a transparently political device. The industry believed that when the time came to implement the decision, two decades later, it would have little difficulty in pointing to an excellent operating record and persuading the parliament of the day to revoke the policy. Even the environmentalists were doubtful whether the phasing-out 'decision' was more than a ritual bow in their direction.

Chernobyl, in April 1986, and the radioactive contamination it caused in Lapland in the far north, changed everything. Suddenly phasing-out was no longer a distant prospect, but something which had immediate political priority. It overshadowed the official opening of the central nuclear waste storage facility CLAB three days later. The Centre and Communist parties demanded the immediate closure of the two reactors at Barsebäck, which are only 30 kilometres from Malmö and even closer to the Danish capital of Copenhagen. The government set up a Review Commission to evaluate the Chernobyl accident and draw lessons for Swedish energy policy. It reported in November 1986, expressing satisfaction with the safety of Swedish nuclear reactors. Nevertheless all the political parties except the Conservatives felt that changes had to be made.

On 15 May 1987 the government presented a Bill dealing with general principles governing the phasing-out of nuclear power[35]. It said that *if* there were enough new power resources, and *if* the conservation programme had been successful—a prudent choice of wording!—then the first nuclear units would be closed between 1993 and 1995. Ten months later the government made a firm announcement that two reactors were to be closed, one in 1995 and one the following year.

The dates reflected a compromise between elements within the Social Democratic Party itself: the women's, youth, and Christian movements wanted a quicker shut-down; while the trade unionists sought deferral because of worries about jobs. Outside the Party the compromise pleased neither industrialists nor environmentalists. The former warned the government that closing nuclear reactors would be likely to cripple industrial sectors like paper and pulp, chemicals, and steel, which are heavily dependent on cheap nuclear electricity. The environmentalists were displeased because they were looking for complete closure of all twelve nuclear stations within three years—ridiculous though that was in view of the lead times needed to provide new generating capacity.

The three-year duration of their parliament induces short-term attitudes in Swedish politicians, in sharp contrast to the strategic approach of their industries. So the government was in no position to listen to those who wished for delay. It was conscious that there would be a general election in September 1988; and there were indications that 5 per cent of the electorate might switch its allegiance from the ruling Social Democrats to the Greens. That could bring the Green Party above the 4 per cent voting threshold and so into parliament, where it might conceivably hold the balance of power between the Socialist and non-Socialist blocs, especially if the traditional allies of the Social Democrats, the Communists, failed to get in. Moreover, the advance of the Greens was making all the other parties more environmentally conscious. The result of the election was that the Greens did indeed enter parliament, though with only 5.8 per cent of the votes—above the 4 per cent threshold but fewer than they had hoped for. The Left's majority of Social Democrats and Communists survived, and the Social Democrats remained in power, with support on specific issues from other parties.

This may be regarded in political terms as justifying the strongly anti-nuclear line taken by the government prior to the election. It had outfaced the Greens by stealing their clothes, going beyond insisting that the closure programme must proceed by forbidding the industry to make any plans for future nuclear projects. To do so would be illegal, a 'thought police' measure worthy of George Orwell. Plant improvements in the context of life extension were equally frowned upon, though 'life assurance' was a permissible subject for study.

But in practical terms the government's problems were only just beginning. There was no confidence in the technical merit of the closure decision. The commission set up after Chernobyl had concluded that the safety of Sweden's twelve reactors was satisfactory, and that closing them down would reduce industrial competitiveness, as well as destroying the highly efficient Swedish reactor construction industry. The closure programme was also estimated to cost 25 billion Swedish kroner for the first two closures, or 100 billion kroner for the total abandonment of nuclear power; and the loss of 60,000 to 100,000 jobs in the energy-intensive industries. The government disputes these figures, which may be tested in the Swedish courts if the utilities claim for compensation.

The Swedes have amongst the highest electricity consumption per capita in the world; and despite the long-standing political rhetoric in favour of conservation it has continued to increase, at over 6 per cent in 1987. There is little hope of achieving energy savings sufficient to close the gap left by the two closures planned for the mid-1990s. There has been a steady uprating of the performance of some of the nuclear power-stations, which has been proceeding quietly and with hardly any publicity; but it is doubtful whether this alone could see Sweden safely past 1995. Some more tangible replacement would be necessary if the closure programme were to continue and eventually encompass all twelve reactors.

Table 4.2 Swedish Generation Options

	Terawatt-hours per year
Total power generation	141
Nuclear contribution	66
Fossil contribution	6
Hydro availability	69
Hydro potential from four remaining major rivers (almost impossible on environmental grounds)	20–5
Hydro potential from small rivers	2
Wind power (by 2010)	3
Maximum additional CHP, wind, hydro (by 2010)	15

Note: Figures refer to 1988 unless otherwise stated.
CHP: combined heat and power (p. 159).

As Table 4.2 shows, hydropower could provide a partial alternative, but only at the cost of major changes to the four remaining large rivers, which so far have been staunchly protected by the environmental movement, and by Parliament. In any case they could not supply sufficient capacity to replace more than a third of the nuclear stations; and moreover hydro production has to be severely curtailed in dry years, throwing even greater reponsibility onto nuclear generation. The 'renewable' energy sources, like wind, cannot offer an answer on the scale and in the time required, for the technical reasons discussed in Chapter 12. Imported coal would be a possibility, though the government, for environmental reasons, is also against its use for electricity production, unless the waste heat can be utilized. Moreover, it would almost certainly be dearer than continuing with nuclear power, particularly if full protection against sulphur and nitrogen oxides were provided. Extensive drilling in the Siljan Lake area north of Stockholm, where a meteor crashed 350 million years ago, has failed to provide evidence of the predicted supplies of deep natural gas. Importing more natural gas from Denmark, the Soviet Union, and Norway might provide an escape route once the necessary infrastructure had been installed, though at a cost.

But in any case the Riksdag (the Swedish parliament) in the spring of 1988 had constrained coal and gas by adopting a policy requiring that the release of carbon dioxide to the atmosphere should not increase—thus effectively painting the government into a corner. The Swedish parliament signalled its awareness of some confusion by agreeing in June 1988 to debate the issue again in mid-1990, after a full review, and before any final decision was taken on which reactors should be phased out. Preparatory work for the review immediately made apparent the incompatibility of the three main tenets of current Swedish energy policy: no nuclear power, no extension of hydropower, and no increase in carbon dioxide emissions. Voices were raised proposing that a further referendum should be held on the nuclear question in the 1990s, though there was little confidence that this is a reliable way of deciding policy.

The major loss of public confidence in the post-Chernobyl period, which had led the government to take its phase-out decision in a moment of populist opportunism, had lasted only a little over one year[36,37]. Thereafter the figures had settled back into the pre-disaster pattern, with only 29 per cent of the population (16 per cent men and 41 per cent women) 'strongly concerned' about nuclear power—close to the pre-Chernobyl figure of 26 per cent, and well below the 42 per cent reached in the immediate aftermath (page 284). Other issues had begun to concern the public more.

Against that background, the abandonment of a nuclear programme which had served the country well would be a triumph of dogma over common sense. *Forbes Magazine*, the leading American business journal, described the policy as 'reckless' and 'foolhardy'. Economically it would be disastrous, given the high front-end capital costs of nuclear power which would be thrown away. Householders' electricity costs could be increased in real terms by 50 per cent, industry's possibly by as much as 100 per cent (the figures come from the Swedish National Energy Administration); and this would affect consumption patterns in ways difficult to foresee. Fears of a loss of access to cheap electricity have already (1990) led Swedish industrialists to relocate some of their energy-intensive investments in other countries: a cement factory has gone to France, an aluminium smelter to Iceland. A wealthy and more unified post-1992 Europe, with its strong commitment to nuclear power, could reinforce such doubts in the Swedish industrial mind. The trade unions made clear in August 1989 that they too were concerned about the indirect employment implications of the phasing-out decision.

The government sensed that it was no longer a secure one-way bet to offer total opposition to nuclear power, particularly for a country whose economy was increasingly in disarray. A first sign that realism was dawning appeared on 9 January 1990. Mrs Dahl, the firmly anti-nuclear Minister of Environment and Energy in the troubled minority Social Democrat government of Ingvar Carlsson (who had succeeded as Prime Minister after Olof Palme's murder in February 1986) had her portfolio reduced to cover Environment alone, though she retained oversight for nuclear safety. Her place as Energy Minister was taken by Rune Molin, a prominent trade unionist, who was opposed to starting the nuclear phase-out as early as 1995—though in his public statements he still upheld the doctrine of complete phase-out by 2010.

The quartet undertaking the energy review, which included the Prime Minister himself along with Dahl and Molin, reported in April 1990. Carlsson was forced to concede that the phase-out timetable could be adhered to only if the Riksdag's ban on additional carbon dioxide releases could be lifted.

The option remains to postpone some or all of the reactor closures. Should a further accident occur meanwhile, that would be the end of nuclear power in Sweden, even if not elsewhere. The policy would then have had the effect of providing an essential 'vaccination' for politicians whose primary purpose is to retain power. In party-political terms the declaratory policy regarding closure seems more rational than it could possibly be in terms of economic logic.

Italy: The tragedy of Montalto di Castro

Montalto di Castro is a small village lying on Italy's west coast, a little north of the mouth of the Tiber, about 100 kilometres north-west of Rome. It has an Etruscan museum. It is also the site of what had been planned as Italy's largest and most modern nuclear power-station, before it was halted in mid-construction following a decision of the Italian government in November 1987. Montalto had been the symbol of the nuclear aspirations of the state electricity utility, Ente Nazionale per l'Energia Elettrica (ENEL). If it could be completed and safely operated for a few years the nuclear programme might at last begin to roll. If not, the outlook would be bleak. Every precaution was taken in the design to satisfy the most stringent safety requirements, even to providing special protection against terrorist attack or crashing aircraft. To no avail: it was not proof against the instability of Italian politics, which by May 1989 had witnessed the comings and goings of no less than forty-eight different administrations in the forty-five years since the end of World War II.

Nuclear power had figured prominently in ENEL's plans in the early 1970s. A 1973 OECD report spoke of plans to build 18 nuclear GWe by 1985, 44 GWe by 1990. Wildly exaggerated though such figures were, they indicated strong commitment, based on some experience, and an outstanding national tradition in mechanical engineering. First generation stations had been started in the 1960s—Latina (a British gas-cooled Magnox design), Garigliano (BWR), and Trino Vercellese (PWR)—and relations between ENEL and the local communities were good. The Caorso BWR station near Piacenza in the Po valley, begun in 1970, was less lucky. It aroused some local hostility during construction due to social aspects of the project; but no reservations about safety were evident. Following the practice for conventional stations ENEL signed an agreement with the local commune which covered contributions towards developing the local infrastructure, and agreed to supply information on health aspects[38].

The subsequent nuclear projects provided for in the *piano energetico nazionale*—PEN or energy plan—approved in the mid-1970s fared considerably worse. For some years there had been growing public disquiet about problems of industrial pollution, notably but not exclusively those created by Mestre, immediately to the north of Venice. Environmental groups grew in strength as a consequence, and were able to whip up local opposition to new projects, including of course nuclear stations. Local politicians were also concerned. A new law on siting and licensing was passed in 1975, increasing the participation of local authorities. The licensing procedure allowed construction to start about two years after the approval of ENEL's plans by the government. A speedier procedure was contemplated for two regions, Molise and Lazio. The former refused to co-operate, but Lazio agreed to a site in the commune of Montalto di Castro. Unfortunately the accelerated procedure failed to provide for consultation with the locals, who became upset until ENEL signed an agreement similar to that for Caorso. Negotiations began with two other regions, Piedmont and Lombardy.

ENEL identified a number of public concerns at this time: waste disposal, the possibility of sabotage, decommissioning, the environmental effects of waste heat, radioactive effluents, and the need to demonstrate the justification for nuclear power through risk-benefit analysis. A public information campaign was begun.

By 1981, in the aftermath of the second oil-price shock, a majority of the Italian parliament was ready to approve a new energy plan, which included the construction of 12 GWe of new nuclear plant, and a reduction of dependence on imported oil. But the problems of obtaining local acceptance remained, even for conventional power-stations. A new law, approved in 1983, provided for a package of financial aid to towns and regions hosting new power-plants, as a way of offsetting any adverse socio-economic impacts. However, by 1985 only 3.3 GWe out of the 12 GWe of conventional stations which had also been envisaged in the 1981 plan had begun construction. Nuclear fared even worse: in four years only the siting procedure for one new two GWe station in Trino (Piedmont) was completed. But at least the affirmative decision by the regional council was clear-cut, by forty-three votes to six.

Elsewhere ENEL faced still more serious difficulties. The Italian political system is characterized by considerable devolution of power to local councils, this being a constitutional memory of the days of the self-governing states, which were only consolidated into the Italy we know today as recently as the nineteenth century. Local authorities often opposed the government's energy plans, being driven by local electoral considerations resulting from opposition by environmentalists and farmers. Stalemate was a frequent result of such opposition. 'Interpretation' of the law became a prime tactic for asserting one's opposition, irrespective of the exact reasons. Claims and counterclaims based on procedure or substance were filed by regions, communes, pressure groups, local mayors, and individual citizens.

ENEL did its best in the circumstances. A main plank of its policy was to take on the burden of the costs which a local commune would have to bear if the nation was to benefit from additional generating capacity. For instance, in Piedmont ENEL undertook certain obligations relating to soil and water management (Piedmont being a rice-growing area), local infrastructure, safety and health, information, and additional energy projects locally in the form of hydro and renewables. The emphasis was on the real problems of the district, which an organization as powerful as ENEL was often able to alleviate. For their pains this was described by opposition groups as 'the wages of fear'. Those who wished the Italian countryside to remain as it had been for centuries could never be won over. By 1985 the nuclear question was once again before parliament[39].

In 1986 the government adopted a new national energy plan, designed to increase substantially the use of coal and nuclear power for electricity generation, while developing the use of natural gas in other energy sectors. But the totally unforeseen event of Chernobyl in April of that year, and rising public concern about the environment, led to an almost immediate reassessment of the plan's provisions. The result in June 1986 was a moratorium on further nuclear developments. A national energy conference held in February 1987 discussed possible options, but reached no final conclusions.

A semblance of political stability existed during the three and a half years that the Socialist Bettino Craxi presided over a five-party coalition that also included Christian Democrats (the largest group), Social Democrats, Liberals, and Republicans. His resignation in April 1987 was followed by a period of uncertainty, leading up to a general election in June. Giovanni Goria took over as Premier.

Montalto's difficulties were growing. At the begining of 1987 the *Corriere della Sera* had conducted a poll which showed that 72 per cent of the public were anti-nuclear. In 1978 the figure had been only 26 per cent, and still only 41 per cent soon after Three Mile Island. The Christian Democrats, the largest political grouping, campaigned against nuclear power. In the circumstances it was hardly surprising that a referendum on 8 November 1987 produced a large majority against the nuclear power programme.

It was concerned with the possible abrogation of laws regulating nuclear power, as regards siting procedure, contributions to local authorities accepting power-stations (not only nuclear) in their area of jurisdiction, and ENEL's overseas collaboration in nuclear matters. The electoral turnout was low: 43 per cent did not bother to vote, 11 per cent were in favour of the existing laws, and 46 per cent voted for abrogation. The motivation of the 'antis' was not entirely clear. They might have been indicating their desire to safeguard the environment; or they might have been protesting against the direction in which this advanced industrial society was evolving. Abstentions could also have been a sign of confusion regarding nuclear matters generally: a poll taken just before the vote showed that 80 per cent of those interviewed did not know what the referendum was about, or what the consequences of a vote either way would be. It also showed strong agreement by most of those interviewed that local authorities close to power stations should receive a subsidy, in apparent contradiction to the subsequent referendum results.

A month later, in December 1987, the government announced guidelines for a new five-year national energy plan, which was strongly anti-nuclear. There were to be no new nuclear projects for five years. The Trino 2 station (2 GWe PWR) was to be halted, the old Latina Magnox station decommissioned, the safety of Trino 1 and Caorso reviewed, and the possibility of converting Montalto to coal or gas explored: if this proved impracticable the possibility of improving its operational safety was to be studied. There was an exhortation to consider the possibility of inherently safe reactors. Work at Montalto was suspended, at a cost of a billion lire—nearly half a million pounds—a day.

ENEL did not take long to report that conversion of Montalto to fossil fuel was economically impracticable. The International Atomic Energy Agency confirmed that Caorso's safety was satisfactory. Early in March 1988, after the Council of Ministers had overridden strong opposition, the government ordered work to be restarted at Montalto di Castro—only to have their wishes flouted by the local Socialist mayor, who revoked the local authority's permit to build. Labour unrest spread amongst the construction workers, who were anxious for their jobs, and led to a march by about 500 on the Prime Minister's offices at the Palazzo Chigi. The Goria government fell.

His place as Prime Minister was taken by Ciriaco De Mita, leader of the Christian Democrats. The new government was formed from the same five-party coalition, some of whose members (particularly the Christian Democrats, Republicans, and Liberals) were beginning to express concern about the demise of nuclear power. De Mita proposed that the future of Montalto should be decided in the framework of yet another new national energy plan—possibly indicating a reluctance to confront the leader of the Socialists, Bettino Craxi.

De Mita's administration showed little willingness to fight for nuclear power on its merits, or for Montalto on the grounds of the expenditure already committed to the project. Three decrees during the autumn and winter of 1988, and a confirmatory law passed on 10 February 1989, marked the formal abandonment of the attempt to carry through Montalto to completion, despite the fact that three-quarters of the cost was already sunk, and that conversion would incur a further four billion dollars and take until 1994. Work on the Trino–2 PWR 2 GWe station, which was still in an early stage, was also stopped. The Latina Magnox plant was permanently shut down. An emergency programme of thermal power stations was instituted to take the place of the cancelled units. A ritual bow was made to the future of nuclear power by a reference to the possibility of turning to 'inherently safe reactors' (see Chapter 9). The De Mita government collapsed in its turn in May 1989. In July he was succeeded by Giulio Andreotti.

The decision to cancel Montalto and Trino–2, which was taken despite a 4 per cent annual growth in electricity demand, destroyed any hope of new Italian nuclear power this side of the year 2000. Of the total of 65 GWe of electricity needed by then only just over 1 GWe will be nuclear—little more than the contribution from geothermal energy. Imports from France, which have grown rapidly—to 9.7 billion Kwh in 1988—will be equivalent to about a further 1 GWe; but the transmission lines are already working at their safe limits. Hydro will account for 15 GWe. The rest will be conventional coal, oil, or natural gas.

Italy is overwhelmingly (81 per cent in 1988) dependent on energy imports, but the country has yet to implement a coherent energy strategy. Oil accounts for 60 per cent of primary energy. This may have been acceptable while oil prices were low, but could hold dangers in the tighter market conditions expected in the 1990s. The most recent energy plan, which received government approval in August 1988, had as one of its objectives reducing independence on imported energy to 75 per cent over fifteen years.

This was a modest enough target when set alongside France's achievements; but a year later it was still in the legislative queue. 'Greenhouse' concerns may possibly focus attention on the fact that less than 10 per cent of Italy's energy production is 'greenhouse-free', compared with around 36 per cent in nuclear France[191]. A reappraisal of environmental criteria at the political level is certainly desirable. Whether this will indeed happen in a way which benefits nuclear power will depend, as elsewhere, on an absence of serious reactor accidents anywhere in the world, better public understanding about the global-warming issue, and strong leadership, if it can be found. What seems more probable is a sharp reminder some time in the 1990s, if the oil market tightens, of the economic penalties of excessive energy-import dependence.

At that point the Montalto di Castro cancellation, and the destruction of the nuclear programme on which Italy had embarked with such high hopes, may engender anxiety even more than regret. It is this fear of excessive foreign energy dependence which underlies the efforts being made by ENEL and its associates to be ready with fresh plans, for reactors of wholly acceptable safety standards, as soon as the five-year nuclear moratorium ends in 1992.

Germany: birthplace of uranium fission

The post-war political structure of the Federal Republic of Germany is unusually complex. The constitution devolves considerable powers to the eleven (including West Berlin) states or länder. The latter participate in central government through the Bundesrat, the second house of parliament (the other being the directly elected Bundestag). The Bundesrat, an institution unique to Germany, is composed ex-officio of selected ministers of each of the Länder. Since about half of all legislation requires the Bundesrat's approval, a change of government in the constituent states therefore has direct implications for the way the whole country is governed.

There are five main political parties, with confusingly similar titles: the centre-right Christian Democratic Union (CDU); its Bavarian sister party, the Christian Social Union (CSU); the Liberal Free Democrats (FDP), who have held the balance in government for all but seven years of the country's post-war history; the Social Democratic Party (SPD); and the Green Party, which emerged from an environmental pressure-group in 1979. In the recent past a far-right Republican group has begun to exert its influence. A form of proportional representation frequently causes government to be a matter needing coalition. As in Sweden, this provides political if not moral justification for a good deal of 'trimming' over an issue as sensitive as nuclear power. A further constitutional factor which has had a considerable bearing on German nuclear history is the way in which pressure groups can use the legal system in the courts to block actions or projects of which they disapprove. Programmes for waste storage, plutonium recycling and fast reactor development have all been pursued by objectors through the courts.

Germany was where the crucial experiment leading to the discovery of uranium fission had been made in November 1938 by Otto Hahn and Fritz Strassmann; so it was hardly surprising that the country was one of the earliest to take an interest in commercial nuclear energy, and in particular light water reactors. French efforts around 1960 to interest the other Euratom countries, including Germany, in standardizing on graphite-gas-cooling technology fell on deaf ears; arguments about the need for economic concentration, and for avoiding undue dependence on the USA, did not carry the day. The economic advantages of the PWR and BWR were already too apparent, particularly when backed by high-pressure salesmanship and a Euratom–USA accord. France within a few years, and the UK after a long policy struggle (see Chapter 5), both eventually reached the same conclusion.

Two research centres, at Jülich and Karlsruhe, were set up in 1956. A number of research reactors were built, a nuclear-ship project begun, and an agreement reached with the USA on breeder-reactor collaboration. In 1962 the first commercially significant order was placed for the 250 MWe Gundremmingen BWR, with nuclear components supplied under the Euratom–USA agreement by the American company General Electric. An important step towards consolidating Germany's own nuclear industry was taken by the creation in 1969 of a strong reactor construction company, Kraftwerk Union AG, formed by merging the nuclear interests of Siemens and AEG. By 1977 nine reactors generating 6 GWe were in operation, and a dozen others were being built.

But the country was not to escape the wave of opposition to nuclear energy which was the dominant international environmental issue of the mid 1970s. President Nixon's 1970 'State of the Union' message, singling out the environment for special consideration, had chimed with Germany's own anxieties about the deteriorating environment. In 1976 a thousand organizations took part in picketing nuclear sites, and the Free Democrats, junior partners in the ruling coalition, declared their opposition. The anti-nuclear movement reached its first peak in 1977. The need to take the opposition seriously was rubbed in by riots at the nuclear power-stations at Grohnde and Brokdorf. Demonstrations effectively blocked the construction of another station at Wyhl. 'Bürgerinitiativen'—citizens' initiatives by environmentalists—added to the uncertainty. The Federal Constitutional Court was asked to decide whether the Kalkar joint German-Dutch-Belgian fast reactor project contravened Germany's basic Atomic Energy legislation. Work on six light-water reactors was held up by litigation.

At the November 1977 conferences of both ruling coalition parties (the Social Democrats under Helmut Schmidt and the Free Democrats) a substantial number of delegates asked for the nuclear programme to be held up until approval could be given for a waste disposal and reprocessing plant to be built at Gorleben, on the Elbe south-east of Hamburg, in Lower Saxony. In December 1977 the government reached a compromise. The FDP accepted that there should be no formal moratorium. The SPD agreed to give priority to indigenous coal, while continuing the nuclear programme to supply the balance of electricity needs. It was of some assistance in reaching this compromise that the reduction in economic activity following the 1973 oil-price shock had made the original nuclear programme seem unrealistically large: in March 1977 the capacity planned for 1985 was cut back by one-third.

In deference to political and public opinion the Federal Ministry for Internal Affairs held up licences for construction or operation of nuclear-power projects until progress had been made on fuel reprocessing and storage. Interim storage arrangements were put in hand by the twelve main electrical utilities intending to operate nuclear stations, pending the completion of Gorleben.

These compromise arrangements did not satisfy the hard core of nuclear opponents. In truth, their target at this time was not so much nuclear power itself as the general direction modern life was taking. It was the industry's ill-luck that nuclear opposition was a symbol of this wider concern: to ask the 'antis' to abandon their campaign would be like asking a company to abandon the 'logo' which had successfully established its corporate identity. Nevertheless nuclear power was not wholly without friends. The trade unions recognized that it provided employment, both directly and indirectly through its effect on electricity costs. They staged a rally in Dortmund in November 1977 at which 35,000 people lobbied for a sound energy policy and for safe nuclear power. This helped the government to reach its compromise a month later. One way and another a period of peace was bought, and the summer of 1978 was relatively calm, at least when compared with the events of the previous year.

Nuclear power was nevertheless still capable of rocking the government, whose coalition was by no means safe, despite the towering reputation of Chancellor Schmidt. The Free Democrats failed to obtain seats in the Hamburg and Lower Saxony state governments in June 1978, having fallen below the 5 per cent voting minimum as a result of interventions by ecologists. However, they managed to retain their seats in Hessen later in the year. Had they not done so the Christian Democrat opposition in the Bundesrat would under the German constitution have increased to two-thirds, at which point all legislation would have been at its mercy.

Schmidt had a majority of only eleven, and came near to defeat in December 1978 over the issue of approving the third stage of the Kalkar fast reactor, which a number of the Free Democrats opposed. The Federal Constitutional Court had ruled a few days earlier that Kalkar did not, after all, contravene the basic atomic law; and that when parliament gave its approval in 1959–60 for nuclear energy it had clearly foreseen the possibility that fast reactors would be part of the long-term programme. The political difficulty was that the Free Democrats in their annual November conference had shown they were aware of the threat posed by the ecologists, by deciding in favour of a moratorium on Kalkar for several years. Only a threat of resignation by the Economics Minister, Count Otto Lamsdorf, headed off a call for a complete ban on nuclear energy. This would have presented the federal government with a considerable problem, since nuclear power was already producing 10.8 per cent of Germany's electricity.

The following year, 1979, was the year of the Three Mile Island accident. Understandably it saw the government still under threat from the Greens. Seventy per cent of Green supporters approved of

Schmidt, but were nevertheless prepared to vote his party out of office. When the Greens were transformed from a pressure group into a formally constituted party in November its members were found to include a number of 'Reds' as well. Meanwhile only ten nuclear plants were operational, and plans for new reactors were still held up in the courts. The reactor-construction industry was starved of orders. Problems of waste disposal remained unresolved. An important Risk Study, the German equivalent of the US Rasmussen Report[46], was published by the Commission on Reactor Safety (RSK).

The position of the Schmidt-led coalition improved in 1980, and in the light of the second oil price shock the government was able to bring in a revised energy policy, aimed at lessening dependence on energy imports. Priority was given to indigenous coal, despite its high cost, but there was still to be a place for further limited development of nuclear power, though rumblings of opposition continued. Curiously, in the federal elections in October the Greens, now a fully-fledged political party, seemed less of an obstacle than when they had been merely a pressure group: they polled only 1.5 per cent. One reason may have been that economic considerations had become uppermost in people's minds: the recession brought about by OPEC's taxation of the West was starting to bite into the German miracle. Unemployment in 1981 was the highest for twenty-six years. That year saw the effective launch of the first 'convoy' of a standardized class of reactors, which had been under discussion with the electrical utilities since the early 1970s; three such reactors were ordered.

Chancellor Schmidt's reign came to an end on 1 October 1982. He was succeeded by Helmut Kohl. Six months later a federal election brought twenty-seven Greens into parliament. Kohl, leader of the Christian Democrats, ruled with the support of the right-wing Christian Social Union led by Strauss. Energy issues still surfaced from time to time, but nuclear power was no longer the only target. Acid rain and the dying forests had taken its place in the spot-light—so much so that during the summer recess of 1984 parliament was recalled for a special session to discuss the start-up, prior to the fitting of its stack filters, of a coal-fired station at Buschhaus near the eastern border.

Later in that year the Greens in Hessen refused to join the SPD in supporting two nuclear projects. But dissent broke out shortly afterwards in their own ranks between the 'realists' and the 'fundamentalists', over co-operation with the SPD. The Green Party was left considerably weakened—but still profoundly anti-nuclear, opposed to centralized electricity supplies, and in favour of 'soft energy paths' like solar energy. Perhaps fortunately for the party it was in opposition, and the impracticability of such policies was not closely scrutinized.

When the Chernobyl disaster came in April 1986 it provided an unlooked-for test for all the political parties. Initially there was hysteria and confusion. Wildly different regulations for the protection of the public against radioactive contamination were promulgated by the different state and federal authorities. Milk sold in Bavaria would have been taken off the market in Hessen[40]. Cattle were treated differently in Germany and Switzerland, only the width of the Rhine away. Such discrepancies could not be concealed from the public. In May there was pressure from the Greens to close the big Biblis station on the Rhine near Worms, 150 kilometres south of Bonn. June saw violent clashes at the Wackersdorf reprocessing plant construction site in Bavaria, and 300 Austrian demonstrators were refused entry at the frontier. July brought protests against loading fuel into the new French reactor at Cattenom, just over the border in Moselle, and demonstrations in Hamburg against the start-up of the big Brokdorf PWR reactor on the Elbe. Chernobyl stayed in the headlines for many weeks until, as Thomas Roser of the German Atomforum drily observed[41], it was displaced by the world football championships.

The political parties were in the interesting and not altogether comfortable position of having to fight a number of state elections, the first only a few weeks after the disaster, and a federal election in January 1987. Election platforms had to be prepared before reliable opinion polls could be available, and before the public could possibly have had time for mature reflection. The Greens had no problem: they stayed even more resolutely anti-nuclear. The first Green politician to be appointed as a minister in a state government (Hessen) exercised the power of his environmental portfolio by taking action against a plutonium fuel plant at Hanau (about 25 kilometres east of Frankfurt) for alleged non-compliance with the letter of regulatory procedures. Like their Swedish colleagues the Social Democrats, once the nuclear industry's supporters, opted at a rally in Nuremberg in August for closure of all nuclear stations, starting in 1987 or 1988, and phased over ten years. The Free Democrats, who shared government with the Christian Democrats, remained the party of the status quo: cancel nothing, construct nothing further. It was left to the Christian Democrats, the largest single party, with 40 per cent of the votes, to decide how the country should react to this unexpected threat from a foreign disaster.

The decisions which the government took were sensible and to the point. A comprehensive review of the safety of German nuclear stations was put in hand, and led to a report expressing confidence. It further asserted that with German reactors a Chernobyl-type disaster was not technically possible. Nevertheless some additional safety measures were recommended, to take the degree of protection even beyond the 'maximum credible accident'. In particular controlled containment pressure relief systems were to be fitted to reactor containment vessels, and in the case of boiling water reactors there was to be a system of flooding the containment space with an inert gas. A new Federal Ministry for Environmental and Reactor Safety was established in January 1987, *inter alia* to exercise sole authority for setting acceptable dose limits for human and animal foodstuffs throughout the country, in place of the hotch-potch of state regulations which had so confused the public in the weeks after Chernobyl. Substantial and immediate compensation was offered to farmers.

Chancellor Kohl also took the opportunity afforded by the 1986 Tokyo summit to appeal for better international co-operation on matters of nuclear safety, and so smoothed the way for the two international conventions—one on the early notification of a nuclear accident, the other on mutual assistance in case of an accident or radiological emergency—that were signed at the International Atomic Energy Agency's General Conference in Vienna on 26 September 1986.

The overall impression was of a government acting sensibly and constructively at a difficult time. Nevertheless, the general line was pro-nuclear, at a time when the generality of public opinion took an opposite view; and a federal election was pending. Believing that politicians do not like to defend lost causes, the German nuclear industry decided to do what it could to improve the level of public understanding on nuclear matters. Weekly advertisements were inserted in 300 newspapers, the emphasis being strongly on information rather than propaganda. It is impossible to say whether the campaign had any significant effect on the electoral outcome in January, but it certainly elicited a favourable response from Christian Democrat politicians.

In the event public duty and political advantage for once went together: in the one federal and six state elections that took place between Chernobyl and the autumn of 1987 the Christian Democrats had no reason to regret the line they had chosen. For their part the Social Democrats lost votes, yet nevertheless reaffirmed their anti-nuclear policy at their mid-1987 rally. The pattern of voting departed significantly from that of the immediate post-Chernobyl opinion polls. The implications of this discrepancy were not entirely clear. It could be that casting a vote is something demanding more conscious reflection than answering a pollster's questions; or that with the passing of time the public was able to see Chernobyl more clearly and in its true perspective—as a regrettable disaster, but one brought on themselves by the Russians, and not necessarily an indication of what might happen if a better-engineered and contained reactor were to have an accident. Whatever the reason, the German nuclear industry, which was by then operating twenty-one nuclear stations and generating 36 per cent of the country's electricity, began to feel that it might be able to breathe more easily.

Any such complacency was short-lived. In December 1987 a scandal erupted at the Transnuklear nuclear transport company. The management discovered that a few of its employees had been guilty of falsely describing several hundred barrels of nuclear waste in the shipping documents, and quite properly reported its findings to the government. It transpired that there had been bribery and fraud on a grand scale, involving DM 5 million between 1982 and 1986. Some of the waste from German power-stations had been intended for treatment (volume reduction and conditioning) in Belgium, so there were international implications. While there had been no real risk to human health, nor any conceivable threat of unauthorized nuclear proliferation, that was not the impression that the popular press conveyed to the public: it even went as far as speculatively linking the scandal to Libya. The public were understandably disturbed; an inquiry was instituted; a guilty employee and an accomplice from an electrical utility committed suicide; the company was put under new management.

Politically there was an immediate loss of trust in both the federal government and the nuclear industry, and a boost for the Greens. A release of radioactivity from the Biblis plant at almost the same time, although minor, did nothing to assist the cause of nuclear power. Moreover, the Transnuklear scandal had the side-effect of focusing attention once more on another thorny problem, waste disposal. Work on the Gorleben waste storage site had been halted for some months, following a fatal accident in June 1987 when an iron ring had collapsed in the No. 1 shaft, apparently through a welding failure under ground pressure. Construction was halted for almost two years.

The future of the Wackersdorf reprocessing plant in Bavaria, though staunchly defended by the powerful political figure of Franz Josef Strauss, also remained a focus of contention. For the time being German nuclear waste was being handled at the French facility at Cap de la Hague, but was due to be returned, starting in 1993. With the 'back end' of the nuclear fuel cycle falling behind schedule this was becoming a politically unwelcome prospect, particularly as German nuclear legislation requires reactor operators to demonstrate effective plans for spent-fuel management six years ahead of fuel discharge.

Nuclear power once again became a political football. The Christian Democrats won the 'plutonium election' in Hessen, after supporting plans for the Alkem company, against a combined SDP-Green attack. But there were demonstrations over the safety of the Fessenheim (French) and Neckarwestheim (German) reactors. The local Hamburg electricity utility came under pressure to sell its shares in four nuclear power-stations. In Schleswig-Holstein the State government refused to allow the Brokdorf reactor to start up after a routine maintenance period, and the federal Energy Minister had to intervene. All this time nuclear-electricity production was growing rapidly, accounting for an extra 7 per cent of generation in 1988, compared with 1987; but this led to problems with the coal-mining states. Nordrhein-Westfalen, the major coal-producing state, sought a 10 per cent cut in nuclear power to reduce the threat to 2,000 mining jobs: despite the DM 150 per tonne subsidy the price of German coal was far above the world figure, and nuclear power was cutting into its market.

The summer of 1988 saw allegations of the sale of nuclear

technology to Pakistan, India, and South Africa; and a former IAEA official told a Bundestag committee that Germany had exhibited 'insensitivity' to non-proliferation questions in its exports. There was also a long-delayed political reaction to the minor radioactive leak from Biblis a year earlier. Biblis A and B were both shut down on government orders, and stayed closed until February 1989. Altogether 1988 was not a happy year. Despite the country's dependence on nuclear power a poll indicated that three-quarters of the population felt that it should be discontinued either immediately or in the medium-term.

None of these events were major in themselves, but they were occurring at a time of political flux, when the stability of the ruling coalition was breaking down. There was scant thanks from the electorate for the affluence that the CDU/CSU/FDP coalition had sustained. Politics were polarizing, the centre weakening, while the extremes gained strength. Politicians intent on both retaining and gaining power began to review their attitudes towards nuclear energy.

The sudden death of Herr Strauss on 3 October 1988 removed a major politician who had been an unflinchingly loyal supporter of nuclear energy, and in particular of the Bavarian Wackersdorf reprocessing plant, which was due for completion in 1996. A Franco-German spent fuel reprocessing plan mooted at the Paris summit six months after his death was found to offer major economies over Wackersdorf, which cast an ominous question mark over the project's future. A further reprocessing agreement was discussed with the United Kingdom.

Even before the summit economic doubts over Wackersdorf had been growing in the minds of the German utilities. The technical case was being eroded by improved fuel-element performance, which made reprocessing less necessary; the economic case was undermined by the competing services offered more cheaply by the French and British. These concerns chimed with the political interests of the beleaguered Chancellor, who was seeking a politically anodyne way of dealing with this awkward problem, at a time when death had taken his strongest ally, and when his own political future was uncertain. His ability to retain power depended on a good showing in the 1989 European and state elections. For a tenacious politician winning them, and fighting off the threats from both ends of the political spectrum, took precedence over driving through nuclear projects—particularly as a general election was due in December 1990. A week before the European elections Wackersdorf was formally abandoned, at a total cost, if all the necessary support is included, of DM 6 billion. The German public drew the inference that the country's spent-fuel and waste-management problems were still unsolved. But Kohl's party, the Christian Democrats, did just well enough in Europe for him to stay at the helm, though with substantially reduced support.

Meanwhile, in the summer of 1989, the Free Democrats were beginning to show signs of distancing themselves from the Christian Democrats' commitment to nuclear power. The Social Democrats sensed they had a chance of detaching the Free Democrats from the coalition with the CDU within a few years, and were ready to use their own, by now, strongly anti-nuclear policy as a lever. The SPD had been partners with the FDP in the thirteen-year governing alliance which had preceded the Kohl administration, and entertained hopes of reviving it. If they succeeded, the nuclear industry would lose another powerful patron. But November 1989 brought the extraordinary events in East Berlin, the effective removal for practical purposes of the Berlin Wall, and rapid moves towards German reunification. It was a once-in-a-lifetime chance for the Federal German Chancellor to consolidate his position, and he seized it eagerly.

The position of the German nuclear industry at the beginning of 1990 remained vulnerable. No new reactors had been ordered since 1982. The European Commission's plans for opening up a free market in electricity, post-1992, might well mean an influx of French electrical energy at prices which the German generating companies could not match. On the other hand the nuclear component of the generating industry could justifiably congratulate itself on providing more than one-third of the country's electricity. In the extraordinary period of political flux that lay ahead this single fact probably constituted the industry's most effective protection.

Switzerland: Conflict in the cantons

Hairbreadth majorities are one way of ensuring that governments remain sensitive to public anxieties. A constitutional obligation to hold frequent referendums is another. A former British ambassador to Switzerland held the country's constitution to be the finest example he knew of a perfectly functioning democracy. Power is devolved on a generous scale from the federal government—headed by the seven-man Federal Council, which holds office for four years without fear of removal—to the cantons and communes. A reference to the ordinary people for a decision is described in Swiss parliamentary language, in all seriousness, as a reference to 'the sovereign'—a shining example to other democracies! All bills approved by the Federal Assembly—the bi-cameral parliament—must be submitted to a referendum if an objection is lodged within ninety days and backed by 50,000 signatures. Any group of 100,000 citizens can take an 'initiative', and demand a referendum dealing if necessary with an amendment to the constitution. As a further political check on the federal government, considerable powers are possessed by the regional cantonal administrations, both directly and via the upper house of parliament, the Council of States, whose forty-six members represent not the electorate directly, as is the case with the lower house (the National Council) but the cantons *per se*[32,42]. Since 1975 these constitutional safeguards have been given an almost non-stop test by the nuclear-power issue.

The Swiss are fine engineers. Despite their land-locked geography they have wrested a leading place for themselves as suppliers of heavy marine engines. Dr Diesel himself once worked for Sulzers. Nuclear power was welcomed as both a challenge and an opportunity by the country which had played host to the Geneva 'Atoms For Peace' conferences. It was also timely, because hydroelectric resources were almost fully exploited, and unable to satisfy a demand for electricity growing at around 3 per cent annually. Electricity supplies in winter were a particular problem. Coal had the disadvantages of pollution and acid rain, important for a country where tourism contributes so much to the economy. There was no natural gas. Oil in the 1960s was still cheap; but for a country which imported five-sixths of its energy the political instability of the Middle East was a constant worry.

Given the size of the country the nuclear programme that was started in the 1960s—before the 1973 oil shock—was certainly ambitious. The reactors were concentrated in the north. The first two to be completed, in 1969 and 1972, were medium-sized PWRs (350 MWe) at Beznau, 30 kilometres north-west of Zurich. A boiling-water reactor of about the same size followed later in 1972 at Muhleberg, only 15 kilometres from Berne. A large—920

MWe—PWR was completed in 1978/9 at Goesgen, 40 kilometres south-east of Basel; and a 950 MWe BWR at Leibstadt, only a little further away to the east, at the end of 1984. This concentration of reactors so close to three major population centres bears witness both to the difficulties of finding more remote sites in this small country, and to the confidence of the Swiss in their engineering prowess. It has incidentally allowed the Swiss to use the waste heat from nuclear power stations for district-heating.

In the summer of 1974 the Federal Council, in the aftermath of the first oil crisis, appointed a commission to examine the country's energy needs. At the time 84 per cent of primary energy was imported, behind only Denmark (99 per cent) and Japan (89 per cent) amongst the industrialized countries. The bulk was oil. The energy commission proposed ways of cutting the proportion to less than 50 per cent by the year 2000, including another 3 GWe of nuclear power. Its final report, in December 1978, envisaged a much-expanded role for the federal government in energy policy, which in this cantonal country was a suggestion that involved an element of controversy. The only concession to the nuclear opponents was a requirement that any reactor proposals should stand or fall by the tests of need, safety, and ability to dispose of the resulting waste. The government also prepared draft proposals for amending the 1959 Federal Atomic Energy Act. Preparations began for a referendum on a revised Act, and this was eventually held in May 1978. The revision came into force in October.

The opponents lost no time in attacking the constitution of the energy commission, which was unsurprisingly drawn mainly from the energy industry; the one anti-nuclear commissioner had resigned before the report was presented. The opponents pointed out that Switzerland actually had a surplus of electricity in the summer months, which it exported. They made much of the fact that Swiss nuclear waste was currently being stored in France, for lack of suitable Swiss facilities. They prepared their own anti-nuclear initiative for submission to the electorate.

Meanwhile not everything was going according to plan. The three earliest reactors at Beznau and Muhleberg had experienced little opposition. But beginning in 1975 Goesgen and Leibstadt proved more controversial. The problems arose partly from local political reactions to the heavy concentration of nuclear sites in the north-west of the country; but they were also partly in emulation of similar reactions in the USA, Germany (FRG), and Sweden. More specifically, once it was realized that for reasons of ecology the waters of the Aare and the Rhine could not be accepted as dumps for waste heat, the only alternative was to build unsightly cooling towers, which meant that the constructors had to go back to the local commune for approval to the amended plans. There had also been an intention to build further reactors, at Graben, roughly half-way between Berne and Basel, and at Verbois near Geneva; but difficulties had arisen over both approvals.

A 925 MWe boiling-water reactor was also planned for Kaiseraugst, 15 kilometres east of Basel, with construction starting in 1974, and finishing in 1980. In fact virtually no work was ever possible. Kaiseraugst became the symbol of Swiss opposition to nuclear power.

Once permission had been granted for Kaiseraugst to proceed, those with other views were determined to make their voices heard. On Easter Monday 1975 the construction site was occupied by 15,000 people in a peaceful 'sit-in'. A 'sovereign' general assembly was convened, and the Gewaltfrei Aktion Kaiseraugst (Non-violent Kaiseraugst Action Group) was born. There was full media coverage. The Grand Council of Basel called a halt to further work. The Federal Council in Berne—the government—insisted that the site should be cleared before negotiations could take place. There was deadlock. Legal proceedings began. Eventually, in June, the construction consortium agreed to GAK's demands, and the demonstrators left the site. The federal parliament debated nuclear-energy policy a couple of weeks later. It was argued for the GAK that parliament had become 'remote', and could 'no longer hear the language of the people'. The objectors charged the government with having failed to introduce an appropriate legal framework for atomic energy. Some deputies felt that the whole thing had been staged by extremists; but from that time forward it proved impossible for any effective work to be done at Kaiseraugst, while the costs of the project continued to soar.

The next few years were far from placid. The plant at Goesgen was stormed by objectors in June 1977; and in November 1979 a pylon was demolished by explosives, during the power build-up period; fortunately the plant was not on load at the time. There was also sabotage at Graben.

Two referendums were ready for submission to the electorate in

1979. The first, held on 18 February, was the anti-nuclear initiative, whose effect if approved would have been to shut down nuclear electricity production within three years. It was narrowly defeated, 51.2 per cent being against the initiative (i.e. *in favour* of nuclear power). Confusion was caused by the wording of the proposition placed before the public, and a substantial number voted in the opposite sense to which they had intended. The majority remained silent, only 49 per cent of the electorate bothering to vote.

Overshadowing this initiative by the activists was the new policy and legislative statement which the government intended to bring forward shortly afterwards, after some years of preparation, as a basis for its own referendum. One of its effects would be to facilitate local and regional consideration of objections to new nuclear stations. The referendum was held on 20 May 1979, and was strongly supported, at least by those who chose to vote: 68.9 per cent in favour of the government's proposals, only 31.1 per cent against. But the majority remained even more silent than in February, only 36.9 per cent taking part. Evidently nuclear power in Switzerland was less controversial than the activists had tried to make out. One reason that has been seriously suggested is that all Swiss men serve for a time in the Army, where protection against nuclear radiation is part of the training syllabus. Thus there is greater familiarity with the issues than in countries without conscription.

With the two referendums out of the way the Federal Council confirmed its agreement to an enlarged (1 GWe) reactor at Kaiseraugst (in October 1981), and work continued on the Leibstadt reactor. But at the same time fresh initiatives involving further referendums were launched. Two came before the electorate on 23 September 1984. The first, demanding that there should be no further nuclear construction, was rejected by 55 per cent to 45 per cent, with only 41 per cent of the electorate participating. A second, eliminating nuclear power as a national energy option, was defeated by almost exactly the same ratio. Although a significant part of the electorate remained anti-nuclear—particularly the churches, the ecologists, and the pacifists—there was a good deal of apathy. The peak of opposition seemed to have passed.

Leibstadt was completed in December 1984, bringing the country's nuclear electricity proportion to approaching 40 per cent; and the steady growth in electricity demand led parliament in

March 1985 to approve (by 118 to 73) the construction of Kaiseraugst for the second time, provided it used known and proven technology. No work had been done on the site since the 1975 occupation; but new tenders were submitted in 1986, and building was planned to start in 1989, with completion due in the mid-1990s. For the electrical utilities the decision to proceed with Kaiseraugst was a battle apparently won, though not yet a struggle successfully concluded.

The reactivated project focused attention on the Nagra waste disposal studies (Chapter 10). Three specific sites for low-radioactivity storage which had been identified in 1985 produced a barrage of local protest. Proposals for a high-level site were still awaited. Some environmental considerations were still working in favour of nuclear power, particularly acid rain and fears for the death of forests, which the Swiss treasure quite as much as their German neighbours. But the canton of Basel was still opposed, and had voted against nuclear power in the 1984 referendum.

Then came Chernobyl. The North-West Action group adopted the slogan: 'Chernobyl 2,000 km away, Kaiseraugst 10 km'. A special session of the federal parliament discussed the implications of the disaster. Some were immediate: milk was banned for pregnant women and children. Motions to close the existing five Swiss nuclear reactors were rejected, but the outlook for two new projected plants was clouded. The Berne canton hardened its opposition to any further nuclear construction on its territory, while Geneva adopted a constitutional amendment banning nuclear power. The Socialists launched two more anti-nuclear referendums: 135,000 signatures were collected in favour of a referendum intended to lead to a ten-year moratorium. Chernobyl made it more and more certain that Kaiseraugst was doomed; and without it the broader future of nuclear power in the country would also be at serious risk. The serious chemical pollution of the Rhine in November 1986 further lowered public confidence in advanced technology, and did nothing to help the case for nuclear power.

By Easter 1987, twelve years after the original occupation of the reactor site, Switzerland still had only five nuclear reactors in service, and none under construction. The Federal Council appointed an expert group to examine the energy options up to the year 2025. It reported in February 1988. Three options—more nuclear power, less nuclear power, or a policy of no change—all proved to need increased taxes on energy. With the pro-nuclear bourgeois parties sharing power with the anti-nuclear Socialists, reaching any political conclusion was difficult. As a way of escaping from the impasse, three members of parliament suggested that construction at Kaiseraugst should be halted, and the owners compensated for their nugatory expenditure—which by the end of 1987 had reached 1.33 billion Swiss francs, of which half a billion were financing charges—in return for permission to proceed with further nuclear construction.

The Swiss electricity industry is in a difficult position. After the energy crises of the 1970s energy growth restarted in 1983, and consumption continued to rise at around 3 per cent a year. Even at a lower growth rate of 2.5 per cent, demand would still double in less than thirty years. Nor is the country extravagant in its per capita use of electricity, which is 30 per cent less than in West Germany, and only one-third of that in the USA. The alternatives are to rely on electricity imports from France, which ran at over 9 billion kilowatt-hours in 1988, and could provide as much as 15 per cent of the country's electricity (the ecologists regard this option as morally repugnant, as French electricity comes from nuclear power); to cut back the rate of energy growth by financial disincentives; where possible to introduce further conservation (district heating schemes could use the waste heat from nuclear reactors); or to use coal, which has its own ecological difficulties. The death of trees is an issue which touches more than aesthetics or ecology: it is also of practical significance in the areas where trees afford protection against avalanches, and where in some cases half of them are already affected. That is a strong argument against further reliance on fossil fuel. It would be difficult to expand hydroelectricity by more than 15 per cent. Meanwhile there was little hope of proceeding with the Graben and Verbois proposals, which have remained at the planning stage. Blooded by the success of their delaying tactics so far the Greens were in no mood to give up the chase.

Against this background of an absence of good and easy answers to Switzerland's energy problems the Federal Council produced[43] a memorandum in September 1988, which reviewed the conflicting issues, with particular reference to the legal position, and proposed its own solutions. Some way forward was necessary in any case because the validity of the existing law on atomic energy was due to expire on 31 December 1991.

The memorandum made clear the Federal Council's conviction that the nuclear option should be maintained; that research and development on small reactors for district-heating should be continued; and that studies for the management of nuclear waste should be extended. The Council's reasons for recommending the rejection of the two further anti-nuclear popular initiatives asking for nuclear phase-out, which had been presented in 1987 and which would be voted on in September 1990, were not only technical but also political: only a minority of the population had so far shown their opposition to nuclear power by registering their votes when they had a chance to do so. The reasons were also partly economic: phase-out would mean increasing imports of electricity.

The Council recognized that popular assent for its views on the necessary scale could only be assured if all reasonable steps were also taken to explore other alternatives. In particular, it was necessary to provide for public endorsement from the earliest stages of planning energy policy. Reports on future energy supplies were a matter for experts; but care would be taken to see that their reports were submitted to broad scrutiny.

The troubled reactor site at Kaiseraugst presented unique problems. The company had done nothing wrong. The approvals were still valid, and revocation for political reasons only would be contrary to Swiss law. Nevertheless political action had led to a situation where huge expenditures were clearly unlikely ever to result in anything useful. As it would be manifestly unjust to leave the whole of this burden to the shareholders, the Federal Council signalled that it intended to enter into discussions with the Kaiseraugst company with an open mind, but with a determination to lance the abscess. Eventually, on 8 March 1989, the Swiss parliament agreed the terms of settlement, with the owners receiving 350 million Swiss francs (about 220 million US dollars) in partial mitigation of their loss of 1.3 billion Swiss francs. An attempt to challenge the decision via a referendum failed for want of sufficient signatures within the ninety-day time limit.

The need to revise the legal and constitutional basis for atomic energy before 31 December 1991 provides its own spur to the resolution of the wider problem. Furthermore, the sudden and world-wide realization of the importance of the 'greenhouse effect' (Chapter 13), which unexpectedly manifested itself as a political force in the course of 1988, can hardly fail to influence the contest with the environmentalists in a direction favourable to the Federal Council's views on nuclear power. Parliament agrees that the nuclear option should be kept alive; but following Chernobyl it will take many years to restore confidence in nuclear technology in the minds of many of the Swiss public. Those living in the north-west have yet to accept in their heads, still less in their hearts, that a forest of cooling towers is the price that must be paid for preserving natural forests and for energy security. Energy policy will remain a fruitful training ground for Swiss radicals. Despite the need for more generating capacity, and the Federal Council's strong endorsement of nuclear energy, the country's constitution will ensure that progress will continue to depend on a slow process of grinding between the upper millstone of energy needs and the lower millstone of activist political opposition. Predicting the future is always dangerous, but this political issue seems destined to run and run.

5 Three English-speaking Countries

As the previous chapters have been showing, the treatment accorded to nuclear power reflects to a fascinating degree the social and institutional characteristics of individual countries. The way they do things reflects their histories and traditions. So it is not surprising that three English-speaking countries as different as the mother country and her healthy progeny, the USA and Australia, should still show some common attitudes to policy-making. Despite their constitutional differences, these are countries which on the whole favour strong political parties, with sharply contrasted views, between which the electorate is invited to choose at periodical general elections. Such a political framework does not lend itself to consistent target-orientated long-term planning. Policies are always at risk of being upset the next time a party has to give way to its opponents. Coming elections discourage bold and radical solutions. A middle course is more likely to stick. Inquiries and committees are useful ways of defusing contentious issues. There is a good deal of 'muddling through'.

Institutional entanglement in the United States

The United States, the birthplace of nuclear energy, assumed the role of industry leader from the moment in the late 1960s when it became obvious to the Europeans—Britain excepted—that the future lay with water-cooled reactors. The American electricity industry gave a massive vote of confidence in the new technology by ordering 100 nuclear power plants even before the 1973 oil crisis. Despite many cancellations the USA still has by far the largest number of reactors of any country: 110 reactors with operating licences by the end of 1989, twice as many as France. And yet, despite this, the US reactor industry has been struggling for over a decade to stay alive.

Unlike France or Japan, the USA—except perhaps in military and foreign affairs—seems reluctant to encourage strong central policy-making. This has been conspicuously true of energy policy in general, and nuclear energy in particular. The reasons are primarily institutional. This is a country of continental dimensions, with a great diversity of regional interests. Its constitution is based on a separation of powers which guarantees both balance and tension between the administration and the legislature. The president may propose, but he cannot always dispose. There are further tiers of government at the state and local levels; a judicial system tailor-made for use by 'intervenors'; and powerful quasi-independent government agencies. These agencies are not headed by an effective permanent civil service to give continuity to policy, as in France and, within limits, Britain. Incoming presidential political appointees spend their first two years learning on the job, and not infrequently *un*learning the dogmas of their party's electoral campaigns. Few of them serve for a whole term. A multiplicity of policy-making centres, with views not necessarily consonant or mutually supporting, takes the place of the powerful central governments of most other countries. Even if it wished to do so, the White House is in no position to wave a magic wand that would change policies overnight. Progress towards providing nuclear power with a more rational policy framework has had to depend on the altogether slower, often frustrating, and sometimes abortive process of argument, persuasion, and not a little horse-trading. So in the case of the United States we find ourselves more concerned with administrative minutiae than with broad sweeps of action by political parties and their leaders.

There are other structural features of the United States that have influenced nuclear power. It is the most litigious nation in the world, with a commensurate number of lawyers—more in the District of Columbia alone than in the whole of Japan. They are a powerful force, ready and willing to arm objectors and intervenors with the means to resist change, often on a contingency no-success-no-fee basis. It is also a country which for many years laboured under a sense of collective guilt, stemming from past scandals of race and civil rights, and the traumatic memories of Vietnam and Watergate. The environmental movement gained enormous public esteem not only for its own work, but also by offering some kind of national catharsis. The attacks on nuclear power began as an offshoot of these wider anxieties. Before long they became the symbol and rallying-point for a popular movement deeply concerned about the country and its future.

Not the least significant feature of the United States for the rest of the nuclear world is its missionary zeal. The USA was born in the eighteenth century out of a yearning for reform, and a conviction that national effort should be devoted to improving man's lot. Today it still retains that conviction, and moreover commands the media resources enabling it to export whatever it holds for the time being to constitute the new enlightenment. The whole globe is its audience, but particularly its cultural and economic friends in OECD. As long as nuclear power enjoyed the backing of a United States consensus it was able to flourish everywhere. When that disappeared difficulties began, and not only in the USA.

The foundation for American civil nuclear power was laid in the 1954 Atomic Energy Act, which permitted private ownership of power reactors, and opened the door to international co-operation. A central feature was a regulatory process intended to foster public acceptance by providing the public with opportunities for participating in regulatory decision-making and licensing—even to the extent of inventing a special type of hearing when no member of the public had asked for one[44]. For each nuclear power plant the approval system required two steps. First, a utility had to obtain a construction permit; and then at a late stage, when the plant was largely complete, it had to apply again for an operating licence. This approach allowed a measure of 'design-as-you-go', which may have been appropriate for a still-developing technology, but was a discouragement to the standardization of design which is the key to achieving manufacturing economies of scale. The regulatory authority was required to hold public hearings at both stages should any intervenor so request. The system worked well enough for a decade; but difficulties arose in the early 1970s, soon after the first oil crisis—paradoxically at a time, well before Three Mile Island and Chernobyl, when nuclear power should have been riding high.

Regulation necessarily involves analysing what a range of possible accidents might involve. It does not, however, automatically require the entire focus to be on hypothetical 'worst cases'. Because it was certainly part of their task, but perhaps also because it was conceptually easier, the regulators chose in the early years to concentrate their studies on accidents with very low probabilities but major potential consequences—as in the Brookhaven report[45] of 1957 and the long drawn-out emergency core-cooling controversy.

Given good design, the consequences of more common accidents were unlikely to be serious, unless a dangerous combination of multiple faults happened coincidentally. Because of difficult analytical issues of statistical probability such combined-fault accidents were neglected until the appearance of the Rasmussen Report, published[46] in 1975 under the aegis of the recently appointed Nuclear Regulatory Commission (NRC). This agency had been created by splitting the regulatory functions of the Atomic Energy Commission (USAEC) away from its operational responsibilities— a feeling having developed that those who promote the technology should not also be its regulators. This view, which is shared by most other countries, is entirely consonant with the general US pattern of checks and balances. The Energy Reorganization Act[47] of 1974 brought the NRC into being on 19 January 1975, while the Energy Research and Development Administration took over other functions of the AEC (ERDA has since been absorbed into the Department of Energy).

The Rasmussen report used risk-assessment methods to estimate accident probabilities and their consequences, and tried to set nuclear risk in the context of other normal risks of living. The methodology was complex, and the report stirred up a good deal of controversy. Altogether the results of the safety analyses of the 1970s failed to convince the American public that nuclear power was in safe hands. The people's native shrewdness led them to a contrary conclusion, that nuclear power was a catastrophe waiting to happen. The consequences of this change of attitude reverberated around the globe.

Other aspects of the regulatory process told against nuclear power. Procedurally it included a good deal of theatre, with an adversarial flavour which provided opportunities for opponents to use regulatory hearings as vehicles of propaganda, if not outright obstruction. Hearings could last for months or even years, enormously increasing the delay before a licence could be issued. The process was hampered by the lack of any defined measure of the degree of public risk that would be acceptable, and by a reluctance to apply cost-benefit techniques. The result was a corpus of regulation which piled Pelion on Ossa, adding to construction costs without any obligation to justify the additional safety which was being bought. With only a few honourable exceptions average times for completion stretched out from eight years to as long as fourteen or fifteen years[48]. To be fair to the regulators, their bureaucratic complexities were not the only cause: massive inflation and reduced demand for electricity had both decreased the incentive for utilities to push for early completion. (The 7 per cent annual electricity demand growth that was typical of the 1950s and 1960s fell for a while to 3 per cent after the 1973 oil crisis). But whatever the exact reasons, the result was that during the extended period of construction the regulatory authorities' growing knowledge of previously unexamined types of possible accidents led to a stream of requirements for modifications, adding to the cost. Even when construction was complete the granting of an operating licence was not automatic, but required another inquiry of its own, which could take a further three or more years.

The result of this regulatory regime was that enormous and structurally complete capital investments could be left lying unused and financially unproductive for years, driving utilities into severe financial problems for reasons which were fundamentally procedural rather than technical. Moreover, under US financial regulations most shareholder-owned electrical utilities cannot recoup investment costs until a power-station is actually in use. Thus utilities had to borrow very heavily, at a time when long-term interest rates were above 15 per cent. With the long delays being experienced, bank charges alone could double the original capital cost. Common prudence and an obligation to defend stockholders' interests then led to cancellations and deferrals becoming the order of the day. As one utility Chief Executive Officer observed[49] as the 1980s began: 'Without a drastic change in the political environment as it affects nuclear power, one cannot determine how much a nuclear plant will cost or when it can be completed . . . other factors are beside the point.' This reluctance to place new orders effectively started in 1974, became complete in 1979, and was still continuing ten years later. Such growth as took place in nuclear generating capacity was the outcome of the wave of orders placed in the early 1970s, which resulted in reactors being brought up to full power at a rate of one every seven weeks throughout the mid-1980s.

By the second half of the 1970s nuclear power had become a source of bitter national controversy. President Carter, who assumed office in January 1977, spoke of it as the energy source of 'last resort'. Although offering token support for a programme of light-water reactors, he set his face against the commercial use of plutonium and the technology of reprocessing, for fear that they might lead indirectly to further nuclear proliferation. He thereby fuelled the opposition to nuclear power in general. At a time when nuclear power was already providing 12 per cent of the nation's electricity, he appointed a number of undisguised nuclear opponents to key energy decision-making jobs.

Briefly at the beginning of 1979 there was a glimmer of hope that the situation might improve. Then came the accident to the Three Mile Island (TMI) reactor. No one has been positively identified as having been harmed; and the containment did its job, preventing the overwhelming proportion of fission products from reaching the atmosphere. But TMI greatly discouraged the public, conferred a new aura of respectability on the objectors, and led to a *de facto* moratorium on new licensing. The *New York Times* admitted that the accident was also a journalistic disaster: not only were the press uninformed on the key issues of nuclear safety, but attempts by the authorities to shed light on what was happening were confused and inaccurate. For the utility it was a disaster of a more serious kind: the State Public Utility Commission ruled that the owners must bear the whole cost. The industry was quick to draw the inference that this was a scale of risk which no company should incur without proper insurance protection.

Despite this, the licensing hiatus which followed TMI can now be seen as having provided the essential spur needed to begin the long process of directing the regulatory approach on to a more realistic course. The pressures were financial: more than a dozen completed plants were idle because of regulatory inaction, at a cost of a million dollars per day per plant.

In most countries the government would have taken overall command and hammered out new guidelines. But the USA's complex system of checks and balances made direct administrative action virtually impossible. The autonomous NRC was in no mood to offer positive direction. It operated collegially by consensus, and could not be coerced, since the commissioners were not responsible even to the US president who had appointed them. The industry was therefore left largely to itself to make most of the running. In the long run this may be the best thing that could have happened: a debate was opened on what constituted acceptable and unacceptable risks—in contrast to attempting to proceed on the unrealistic basis of engineering for virtually zero risk. For its part Congress set about the long process of creating a more appropriate legislative framework. However, despite an enormous investment of effort on the part of both industry and the politicians, the task was still only partly finished a decade later. Meanwhile nuclear power in the USA remained under a cloud, even though it was forging ahead in countries where the institutional and regulatory framework was more favourable.

The self-examination which followed Three Mile Island showed that the context in which nuclear power had to try to operate was deficient in several vital respects[48–51]. Unless these could be dealt with there was little doubt that those who asserted that 'nuclear power was dead' were uncomfortably close to the truth. Progress was needed on half a dozen fronts:

- operating standards
- third party insurance and indemnification
- new arrangements to spread financial risk
- more equitable arrangements regarding cost recovery
- decisions on how to deal with nuclear waste
- more streamlined regulatory procedures, including advance type approval of standardized designs

Operating standards were primarily the nuclear industry's responsibility. In the early days an élite work-force and a limited number of reactors ensured that there would be few problems. But the competing adventures of space technology, aviation, and microelectronics had since directed the interest of many skilled engineers elsewhere. By 1978 operating standards had fallen in some cases to unacceptably low levels. Moreover the American electrical generating industry included no organizations with the strength of a national utility like Électricité de France. Of the fifty-three American utilities operating nuclear stations in 1988, only fourteen had more than two reactors. Such a fragmented generating industry could not match the career prospects originally offered by the US Atomic Energy Commission in the 1960s and 1970s. It was hardly surprising that staffing standards had fallen, and that average US operating performance—as measured, for instance, by reactor availability—was well below world standards. The fact that there were some shining exceptions showed that this aspect of the problem was not primarily technical or institutional, but managerial.

The TMI accident led to a series of investigations, including the government-appointed Kemeny Commission[52]. A new awareness led to a realization that some earlier less serious incidents should have been taken as warning signs; but there was no effective machinery then in existence for disseminating analytical warnings and operational experience amongst users. The creation of such machinery, which had long existed in the world of aviation, was a major positive step brought about by TMI.

The root cause of the TMI accident was operator failure to appreciate the actual condition of the plant, in the face of confusing indications on the control panel. An error during maintenance on the non-nuclear equipment had affected two main feed-water pumps. As part of the protection system a pressure relief valve had opened automatically, and the reactor was shut down, also quite correctly. The operators believed the reactor to be in a safe condition. However, they were under the false impression that the relief valve had shut again, when in fact it was still open: the indicator light was merely confirming that a SHUT command had been sent, not that it had been effective. Over one hundred alarms went off, leaving the operators no easy way of recognizing which indications were important. Several instruments went off-scale. It took two hours for the fault to be understood, and during that time water was leaking from the core, leaving the fuel exposed and in danger of melting—because of the radioactive heating which continues even when a reactor is shut down (see Technical Appendix). Furthermore, in the confusion the operators had overridden a high-pressure injection system that had automatically tried to maintain the correct water level in the core. Nearly one million gallons of cooling water escaped. The core was ruined, half the fuel elements having melted. TMI forcibly drew attention to the importance of proper design of the man-machine interface, operator training, and technical back-up in depth.

Three months after the accident a new Institute of Nuclear Power Operations (INPO) was set up by the nuclear and electricity industries to promote excellence in nuclear power-plant operation. To reinforce the emphasis on regulatory and human factors the industry in 1984 also set up NUMARC, the Nuclear Utility Management and Resources Council, to consider policy on a whole range of related issues—including emergency preparedness, operator fitness for duty, operator re-qualification, seismic design, containment integrity, guaranteed control-room power supplies, plant standardization, and radiological safety—and to maintain close relations on such matters with the regulatory authorities. It was formally incorporated in 1987 as a permanent body with its own staff. Two years earlier, after a lengthy review of the problems of sustaining exemplary operating performance, a new National Academy for Nuclear Training was established to improve the training and accreditation of key nuclear workers.

These well-intentioned actions went some way towards dealing with the man–machine problems that TMI had exposed. The problem was how to make them bite at the working level. Eight years after TMI it was still possible for the NRC to discover major lapses in operating discipline on a number of reactor sites. The most serious occurred in March 1987, when the NRC ordered the closure of the Peach Bottom station, managed by Philadelphia Electric on behalf of a consortium of utilities. The operators had been caught reading and sleeping while on duty in the reactor control-room. Over-confidence in the reliability of the plant had led to complacency, which was reinforced by group loyalty amongst the work force. This went as far as arranging for the security guards to alert the operators when regulatory officials entered the station to make spot checks. Once the facts were established heads rolled at the top of the utility; a fine of over a million dollars was imposed on the company; and thirty-three operators were fined up to $1000 each. But a far larger financial penalty lay in the enforced withdrawal of the plant from commercial generation for more than two years. In addition, the $250 million spent on improvements and retraining were not admitted into the rate base by the regulators. INPO wrote to the utility saying that the case was 'an embarrassment to the industry and to the nation'.

Third-party insurance had been dealt with since 1957 under the umbrella of the Price-Anderson Act. This made nuclear plant operators liable for damage to third parties, while setting a limit on their total liability. Beyond this government indemnification took over. Without this legal protection the operators would have had to rely on a limited pool of commercially available insurance funds for what could well have been essentially unlimited liability, given the very high awards that claimants could expect from the American courts. The opponents of the Act argued that it provided an unjustified subsidy. A federal judge in 1977 found the limitation on liability to be unconstitutional, but the Supreme Court later reversed that ruling. As a matter of practicality rather than law, without this 'cap' on industrial liability no shareholder utility would dare risk investing in nuclear power. As a matter of record, no accident in the USA, not even Three Mile Island, has yet exceeded the required private liability insurance (though 2,000 TMI claims were still outstanding as late as 1989). The Act was extended in 1965 and 1975. When it expired in August 1987 it took a further year, until September 1988, before Congressional agreement could be obtained for a fifteen-year extension (in the meantime existing reactors were 'grandfathered').

The renewal debates over Price-Anderson led to expanded benefits for third parties; but they also reflected the increasing power of the anti-nuclear community. In the 'no-fault' form the Act has taken since 1966—compensation without the need for litigation —and following the 1988 revision, compensation for an accident at a nuclear power plant would be provided by private insurance up to a total of about $160 million dollars, plus further mandatory contributions if necessary from all American nuclear utilities. These would be paid retrospectively after an accident, at an annual rate not exceeding $10 million per licensed reactor, with a 'cap' on the total contribution per reactor of $63 million. With over one hundred reactors licensed, the total available from these sources would therefore be about $7 billion per accident, a sum which would be inflation-indexed. So the limit of the industry's legal liability is already about ten times greater than in the previous version of the Act, and it will grow further as new reactors are brought into service. If more funds were needed in the case of a particularly severe accident, Congress would 'take whatever action is deemed necessary and appropriate'. Non-lawyers will note with wry amusement that part of the debate in Congress was concerned with defining the point at which legal costs could be paid out of the sums so provided!

New ways of spreading financial risk have been sought by the industry, to reduce the financial exposure of the nuclear generating companies. The majority are privately owned and financed, but have limited resources and do not enjoy a 'deep purse'. Joint ventures between groups of companies to build and operate several nuclear units are one obvious way forward. Generating companies specializing in nuclear operations should be able to provide a greater depth of expertise than that enjoyed by many of the smaller US utilities.

Cost recovery for nuclear facilities has been a serious problem facing the electrical industry, in two major respects. The state Public Utility (or Public Service) Commissions (PUCs) have the power to disallow costs which they consider to have been 'imprudently' incurred. They are frequently accused of abusing their 20/20 hindsight, which was unavailable to the utility managers at the time they had to take their decisions. Furthermore, most of the PUCs have been reluctant to allow more than a small part of the cost of 'work in progress' into the electricity rate-base, on which charges are calculated. In this respect the US industry has been at a major disadvantage compared with its European colleagues, most of whom not only enjoy a more predictable regulatory regime and are therefore better able to judge the costs of their projects, but can also use the revenue from electricity sales to finance capital expenditure as it is incurred. In the USA full cost recovery has been unavailable to most privately-owned utilities until a plant is complete, approved for operation, and brought into service—the 'used and useful' principle by which private US monopoly services are regulated. This AFUDC method of re-imbursement (allowance for funds used during construction), particularly in a context of lengthy regulatory delays, has the inevitable and undesirable consequence that a 'rate shock' occurs immediately a utility is authorized to begin cost recovery. In such a context the practical importance of a more stable, more predictable and less time-consuming regulatory climate for shareholder-owned utilities hardly needs to be spelt out. (The relatively few publicly-owned generating corporations are mostly under federal regulation, which takes a more European view; many of the small municipally-owned utilities are also outside the PUC net, but have limited importance for nuclear power.)

From an economic viewpoint the 'used and useful' legal basis for cost-recovery systems has the effect of tipping the scales between energy sources with different distributions of capital and running costs, to the advantage of coal and the disadvantage of the more capital-intensive nuclear electricity. From a policy viewpoint this economic consequence happens to be biased towards decisions which contribute to the 'greenhouse effect'. The inclusion of work-in-progress in the calculations on which electricity prices are based would help to remove this bias, and in the process transform nuclear economics. It would be a matter of 'paying more now for use later', rather than 'paying nothing now but paying still more later'.

The problem being institutional, so is the partial solution. Ways are being sought (not always with success) to create assemblies of generating organizations to produce wholesale rather than retail electricity: under US law they could then be subject to the regulatory approval of the Federal Energy Regulatory Commission, rather than the local PUCs. The expectation is that a federal body could take a longer view than a State PUC, particularly one whose members are elected rather than appointed: for instance FERC is prepared to admit 50 per cent of 'prudently-incurred' capital expenditure into the rate base. The Eastern Utilities Association, which operates in New England, is an example of a multi-utility corporation selling electricity on a wholesale basis under FERC regulations.

Waste management has been, and still is, the focus of some of the most contentious debates between the nuclear industry and its opponents. Chapter 10 recites the moves which have taken place since the passage of the Nuclear Waste Policy Act in 1982, a measure which was the culmination of work spread over three Congresses. At the beginning of 1990 preliminary steps were being taken to build a permanent repository for highly active waste, with Yucca Mountain, Nevada as a prime candidate site; while under other legislation applying to waste of lower radioactivity, individual States or groups of States ('compacts') were made responsible for providing disposal sites for lower-level radioactive waste by the end of 1992. Problems still exist, but their resolution is on the way, if haltingly.

Reforming the reactor licensing process has been an aspiration of five presidents, but given the political difficulties nothing could be achieved without a favourable conjunction of circumstances. Progress began to be made in the 100th Congress, but much remained to be done when it ended at the close of 1988. It was left for the Nuclear Regulatory Commission itself to decide that it possessed, after all, the authority to institute a major procedural reform, without the need for additional legislation. This it did, as we shall see later, in April 1989.

The need has been for a licensing process that would be as far as possible one-step instead of two-step; advance approval of standardized designs and sites; and regulatory stability once a licence has been issued, including the limitation of mandatory back-fitting to instances where substantial safety benefits would result. The way would then be open to cut average construction times to a reasonable six years, which would go a long way towards unshackling the US nuclear industry, and allowing it to engage effectively in competition with other forms of electricity generation. There has, however, been considerable Congressional reluctance to eliminate two-step licensing entirely, at least until public anxieties over nuclear power have substantially diminished. The industry's view has been quite simple: unless there could be greater certainty that operations would be permitted despite the second (post-completion) licensing step, which is mandatory under the Atomic Energy Act, the realistic prospect would be that few, if any, nuclear stations would be ordered.

The long period of reappraisal of nuclear power after TMI threw into sharp relief the issue of securing a rational relationship between the money the Nuclear Regulatory Commission required to be spent on safety and the nature of each particular risk that was being prevented. The industry took the lead in suggesting criteria that might be adopted: for instance, no one living near a nuclear plant should be subjected to 'a significant increase in the individual's annual mortality risk'. This approach received the endorsement of the NRC on 14 March 1983, when a policy statement was issued establishing safety goals. The statement was notable for its guidance on the cost-benefit issue: 'the likelihood of a nuclear reactor accident that results in a large-scale core-melt should normally be less than one in ten thousand per year of the reactor operation'; and 'the benefit of an incremental reduction of societal mortality risks should be compared with the associated costs on the basis of $1,000 per averted person-rem' (a measure of radiation dose—see Chapter 8). This was a step into an area that had long been regarded as highly controversial—the apparent weighing of the value of life in monetary terms. It was, however, no more than what must be done in every risk area where resources are limited: they need to be allocated to the areas of greatest need or effectiveness. The Commission also backed up this approach with a requirement that probability risk-analysis should be a normal part of construction permit applications, forcing all concerned to focus their minds on quantitative aspects of safety from the beginning of every reactor design.

Many took the view that changes were needed in the Nuclear Regulatory Commission itself. Its independence of action, coupled with its collegiate structure, defied the normal administrative principle of clear-cut head-on-the-platter accountability. The Kemeny Commission set up after TMI recommended that a single administrator should replace the system of jointly responsible commissioners. The Carter administration, before it ended at the beginning of 1981, had somewhat strengthened the position of the Commission's chairman, but had otherwise accomplished little. By the mid-1980s even the commissioners themselves were arguing for reform on Kemeny lines. New appointments by President Reagan began to move the Commission in this direction. Two former admirals from the nuclear navy were brought in—Admiral Lando Zech in 1984, and Admiral Carr two years later. On becoming chairman in 1986 Admiral Zech made it clear that he intended to be a strong manager. These appointments were interesting for the way they brought into the Commission, at the very top, the experience of man-management in the context of handling high technology which TMI had shown was seriously deficient in the US nuclear electricity industry. However, despite Admiral Zech's apparent personal preference for a single administrator the 100th Congress closed in 1988 without any changes to the NRC's structure. There were signs that Congress preferred, after all, a collegiate structure like the old Atomic Energy Commission, where a variety of views could be aired before difficult decisions were collectively taken.

Meanwhile the NRC had begun to set its own house in order. In late 1985 it brought in a new back-fit rule which required that safety benefits should be assessed in the light of probable costs. It also adopted a Severe Accident Policy Statement, setting out criteria for new licensing applications, but also concluding that existing plants posed no unacceptable risk to the public. Perhaps because of this, when the Chernobyl disaster occurred early in 1986 there was no NRC-imposed licensing moratorium such as had followed TMI.

However, the Russian accident did inflame the long-running controversies over the Seabrook (New Hampshire) and Shoreham (Long Island) plants. In both cases the reactors were complete, but problems had arisen over planning for emergency evacuation, which needed to be agreed with the local communities within a radius of ten miles. At Seabrook this circle took in part of Massachusetts, which under Governor Dukakis was resolutely opposed to nuclear power. Starting in 1986 the responsible utility—the Public Service Company of New Hampshire—found itself without the co-operation of six communities living over the state line. Seabrook's warning sirens were removed in an effort to invalidate the emergency arrangements which are an essential part of an operating licence. The utility drew up its own plans, which were approved by the Federal Emergency Management Administration and the NRC, and upheld by the US Court of Appeals, and by a presidential order signed in November 1988. Meanwhile the utility, crippled by the costs of failing to start up the reactor since its completion in 1987, and prohibited by a court ruling from offsetting the costs from its general sales of electricity because the reactor was not 'used and useful', had applied for bankruptcy—the first to do so since the Great Depression. Eventually a full-power operating licence was granted, and early in 1990 preparations were made for starting operations.

The 809 MWe Shoreham boiling water reactor on Long Island was granted a low-power licence in 1985, and a full-power licence in 1989—fifteen years behind the original target date. Meanwhile the Long Island Lighting Company had been driven by public opposition into such severe financial straits that the State of New York offered to buy the $5.5 billion plant for one dollar as a preliminary to dismantling it, and in return to assist the company in building new non-nuclear plants, and to authorize a substantial phased increase in charges for electricity (60 per cent over a decade). The new Bush administration expressed its opposition to such a waste of resources, and a bizarre struggle developed in the summer of 1989 between the Department of Energy and New York State, with the NRC watching from the side-lines. LILCO's shareholders' interests favoured settlement rather than further indefinite uncertainty, and in July 1989 workers began to remove the fuel from the reactor.

These two confused cases highlight the urgent need for a more rational system for site approvals and reactor licences. The industry's hopes are that a limited number of new advanced reactor designs, incorporating significant improvements in ultimate reactor safety, will in time receive the NRC's blessing. If such designs could be built with no more than the site planning, design, and approved construction checks that are normal elsewhere, this would enormously improve the economics of American nuclear power-stations. A degree of standardization would at last make it possible to climb up a learning curve, as France has done, instead of constructing reactors that are almost always different. It would also simplify the training of operators, particularly as regards operation under fault conditions. The NRC very properly took the view at the end of 1988 that despite these important potential benefits, its quasi-judicial function meant that no promises could be given prior to receiving full details of the proposed designs.

However, a few months later, on 18 April 1989, the Commission published new regulations which went a long way towards meeting the industry's wishes, without derogating from the NRC's own regulatory role. *Early site permits* would resolve siting issues before major expense was incurred, and would make it possible for a utility to 'bank' a site for future use for a period of twenty years. *Certification* would be available for standard reactor designs which represented an 'evolutionary change' from existing and operating light-water reactors. Designs which 'differed significantly' from existing reactors would not be barred, but would require additional study before certification. Most significantly, a *combined licence*— a combined construction permit and operating licence—could be issued at the beginning of construction. Under the new procedures the second, pre-operational, licensing step required by the Atomic Energy Act would be limited to resolving any issues of non-compliance with the terms of the combined licence. The interests of the public are still safeguarded under the new procedures. An adjudicatory hearing will be held on each combined licence application, at which persons whose interests are affected could be heard. The public may also petition the Commission at the time of the pre-operational hearing, though subsequent action would be at the Commission's discretion. The first industry application for standard design certification was made by the General Electric Company for its Advanced Boiling Water Reactor design.

The anti-nuclear lobby unsurprisingly opposed the new regulations, and seven groups joined together with the State of Massachusetts in opposing them before the US Court of Appeals for the District of Columbia, on the grounds that they violated the legal requirement for two-stage licensing. The industry filed a countervailing petition. Should the Court eventually find for the objectors, the Congress would almost certainly have to review the state of the law. In some ways the electrical utility industry might well feel happier if the new procedures were firmly backed by Congress.

As this brief review has shown, the problems of nuclear energy in the United States have been not only technical and managerial, but also profoundly political—though from a standpoint more concerned with institutions and the behaviour of government regulatory agencies than with party politics. Party views are, however, not entirely irrelevant, since the Democratic Party is much more responsive to the arguments of the anti-nuclear opposition than are the Republicans. But, generally speaking, the issues which will determine nuclear power's future are not such as any incoming government can quickly influence: they are too deeply enmeshed in the whole administrative nexus. Putting things right is best done by steady unspectacular work well away from the media's spotlight. Lobbying for changes to be made is a task for the industry associations, which include the US Council for Energy Awareness, a broadly-based grouping of manufacturers and electrical utilities concerned with the nuclear future. The fact that the US Congress is not noticeably anti-nuclear should be helpful: of its 535 members four-fifths are regarded by political observers as probably neutral, desiring only a sensible resolution of the legislative issues. Success will have come when the Edison Electric Institute, the industrial association of the major US electrical utilities, is prepared to withdraw its 1985 comment[53] that 'under present regulatory and institutional arrangements, no American electrical utility would consider ordering a new [nuclear] power plant'.

The solid work that has been applied since TMI to redesigning the institutional framework has resulted in significant progress, even though it is still (1990) unfinished. However, it has yet to win the public recognition that it deserves. In February 1985 that oracle of the business community, *Forbes Magazine*, under the headline 'Nuclear Follies', described the US power programme as 'the largest managerial disaster in business history'. Four years later it was still a commonly held view in the USA that nuclear power was a technological pariah, and moreover one that was economically superfluous. For the future the key will be how far the perception of need can be restored in the public mind. That will *inter alia* depend on the speed at which economic growth promotes demand for electricity, eroding the capacity margin in the electricity networks and increasing the risk of voltage reductions and eventually grid disconnections. Forecasts suggest that the capacity margin, particularly in the north-east, might come close to its safe lower limit early in the 1990s. This is one reason why the Department of Energy launched work on a national energy plan in July 1989, with the intention of presenting it to President Bush in December 1990.

The US public's perception of whether nuclear power is needed may also receive a shove from a number of other directions: the steadily growing interest in the 'greenhouse effect'; inflation, which has the effect of gradually improving the economics of nuclear power in historical accounting terms compared with coal; and the greater institutional readiness which the Nuclear Regulatory Commission is showing to avoid needless burdens on the economics of the energy source whose continued existence is its own long-term *raison d'être*. The least that can be said of the painstaking work of the 1980s is that when the time comes for the USA to build more nuclear stations, the institutional framework will be better matched to the task.

The British history of politically induced decline

No one reading the history [54–7] of British civil nuclear energy since 1947 can fail to be struck by the sad contrast between the extraordinary efficiency of the technical operations in the early years, and the seeming inevitability with which the politicians and the atomic engineers together gradually painted the British reactor industry into a corner, by standardizing on an unexportable design in the late 1960s. Twenty years further on, too late by far in commercial terms, the pressurized-water reactor was at last taken up. Its fault had been, quite simply, that it was 'not invented here'. But no sooner had the first PWR begun construction at Sizewell, than the whole future of the British nuclear programme was thrown into confusion by the knock-on effects of the electricity privatization of 1989–90. Instead of being the start of a nuclear renaissance, Sizewell risks becoming yet another symbol of the country's failed nuclear dream.

A prime purpose in the early years, once a nuclear deterrent had been created, was to establish a new export industry. At the beginning policy was made by the nuclear technologists and their Whitehall colleagues, rather than the national electricity undertaking. In later years the Central Electricity Generating Board played a more significant role, and did have one real chance of changing the direction of events. That was in 1964, during the assessment of the seven tenders—three for Advanced Gas-Cooled Reactors (AGRs), four for light-water reactors—submitted for the Dungeness B reactor. In the event it chose an AGR, and moreover a singularly ill-starred version, put forward by a contractor known to be managerially and financially weak. Whatever the pressures or reasoning that led to this decision Dungeness B became the rock on which British hopes of reactor exports foundered. The contrast with the events taking place just over the southern horizon from that reactor is striking. France started down the nuclear road a few years after Britain; but as the case built up against continuing with gas-cooling she showed much greater flexibility, swallowed her pride, and switched at the right time to a programme of light-water reactors. The results recorded in Chapter 3 speak for themselves, and for the effectiveness of the PEON commission, which from 1955 brought together the providers of nuclear technology and the users, to discuss policy on an equal footing.

Why did Britain not do the same? There were many contributory causes: the extraordinary dominance of the government's nuclear technocrats at the outset; a desire to bolster Britain's crumbling world position by showing that the old lion was still capable of splendid new tricks, that America was not the only country with nuclear competence, and that Britain could manage quite well without Euratom; the almost entire lack of technical knowledge at the time amongst parliamentarians and the higher Civil Service; a frequently changing structure of advisory committees; an engineering industry whose separate units, though sound enough in their traditional roles, lacked the muscle needed for this new development; a cossetted nationalized coal industry, with high production costs, offering weaker competition than in the USA; a controlled economy, with very low rates of interest which blinded decision-makers to the commercial importance of capital cost when customers abroad came to choose between reactor types; the almost complete lack of any tradition of long-term planning, based on consultation with a broad spectrum of industry and commerce. In a word: the country's institutions.

What cannot be blamed in the British case, for at least the first thirty years, is inter-party warfare. Nuclear power from the start enjoyed generally bi-partisan support, in a House of Commons where only two parties really mattered, and where the 'first-past-the-post' system of voting frequently assured comfortable majorities for the party in power. Governments did of course change from time to time, after general elections. But the combination of government-funded development and nationalized utilities virtually guaranteed the support of the permanent Civil Service; and the long lead times of any nuclear programme limited the ability of an incoming party to meddle with the programme it inherited. In any case post-war British governments never felt sufficiently certain to cancel what had already been started; nor would a manufacturing nation have wished to make such a repudiation of its own competence. It was only with the coming of the Thatcher era, and her government's determination to privatize electricity, that party politics came, almost by accident, to play a determining role in nuclear policy.

The early years

The British civil nuclear energy programme was an offspring of the country's military and political aspirations of the immediate post-war years. Once the decision had been taken by Attlee's Labour government to manufacture nuclear weapons the first requirement was for military plutonium. Two reactors were built at Windscale in record time, and plutonium production started early in 1951. The first British bomb test took place at Monte Bello, off the north-west coast of Australia, on 3 October 1952. The plutonium production 'piles' used straight-through air-cooling: water-cooled graphite-moderated reactors of the type used for this purpose during World War II in the USA had been rejected as potentially too dangerous for a small highly-populated country. What was feared was exactly the kind of accident which took place in 1986 at Chernobyl. Britain was thus launched down the road of gas-cooled reactor technology, which in the end was to prove a commercial cul-de-sac.

So far as design is concerned gas-cooling is in some ways the easier technology. In BWRs and PWRs water has to do the job of both coolant and 'moderator' (see Technical Appendix). Optimization of the design is therefore more complicated than in gas-cooled reactors, where the gas (because of its low density) takes only a minor part in the nuclear physics, so that cooling and moderation can be separately optimized. But gas is a poor heat-transfer agent. That was hardly a major consideration for the early plutonium production reactors, which were of limited power, and built to satisfy a military rather than a commercial requirement; but for a commercial electricity-producing reactor it was vital. To improve heat-transfer in the interests of keeping the size of the reactor within manageable proportions the gas pressure needed to be increased, the temperature raised (thus improving thermal efficiency), the coolant changed from air to carbon dioxide (to minimize chemical reactions with the graphite moderator), and the whole enclosed in a large pressure-vessel—too large unfortunately for easy fabrication off-site in a factory.

In 1956 the first of the Calder Hall reactors, built with customary efficiency in only three years on these improved gas-cooled principles, added its output to the supplies of both military plutonium and electricity. The Queen threw the switch connecting it to the grid on 17 October; the reactor was still operating thirty-three years later. Calder Hall was not the first reactor to produce commercial quantities of electricity. That honour is held by a small 5 MWe graphite-moderated water-cooled plant which was commissioned at Obninsk in the USSR on 27 June 1954. (Irony abounds in this field: it was this reactor which set the Soviets down the path which eventually led to Chernobyl.) Calder Hall was much larger, and its electricity sales subsidized military plutonium production: the reactor was officially described as 'dual-purpose'. In October 1957 one of the nearby Windscale military production 'piles' (i.e. reactors) caught fire, spilling radioactivity over the Cumbrian landscape. That reactor was abandoned and sealed. There was surprisingly little effect on the rest of the programme.

Even before Calder Hall had begun producing electricity sufficient euphoria had been created to launch the first programme of civil power-stations in a White Paper[58] published in February 1955, which daringly proposed a 1.5–2.0 GWe programme of electricity-producing pressurized gas-cooled reactors, to be completed by the mid-1960s. It was a government decision in which the national electricity authority played only a minor part. The first four reactors were to build on Calder Hall experience, but would use improved fuel elements capable of withstanding higher temperatures. They were known, after the fuel-element canning material, as the 'Magnox' family of reactors. Providing they were built in sizes large enough to obtain economies of scale, and provided also that a substantial 'credit'—initially around one-third of total generating costs—was included for the plutonium produced, they were forecast to be competitive with coal stations. However, electricity costs were not the main focus of the 1955 White Paper. The purpose was to get nuclear power launched, as a contribution to fuel diversification, and in that it succeeded. The White Paper also opened the door to the possibility of building some water-cooled reactors, but the option was not pursued partly because the British engineering industry was ill-prepared.

The energy outlook changed radically in 1956 following the Suez Canal closure. There was a serious oil shortage, and a suddenly increased awareness of the political desirability of reducing dependence on imported energy. In March 1957, some months after the successful switching-on of Calder Hall, but before the Windscale accident, the programme was trebled to include 5–6 GWe of construction by 1965. Further adjustment in 1960, in the light of the somewhat disappointing costs of the Magnox stations, slowed down the construction programme to complete 5 GWe by 1968. The discovery in 1968–9 that mild steel reactor components were corroding faster than forecast led to an operating temperature limitation, which further reduced the effective Magnox total. The Wylfa reactor lost 30 per cent of its output.

The extent of the economic loading against the gas-cooled reactor, when judged in a fully commercial context, was not properly understood in the early days, partly because of over-optimism in costing, but also because of the way the British public sector made its economic assessments. In the immediate post-war years the economy was tightly controlled. Interest rates were very low—only 3 per cent in 1954. It was even possible to borrow money from the Public Works Loan Board for fifteen years at 3¾ per cent. Such rates gave gas-cooled reactors, with their high capital costs but low running costs, the best possible chance of succeeding against their water-cooled competitors, which had lower capital but higher running costs. Unfortunately such money rates were not typical of what would be incurred later by overseas purchasers when there were export opportunities. By 1964 it was already clear to most of the Euratom countries that light-water reactors, like the American Shippingport PWR which had started generating electricity in 1957 only 14 months after Calder Hall, were likely to be economically preferable, given commercial rates of financing. France, which had also started down the gas-cooled route, altered course by 1968–9, having decided that it would be unwise not to follow the course on which the USA and the rest of the Euratom countries were embarking. So although the British civil programme had from the beginning been intended to establish a new export industry, it fell at the first economic fence. For what was still, at the beginning of the nuclear story, the world's leading trading nation this failure to recognize commercial realities was an extraordinary oversight.

Although the institutional pressures to maintain course were enormous, doubts about a programme which did not include light-water reactors continued to arise periodically. One occasion was a report published in 1974 by the short-lived Nuclear Power Advisory Board, which dismissed the Advanced Gas-Cooled Reactor as a contender for future orders; but it took another five years of pressure from the user, the Central Electricity Generating Board, before reactor policy changed. It will be the mid-1990s before the first British PWR begins to produce electricity; and that may also be the last for a considerable time.

The reactors at Windscale and Calder Hall had been built with remarkable speed and efficiency by a corps of government engineers and scientists, who in August 1954 were transferred from the Civil Service to the newly-created UK Atomic Energy Authority (UKAEA). They did not have the industrial resources to handle the expanding programme, and encouraged the government to create competing engineering consortia, which would then take the lead in seeking export markets. We can now see that this was the beginning of the British failure: what was actually needed was a single strong national nuclear-engineering entity. There would be competition enough from overseas.

The competing-consortia approach, while superficially attractive, had serious flaws. No less than five consortia were eventually created, far too many for the work-load; and—despite the training arranged by the UKAEA—far too weak to master successfully the design problems of gas-cooling technology. Financially the consortia were 'men of straw', whose performance guarantees had little commercial value unless there could be recourse to the parent companies. Mergers quickly took place; but once the number had fallen to three the original intention of using competition in tendering as the spur became more theoretical than real. 'Buggins's turn' became the order of the day. The third consortium collapsed in 1969.

Competition in design did, however, undoubtedly have the effect of radically improving station efficiency, and therefore output. The seven Magnox stations which were under construction by 1961 represented over 3 GWe of generating capacity, well over the original target, and half-way to the revised 1957 target. Fewer stations were going to be needed than originally foreseen, which was an additional reason for reducing the number of consortia. The later stations incorporated innovative arrangements, notably the first British use of pre-stressed concrete pressure-vessels, which the French had pioneered.

What the competitive environment did not succeed in doing was to keep down capital costs. That nuclear power requires more capital than coal-firing is self-evident, given the differences between the two technologies; but in 1962 there was a disturbingly high threefold differential. Part of the reason must have been the lack of standardization created by the multi-consortia approach. Almost every reactor was different, and there was little possibility of climbing up the learning curve. When in later years some of the Magnox stations, with their low fuel costs, rose to near the top of the CEGB's preference rating, it was not only due to the reliability with which on the whole they performed, but also as a consequence of bookkeeping amortization in a context of rapid inflation.

The Advanced Gas-Cooled Reactor programme

A major design limitation in the Magnox reactors was the uranium metal fuel. By using ceramic uranium oxide in its place higher gas temperatures and thermal efficiencies could be obtained. A small pilot-scale reactor incorporating this change was ordered in 1957 and reached full power at Windscale in January 1963; it became the first of the Advanced Gas-Cooled Reactors (AGRs), which were intended to be the British answer to the PWR. Policy for a second nuclear-power programme was outlined in April 1964 in a White Paper[59]. It proposed that plans should be based on commissioning 5 GWe of additional nuclear capacity between 1970 and 1975. The paper noted that American light water reactors were said to have lower capital costs than those expected for the AGR; but concluded on balance that it would be right to continue with the British line of development, and that CEGB would issue tender enquiries for AGRs. However, they would also 'be ready to consider tenders from British industry for water-moderated reactor systems of proved design . . .'.

Seven tenders—three for AGRs, four for light-water reactors—
were submitted for a 1 GWe station to be built on the south coast
alongside an existing Magnox plant; it would be known as
Dungeness B. After an examination of rival tenders, said at the time
to be 'the most intensive in British industrial history', and despite
an initial preference for the boiling-water reactor, CEGB's choice
fell in May 1965 on an AGR, for a variety of technical reasons:
higher thermal efficiency, better steam conditions, on-load refuelling,
inherent safety, a pre-stressed concrete pressure-vessel; in all,
'greater development potential'—always assuming that the promises
would be fulfilled. If there were political reasons as well, they were
not emphasized. The responsible Minister, Fred Lee, told Parliament in a moment of hyperbole: 'We have hit the jackpot . . . the
greatest breakthrough of all time.' The normally sober *Annual
Register* commented euphorically[32] that 'the winning of the
Dungeness contract was one of the most significant and hopeful
events for British industry for a long time . . . it was expected to
have a very big influence on the future choice of reactors'. These
last words came true, though in the opposite sense to that which the
author intended.

The overall generating cost of the AGR was estimated as about 7
per cent less than for a competing boiling-water reactor design.
This was well within the margin of error of cost-forecasting at such
an early stage in nuclear history; and even this slight advantage
existed only if the capital costs were realistic. The BWR costs were
based on a 600 MWe American design for the Oyster Creek
reactor, and in comparison the quoted AGR costs seemed surprisingly
low. The chairman of the CEGB was sufficiently concerned to ask
for private reassurances from the directors of the winning consortium[54].

We now know that CEGB's acceptance of the Dungeness B
tender was an unmitigated disaster. There should have been far
more emphasis on verifying the engineering design. The reactor was
far too large an extrapolation from the 34 MWe Windscale
prototype. In addition there were a number of inexcusable
construction errors, and as a result the station did not produce any
electricity until 1985, and was still experiencing teething troubles as
late as 1990. The construction consortium collapsed in 1969,
leaving the job to be completed by one of its rivals. Although the
collapse eventually facilitated a belated reconstruction of the

engineering industry, the débacle could not be concealed. In a tough competitive world British industry lost all further hope of gaining entry to export markets with gas-cooled designs. Even at the time of the decision strong criticisms were made of the CEGB appraisal. In retrospect its claim that the chosen design had fewer unproven features than its competitors seems particularly hard to justify.

Six months after the 1964 White Paper the government changed, and Harold Wilson formed a new Socialist administration. In his election speeches he had caught the public's imagination with talk of a 'white-hot technological revolution'. These were mere words, unsupported by detailed groundwork; but they helped him to gain power in October 1964. He consolidated his hold eighteen months later. In frank imitation of the French economic-planning process, which had proved so successful, but without the benefit of its accumulated experience, a British National Plan was commissioned. It was hurriedly put together in just under a year. When it appeared, in September 1965—a month before the first discovery of North Sea oil—it was predicting a sharply increased rate of growth. As a natural corollary a further White Paper on Fuel Policy[60] was published, lifting the nuclear-programme target to 8 GWe, based on the AGR. Unfortunately the National Plan, the first British excursion into the realm of 'indicative planning', was hardly a plan in the true sense, more a collection of aspirations poorly tested for internal consistency. While it was possible to hope that it might become self-fulfilling, which had been the French experience, the root causes of British economic decline had not been tackled. Nor could they be under a Labour government whose political organization relied for financial support on the trade unions, and which was therefore unable to dismantle their crippling panoply of restrictive practices which the law had protected since 1906. The actual outcome was disappointing economic growth and a period of excess generating capacity.

The 1965 Fuel Policy White Paper was blunt in its criticism of the first nuclear programme: ' . . . the earlier expectations about the economics of nuclear power have proved premature . . .'. Nevertheless it accepted that a steady fall in capital costs could be ensured by continuing along the AGR route, at a rate of one station a year for the years 1970–5. It also accepted a run-down in coal production.

Orders for AGR stations at five sites were placed by 1970. Hinkley Point and Hunterston shared a common reactor design.

Heysham and Hartlepool formed another pair; but the phasing of their construction, and the need for substantial modifications, meant that once again there was little chance of benefiting from replication. This is evident from the building record. The planned building times were four to five years. What was actually achieved was a minimum of ten years (the Hinkley Point-Hunterston pair), an average of around fourteen years, and in the case of the first AGR at Dungeness B an appalling record of unsatisfactory construction and subsequent rectification extending over twenty-five years. The policy consequence of the competing-consortia approach was that the country was committed to sorting out the complications of the three different AGR designs which made up the second nuclear programme. Moreover they had been inadequately specified at the outset, and the Nuclear Installations Inspectorate insisted on substantial design changes—it was a case of design-as-you-go. The contrast with the smooth progress of the Framatome family of PWR reactors in France, with their steadily falling construction times, was there for the world to see.

The disappointments with the gas-cooled programme that were already evident by 1971 led to further talk of a new programme based on pressurized water (PWR) technology. But at the time there were doubts on environmental and safety grounds, particularly the integrity of the large primary pressure-vessels. It took more than a decade to lay these worries completely to rest. The government—by now the Conservatives once more under Edward Heath—set up a working party, the Vinter Committee, to examine future power reactor policy. Its report in 1972 was in some respects inconclusive, because it was short of hard facts to go on. What was clear was that the British industry was in serious need of reorganization. Steps were taken to consolidate the two remaining design and construction companies into a single stronger unit. But the home market that such a company would need was missing, and there was still no consensus on reactor choice.

An alternative to the PWR existed in the shape of the Steam Generating Heavy Water reactor, a 92 MWe prototype of which had been operating at the Winfrith research establishment since 1968. Its potential attractions were better steam conditions and efficiency than could be obtained with the PWR; and the substitution of numerous small pressure-tubes for the single large pressure-vessel of the PWRs. This was a safety feature—it is easier to be certain about the integrity of pressure-tubes—though there were doubts for other reasons about the design and ultimate safety of a scaled-up version, and also problems over heavy-water supplies. The Dragon high-temperature project which had been operating at power since the mid-1960s was also proceeding at Winfrith, in collaboration with other European countries, but was a long way off its commercial stage. The 250 MWe prototype fast reactor at Dounreay was making real progress—it became operational early in 1974—but its commercial market seemed to be coming no nearer as the years went by. Little was being done towards providing the CEGB with the light water reactors that it needed.

A push was provided by chance from another direction. A sometimes violent and occasionally lawless coal strike led to widespread power cuts early in 1972 and, despite a degree of public sympathy for the miners, reminded the country of its vulnerability to an energy policy based mainly on fossil-fuel resources. At almost the same time a new chairman was appointed to the CEGB. He quickly announced tentative plans for ten or eleven new nuclear stations to be built within ten years. Six or seven of them would use a 'proven' type of reactor—it was generally assumed that Sir Arthur Hawkins meant some form of light-water reactor. The formation of the National Nuclear Corporation in June of the following year appeared at last to provide the muscle needed to carry through the programme. A further sign of government interest was the creation of a Nuclear Power Advisory Board, under ministerial chairmanship. But energy was about to become intertwined with world politics. On 6 October 1973 the Yom Kippur War flared in the Middle East. Oil supplies were affected; prices rose; serious inflation was in prospect. The Heath government brought in measures to control inflation, including a legal limitation on wage increases. This cut short wage negotiations by the National Union of Mineworkers. The result, by 12 November, was a union ban on overtime working in the pits. On the first day of 1974 Heath imposed a three-day working week to save fuel. The economic situation deteriorated, and within a few weeks he called a general election to settle who should run the country—and lost. Labour returned to office.

In the dying weeks of the Heath administration the CEGB had published a more ambitious proposal, involving eighteen large

PWR stations, to be built by 1983. The South of Scotland Electricity Board was at the same time planning a further eight nuclear stations, but did not favour the PWR. Suddenly the outlook for nuclear power seemed almost unbelievably more propitious. But the controversy about the best choice of reactor remained, and primary pressure-vessel failure in PWRs was still a matter for concern. The Steam Generating Heavy Water reactor (SGHW), with its pressure-tube design, would avoid that difficulty, and was favoured by the South of Scotland Electricity Board. When the new Energy Secretary announced a third nuclear programme in July 1974 it was based on the SGHW; but it was smaller than had been expected—only six reactors of 600 MWe capacity, to be built over the next four years. It was put forward as a first step to gain experience with the new design; but it seemed that the government, and not the main user—the CEGB—had made the choice. The government also disagreed with CEGB's optimistic projections of electricity-demand growth—justifiably as it turned out, in view of the effects of the economic depression created by OPEC's oil-price 'tax' on all western industrial nations.

Hopes that a 'home-grown' reactor type could form the basis for British nuclear efforts soon withered. The CEGB pressed for changes in the design of the SGHW, on operating and safety grounds. Its size, complexity and cost escalated. At much the same time—1976—doubts about PWR pressure-vessel integrity were eased by a report by the distinguished physicist Sir Walter Marshall, who was later to become chairman of the CEGB. The Nuclear Installations Inspectorate reported favourably on PWR safety in July 1977. The CEGB suggested cancelling the SGHW programme. The continuing effects of the oil crisis and the poor economic performance of the country held back economic growth and removed the pressure for a rapid decision. In the summer of 1977 the CEGB's Chairman, who had advocated the purchase of large numbers of a reactor type that was of foreign design, even if it would be largely British built, and had perhaps thereby frightened the increasingly influential environmentalists, did not have his contract renewed. The new Energy Secretary, Tony Benn, trimmed back the nuclear research programme. In January 1978 the Government agreed in the House of Commons that 'it would be right to discontinue work on the SGHWR . . . that two early nuclear orders are needed and that these must be AGRs . . . and that in addition to the AGR we must develop the option of adopting the PWR system in the early 1980s'. But the Labour government was disintegrating, and in the summer of 1979 a Conservative administration under Margaret Thatcher took over. The last two AGRs, at Torness and Heysham, ordered in 1980, were able to build on the successful features of Hinkley Point and Hunterston.

The first PWR: the Sizewell inquiry

Despite the Three Mile Island accident at the end of March 1979 the new government quickly affirmed its support for nuclear power, and in December announced that the next nuclear station would be a PWR, but that a public inquiry would first be held. On 30 January 1981 the CEGB applied for a licence to build a pressurized-water reactor at Sizewell, 100 miles north-east of London, to be the first of a limited programme of similar reactors. It would be basically an American (Westinghouse) design, but the construction responsibility would be shared with the National Nuclear Corporation. The terms of reference of the inquiry showed that despite its substantial parliamentary majority the government was intending to use the occasion to play for safety, and if possible defuse the nuclear controversy once and for all, by asking the Inspector, Sir Frank Layfield, to answer all relevant questions: economics, safety, alternatives, environment. The government was in no hurry— another general election was not far off—and the inspector took his time[61]. The main hearings started on 11 January 1983 and lasted until 7 March 1985; the Inspector's report[62] was finally published on 26 January 1987. The cost was ten million pounds. Although it was nominally a public event, the audience usually numbered less than ten. It is a procedural curiosity that although Chernobyl occurred during the writing of the report, the Inspector was, strictly speaking, not allowed to take cognizance of that event, because it occurred after the formal evidence had been completed.

If Sizewell was intended to act both as a lightning-conductor for nuclear issues, and as a provider of authoritative information for the future, it appeared at the time to have succeeded admirably. Everyone was free to speak. Time was not limited. Nothing was excluded. The only complaint was that public funds should have been available to help the protesters prepare their case; but at least some facilities were offered by the CEGB.

The inquiry was useful in clarifying certain key criteria. Would

Sizewell save money? Was it needed anyway? Were the hopes pinned by environmentalists on further conservation realistic? Were we right in importing French electricity, or would we be placing ourselves 'in hock' to France? What were the alternatives? The Inspector recognized that the improved second-generation AGR might still have a case, but that because of construction delays experience was still too limited to be certain: it could not compare with the accumulated knowledge about the PWR. Economics were closely studied. The analysis showed a 75 per cent probability that the PWR would be cost-saving when tested against expected world coal prices, even if built in advance of actual need. The inquiry placed considerable weight on fuel diversity for its own sake: by staging a major strike during the inquiry the miners helped to underline its importance. As for safety, the lesson of Chernobyl was that human error could never be wholly discounted; but the inquiry had every reason to believe that British control-engineering and safety practice were far ahead of the managerial shambles that had led to the Soviet disaster.

The downside of the whole quasi-judicial process of inquiry was its detachment from the normal accountability of the world of action, and the resulting commercial uncertainty and cost. Design teams and spare manufacturing capacity had to be kept in being while the stately dance reached its conclusion. The procedure could be justified in commercial terms only if it opened the way for future policy decisions to be taken in timely fashion where they properly belonged: inside government, and round the utility's boardroom table. But within two years some of the same ground was being retrodden in the Hinkley Point inquiry regarding a virtually identical reactor.

By the time Layfield reported Mrs Thatcher was in a politically impregnable position, having roundly defeated the miners' leader, Arthur Scargill. Some kind of a clash had been inevitable. The steady increase in nuclear power as the AGR stations were one-by-one brought on stream was digging into coal's main remaining market, now that the railways no longer ran on steam. Once the 9.8 GWe of nuclear power installed by the time of the miners' strike in 1984 were fully commissioned they would be the energy equivalent of about 20 million tonnes of coal annually—lost work for 15,000 miners. For comparison the annual output of the National Coal Board just before the strike was 120 million tonnes, compared with almost 200 million tonnes in 1960, before the railway market had been lost. Success with nuclear power almost inevitably fore-shadowed further hardship in the mining areas of Yorkshire (Scargill's power-base), Wales, and Scotland. It was hardly surprising that miners could be seen supporting the anti-nuclear groups at Sizewell and elsewhere—though rarely declaring their direct personal economic interest. The existence of nuclear power as an alternative to coal was also strengthening Thatcher's hand in pressing for vast improvements in the way the nationalized coal industry was run. Many uneconomic pits were closed.

Against a background of declining union membership and vanishing political influence the miners' leader finally decided on 10 March 1984 to give battle, to secure a better bargain before his position weakened further. But he had left it too late. The winter was almost at an end, and moreover the CEGB was unusually well prepared, with ten million tonnes of coal in stock at the power-stations. It was his additional misfortune that when the lines were drawn the Prime Minister had only recently vanquished a more dangerous opponent—General Galtieri—during the Falklands conflict. She also knew that in this confrontation with the miners she once again had the country behind her. After a bitter struggle lasting five days short of a year Scargill was decisively beaten, and the miners capitulated. They lost not only because they were badly led, but also because fuel diversification—oil and nuclear—had made it possible to eke out coal stocks at the power-stations far longer than the miners had expected. The cost to the country had been £2 billion; but the lights had not gone out. The Coal Board's work-force fell from 208,000 in 1982 to 88,000 in 1988–9.

The political lesson for the future was clear, and the way seemed to be set for the smooth translation of the Layfield recommendations into action. A site licence for Sizewell was granted on 4 June 1987, and building started. Within a few months a further application was made to build a second PWR at Hinkley Point, due for completion in 1998; and two more PWRs were planned to follow. Britain at last seemed to be coming back into the nuclear mainstream, after Byzantine complications which in retrospect can only excite astonishment and regret. As a result she had done far worse on the reactor side than most other European countries, despite a splendid start, worse indeed than developing countries like Taiwan and Korea that had been content to buy in their technology. The successful countries had been those whose national ambitions had been guided by attention to the commercial imperatives of electricity generation.

Other aspects of nuclear policy

The starker political and economic realism which the Thatcher government stood for inevitably had its effect on other aspects of nuclear policy. In particular the fast reactor was placed on the back burner, in an announcement in July 1988 that government support for the 250 MWe Dounreay Prototype Fast Reactor was to be terminated after a five-year warning period. The long-term economic justification for the fast reactor is as a hedge against uranium supplies becoming constrained. But in the late 1980s uranium prices were very low and still falling, and there appeared little prospect that the fast reactor could compete with existing designs for as long as that was the case. Nor were the price rises needed to put the fast reactor in business expected before the year 2030. The decision to withdraw funding from the reactor, in an area in the far north of Scotland which had grown to depend for its livelihood on the local atomic establishment after three decades of considerable technical success, was not an easy one, nor one that went unquestioned; but the government was bent on reducing the cost of the public sector, and a technology that might not be needed commercially for another thirty to forty years was an obvious target. The official view was that the only sensible way forward was through international collaboration. In March 1989 officials from Britain, France, and Germany signed an agreement to pool research and development programmes aimed at the joint development of a European fast reactor. The view was soon confirmed that the Dounreay PFR was too valuable a research tool to be lightly abandoned, particularly as it was nowhere near the end of its engineering lifetime. Moves began to seek other sources of funding after British government support terminated in March 1994.

One major and fairly successful British speciality remained: fuel reprocessing and plutonium recycling. In contrast to the vacillations over reactor policy, the reprocessing plant at Sellafield, alongside the Windscale reactor site, had enjoyed consistency of policy for many years. It had come out well from an inquiry into its expansion plans in 1977: the inspector's report constituted a 'lucid, sweeping, and almost unequivocal support of British Nuclear Fuels' case'—to

a contemporary comment[32]. Since then BNFL had been
dily accumulating commercial experience in a difficult tech-
logy, which in its civil applications had defeated the Americans.
Only the French had gone further. Sellafield was gearing itself up to
meet the steady growth in uranium and plutonium recycling that
was expected during the next century, while the Dounreay site and
plant were admirably suitable for reprocessing fast reactor fuel.
British government support for the reprocessing side of Dounreay's
activities is assured until March 1997.

The Sellafield operating record was not without blemish. In 1979
20,000 gallons of radioactively contaminated water had leaked;
and in the following years there had been further intermittent
scares, and a prosecution in the Crown Court at Carlisle. At one
time the Nuclear Installations Inspectorate warned the company
that unless standards could be improved, the plant might be shut
down. The proper technical response was made, and BNFL set
about restoring its public image with a successful programme of
television advertisements and public visits, intended to dispel the
damaging image of Britain as the nuclear dustbin of the world. The
prize was not only the immediate market for reprocessing and fuel
recycling: the technology was an essential part of the long-term
fuel-saving potentialities of the fast reactor. Despite the débacle
over the AGR, and the placing of the fast reactor on the back
burner, it would ensure that Britain remained a significant force in
nuclear technology; and it satisfied the country's desire to make a
contribution that was truly home-grown. Unfortunately for BNFL,
the task of maintaining public support was hampered by recurring
and well-publicized anxieties about a possible causal connection
between the plant's operations and the unexpectedly high incidence
of childhood leukaemia in the local area (Chapter 8).

Electricity privatization

The circumstances of the British nuclear electricity programme
were sharply altered by the February 1988 decision of Margaret
Thatcher's government to 'privatize' the British and Scottish
electricity utilities. For several decades past they had been part of
the nationalized industries. As such they had been protected from
the financial consequences of the poorly performing AGRs by the
Treasury, which acted as their banker of last resort. The Thatcher-
ites wielded a new broom. It was their political creed that

privatization could and should make the whole financial position more 'transparent', as it had already done for other nationalized industries; and that this would provide an excellent discipline and guide to future policy. Dogma apart, there was also the sweetener that privatization of the publicly-owned generating industry and national grid might realize £20 billion for the Treasury, and so help to hold down taxation.

The Scottish generating boards and their distribution networks were to be sold as going concerns; but in England and Wales the much larger CEGB was to be broken up into two competing organizations of unequal size, with nuclear power going to the larger portion, National Power (the smaller portion was to be called PowerGen). The grid would be split off as a separate entity, and jointly owned by twelve regional distribution companies. The generating companies would no longer bear the responsibility for seeing that the lights did not go out. That responsibility was to be nominally transferred to the distribution companies, though in circumstances which cast doubt on their ability to discharge it effectively. The industry was launched on an ill-prepared voyage into the unknown.

It was recognized that after the difficulties of the AGR programme nuclear power might need special treatment, and at the outset the government let it be known that a proportion of electricity would initially come from non-fossil-fuel sources. This quota, which was eventually fixed at 8 GWe, would include a small amount of hydroelectricity, and in time a few megawatts of wind generation; but it would be mainly nuclear. For a time a 'nuclear levy' would also be charged on fossil-fuel generation (it was initially set at 10.6 per cent of final sales, though with the expectation that it would later fall). The announcement regarding the levy created presentational problems: if British nuclear power was about to become economic, as asserted at the Sizewell Inquiry, why did it need this double protection? A possible answer was that this was the price of diversity. The harsher truth was that while well-built and well-run PWRs could be broadly competitive with fossil fuel, the British AGR programme was still a financial burden. Nor could Sizewell, the first of the new line of PWRs, hope to match the economics of the long French production run.

But any marginal inability to compete with fossil fuel was as nothing compared with the effects of the organizational upheaval that this particular form of privatization brought with it. All the assumptions on which the electricity industry had been run for decades were to be abandoned. The traditional world-wide pattern is of a vertically-integrated industry, with a generating company enjoying a regulated monopoly, in return for an 'obligation to supply' (OTS), or 'an obligation to serve in a defined geographical franchise'. This requires the supplier to give a firm guarantee—in both the short term and the long term—that when a switch is operated the lights will always come on. This is broadly how CEGB has functioned within its designated area—England and Wales combined. It is true that, unlike the vertically integrated Scottish boards and many overseas utilities, the CEGB had not handled distribution at the point of sale. That had been the task of the Area Boards; but as the CEGB looked after the national grid south of the Scottish border, which supplied the distributors, the effect was much the same. This arrangement provided a firm basis for demand forecasts, and for the planning needed by the long-term implications of the OTS. The introduction of competition in generation (though not in electricity sales) that had already been allowed by the 1983 Electricity Act in the UK had in practice done little to disturb this general pattern.

Privatization *per se* need not have disrupted this pattern. Examples abound elsewhere of regulated private utilities which operate nuclear-power units. But the particular form of privatization adopted by the Thatcher government broke new ground, bringing competition to every part of the electricity industry. Neither National Power nor PowerGen would have an area franchise, nor the ability to pass on costs automatically to their customers in the twelve areas. In future, sales would be on the basis of competitive bidding. Neither generator would any longer have an obligation to supply. According to the reorganization scheme, the OTS would be transferred to the distributors; but it would no longer take its traditional form, since in the fully-competitive environment to which they would be exposed after a transitional period of eight years no one could any longer reasonably be held responsible for guaranteeing that the lights would not go out. It would be necessary to rely on a quite different market mechanism, with electricity being in effect auctioned throughout the day on the basis of bids from the various grid suppliers—including the Scottish generators and the nuclear 2 GWe imported from France via the Channel link. The proponents of privatization believed that frequent variations in price could have the effect of smoothing demand, by discouraging large industrial consumers from taking current from the grid at times of peak-load. What was left of the OTS concept was an obligation placed on the distribution companies to connect a customer to the grid on request. Major customers with a peak demand of more than one megawatt would be free to buy their electricity from any grid-connected supplier, not just from their local distribution company: the new grid company would transmit the necessary current from the point of generation. The first major user to announce its intention of making use of this new freedom was London Airport. The obligations of the distribution companies, should a customer leave them and then wish to return, had still to be defined.

It is hardly a matter for surprise that this novel pattern has many novel consequences. In theory at least, the twelve new distribution companies will no longer have a firm basis for short- or long-term planning, any more than the generators; though no doubt a future government would intervene if things started going obviously wrong. Nor will they be under a prior obligation to purchase stated quantities of electricity from National Power, PowerGen, or any other supplier; indeed, they may be generators in a small way themselves—up to 15 per cent of their requirements. That in turn implies that the two major generators, National Power and PowerGen, can no longer know for certain in advance exactly what they should produce, and what reserve capacity should be retained; still less what the demand might be in ten years time, after a number of new independent generating companies have started to feed the grid. In this new context of uncertainty all plans for new long-term capital-intensive investments are vulnerable, whether for new nuclear power stations, large coal stations, or possibly even the long-mooted Bristol Channel barrage for tidal electricity generation. Henceforth demand growth can best be met by low capital-cost, quickly constructed small stations; whether they add to 'greenhouse' emissions will be a secondary consideration.

There are concomitant financial difficulties, and new consider-ations of tax, debt, equity, risk, and required return on capital. As part of the process of privatization it was necessary to produce a prospectus, showing (as required by law) a true picture of the state of the privatized 'fission fragments' formed from CEGB. It would have been inappropriate to transfer the financial obligation for the used fuel awaiting treatment at Sellafield to National Power, when the purpose of privatization was to secure an easy and profitable sale of a company with no crippling inheritance. It was therefore necessary for CEGB, in its final accounts, to provide fully for the costs arising from its past activities. Two difficulties arose. One was that CEGB had always been required to return any financial surplus to the Treasury, as is normal for British nationalized industries. Although notional 'provisions' for reprocessing and decommissioning had appeared in past accounts, the reality was that no cash funds existed for these purposes. Secondly, the costs for post-irradiation fuel treatment quoted by British Nuclear Fuels grew very rapidly, once the extent of the new uncertainties was fully appreciated. BNFL abandoned its cost-plus approach, and instead quoted CEGB on a fully commercial basis, taking into account all possible risks. These now even included the possibility of having to return Sellafield to a green-field site. Unlikely though that seems for a country which has invested so much in reprocessing technology with an eye to its future trading possibilities, it is what a House of Commons Select Committee had recommended.

The escalation of costs was particularly great for the Magnox stations, which were coming to the ends of their lives, when it would be necessary to de-fuel them and deal with the relatively large tonnage of uranium which these low-rated reactors use. In their case this would be the main decommissioning cost. The discharge of used fuel on final shut-down would be eight times the normal annual discharge, and because of the poor corrosion resistance of these particular fuel elements, reprocessing could not be long delayed. These large tonnages made any cost escalation a serious matter. It became clear that there was no possibility of meeting the closure charges associated with fuel treatment out of revenue earned during the stations' short remaining lifetimes. On 24 July 1989 the government decided to withdraw the Magnox reactors from the privatization sale.

The PWR programme posed a different problem. The largest single contribution to the price of electricity from a PWR comes from capital charges. For a decade from 1977 the Treasury had recommended using a charge of 5 per cent in real terms for the purpose of future investment planning. In 1988 the figure was raised to 8 per cent. With an assumed lifetime of forty years the average price of electricity then came to 3.2 pence per kWh, if the costing was done on a 'public-sector' basis[63]. But the transfer to the private sector changed the financing considerations completely. In the circumstances laid down by the government no financier could regard an investment in a PWR as safe: there would be neither a monopoly franchise, nor a firm cost-plus contract with the distribution companies, nor a government guarantee. The required return on capital would accordingly rise to reflect the risk. It might be possible to borrow money at a reasonable rate for a term considerably shorter than the operating lifetime; but in that case very high initial electricity prices would be needed to pay off the debt in the time available. Later in the station's life the accounted cost, freed of capital charges, would fall to a very low figure; but it was the initial hurdle which counted in the privatization debate, and which created a furore. National Power advised the government that the best compromise it could suggest was a price of 6.25 pence per kWh, on the basis of cost recovery over twenty years and 10 per cent real return on capital—almost twice the 'public-sector' price of nuclear power.

On 9 November 1989 the government announced that it was not willing to provide the guarantees that National Power would need if it was to quote a more competitive figure, or one more in keeping with the expected operating lifetime; that the Sizewell PWR would be retained in the public sector; and that any further PWR orders would be deferred for at least 5 years. With the Magnox and the PWRs both removed from privatization, it was inevitable that the AGRs should also stay in the public sector, in a new government-owned organization, Nuclear Electric. How that organization should articulate with the competitive environment which was being created, and on what pricing basis, was not immediately clear.

Rarely has economic theory interfered more completely with an established and tested way of doing things. It is to be hoped, for the sake of the country, that the theoreticians are right; or at least that a safety net can be established under British electricity generation as a whole—quite apart from the special case of nuclear power—in case they are wrong. Fortunately, the full surge of competition will not be felt for 8 years, which gives time for learning how to make the new system work, and if necessary for fresh institutional change, particularly as two general elections will have been held by then. Meanwhile British nuclear power is 'on hold'.

On 30 November 1989 Lord Marshall, who had been appointed

to the chairmanship of the Central Electricity Generating Board in order to establish British nuclear power on a firmer footing, and who had also been elected by virtue of his international reputation as the first chairman of the World Association of Nuclear Operators, said this: ' . . . the broad story of nuclear power in this country is the most powerful argument in favour of privatization that I have ever seen. Over the last forty years governments have interfered with this business so continuously, and with such appalling effects, that I am thoroughly convinced that it must be best to do everything that can be done in the private sector.' A sad conclusion, but one borne out to the letter by this history.

Uranium mining in Australia

Australia's contribution to nuclear power is as a supplier of uranium, which was first discovered there almost a century ago, in New South Wales. There was some small-scale mining (for the radium content) until the 1930s, but serious commercial operations did not start until the weapons boom following World War II. Production began at Rum Jungle near Darwin in 1953, and at Radium Hill in South Australia in the following year. But by 1971 mining had come to a halt as a result of the collapse in the market described in Chapter 2. By then a number of excellent ore-bodies had been located in the Northern Territory in particular, and also in South and Western Australia[64]. In the ordinary course of events the renewal of interest in nuclear power which occurred in the early 1970s would have led to the speedy development of these potential mines. All the Northern Territory mining companies were in the process of negotiating agreements when the Liberal-National Country Party government fell in November 1972.

While in power this coalition had begun to shape a new policy for mineral exploitation. As mining was of profound economic importance to the country, mining companies generally were given favourable tax advantages. Because of their strategic significance uranium exports were regarded as a special case. The 1953 Atomic Energy Act had made uranium in the Northern Territory the property of the Commonwealth (i.e. federal) government, and the government participated actively in uranium activities. This reflected the constitutional position that the Northern Territory is under the jurisdiction of the Commonwealth government in Canberra; the NT happens to be the country's principal uranium-bearing area.

Extensive foreign participation in uranium mining, as with other minerals, was having the effect of bringing large amounts of capital borrowed from overseas into the country. Late in 1971 the Treasury began to be anxious about the monetary consequences of the build-up of liquidity. There were also understandable political concerns about allowing Australia's natural resources to fall into foreign ownership. The government therefore enacted the Companies (Foreign Takeovers) Act 1972, which made acquisitions of 15 per cent of voting power by foreign interests, or 40 per cent in aggregate, subject to examination. This was not intended to be the end of the coalition's study of foreign ownership; but before further action could be taken the McMahon government fell, and after twenty-three years of opposition the Australian Labor Party (ALP) came to power under Gough Whitlam.

By tradition the ALP was rather more ideological than its right-wing opponents. It criticized the outgoing government for having granted tax concessions to mining companies without demanding equity participation. The nationalization ambitions briefly took the form of a wholly impractical scheme, soon laid to rest, of mandatory local enrichment of Australian uranium prior to export. Part-public ownership of uranium was a more realistic possibility. The government negotiated an agreement with the owners of the large Ranger deposit in the Northern Territory, under which the Australian Atomic Energy Commission would receive a half-interest in the net profits, in return for providing the majority of the production financing and waiving all royalties. The Commission was to be the sole marketing agent, under legal authority derived from the Atomic Energy Act. Meanwhile, export contract approval was withheld, owing to the 'unsatisfactory nature of the market'. Relations between the industry and the government became strained. In 1975 nationalization policy required all new uranium projects to be wholly Australian owned; earlier projects were to have at least 50 per cent Australian equity participation.

The Labor government combined this nuclear stance with being strongly pro-Aboriginal and pro-environment. A Ministry of Aboriginal Affairs was created, and began to study the question of Aboriginal land-rights in the Northern Territory. It soon became clear that they would be a complicating factor in the future of uranium mining. There was also a new interest in the environment: an Environmental Protection (Impact of Proposals) Act was passed at the end of 1974, requiring all new mining projects to submit an environmental statement, showing the extent of a project's impact on the environment. This limited Ranger's further development until such a statement could be prepared and approved.

The Whitlam government was short-lived, and fell at the next general election in November 1975. The incoming coalition under Malcolm Fraser quickly declared that its role was not to seek ownership on its own account, but to provide a suitable legislative and economic framework which would allow the mining industry to flourish. An element of nationalism still remained as regards share-ownership, which in future was to be 75 per cent Australian for all new uranium projects that resulted in production. However, the shortage of capital in the country soon led to some easing of the rules. Production restarted at the Mary Kathleen mine in 1976.

Before the demise of the Labor government it had set in train an environmental inquiry into the Ranger project. Ranger is situated in the coastal plain of the Northern Territory, in an area which was becoming a symbol of the 'dream-time' of the Aborigines. Only 800 of Australia's 200,000 Aborigines were living in the uranium-bearing region, but the land-rights issue which they symbolized carried great political weight, despite the small numbers directly involved. A Royal Commission, under Mr Justice Fox of the Australian Capital Territory Supreme Court, started work in 1975. He interpreted his terms of reference widely, to allow study of all aspects of the nuclear debate. This provided an easy entry for the radical environmentalist groups opposed to mining development, including the Friends of the Earth and the Australian Conservation Foundation. Parts of the trade union movement also took an opposing stance, which was politically significant in view of their close association with Labor.

While the Ranger Uranium Environmental Inquiry was sitting the legislative framework was modified by the December 1976 Aboriginal Land Rights (Northern Territory) Act, resulting from earlier studies begun by the previous government. It recognized tradition as a basis for land-rights, and brought the proportion of Australia's uranium reserves that were subject in one way or another to restrictions stemming from Aboriginal rights to nearly 80 per cent.

Mr Justice Fox took two years before presenting his final report in May 1977. It dismissed some of the widespread fears about uranium[65], but called for the fullest discussion on three issues:

nuclear proliferation, the safe disposal of nuclear waste, and the impact of mining on the life and culture of the Aborigines. In particular he proposed that a national park—Kakadu—should be created, and that land should be granted to the Aborigines. Under the Aboriginal Land Rights Act this would require negotiation and payment of compensation by the mining companies. He also recommended a 'sequential' process of development of the various known Australian ore-bodies, five-sixths of the country's reserves being in the Northern Territory.

Malcolm Fraser's Liberal-National Country Party government, which had been returned to power while the Royal Commission was still sitting, was in favour of uranium development, and in August 1977 lifted the ban on uranium exports which had applied for four years. The restriction on private-enterprise exploration for uranium in the Northern Territory was also lifted. The parliamentary members of the ALP—now in opposition—made it clear that they would oppose new mining developments until they could be satisfied that storage and other safeguards were satisfactory; and that the next Labor government would not be bound to honour any future contracts for uranium entered into by its predecessor. However, the influential president of the Australian Congress of Trade Unions, Mr Hawke—later to become Prime Minister—was not himself opposed to mining, provided there were adequate safety and environmental controls. The Fraser government, seeking a firmer mandate on the uranium issue, called an election in December 1977, and won an unexpectedly large majority. Gough Whitlam resigned as ALP leader.

During the months before the election a new influence had come on the scene, in the shape of President Carter's policy on nuclear proliferation. By focusing on the dangers of plutonium, and extolling the benefits of relying only on uranium, the President drew attention to the potential influence of the uranium-producing nations towards slowing down and possibly preventing further proliferation. The Australian public were quick to appreciate that this could provide the country with an opportunity of exercising its influence on the world scene—which it could certainly not do through non-participation. This new perception came to the rescue of the mining industry, which had felt itself under threat from a powerful nation-wide anti-uranium movement with non-proliferation objectives, quite unconnected with the Aboriginal issue. The Prime

Minister announced in May 1977 a comprehensive policy on nuclear safeguards, to guide export policy, and the government commended negotiations with possible overseas purchasers. Against opposition from the communist-led transport unions the Northern Land Council—the body representing the interests of the Aborigines living in the area—agreed to the start of uranium mining at Ranger, with the Aborigines receiving significant financial compensation.

On the Labor side the old guard was giving way to the new, and in 1979 Bob Hawke decided[32] to take up federal politics. The Party was giving further thought to uranium policy, and a strong left-wing anti-nuclear influence was reinforced by the Three Mile Island accident. For a time the ALP's policy, if returned to power, was to close all uranium mines and repudiate without compensation any existing contracts; but expediency soon shouldered ideology aside. After the possibility appeared of creating a major new copper, gold, and uranium mine in South Australia—Olympic Dam—it became clear that the Labor Party in that state could not win the state election due in 1982 unless they supported the new project. The 1982 ALP Federal National Conference therefore modified the Party's uranium policy substantially, to permit the continued operation of existing mines, though not their expansion; and to allow new mines where uranium was extracted incidentally to other mineral production—which of course opened the way for Olympic Dam.

The ALP was able to damage the Fraser government by pointing to a large federal deficit in 1982; and in March of the following year gained a sweeping victory, which brought in Hawke as Prime Minister. The ALP's new 'three mines policy', adopted in November 1983—the three mines being Ranger and Nabarlek (both in the Northern Territory), and Olympic Dam—was distinctly more forthcoming than the views Labor had expressed while in opposition: evidently the 250 million or more US dollars per year which were obtainable by Australia even in the somewhat subdued uranium market of the mid-1980s were of political significance. Other aspects of the earlier Labor policy continued to apply: strict non-proliferation safeguards; a refusal to supply France for as long as that country held weapon tests at Mururoa Atoll in the South Pacific (the policy was eased in 1986); vigorous opposition to the dumping of radioactive waste at sea; and the maintenance of the government-imposed floor price for uranium.

The policy was encapsulated in a 'platform' on uranium[66], carried by the biennial Federal National Conference of the ALP in July 1984. Such policy statements are politically binding on the Party. This one provided a firm foundation for the development of a major section of the mining industry—though the owners of the mines which had not received approval were understandably unhappy. Part of the quid pro quo was the prohibition of 'the establishment in Australia of nuclear-power plants and all other stages of the nuclear fuel cycle'. It is a wise Party which knows when to make political capital by prohibiting something for which there would be little commercial justification!

The doubts about the future which the ALP had engendered while in opposition were set at ease by its performance in office. The realization that Australia could exploit its uranium exports and still exert a beneficial influence on non-proliferation policy proved a turning-point: for once there was political advantage in being seen to support part of the nuclear industry. Labor's uranium-mining policy, as it evolved in office, was clear and workable, and the previously hostile stance of some trade unions was defused.

Despite—or perhaps because of—a very small parliamentary majority after the election in December 1984, the uranium policy survived the next biennial National Conference of the ALP in July 1986; and after Labor had won the general election of 1987, continued without major problems until the following conference at Hobart in June 1988. By then events had begun to create difficulties. The Nabarlek deposit had been mined out: should the policy become one based on two mines only, with the loss of revenue to the country which this might imply? Or should the owners of Nabarlek be allowed to exploit another nearby deposit; and if so, could this be justified politically in view of the gross unfairness it would represent to its neighbour Jabiluka? Jabiluka is one of the largest uranium ore-bodies in the world; it is outside the boundaries of the Kakadu National Park; and mining plans have been ready for a decade. However, it was excluded from the three mines policy, and the property's only contribution to the Australian economy up to the time of the 1988 conference had been as a location for the film *Crocodile Dundee*.

The Uranium Policy Review Committee that the ALP National Conference appointed to review the options was instructed to consider all issues relevant to the Party's 'platform' on uranium, including the current three mines policy, the possibility of 'upgrading' yellow-cake to hexafluoride prior to export, and the pricing policy for exported uranium—which was causing problems for Australian producers at a time of market weakness world-wide. The floor-price regulation stemmed from the 'pro-uranium' Fraser government, and had been retained by the ALP on coming to power possibly because of its constraining consequences. As one observer close to the industry observed, the astute members of the ALP could see that the floor price might achieve painlessly what political action would not do: stop the growth of the uranium industry.

The review took place against a fascinating political background. Within the ALP there were three factions: the strongly anti-nuclear Left (the remains of the old quasi-communist ideologues); the Right (the descendants of anti-communist traditional trade-unionists); and the balancing Centre-Left, which was a newer growth. The Centre-Left undertook to 'manage' the review so as to yield a rational result with a minimum of intra-party tension.

The federal constitution of Australia also played a significant role. The owners of Ranger and Olympic Dam were happy with the status quo. Ranger was in production, and able to expand its output. Development of Olympic Dam was well advanced. Both mines were fighting for contracts in a depressed world uranium market, and the last thing they wanted was further competition. They were strongly supported by the Labor government of South Australia. But there were other considerations. The Labor government of Western Australia was anxious to press the claims of its own potential uranium mines—Kintyre and Yelirrie. The Northern Territory was not a Labor stronghold, but it possessed a remarkably powerful lever in the Aboriginal issue. If new developments were not authorized there, the Aborigines would ask why the federal government was not supporting them. Reaching a decision was not made any easier by a clear split within the Aboriginal ranks. There were those, mostly from outside the Northern Territory, who opposed any further encroachment by the white men on their traditional lands; and those inside, led by the Chairman of the Northern Land Council, Garrawuy Yunupingu, who had a lively appreciation of the value of mining royalties—which had amounted[67] to US$73 million by 1988.

There was also the issue of market confidence. Purchasers of Australian uranium appeared less ready to place large long-term orders than the mining companies would wish. One reason was the depressed state of the market generally, and the ability to buy spot uranium easily at favourable prices; but there were grounds for believing that uncertainties over the ALP's depth of commitment to uranium also had something to do with it. At a time when the large United States market seemed to be on the point of being fully opened to Canadian uranium, the Australian mining industry would have appreciated firmer support from its own government.

Yet another issue became politically significant while the review committee was sitting: the 'greenhouse effect'. Australia is one of the countries best placed to benefit from world trade in coal, which prior to 1988 seemed destined to grow rapidly. The 'greenhouse' considerations that suddenly came to political prominence in that year, through the limitations they might induce governments to set on future carbon dioxide emissions—as Sweden has already done—might possibly modify such prospects. The normal momentum of the world economy is of course on the side of Australia's coal industry; but 'greenhouse' considerations might improve the relative long-term prospects for nuclear power, and thus for Australia's uranium, though at the expense of its coal. The Prime Minister began to take a personal interest.

The review committee's report was expected to appear in 1990 (after this book went to press), after which it would have to be debated before adoption by a subsequent ALP National Conference. Meanwhile Labor had won an unprecedented fourth term in the March 1990 election, but only by a wafer-thin majority. In the circumstances the review committee's decision to 'make haste slowly' seemed entirely appropriate.

PART TWO

THE MAIN POLICY ISSUES

6 Nuclear-Power Economics

THESE nine political histories show how different countries have pursued bewilderingly different policies towards nuclear electricity. Even allowing for the varied influences of national politics, it is clear that nuclear power has been unusually difficult to assess in economic terms. The politicians deserve some sympathy. The technology has been constantly evolving. So too has the understanding of what is involved in going nuclear successfully, in the light of two very different major accidents. Costs have escalated as safety has been bought by ever more stringent regulations. It is only since the early 1980s, as nuclear technology has stabilized, and the full range of costs and benefits become more predictable, that it has been possible to base nuclear investment analysis on something more than inspired guesswork.

Today the view can be heard that the lower fossil-fuel costs of recent years have destroyed the economic case for nuclear power. The public, observing that nuclear power is nevertheless still expanding, albeit slowly, is confused and would like the facts in some simple and understandable form. The truth, unfortunately, is boringly complicated. There are certainly circumstances where nuclear electricity can be regarded as cheaper; but whether this is so in any particular case depends on the weight attached to many factors, including interest rates and future coal prices; very much on how a nuclear project is run and regulated; and not least on how the assessments are carried out. Every businessman knows the problems of looking into the future, and how easily a forecast can be massaged to produce a desired conclusion. The additional difficulty in the case of electricity supplies is that we are concerned with generating-plant which is intended to function for thirty, or even (for a coal station) forty-five years, after a planning and building period of a further 5 to 8 years; and where the 'most economic choice' depends fundamentally on assumptions about both nuclear performance and how the alternatives are likely to fare in the meantime. The difficulties can be appreciated by casting a look backwards over a comparable period—to 1960 or even

1950—and considering how the energy scene has changed in the meantime.

Major influences affecting the relative economics of new nuclear and non-nuclear power

From an investment viewpoint there are several alternatives to installing a new nuclear power-station: conventional coal-firing; new forms of coal-burning (e.g. fluidized-bed burning, which has some advantages in controlling undesirable emissions); burning coal in combined heat and power schemes, where the normally wasted heat is piped away for district-heating; heavy oil-firing for conventional boilers; combined-cycle gas turbines, where the waste heat from the gas turbine is used to raise steam which is passed through a turbine to produce extra electricity; burning lighter oil in gas turbines at times of peak-load; hydropower, if it is available; and, for the future, a whole range of novel energy technologies based on 'renewable' resources. In a large and diversified system some or all of these options will be switched in or out, depending on demand, according to a 'merit order', whereby stations are called up in order of increasing running costs in order to minimize total system costs. Once built, a hydro plant or a nuclear reactor will be used preferentially for the 'base-load'—that 30 per cent or so of maximum demand which is always present, whatever the time of day or season—because of the saving on fuel costs.

In practice the choice of energy investment has some constraints. The novel ways of dealing with coal have yet to establish a clear economic advantage over tried and tested technology, at least for base-load generation. District-heating schemes using the waste heat from electricity generation are almost unknown in the UK, though commoner in the rest of northern Europe. There are uncertainties about the long-term supply of natural gas at competitive prices. The 'renewables' have their difficulties, as we shall see later. Conservation—the alternative to new investment—needs the co-operation of large numbers of people, and is not quickly organized. While a large national system will have room for some of these alternatives, to meet or avoid particular segments of demand, conventional coal-firing is likely to remain the dominant alternative to nuclear power in many countries, and the competition it offers will largely determine nuclear's future in Europe—though oil and gas m. alternatives elsewhere[68].

Nuclear and fossil stations both make the same pro electricity, but have very different patterns of cash expenditure over time, particularly as regards the *balance between capital and fuel costs*. Capital costs, which are nearly all incurred before any electricity is produced, are relatively much higher for nuclear stations than for fossil-fuelling: from 45 per cent of the total costs for nuclear, to as much in some cases as 70 per cent, against 20–40 per cent for coal. Conversely nuclear running costs are lower, though the exact figure for coal depends very much on the location[69–71]. The highly capital-intensive nature of nuclear power means that it is more sensitive than coal to taxation regulations affecting investment allowances. The 1986 tax changes in the USA, which cut depreciation schedules and eliminated investment tax credits, bore more heavily on nuclear- than on coal-plants.

As regards *nuclear fuel costs*, uranium as mined accounted in the market circumstances of 1989 for 10 per cent or less of the cost of nuclear generation. Even with a threefold increase in the price of uranium the cost of nuclear electricity would rise by no more than 20 per cent. Hence France's claim that, by switching to nuclear electricity so completely, she has virtually insulated herself from the adverse effects of raw material cost fluctuations, and given her industries a sound long-term basis for planning, especially those which are large consumers of electrical energy. For a coal-fired station, where the fuel component may account for over half the total cost—except close to sources of unusually cheap coal (mines or deep-water ports)—a similar change in the cost of coal would lead to a doubling in the price of electricity, a vastly greater degree of sensitivity.

The capital-intensive nature of nuclear energy and its complicated technology make it vulnerable to the effects of *delays in construction*, and so to *interest rates*. In the USA in the early 1980s, when many new reactors were held up pending a full evaluation of the safety lessons of the Three Mile Island accident, their owners had to borrow at money-market rates above 15 per cent. At such rates it matters greatly whether a nuclear-plant is constructed efficiently, in the six years taken for the St Lucie 2 plant in Florida, or in the even shorter times—just under five years—which have been achieved in

France; or whether, at the other end of the scale, construction times follow the US average in the mid-1980s of ten to eleven years; or the appalling record of twenty years taken for Dungeness B in the UK[72]. In the United States, with institutions and traditions which have allowed intervention by objectors at the district, state, and federal levels—even after a reactor was in all respects complete—persistent and continuing assertions that a particular nuclear station would be uneconomic have made this true in fact, through the ineluctable accretion of financing charges. As a result the cost for similar units has varied, between the best and worst US performers, by a factor of more than three. Such an uncertain climate does not provide a valid test of the competitive qualities of nuclear technology; but it is what has shaped the industry's reputation. That is why the revised US licensing procedure announced by the Nuclear Regulatory Commission in 1989 is so important to the nuclear future (page 118).

The time taken to construct a nuclear station depends to some extent on its *type and design*. Light-water reactors (LWRs) are relatively compact, and can be largely fabricated off-site in factories where manufacturing conditions are controlled and optimized, and where the advantages of series production can be won. In contrast, the advanced gas-cooled (AGR) reactors required massive on-site 'one-off' civil engineering and pressure-vessel fabrication, which made it more difficult to achieve production economies.

Apart from design differences, there is also the issue[80] of *standardization*. All manufacturing history shows that the time spent in manufacture falls as experience is gained, provided a standardized design is being produced. The lead time for constructing French pressurized-water reactors (PWRs) fell steadily from seventy-five months in 1977 to just under sixty months. The German 'convoy' programme showed similar benefits, though unfortunately the programme shrank to a mere three reactors. In contrast, as we saw in the previous chapter, the strategy for the British AGRs was based on a misreading of the supposed benefits of competing designs, against a background of over-optimistic predictions of economic growth. Too many different versions were commissioned, from too many companies: at one stage, briefly, there were no less than five organizations competing in a market which we can now see, with hindsight, was more suited to a single national entity. In the USA there was an even greater multiplicity of suppliers: ten architect-engineers, four reactor vendors, and hundreds of system component manufacturers. Hardly any two reactors were identical, so learning from experience was all but impossible. The few honourable exceptions included Commonwealth Edison's twin stations at Byron and Braidwood, and the three at Palo Verde in Arizona. At Palo Verde unit 2 was 5 per cent cheaper than unit 1, and the start-up time was cut from fifty-six to thirty-five weeks. A country which does not standardize its reactors finds it much harder to climb up the learning curve.

Although standardization could in theory be promoted by manufacturers, historically the *structure of the generating industry* has had a greater influence. Unlike the huge Électricité de France, with over fifty reactors already operating, small utilities are in no position to establish a national policy of standardization. Nor do they all have the financial muscle needed to carry them safely through teething troubles. Many of the fifty-three US utilities which were operating nuclear reactors in 1988 found that the commitments they had entered into in the early 1970s were more than they could safely shoulder. Their subsequent behaviour has tended to be increasingly averse to taking on further nuclear commitments. That is not an environment where standardization can flourish.

Efficiency of operation is as important as efficient construction. There are great differences between the *annual utilization of nuclear-plant* in different countries. Some arise from fundamental aspects of design: reactors like the Canadian CANDU or the British AGRs, where on-load refuelling is possible without the need for complete shut-down, clearly should have an intrinsic advantage in this respect over PWRs and boiling-water reactors (BWRs), which need lengthy shut-downs every twelve to eighteen months, when the pressure-vessel lid is removed to give access to the core (though for other reasons the theoretical benefit of on-load refuelling is not always achieved in practice). But even within the PWR and BWR families there are great differences, with many US reactors (though fortunately not all) showing a surprising inability to match the high plant utilizations regularly achieved in Europe and Japan. In 1987 the best US performers had availabilities of well over 90 per cent; but the country average load factor was still only 60 per cent. In the same year the corresponding figure for Finnish reactors was 91 per cent, for Swiss reactors 84 per cent, and for Japanese reactors 79 per cent. (The load factor is the ratio of the energy produced in a given period to the energy that would have been produced had the plant been run continuously at maximum capacity.) Low plant utilizations are reflected in higher electricity costs per kWh, because the high capital costs are spread over a smaller output. In France availability grew[1] from 63 per cent in 1981 to 79 per cent in 1984, which with thirty-three units then installed was in energy terms equivalent to commissioning a further eight reactors. What is interesting is the absence of any correlation between operational efficiency and the size of the utility: the excellent Finnish and Swiss performances were achieved by small utilities. The explanation may lie in the high professional standing of the industry in those countries, whereas in the USA there are many other competing attractions for high-quality engineers, including NASA and Silicon Valley.

Non-fuel costs for nuclear stations can show surprising variations. In the US routine operating and maintenance costs grew at an average of 12 per cent annually in *real* terms between 1974 and 1984, for a variety of reasons—from a desire to improve performance through a greatly expanded training programme, to government-imposed requirements for more meticulous documentation and for a substantial increase in security staff. The US Energy Information Administration[73] found that the total non-fuel costs in US reactors varied by an astonishing factor of 5.5, between lowest and highest.

Inflation and the *method of assessment* can both have an important effect on the apparent relative costs of competing systems. The years of massive inflation immmediately after the two oil shocks made a tremendous difference to the relative positions of coal and nuclear, when judged on the basis of historic costs. On that basis the early British Magnox stations had a significant economic advantage over coal. The figures for 1983/4 were: nuclear (Magnox) 1.87 pence per kWh; coal 2.32 pence per kWh; oil 4.30 pence per kWh. But if, instead of using historic costing in an inflationary period, the calculations were remade on the basis of 5 per cent 'opportunity cost'—measuring the advantage that would have accrued if the money had been invested in other ways—the picture changes[74], the new figures being: Magnox 2.78 pence per kWh; coal 2.56 pence per kWh; oil 5.79 pence per kWh.

The low-temperature waste heat from any power station, whether nuclear or not, cannot for reasons of basic thermodynamics be effectively used in steam turbines. It is therefore usually discharged to the sea or to a large river, or (via cooling towers) to the atmosphere. But in principle it could still be used for district-heating if the necessary infrastructure were available; and in that case electricity production, whether from coal or nuclear, could obtain a bonus[71] by selling off this useful by-product for district-heating (DH). This is known as *combined heat and power*, or CHP for short. Some reduction in generating efficiency is unavoidable, though acceptable, if the exhaust steam is to be still sufficiently hot to be useful for domestic heating. The larger problem is one of distributing the heat from a power-station to the many places where it is needed. The difficulty is not the long-distance transport of heat, where good technologies are now available, but the construction of the network of mains and meters needed at the point of use. Clearly a political commitment to planning is a pre-condition, and competition from a pre-existing network of domestic gas mains a deterrent. CHP is extensively used in Scandinavia: it provides nearly 40 per cent of Denmark's heating needs, with one million homes connected. The Danish Electricity Supply Act allows the government to insist on the installation of CHP, while the Heat Supply Act very sensibly avoids double investment on both DH and domestic gas mains[75]. In Sweden more than 10 per cent of electricity is generated by CHP/DH. The Swiss, whose nuclear reactors are built unusually close to major towns, have actively pursued nuclear district-heating, though the economics have not always been favourable. 'Greenhouse' considerations (Chapter 13) are bound to change perceptions of what should be considered as economic in the broadest sense, and may lead governments to give greater encouragement for energy conservation measures like CHP through suitable fiscal incentives.

The mirror image of conventional CHP is to allow large industrial users of energy with their own generating stations to export to the grid any surplus electricity. In the ten years after the US passed the Public Utilities Regulatory Policies Act (PURPA) in 1978, with the intention of encouraging such *electricity sales from independent producers* at agreed prices, or at the utilities' 'avoided costs', no less than 62 GWe of generating capacity were built or planned; 7 GWe were added in 1988 alone[76,77]. One purpose of the 1988–90 privatization of the British electricity industry was to create similar incentives towards competition. However, it should not be forgotten that PURPA's apparently successful intervention in the US market-place has been accompanied by some artificialities, with regulated utilities being forbidden to pursue economically sound developments which independent competitors were free to undertake.

There are *other costs which influence the balance* between nuclear- and non-nuclear electricity generation. The cost of reducing the effect of acid rain from coal stations by flue gas desulphurization is an example. It is a major capital item, currently of the order of £250 million for back-fitting a 2 GWe coal station. It also lowers thermal efficiency and adds to running costs.

Again, nuclear expenditure has a 'tail' extending far into the future, for *waste-management and decommissioning*—an extended process likely in most cases to be phased over half a century or more. A number of countries already build a decommissioning surcharge or fee into their nuclear-electricity costs[78]. Fees are based partly on detailed costings, and partly on experience, which is growing steadily. Some uncertainty in costing at this stage need not be a matter for great concern, since the amount of energy produced over its lifetime by a large modern nuclear station is so great that even 200–500 million dollars for eventual decommissioning many years ahead represent only about 1 per cent additional cost per kilowatt-hour[71]. The difficulties suddenly encountered during the British electricity privatization over the decommissioning costs of the Magnox reactors (page 140) are unlikely to be typical, since an unexpected shortening of their working lives and other factors connected with privatization had made it impossible to build up an adequate decommissioning fund in the normal way. Moreover, with their low heat ratings and corrosion-sensitive fuel elements, their closure involved the early treatment of a relatively large tonnage of fuel per megawatt of output, compared with modern light-water reactors. Apart from the charges for dealing with the fuel elements, the remainder of the engineering costs incurred in dismantling are likely to be much the same, whatever the reactor output or type, and therefore bear on the economics of large modern PWRs much less than on these small early reactors.

In contrast, coal's costs have been taken historically as ending with the closure of a station. However, this conflicts with what is now known about the *huge potential costs of the 'greenhouse effect'*, through the civil engineering difficulties of dealing with the rise in sea-level which is now expected to occur before the end of the twenty-first century (Chapter 13), as a result of the effects of carbon dioxide emission on the earth's climate. Even early in the new century this particular external cost could conceivably influence the choice between coal and nuclear power, particularly if governments began to impose 'greenhouse' taxes. The much criticized nuclear industry could in time be viewed as environmentally the more benign!

A further factor which eludes precise quantification, but is nevertheless of considerable practical importance, is *diversification* of energy supplies. If its fuel supplies are not diversified a country may be hostage to unforeseen events or technical failures. France's 46 per cent dependence on oil and gas for electricity production in 1973 made her vulnerable to the oil-price shock when it came. Britain's coal-strike in 1984–5 was a desperate attempt by the miners to maintain their slowly disappearing monopoly of electricity fuel supplies, at costs above world levels. It was defeated by a combination of high coal stocks and the diversification made possible by using some remaining oil-fired stations on base-load, by burning oil in stations which normally used coal, and by nuclear power. The flexibility of oil, and willingness to accept its higher cost, were major factors in the struggle which the miners clearly failed to anticipate. Nuclear power does not have the same flexibility—uranium cannot be used in any other way—but it contributed its own element of strategic long-term diversity. In the present state of electricity production the diversification argument supports further nuclear development in most countries, even if a small premium has to be paid. There could, however, come a time when it becomes an argument for limiting further nuclear investment: it would require only one major accident to a large PWR anywhere in the world for the public to call into question the dependence on nuclear power that is the cornerstone of France's energy policy.

Even this list of variables does not exhaust the factors a full economic appraisal should take into account; for instance:

- rate of growth of demand
- financing method, interest rate, progress-payment phasing
- prospective system order of merit
- plant size and its relation to grid size

- effect of programme size on costs
- assumed plant lifetime
- allowances for cost/time overruns during construction
- commissioning and power build-up time
- effect of exchange rate swings on imported fuel costs
- transport costs for coal; station siting at mine or port
- cost of buffer stocks
- nuclear fuel-cycle processing costs
- achievable uranium fuel 'burn-up' (i.e. utilization)
- possibility of mandatory retrofitting for safety or environmental reasons (could apply to coal or nuclear)
- whether other plant is co-located (to share service and operating costs)
- plant availability and load factor
- transmission costs if from remote site

As we saw in connection with British electricity privatization, the inferred 'cost' per marginal additional kWh can be altered within wide limits by varying such assumptions. All this means that what analysts in one country say about nuclear economics (e.g. 'nuclear power cannot compete with coal' in some parts of the USA) may or may not be 'true' according to another country's criteria: it is always necessary to read the fine print.

Exchange rates create further distortions in inter-country comparisons, because they do not always reflect true purchasing-power parities. Such distortions can be overcome by making comparisons between coal and nuclear within individual countries, and comparing the resulting ratios. That may introduce its own variations in other directions—reactor and coal station design, assumptions regarding fuel costs, etc. But this could actually be helpful, adding to the robustness of any conclusions by, in effect, introducing a series of sensitivity checks.

Quantitative comparison of coal and nuclear generating costs

The different timing of expenditures and receipts for coal and nuclear stations means that some method is needed to take account of the basic fact of investment—that money available today can be made to work, and is therefore more valuable than the same amount received in ten years time. The analytical device used is the *discount rate.* Future flows of expenditure and receipts are adjusted by applying the discount rate for each intervening year, and summing to produce a *net present value*. A zero NPV implies that a proposed investment will yield the discount rate as the rate of return; an excess of PV revenue over PV expenditure implies a return better than the discount rate. This is the discounted cash flow (DCF) technique widely used in business. By comparing the NPVs of two competing options all the technical, operational, and financial differences can be subsumed into a single comparison. The complicating factor of inflation can be eliminated by treating all future cashflows on the basis of constant-money costs, with no inflationary addition.

The concept of discounting can be looked at in two ways. One view is that the discount rate should simply reflect the cost of money in the market. If interest rates are 10 per cent, this could also be taken as the discount rate. A return of $110 next year would then have a NPV of $100 today. Alternatively a higher discount rate can be set, to provide a more stringent test, reflecting a desire to insist on a higher financial performance. This is commonly the case in business, where the objective is to build up resources as quickly as possible in a highly competitive world, despite the constant presence of financial risk. Public bodies like electrical utilities do not normally face the same challenges of competition, which seems to imply that they could live with a lower discount rate than commerce, because of the low level of risk. However, use of a discount rate substantially lower than that used by private industry would open them—or their regulatory authorities—to complaints of diverting money from other uses which might have been more beneficial to the community.

Discount rates are not necessarily static, and a conclusion reached when they are high would not necessarily apply at a time of lower rates. During the 1970s and the 1980s the British government variously instructed the Central Electricity Generating Board to operate at test discount rates of 5, 8 and 10 per cent in real terms. There is no certainty that the present level of 8 per cent, which represents what the totality of British industry has earned in real terms on average over the recent past, will necessarily apply in future. It also does not apply in many OECD countries which prefer a real discount rate of 5 per cent—at which nuclear power is competitive[71].

The protection of electrical utilities against normal commercial competition is no longer something that can be taken for granted. In the USA, as we have seen already, the PURPA regulatory regime is creating changes in the network which would have been considered startling only twenty years ago. In the European Community there are moves towards a free market in the import and export of electricity. In the UK the privatization of electricity (page 136) is clearly intended to encourage independent producers to enter the electricity market. In practice they are likely to act in a commercial manner, with aversion to high initial capital expenditures where these can be avoided; in other words, as though operating in a high discount-rate environment.

The decision to privatize British electricity led to public discussion about the choice of discount rate appropriate for a technology which, it was argued by the nuclear opposition, could if badly handled lead to accidents as severe as Chernobyl. The coal lobby enthusiastically agreed that nuclear power should be penalized by a high discount rate for its 'systematic risk'. The London financial markets took a similar attitude to this unfamiliar form of investment. But it was pointed out that markets use the so-called equity beta-values as measures of the systematic risk associated with holding a particular stock; and that the betas for stocks of US utilities with substantial nuclear capacity suggest that the American stock-market views them as of relatively low risk[79]. What appears to emerge is that discount rates can reasonably be set on the assumption that the technology will work as it should; while in the US at least the third-party aspects of any accidents will be dealt with separately, via insurance plus non-crippling retrospective payments from the whole industry, plus ultimately government backing (the Price-Anderson framework, Chapters 5 and 9).

As this discussion has shown, the exact choice of discount rate is in the last resort a matter of judgement. Its importance for the coal–nuclear comparison is that the outcome is sensitive to the exact figure used. A high discount rate reduces the merit of nuclear power in comparison with coal, because of its high front-end capital cost. A lower rate penalizes coal, because the long stream of high fuel costs throughout a station's lifetime then plays a greater role. Paradoxically, an extremely low discount rate might not be the most advantageous for nuclear power, because the possibly even longer stream of post-operational expenditure would then be more 'visible'.

In the *constant-money levelized cost method* of assessing station costs, the total costs incurred in each year for all purposes, after netting out the effects of inflation ('constant-money'), are discounted to a selected base-date (the ranking of projects does not depend on the date chosen), and the total compared with the total lifetime electricity output, similarly discounted. The 'levelized cost' per unit is then the discounted total cost divided by the similarly discounted total production over the station's lifetime. If charged to the consumer it will exactly repay all the costs, and provide a return on capital equal to the discount rate.

Using this approach, the OECD periodically compares the costs of electricity production from coal and nuclear stations within a number of member countries—avoiding in this way problems of exchange-rate distortions. Table 6.1 summarizes the most recent study, published in 1989. The figures are based on utility estimates of the costs that they themselves would have to bear, for nuclear stations of about 1 GWe and coal stations of about 600 MWe, both reflecting the 'state of the art' for commissioning dates around 1995. The costs include delivery of fuel to the stations, dismantling and waste costs, and for coal-fired stations desulphurization. In North America regional variations are included, to show the economics of coal-fired generation near to a mine mouth.

Alternative assumptions show the effect of altering the discount rate, and also the coal price. Variants B and C in the Table are based on coal costs projected by the Coal Industry Advisory Board (CIAB) of the International Energy Agency.

The reference case of Table 6.1 puts nuclear power ahead of coal—in some countries well ahead—except where coal power-stations are close to very low-cost mines, or where (as in the USA) nuclear power has been held back for a variety of reasons. The pattern has remained broadly similar since the earlier OECD studies in 1983 and 1986, though the increasing availability of low-cost internationally traded coal has somewhat weakened nuclear's position. The variants included in the Table show the extent to which other assumptions about discount rate or coal price can alter the conclusions. Even at a discount rate of 10 per cent nuclear power is still ahead in countries where it has a good construction and operating record. In countries where the conclusion is less clear-cut the question arises as to which discount rate best represents the future. A rate somewhere between 5 and 10 per cent is regarded as a reasonable choice by most OECD utilities[71].

The figures in the Table are of course for new coal-plant,

Table 6.1. Ratios of Nuclear- and Coal-Power Costs

	Reference[1] Case	A[2]	B[3]	C[4]
Belgium	0.56	0.70	0.65	0.80
Canada				
Ontario	0.75	0.94		
New Brunswick	0.94	1.11	0.85	1.02
N. Brunswick nuclear, Alberta coal	1.22	1.31		
Finland	0.83	1.02	0.74	0.93
France	0.69	0.82	0.76	0.88
Germany, FR:				
indigenous coal	0.70	0.88		
imported coal	0.91	1.14	1.01	1.20
Japan	0.78	0.90	0.84	0.96
Spain	1.03	1.30	1.18	1.45
UK	0.94	1.18	0.92	1.16
USA:				
Mid-West	1.10	1.19		
West	1.23			
East	0.93			

1. 5 per cent discount rate; long-term coal prices as judged by electrical utilities in respondent countries. Commissioning date 1995. Station life thirty years. Load factor 75.3 per cent. Costs, at bus-bar, cover all items falling on utility, including fuel delivery to station, dismantling and waste costs, and desulphurization.
2. As reference case, but 10 per cent discount rate.
3. As reference case, but based on the IEA's Coal Industry Advisory Board's price forecasts.
4. As Variant A, but CIAB coal prices.

Note: A figure less than 1.00 indicates that nuclear electricity is cheaper.

Source: Based on reference 71.

compared with new nuclear-plant. It is far harder for new coal-plant to compete against *existing* nuclear-plant (unless the latter is in need of expensive maintenance) because a large part of the expenditure is already 'sunk', and the nuclear forward costs—for operation and fuel—are relatively low. Countries which already have substantial nuclear programmes are therefore unlikely to switch prematurely to coal, provided they base their decision on considerations that are economic rather than political (Sweden's example shows this may not always be the case!).

The long-term price of coal

The average price of coal assumed for the year 2000, as assessed by the coal industry participants in the OECD study (variants B and C of the Table), was $50 a tonne at western European ports, and $47 per tonne in the western Pacific (January 1987 US dollars; coal quality twenty-six giga-joules per tonne). These average figures were based on opinions which covered a fairly wide range: $42 to $70 in the case of western Europe. At the top end of this range nuclear power would have little difficulty in competing in most countries. At $42 it would face a much harder task, except where nuclear performance is exceptionally good. However, because of the still evolving pattern of the nuclear industry, nuclear costs also at present vary widely between countries, and are likely to continue to do so for the next fifteen to twenty years. Consequently there is no single and precise 'break-even' coal price that provides a simple indicator of nuclear power's ability to compete in each and every country.

Cost comparisons are made more interesting by the fact that coal is in a state of transition. As we shall see more fully in Chapter 12, it has only recently come to be traded world-wide on a substantial scale—about 130 million tonnes annually in the late 1980s, or about the output of the United Kingdom. The CIAB foresees the international trade roughly doubling by the year 2000. This view is based on cheap sea-borne coal from sources as diverse as Australia, China, Colombia, Poland, USA, and Venezuela. This new source of competition is leading in turn to a response by the coal industry in older producing areas, and to the closure of high-cost mines.

Coal is a complex market, which does not necessarily respond to market pressures in easily predictable ways, because some important producers—China in particular—seek foreign exchange almost irrespective of price. The still limited traded volume makes the market volatile and vulnerable to interruptions. In 1981 the price for steam coal was briefly over $80 a tonne for delivery to Rotterdam (about $3 per GJ), following unrest in Poland, strikes in Australia, and infrastructure problems in American ports; but it then fell rapidly, helped by heavy over-investment in coal supplies and cheap sea transport using surplus bulk-carriers. Coal was landed in Europe in the summer of 1987 at a spot price of $30 per tonne ($1.2 per GJ), a figure well below the cost of indigenous European coal, and one which, if sustained, would make nuclear energy uncompetitive in many countries. However, this very low coal spot price is unlikely to be typical of the future market; indeed the internationally traded price has since shown some recovery to around $40–45 per tonne ($1.5–$1.7 per GJ).

For electrical utilities considering their investment programme a major question is whether competition and greater internationally traded volume will confer on coal a greater degree of price stability than it has enjoyed in recent years, and if so at what level. The international coal industry is confident[81] that at costs equivalent to a delivered price of just over $50 per tonne (1987 dollars—around $2 per GJ) a large number of mines around the world could be brought into operation, which should stabilize the long-term price at a level still sufficiently low to keep coal in contention for electricity generation. Furthermore, the coal industry points to the very large reserves remaining—something like 200 years of supply at present production levels—and argues that a long-term price of $50 at Rotterdam should be sustainable. On this basis, and its own assertion that a 10 per cent discount rate represents the realities of the modern world, the coal industry argues strongly for the abandonment of nuclear power.

It is ironic, but the inevitable result of supply economics, that nuclear power has itself contributed to the softer coal prices that now seem to threaten its position. It is credited by the Arabs[4] with having done just that to oil in the 1980s, through its displacement of the oil which had been widely used for electricity generation in OECD at the end of the 1960s. World-wide nuclear electricity production is the energy equivalent of 700 million tonnes of coal per annum, which was just about the production of the USA in the mid-1980s. It is easy to see why the coal lobby must try to curb further nuclear development.

Any view of the future can hardly overlook the volatility of commodity prices generally, to which as we have seen coal has been no exception. Moreover, unlike uranium, coal cannot be easily stored in the quantities needed to stabilize the market. Users of imported coal must therefore remain cautious, particularly as the normally designated currency—the US dollar—has also become subject to violent swings on the world's exchanges. Indigenous coal is bound to retain some attractions for reasons of comparative price stability.

Moreover utilities, when evaluating energy alternatives, need to make very firm assumptions about the next twenty years, reasonably firm assumptions about the following twenty years, and in some respects look still further ahead. It is like trying to envisage the 1990s from the time of the Korean war. No one can be sure that world-traded coal will still be cheap; or that shipping costs will still be low (the present fleet of surplus bulk-carriers which helps to keep down costs will have long gone to the scrap-yards). All we know with certainty is what has happened already. As the French poet and essayist Paul Valéry remarked: 'the human race goes into the future backwards'. Experience teaches caution, and not least the importance of a diversified portfolio.

Timing and scale of nuclear investment

Besides the problem of choosing between coal and nuclear, there are also the matters of timing and scale. In France at the time of the 1973 oil shock total electricity generation from all sources was about 160 terawatt-hours per year (one TWh is 10^9 kilowatt-hours). This was already four times the 1950 total from all forms of generation. But by 1989 the total was nearly 360 TWh, with nuclear alone accounting for 285 TWh per year. This is a huge rate of increase. Retrospective assessments of the decision to opt for nuclear have shown that choosing coal when oil became expensive would have led to lower French electricity costs only up to 1981. Thereafter coal would have proved the more expensive option, and the tariffs for 1990 would have been 15 to 20 per cent greater[1]. Such advantages can only be won by a country which encourages long-term planning. They have been unavailable in the circumstances of the USA, with its fragmented utility industry and a regulatory framework that has been exceptionally cumbersome. It is also far from clear that the emphasis on short-term market forces, which is such a feature of the chosen form for British electricity privatization, will prove an effective long-term substitute for a strategic plan.

With station lead times of five or six years, and some uncertainty about the exact utilization achievable, it was always obvious that

France would find difficulties in establishing an exact match between capacity and demand. But she was in the fortunate position of having a solution ready to hand: electricity export. Being part of the European landmass, and connected into the grids of the neighbouring countries, France is able to export electricity in large amounts at the advantageous prices which her modernization programme has made possible—42 TWh in 1989. In the northerly direction the English Channel imposes some technical difficulties; but these have been overcome, with a 2 GWe link into the British grid. Britain, whose national press regularly proclaims that nuclear power is uneconomic, is Électricité de France's largest export customer, taking 13 TWh a year.

The debt incurred during France's change-over to nuclear—232 billion francs at the end of 1989—is criticized by nuclear opponents for having 'crowded out' more profitable investment. The figure is indeed huge, but becomes less daunting when viewed in perspective. EdF's debt/turnover ratio in 1989 was 1.6, closely in line with 1985 forecasts[1]. At the time of the rapid post-war hydropower expansion, the ratio was as high as 3.0; and it stayed around 2.7 until the mid-1960s. Even allowing for the higher interest rates of the late 1980s, a ratio of 1.6 does not present EdF with an unmanageable financial problem. However, to dispel any suspicion of 'dumping' exported electricity at unrealistically low rates, without making proper allowance for debt repayment, EdF undertook at the beginning of 1989 to take measures to reduce its indebtedness more quickly. Barring the unforeseen, EdF's investment has probably provided France with electricity at stable real prices for the next thirty years. In that time her citizens will spend several times as much on their private motor cars.

The Third World

It has been a central assumption of nuclear development that nuclear power is best able to compete with coal if all the possible advantages of scale are exploited. At lower generating-plant sizes both coal and nuclear costs per electrical unit rise, but the change is less pronounced with coal. This has implications for the use of nuclear power in the Third World: the lower the plant size the more we may expect the coal option to be favoured. The successful development of smaller 'inherently safe' reactors, needing less expenditure on elaborate safety precautions (page 242), could challenge this general assumption. However, the outputs currently envisaged are still fairly large by Third World standards, in the range 320 to 600 MWe.

As a rough rule of thumb the largest unit in a generating network should not contribute more than 10 per cent of the total power, since beyond this it becomes difficult to guarantee the maintenance of electricity supplies in the event of a unit failure. Thus even a scaled-down PWR producing 600 MWe is unsuitable for grid sizes of less than about 6 GWe. On this basis there are no more than twenty to thirty countries in the Third World which could become potential users of nuclear energy by the beginning of the next century, in addition to the ten which already have nuclear power programmes or firm plans[82]. The twenty-four reactors built in these countries by 1989 were very unevenly distributed, eighteen being concentrated in only three countries: Taiwan, the Republic of Korea, and India. Another eighteen are expected to be in operation by the mid-1990s[72]. It will take the development of economic small reactors of around 300 MWe to stimulate nuclear electricity in the Third World—and possibly a more pro-nuclear attitude on the part of the World Bank.

Lower coal prices than in the past, and the shortage of capital which is endemic, will also limit nuclear growth in the Third World. However, indigenous coal can also be costly in some circumstances. A 1985 Indian study[83] reached the conclusion that in some parts of the country the overall cost of the coal option could actually be greater, given that some coal-fired stations would be 800 kilometres from the mine-head. This illustrates the importance of considering the totality of the implications when conducting an inter-fuel comparison as a basis for future energy investment.

The greenhouse effect

The same observation applies *a fortiori* to the greenhouse effect (Chapter 13). Assuming that expectations remain unchanged—including a rise in sea-level and changes in climatic zones—it seems probable that a concerted move will be made at some time by the industrialized countries to restrain the use of coal, oil, and natural gas, so far as this is possible in the real world. The prices of these fuels would then be depressed. We could conceivably find ourselves in a situation where a low coal price no longer meant that nuclear power—or for that matter some of the newer renewable energies, even if more expensive—should necessarily take second place. Any predictions can only be speculative; but the possibility is clear— that for reasons of environmental policy costs which might fall on third parties could come to influence power-investment decisions, even though no one knows even roughly what those costs might be. It is sufficient to know from simple inspection that they could be very large indeed. There will be interesting new paths for energy economists to tread in the twenty-first century.

Conclusions

With energy commodity markets so volatile there can never be a final conclusion on nuclear economics; but for the next couple of decades the general picture seems likely to be something like this:

(i) A variety of new ways of using oil and natural gas for electricity generation will be increasingly exploited during the 1990s; but coal is expected to remain nuclear power's dominant competitor, and a useful benchmark for investment analysis.

(ii) Well-engineered, well-managed nuclear power is broadly competitive with coal for base-load electricity generation, except in the lowest-cost coal areas, or unless unusually high rates of return are required. Nuclear power's ability to compete with coal for non-base-load generation is limited, and depends critically on keeping down total costs through efficient design, construction, and operation. There is still considerable scope for nuclear cost reduction in some countries, notably in the USA. Given the high front-loading of nuclear costs there is no economic case for abandoning existing nuclear power-stations, provided they are working well, and replacing them by coal before the end of their economic life.

(iii) Coal's ability to compete for base-load generation with nuclear power depends on the promise of offering secure supplies until about 2020 at reliable prices (1987 money values) of around $50 per tonne, delivered. At this price there is probably not a great deal to choose between the costs of nuclear and coal generation. The coal industry believes it can maintain or better this price for world-traded coal delivered to Rotterdam, though that is not the same as offering bankable assurances. The coal market saw great volatility during the 1980s. Major swings in dollar exchange rates in recent years—dollars being a normal unit of account for coal—add further uncertainty. There is no corresponding problem for nuclear power, which promises constant real electricity prices into the long-term future, provided reactors of proven and standardized design are used.

(iv) With coal, as with oil, there is a stockpiling problem. Dependence on imported coal exposes a country to swings in the coal market against which it would be almost impossible to provide adequate protection via buffer stocks. Stocks may also be insufficient to protect a national utility against a prolonged coal strike, such as the UK weathered with some difficulty in 1984–5. Again there is no corresponding problem with nuclear power: uranium can be bought on long-term contracts, and it is both easy and cheap to hold several years stocks of the raw material.

(v) Coal power-stations can be designed to be easily convertible to oil or gas should cheap supplies become available, even for intermittent periods; this is a flexible feature which nuclear cannot match.

(vi) Nuclear electricity generation displaces 600–700 million tonnes of coal per year—about one-fifth of world production—and thereby contributes to lowering the world-traded coal price.

(vii) Nuclear power in the large sizes normal in industrialized countries is unsuitable for most Third World electricity grids.

(viii) Within two decades anxieties over the climatic effects of large-scale coal burning could begin to alter the balance in favour of nuclear power, possibly via fossil-fuel taxation.

Given the impossibility—for all the reasons mentioned in this chapter—of knowing what is 'right' or 'best' in the long term, we are forced to the same conclusion as that reached by the Inspector, Sir Frank Layfield, at the British Sizewell B Inquiry. After more than four years of work, involving sitting on 340 days, the oral examination of 195 witnesses, and sixteen million words of discussion backed up by 4,330 supporting documents, he concluded that the sensible course was to go for a balanced portfolio of energy resources. It will be necessary to wait for another thirty to forty years to know whether a more selective course would have been better. Meanwhile, given that at present in most industrialized countries there is no dramatic economic advantage either way, and that the preference depends very much on the chosen assumptions and one's view of the future—including the environmental future and the 'greenhouse effect'—a mixed portfolio seems as likely to represent a 'least-regret' course here as it does in most other areas of investment.

7 The Potential Weapons Link

For four decades the history of nuclear power has been punctuated with frequently expressed concerns about the inadvisability of proceeding with the technology. It was not just doubts about safety that gave rise to such thoughts, but also a fear that progress with nuclear power could bring nuclear war closer. The word 'nuclear' created a direct link, an assumed causal connection, in the minds of the public between the innocent production of electricity and military horrors. It is beside the point that since 1945 nuclear weapons have been used exclusively for deterrence rather than fighting; and that having kept the peace in Europe for nearly half a century they must have contributed to the sudden easing of tensions between the USSR and the West which made 1989 as significant a year as 1789. The objectors regard them as inescapably evil; and since they cannot be manufactured without drawing on some of the same materials and techniques that are needed for civil nuclear power, that too must by association be wrong.

How well-based is the belief that the pursuit of civil nuclear power necessarily carries with it dangers of further 'horizontal' nuclear proliferation? (The adjective is used to describe the extension of proliferation to new countries, in contrast to 'vertical' proliferation, in which countries already possessing nuclear weapons add to or modernize their own armouries.) And to the extent that the proposition may be true, what is already being done about it, and what more would be possible?

Historically the chain of causation has tended to run the other way—from military to civil. In America the first reactors were used to produce the plutonium which was eventually to destroy Nagasaki; and ten years later the pressurized water reactor grew from Admiral Rickover's work on submarine propulsion. The British family of gas-cooled reactors began with the military plutonium production reactor at Calder Hall. China provided herself with a weapon in 1964 two decades before beginning to take a serious interest in power production[84]. India's 'peaceful nuclear explosion' in 1974 took place when her civil power capabilities were minuscule. Israel possesses no power reactor, although nobody doubts that she has a sizeable weapons programme. In France, as we saw in Chapter 3, civil and military developments progressed more in step with each other; but the military option was kept open from the start.

Making civil nuclear electricity safely, in large unit sizes and economically, is at least as difficult as running a weapons programme. A civil power programme is therefore not an obvious starting-point, and it has not in fact been so used for the fortunately few examples of 'horizontal proliferation' that have so far occurred. India and Israel used reactors built for 'research' rather than power production. If Pakistan under the late General Zia-ul-Haq harboured proliferation aspirations, as seems almost certain, the key element was not a reactor but a purpose-built uranium enrichment plant.

Minimum facilities needed for a weapons programme

In the context of nuclear proliferation it seems unlikely that a small or medium-size country would aim to provide itself with the range of warheads and delivery systems needed by a fully-fledged nuclear weapons power. The purpose would more likely be political—for deterrence, to allow some muscle-flexing, or to pose a threat to a non-nuclear-weapons state in the context of a regional dispute. In that case a handful of relatively crude weapons might be thought sufficient. However, Israel is believed to have gone considerably further with her clandestine weapons programme, and is estimated to have amassed at least fifty nuclear weapons[85].

Warheads may use nearly pure uranium–235, enriched to 80 per cent or more—as at Hiroshima—or plutonium–239 as at Nagasaki. The quantities needed per warhead are likely to be around 15–25 kilograms of U–235 or 5–10 kilograms of Pu–239. As explained in the Technical Appendix, plutonium production requires a reactor and a chemical separation plant. In a reactor around 1 gram of plutonium is created for each (thermal) megawatt-day of heat that is generated. One warhead therefore needs 5,000 to 10,000 megawatt-days; and if this is to be achieved in one year with a reactor operating for 70 per cent of the time the reactor needs to generate 20–40 megawatts of heat. This happens to be a common size for materials testing research reactors, used to provide a strong flux of neutrons for nuclear physics measurements and investigations of the effect of intense radiation on the structure of materials. There are many such reactors all round the world. A larger reactor would speed up production, and provide the additional material needed for weapons development.

The plutonium route would not necessarily need an enrichment step prior to irradiation in the reactor, provided the 'moderator' (see Appendix) was heavy water or graphite, because in that case 'natural' (i.e. unenriched) uranium could be used as the fuel. The first British plutonium production reactors—they were then known as 'piles'—at Windscale used natural uranium and graphite. Such reactors are large and probably difficult to conceal, in contrast to heavy-water moderated reactors, which are more compact. Moderators of the purity needed in a reactor are not generally available, and would have to be manufactured locally, unless they could be obtained by deception. Norway, one of the few Western sources of heavy water, had her suspicions aroused that some of her production, sold to Israel in 1959, had been subverted without her approval to weapons uses. Israel agreed in 1990 to return to Norway the ten tonnes that remained—half the original quantity. After reports of illegal re-routeing of Norwegian heavy water to India, a Royal Decree adopted on 10 March 1989 generally prohibited its export, except for purposes of research or international co-operation. There are indications that India has clandestinely acquired supplies of heavy water from Chinese and Soviet sources via a German intermediary[85].

Other facilities needed would be a fairly simple fuel-element production plant, a small chemical separation plant to extract the plutonium (located in Israel's case underground in the Negev desert), a heavy-metal fabrication plant (no longer much used in civil nuclear engineering, which has largely switched to using the fuel in oxide form), and a warhead production facility. The post-reactor stages pose considerable safety problems on account of radiation, and require good containment and remote handling facilities. Trained chemical and metallurgical technicians would be needed, though in the early stages the effort could be provided by using a high proportion of graduate staff.

The uranium–235 route avoids the need for fuel fabrication, reactor construction, and post-irradiation chemical separation, but instead requires an enrichment plant. The diffusion plants operated in the USA, France, and for a time the UK, need a good deal of know-how; they are intrinsically large and consume a great deal of electricity; and for efficient production the stage sizes need to be altered along the 'cascade', becoming smaller as the U–235 concentration increases. The centrifuge system developed by the URENCO British-German-Netherlands consortium is smaller, uses less electrical energy, and the units are more capable of working over the entire enrichment range right up to weapons grade. However, a sizeable high-quality manufacturing operation would be needed to produce the many hundreds of centrifuges required for even a small weapons facility. This is the route Pakistan used under General Zia, basing the design on the knowledge of an ex-employee of URENCO to build a plant at Kahuta, near Rawalpindi. General Zia's statement on 21 March 1987 that Pakistan had discarded the nuclear weapons option did not entirely remove the resulting political anxieties. There were too many other signs of co-ordinated progress towards a weapon—such as the purchase of a tritium gas storage and purification plant from Germany in that same year, and the attempt in 1984 to purchase fifty krytrons (high-speed electronic switches used in nuclear weapons). The statement by his successor, Benazir Bhutto, to President Bush on 6 June 1989, that her country was not intending to make nuclear weapons, would have carried more weight if her hold on power had been more robust. Argentina and Brazil are known to be interested in enrichment technology. In its Valindaba plant South Africa uses an aerodynamic variant of the centrifuge process, in which hexafluoride gas rather than the container is made to spin in a number of ingeniously designed large structures. It works, but requires more energy than a normal centrifuge. For a small programme of either weapons or fuel element production this would not be a major consideration; however, South Africa denies any weapon intent. The facility was used to supply fuel for the Safari–1 reactor, after the US stopped supplies in 1977.

After the enrichment stage the U–235 route would require a metal fabrication and machining facility, but because of the much lower radioactivity of U–235 this would pose fewer safety and design problems than plutonium.

Both routes would require a supply of uranium, probably of the order of 50 tonnes per year for the plutonium route; somewhat less, depending on the production rate required, for U–235. Fifty tonnes represent only one-thousandth of current world production, and obtaining such a quantity is unlikely to present much difficulty. Moreover uranium is fairly abundant. Most countries should be able to find deposits within their own boundaries sufficient for a small military operation, even though the ore-grades might be too low to support normal commercial production. The job could probably be done with less than one hundred graduate engineers, plus technicians. The lead time to the production of the first weapon could be as short as from five to seven years, though without a test programme its efficiency would be suspect. There are reports that Israel was able to proceed with some confidence as a result of French help[85].

Regular visits to nuclear-power installations by inspectors from the International Atomic Energy Agency would make it more difficult for such a programme to avoid detection. Obviously detection is simplest when all nuclear facilities in a state are inspected under a 'full-scope' (i.e. comprehensive) safeguards agreement, of the type accepted by parties to the Non-Proliferation Treaty (see below). If an inspector were denied access to some or all of a country's installations a would-be proliferator would theoretically find it easier to keep his intentions secret, and to divert some material from facilities ostensibly set up for civil purposes. However, a safeguards agreement is not so easily shaken off. The IAEA does not have to *prove* diversion. If access is denied the IAEA Board could, under such an agreement, require a state to remove the bar. If it remained in force, the IAEA could reach a finding that it was unable to prove an *absence* of diversion. In addition, national intelligence-collecting methods are nowadays so well developed that maintaining complete secrecy is never easy; and in fact a number of states have been identified through national intelligence means as harbouring proliferation intentions. Unfortunately, in a world no longer policed by the Great Powers, unearthing a proliferator's secret is only one first small step towards preventing him from continuing.

What is virtually impossible is for a small sub-national group to manufacture nuclear weapons, at least without the active co-operation of a host government—and it is hard to see where such co-operation would be available, for the obvious reason that if successful it would then be out of control. There is no possibility whatsoever of the job being done by one man, or even one company—such stories are strictly for James Bond films.

Possible points of linkage between civil and military programmes

Nuclear critics can reasonably point to four ways in which a civil programme might offer some assistance towards horizontal proliferation. First, almost all civil programmes need enriched uranium, and enrichment is also one of the routes towards weapons. Secondly, all civil reactors produce plutonium during operation, and if it is separated in a reprocessing plant it may be usable in weapons, particularly if it has not been kept too long in the reactor (see below). Thirdly, the education and training of the necessary technical and scientific manpower needed for a national civil nuclear programme could hardly fail to be of assistance to the proliferation ambitions of a government bent on acquiring a few warheads. Fourthly, some of the support facilities used for a civil programme might be available for a military programme at marginal extra cost; or electricity sales might provide a subsidy; or civil needs might legitimize the acquisition of facilities whose real purpose was for the weapons programme.

The *enrichment* point is a real one. Enrichment plants are undoubtedly sensitive installations, even though a civil plant would not normally produce the highly enriched uranium needed for a weapons programme. A point which will always be of concern once an additional country has provided itself with an enrichment plant, allegedly for civil purposes, is that the engineering effort required to take the enrichment up from the normal reactor level of about 3 per cent to the weapons-grade of around 90 per cent is actually less than that needed to go from natural uranium to 3 per cent uranium–235 for reactor use. The reason is that as the uranium proceeds through the enrichment cascade the unwanted uranium–238 is progressively rejected into the 'tails', thus reducing the amount of material which needs to be moved around in the later high enrichment stages. A level of 20 per cent enrichment marks the rough boundary between enrichment activities which pose no immediate proliferation threat, and those about which assurances are certainly needed.

At the moment only a few countries are in a position to make weapons-grade enriched uranium even if they wished to do so. The fear is really one for the future: that as nuclear power expands more and more countries will wish to provide themselves with a complete spectrum of fuel-cycle support facilities. This would hardly be in the interests of international stability. But a policy of active discouragement on the part of the nuclear-weapons states has led to charges of 'technological colonialism'. This is delicate political ground, where compromises are needed, accompanied by assurances of continuing availability of enrichment services at reasonable cost. Brazil has made progress with both centrifuge and jet-nozzle enrichment, the former through the efforts of her naval technicians, the latter with help from West Germany (it is therefore safeguarded). The government went some way towards setting fears at rest with an announcement on 5 October 1988 of a new constitution, which prohibits building and stocking nuclear weapons on Brazilian territory—though a future government would unfortunately need only a simple majority to remove this restriction.

There are several points concerning *plutonium* which bear on the problem of horizontal proliferation. First, Argentina, India, Israel, Pakistan, and possibly North Korea have small reprocessing plants which owe, or might possibly owe, their origins to weapons aspirations. Argentina's Ezeiza plant, with completion planned for 1990, is subject to IAEA inspection for as long as it processes fuel from reactors that are themselves safeguarded. The Soviet Union has pursued a simple and effective way of dealing with the plutonium route to proliferation: all fuel supplied to its (former) client states was reimported after irradiation in a power or research reactor—it was the USSR itself which did any subsequent reprocessing. This condition was imposed in 1988 even on India, which had previously shown a reluctance to accept safeguards on foreign-supplied equipment, unless the financial terms were especially attractive.

As regards the possible use in weapons of plutonium produced in civil power reactors: it is a reassuring fact that most commercial reactor cores are located in massive pressure-vessels, which stay sealed for periods of twelve to eighteen months. They are opened only during major shut-down periods, and in practice the fuel cannot be taken out at shorter intervals. Clandestine diversion is virtually impossible if the maintenance and refuelling operations are conducted under IAEA inspection, which is the normal 'safeguards' practice. When the fuel is finally taken out it contains 20 per cent or more of the plutonium–240 isotope of plutonium. As explained in the Technical Appendix, this isotope is spontaneously fissile: in 10 kilograms of plutonium containing 20 per cent Pu–240 there would be about one million fissions per second. Even with a final assembly time as short as one-millionth of a second this would be unwelcome in bomb material, because of the possibility it introduces of premature injection of neutrons at the moment the bomb is being assembled into a critical mass, and hence uncertainty about the size of the explosion, or 'yield'.

This was the basis for the early hopes that plutonium from commercial power reactors would be unusable in weapons: 'weapons-grade' plutonium is made using much shorter irradiations, to keep the Pu–240 content low. However, it is known from an informal statement in 1978 by a US official that at least one demonstration explosion took place in 1962, using so-called 'denatured' material with more than 8 per cent Pu–240 (a figure of 12 per cent has been mentioned unofficially). No information is available on the size of the explosion. In 1976 the US government issued a statement[86] which read:

. . . although reactor-grade plutonium is more difficult to work with than plutonium produced specifically for nuclear weapons, it can be made into an effective nuclear explosive . . . As to pre-initiation, it is more likely to occur in a device using plutonium with a large content of undesirable isotopes that spontaneously fission, but even low technology devices employing reactor-grade plutonium will produce high-order nuclear explosions.

A few reactors, like the Canadian CANDUs and some British gas-cooled reactors, have facilities for on-load refuelling. This in principle opens up the possibility of irradiating fuel intended for clandestine weapons production for the short times needed if the plutonium–240 content is to be kept low enough to allow weapons of predictable performance to be built. Such reactors in the hands of non-weapons states therefore need to be regularly inspected if international confidence is to be maintained.

Research and materials-testing reactors also pose dangers of proliferation. Because they are of relatively low power and incapable of making plutonium on a large scale they might be thought innocuous. But the flexibility with which they are constructed—to allow experiments to take place easily, and to facilitate the insertion and withdrawal of materials from the reactor core—implies a need for international inspection, at least for reactors with powers in the tens of megawatts range.

In order to benefit from the plutonium which is made in any case in civil reactors, '*mixed oxide fuel*' (MOX)—mixed plutonium and uranium oxides—will become more common as a civil fuel by the year 2000. Unlike uranium–235 and uranium–238, which are chemically inseparable, the plutonium in 'MOX' can be separated by chemical means from the uranium. MOX fuel should therefore be a target for non-proliferation inspections, to ensure that the full complement of fuel can always be accounted for.

In spent fuel elements that have recently been taken out of a reactor the intense radioactivity and the associated heat generation provide a physical barrier to proliferation. But as the fuel rods 'cool'—in both the literal and the metaphorical radiological senses—the plutonium slowly becomes more accessible. Waste fuel elements in fact constitute a potential 'plutonium mine', needing permanent safeguarding. This means that the facilities used for their ultimate disposal must be designed and sited with this in mind. It also has a bearing on where such waste should be stored. In January 1984 China expressed some interest in providing storage facilities for other countries' spent fuel, in return for a fee. The offer reportedly did not extend to vitrified waste—a distinction which raises important political questions[87]. The subsequent reminder in Tiananmen Square on 3–4 June 1989 of the country's political unpredictability must have made storage in China unthinkable for most countries, if indeed it was ever practical politics.

A further aspect of the plutonium proliferation issue involves the *fast reactor*. It is the best hope of producing nuclear energy into the very distant future; but as explained in the Technical Appendix, obtaining the fifty-fold increase in energy from a given weight of uranium, compared with what an ordinary reactor can hope to achieve, necessarily involves large-scale reprocessing, and the production of plutonium in concentrated form. It is not difficult to anticipate the extreme caution that will exist in the minds of nuclear-hardware exporters over supplying fast reactors to many countries throughout the world. Fortunately we are speaking of a time still several decades away. What is decided then will owe a great deal to the experience—favourable or unfavourable—ac-cumulated over the intervening years, and to pragmatic judgements by the supplying governments.

Then there is the question of MUF—*material unaccounted for*. No matter how closely a plutonium plant is subjected to international inspection there is a limit to the accuracy with which the materials balance can be drawn up, because there is always some unavoidable uncertainty in the quantity of plutonium and other isotopes produced in the reactor in the first place. It is difficult to measure accurately the intensity of the neutron flux in a reactor, or the nuclear properties of the various materials—both factors we should need to know. The accuracies regarded as normal in everyday life when dealing with weights or lengths are quite unattainable in such nuclear measurements: 1 per cent accuracy is possible; 0.1 per cent would be straining our technical means. The consequence is that there is always a corresponding small uncertainty in the calculated plutonium content of the fuel elements dissolved at the head end of a chemical separation plant. This is of some concern to the management, because accumulations of undetected plutonium must be avoided in case a critical assembly is accidentally formed (the danger is not one of a bomb-like explosion, but of an emission of radiation which would constitute a hazard to the operators). MUF reports are published from time to time by the British Department of Energy, for the fuel cycle plants at Sellafield and Dounreay. In theory the discovery of a positive amount of MUF could mean that some material had been lost or even clandestinely diverted; but it would not necessarily mean either of these things, for the above reason. Each case would be a matter on which an inspecting authority would have to make up its own mind. With good plant-containment and proper boundary control MUF is not in practice a serious worry for an inspecting team seeking to satisfy itself that no deliberate diversion has occurred.

From time to time these considerations are affected by new developments in technology, notably isotope separation using lasers. If one could directly pick out the wanted U–235 isotope from the unwanted U–238, atom by atom—instead of having to rely on the cumbersome process of passing uranium hexafluoride through a diffusion plant cascade, and using the tiny difference in weight between U–235 and U–238 to separate the two isotopes progressively along the cascade—one would have a far more elegant technical solution. Similarly, if Pu–240 atoms could be rejected while leaving the Pu–239, the way would be open to making weapons-grade material from plutonium which had been irradiated in a commercial reactor. This is what AVLIS—atomic vapour laser isotope separation—should in principle be capable of doing. For obvious reasons the details are closely guarded, and it is not known how accessible the technology will become for an intended proliferator[22, 23].

On the general point that *a weapons programme may be able to rely on the facilities installed for a civil electricity programme* there are arguments both ways. It would certainly not be a simple and straightforward route to the acquisition of weapons, if only because civil facilities are by no means all that are needed for a weapons programme. Further, information on the operations of civil nuclear-power plants circulates freely both via personal professional contacts and through the technical press; this is even becoming true within the USSR, following the traumatic experience of Chernobyl. Unusual secrecy surrounding a particular plant would therefore arouse suspicion. This is still more so now that the World Association of Nuclear Operators (a valuable reaction to Chernobyl—see Chapter 9) is in existence. Moreover, all supplier governments, of both nuclear materials and equipment, make their supplies conditional upon acceptance of safeguards inspections on behalf of the purchaser. A proliferator would therefore be faced with a choice between attempting to defeat these safeguards, or accepting a very restricted circle of black-market suppliers. Apart from this, experience shows that it would be difficult to get far without the international intelligence community being aware in broad terms of what is happening—though that, unfortunately, is no guarantee in the real world that effective political action would follow.

The International Atomic Energy Agency and 'safeguards'

Over the past thirty years the institutional arrangements for protecting the world against the unwelcome surprise of further proliferation have been progressively strengthened. Amongst the most important is international inspection of civil power installations. The significance to world peace of the team of inspectors based on the International Atomic Energy Agency is out of all proportion to the resources they need[88]. The nearly 200-strong corps of inspectors cost about $50 million in 1989—a quarter of the Agency's budget, and about the same as a police force in a major city. The diplomatic term of art for the regular inspections they carry out, the records they keep, and the surveillance equipment they install, is 'safeguards'.

The IAEA owes its existence to a proposal to the United Nations by President Eisenhower on 8 December 1953—a modern case of 'swords into ploughshares'. The Agency started work in Vienna in 1957 and developed a three-pronged programme. One major task was the dissemination of technical reactor information. A second was a broad programme of applying nuclear methods in non-power applications, notably agriculture: radioactive tracers have many research uses, while high-intensity radiation can be used to preserve food. Thirdly, the Agency has a corps of inspectors, who by invitation of host governments carry out inspections of nuclear installations. The corps possesses no police powers, and is in no position to veto any activities of which it may disapprove. Its function is one of tracking nuclear-fuel movements, reporting the findings, and so if all goes well building international confidence that civil nuclear installations are being conducted on a bona fide basis. When it began, in a world where nuclear power was still a rarity, there was some scepticism about the value of such a system, devoid as it was of 'teeth'. It was only later that its real importance came to be appreciated. Nor did the absence of teeth greatly matter: they could be supplied by the political reactions which would follow any reported development which might be regarded as dangerous to world peace.

The acceptance of regular 'safeguards' inspections of all nuclear installations is an obligation assumed by signatories of the 1968 Non-Proliferation Treaty (see below), other than the pre-existing nuclear weapons states. Over the past thirty years periodical safeguarding inspections by the IAEA have been increasingly supplemented by automatic surveillance techniques to increase the effectiveness of the inspectors, and to keep operating costs down. Cameras, video-recorders, and sensors are placed so as to increase the chances of detecting any unreported operations or tampering with the plant being inspected. The normal design requirement of plant containment, with restrictions on physical access, is a further assistance to the inspectors. Material accounting is central to the success of the operation: inward and outward flows of material must be tracked, samples taken and analysed where necessary, and inventories checked, in all the significant areas, including inward and outward storage areas. Maintaining familiarity with plant design, reading operating reports, and regular visual inspections remain as important as ever. One hundred per cent assurance will never be obtainable; but the extent and diversity of the methods used, and the simple fact that nuclear facilities are open to inspection, have served to moderate political anxieties about the implications of nuclear energy development.

The IAEA inspectorate becomes interested when uranium enrichment passes the 20 per cent U–235 mark. Higher concentrations than this are not currently found except in a few research reactors of early design, almost all of which are under safeguards. To reduce even this possible loophole, most research reactors have now been modified to take fuel of enrichment below 20 per cent. Fuel fabrication, spent-fuel reprocessing plants, and other parts of the fuel cycle are also inspection targets.

International agreements to block proliferation

The dangers for the world posed by a proliferation of nuclear weaponry was appreciated well before the founding of the IAEA—indeed from the very beginnings of atomic technology[89,90]. It gave rise to the Baruch Plan of July 1946, in which the USA proposed the creation of an International Atomic Development Agency to manage, control, or own all atomic energy activities; atomic weapons were to be renounced. It was a politically non-negotiable measure: the Soviets, who were still three years away from their first bomb-test, were certainly not prepared to lock themselves into a position of potential military inferiority, and the plan was stillborn. Before putting a bridle on nuclear electricity it was first necessary in a different context to make some progress over arms control. It took another seventeen years before the Partial Test Ban Treaty of 1963 signalled the superpowers' readiness to take a step towards reducing world tensions. Five years later the mood of gradually advancing political willingness led to the Nuclear Non-Proliferation Treaty ('NPT') of 1968—a measure that was far less ambitious but far more realistic than the abortive Baruch Plan.

Meanwhile the world was not prepared to accept that the undoubted possibility of proliferation was a sufficient reason for forgoing the important advantages of civil nuclear power. Many nuclear objectors take a different view, and have a right to their opinions. Politics, however, is concerned with making value-judgements in the face of conflicting considerations, which in this case includes weighing the probability of proliferation against the certainty that nuclear power is a valuable energy source. Today's political consensus is that we should continue to aim at getting as far as possible the best of both worlds—nuclear power without substantial horizontal proliferation—through a judicious combination of sticks and carrots, particularly those which the superpowers are able to apply. If there were a spectacular failure of safeguards this view might change; but that has not yet happened.

The encouraging fact is that there are still only five fully capable nuclear-weapons states—the USA, the USSR, the UK, China, and France; with Israel, possibly India, and perhaps Pakistan being 'threshold states' (in the literature of the subject the latter are nevertheless normally included in the list of *non*-nuclear-weapons states). There are a few other 'question-mark' countries which have been suspected of harbouring proliferation intentions, including Argentina, Brazil (prior to the new 1988 constitution), and (for the future) Iraq and possibly North Korea; but they have yet to cross the Rubicon of a demonstration explosion.

The oft-quoted 'explosion', which the Vela satellite is alleged to have detected over the South Atlantic on 22 September 1979, was quickly laid at South Africa's door. The evidence was unreliable, as that satellite was subject to many false alarms. Wynand De Villiers, head of the South African Atomic Energy Commission at the time, laughingly commented that 'if you believe that it was a nuclear test you must also believe that we have the most advanced technology to construct an explosive device without any fall-out'. However, South Africa undoubtedly has the technical capability to make nuclear weapons; indeed, suggestions have been made that this may have happened already without any announcement being made[91].

What we do know is that the overwhelming majority of industrially advanced countries, and also most of the developing countries now entering their industrial phases, have forborne to use their knowledge to make weapons. This encouraging state of affairs has not come about by accident, but through long-drawn-out negotiation, which has created an international consensus in favour of non-proliferation. Almost all countries see this as necessary in the interests of world stability, which in many cases directly touches their own security. Clear signs of this concern can be found in the various international and regional treaties that form an important part of the non-proliferation regime.

The *Treaty on the Non-Proliferation of Nuclear Weapons (NPT)* was signed in 1968 and came into force two years later. It grew out of a general understanding that limits needed to be set, in the interests of world stability, on further horizontal proliferation. It has become in effect a bargain between the Nuclear Weapon States (NWS)—those which possessed nuclear weapons prior to 1 January 1967—and the rest of the world (for text see references 92 and 93). Article IX opens the Treaty to all states, and provides for the necessary machinery.

The NWS pledge themselves in Article I not to transfer any weapon to any recipient whatsoever, nor 'in any way to assist, encourage, or induce any Non-Nuclear-Weapons State (NNWS) to manufacture or otherwise acquire nuclear weapons or other nuclear explosive devices'. All NNWS pledge themselves in Article II not to manufacture or receive nuclear weapons or explosives; and in Article III to accept inspection of all their nuclear activities ('full-scope safeguards', modelled on IAEA information circular 153), 'with a view to preventing diversion . . . to nuclear weapons or other nuclear explosive devices'. In addition Article III requires each state party (both NWS and NNWS) not to provide fissionable material, or the means to make it, to any NNWS (whether or not a party to the Treaty) unless subject to safeguards. This has considerable political significance, as it is the basis for the measures, described below, which exert a degree of international control over nuclear exports.

Article IV (originally included as an incentive to join the Treaty) begins with a declaration that all parties have an 'inalienable right' to use nuclear energy for peaceful purposes; and requires all parties which are 'in a position to do so'—including the NWS—to co-operate in contributing to the further development of the applications of nuclear energy for peaceful purposes, 'especially in the territories of NNWS party to the Treaty'; and in assisting other countries with scientific information, equipment, and materials towards obtaining the benefits of nuclear power.

Article VI pledges the determination of all parties—NWS and NNWS alike—to 'pursue negotiations in good faith on effective measures relating to . . . nuclear disarmament'. As a bow in the direction of equality of treatment the UK and the USA from the NWS have placed all of their civil installations under safeguards; the USSR also permits inspection of some reactors. Article V, which has so far been of no practical importance, is concerned with sharing the possible benefits of peaceful nuclear explosions. Article VII asserts the rights of states to conclude regional non-proliferation treaties.

Under Article X any party can withdraw after giving three months notice if it considers that extraordinary events have jeopardized its supreme interests; none have so far done so. The Treaty is reviewed at five-yearly intervals (Article VIII); in 1995 a decision will be reached about its longer-term future (Article X).

The list of NPT members in mid-1989 totalled 141, plus Taiwan (for which there is a problem of recognition). The membership includes Libya, Iran, and Iraq—which some may find surprising but encouraging—and a number like the Holy See, the Grenadines, and Tuvalu which are reminders of the fascinating diversity of the modern United Nations family. This almost universal support is a political fact of the highest importance; though it must also be remembered that there are some important non-signatories, including Argentina, Brazil, Chile, China, Cuba, France, India, Israel, Pakistan, and South Africa. Pakistan professed interest when Benazir Bhutto came to power. South Africa, under economic pressure from American restrictions on importing its uranium, and to avoid suspension of its participation in the IAEA, announced on 21 September 1987 that it was studying the implications of joining; it had not done so two years later. France[94] is a non-signatory, but has pledged to act as though she were one, and some of her facilities are under safeguards. The People's Republic of China, after long hesitation, made a voluntary safeguards offer for the reactors now under construction, but opposes the NPT as discriminatory.

Although the Treaty has survived for almost two decades there have been distinct signs of strain at the time of the quinquennial review conferences, partly as a result of a feeling on the part of Third World countries that the major nuclear countries have dragged their feet over assistance with nuclear power programmes (Article IV)—though since the technical difficulties have become more apparent this point has been less contentious. A second cause for complaint is over the slow progress the NWS have made with disarmament, contrary to the spirit of Article VI. Concern on this last point is understandable: from the signing of the Partial Test

Ban Treaty[95] in 1963 to the end of 1988 there were 1,244 nuclear explosions, of which the USA made 579, the USSR 451, and the UK 18. Of the non-signatories France made 164, China 31, and India 1.

There was particular apprehension before the Review Conference in 1985, since the previous Review had been far from successful, and only one more (1990) remained before a decision was due in 1995 on the Treaty's future. The world-wide nuclear industry became concerned, because without the relative confidence symbolized by the NPT, trade in nuclear fuel would become more difficult and less predictable. A declaration of support for the Treaty[96] was issued by the Uranium Institute—the international nuclear fuel industrial association—inviting politicians to see the Review as more than a purely political debate, and to recognize that the NPT had become a matter of commercial importance to international trade:

... if the existing international system of safeguards were to be abandoned, the injury to nuclear trade and co-operation would be very great. At best, there would be an extensive period of uncertainty while individual nations attempted to replace the existing international surveillance regime with a plethora of bilateral safeguards ... At worst, international nuclear trade and co-operation, deprived of the natural confidence generated by non-proliferation safeguards, would be very seriously disturbed ... No industry is more dependent on a network of intergovernmental agreements, reflecting a broad consensus on principles. The NPT ... lies at the heart of both the consensus and the network.

In the event the 1985 Review passed off successfully, and the eighty-six participating delegations produced a useful and sometimes thoughtful report. The improvement in East–West relations which has followed Mr Gorbachev's arrival as Soviet leader should provide an important strengthening factor, in the sense of increasing the superpowers' commitment to Article VI, and easing the path of treaty extension when the 1995 NPT conference convenes.

A regional system of safeguards exists under the aegis of *Euratom*, to ensure that nuclear materials are not diverted from their declared uses. Euratom was created in 1951, and when its safeguarding inspections began in 1959 under the authority of Chapter VI of the founding Treaty—pre-dating the operation of the NPT—it was able to take over the bilateral safeguards duties of the

US within Europe. It has proved useful to be able to call on Euratom for an independent view on the rare occasions when some event causes concern—such as the Transnuklear scandal, to which we return later.

On 14 February 1967, a year before the negotiation of the NPT, a regional treaty, the *Treaty for the Prohibition of Nuclear Weapons in Latin America* (the Treaty of Tlatelolco) was opened for signature and ratification. The non-proliferation pledges of the Treaty were to be verified through IAEA safeguards, and special investigations could be called for if necessary. Twenty-two years later (1989) it was still not fully in force, since this would require unanimity of ratification throughout Latin America. Most states have waived the unanimity requirement through a declaration provided for in Article 28.2, but for various reasons Argentina, Brazil, Chile, and Cuba still have difficulties. France, the Netherlands, UK, and USA have signed (but in France's case not ratified) an Additional Protocol I in which, as states having some responsibility for territories in the region, they pledge themselves to assume the same responsibilities as the Latin American signatories towards the denuclearization of the region. The Chinese People's Republic, France, UK, USA, and USSR have signed Additional Protocol II, guaranteeing that they will not threaten the use of nuclear weapons against any of the parties to the Treaty. This Protocol is of some interest in the context of tensions between the UK and Argentina over the Falklands. These islands are also one of the reasons given by Argentina for not ratifying the Treaty.

More recently a further regional treaty, the *Treaty of Raratonga*, was signed on 6 August 1985—the fortieth anniversary of the Hiroshima explosion—by eight South Pacific states, declaring a nuclear weapons free zone covering most of the Pacific south of the Equator. It came into force on 11 December 1987. Individual signatories are allowed to reach their own decisions regarding visits by nuclear-powered or armed naval vessels.' The Treaty has no direct effect on civil power developments. However, it is of interest that prior to its signing there were some tensions between France and Australia owing to continued weapons tests in the Pacific, which in turn led to a temporary suspension of Australian uranium exports to France in the 1980s.

Besides proliferation there is also the question of terrorism. A *Convention on the Physical Protection of Nuclear Materials*, dating from 1979, has been signed by forty-four states, and came into force on 8 February 1987. It is mainly directed towards minimizing the chances of theft or sabotage during international transport, but it also deals with the problem of storage. Parties to the Convention have a duty to assist non-signatory states in protecting nuclear material, and to offer no sanctuary to criminal offenders.

Multilateral reactions to the 1974 Indian nuclear explosion

The satisfaction engendered by the NPT, Tlatelolco, and the regular inspections by the IAEA corps of inspectors was rudely jolted on 18 May 1974 by India's 'peaceful nuclear explosion' in the Rajasthan Desert, in the north-west of the country not far from the Pakistan border. The material for the device came from about 15 kilograms of plutonium which had been produced in a natural uranium-fuelled, heavy-water-moderated research reactor, which had been supplied by Canada four years earlier, and which used heavy water provided by the USA. The reactor had the capability of producing about 10 kilograms of plutonium per year, which was separated in a pilot reprocessing plant at Trombay, near Bombay. This was the first example of production of an explosive device from a nuclear reactor which had ostensibly been installed for non-military purposes. It was not under safeguards, though assurances had been given to Canada and the USA that the material they had supplied would be used for peaceful purposes only. Hence no doubt the tongue-in-cheek designation of the event by the Indians as 'peaceful'.

The political reactions were immediate. Canada suspended all assistance with the building of a heavy-water plant and of two reactors at Rajasthan, one of which had been under IAEA safeguards. Further co-operation was made dependent on IAEA inspection of all India's facilities. The demand was refused, and two years later all co-operation between the two countries was suspended. Relations with the USA were also damaged. However, although the restrictions did not stop India's nuclear development, there have been no more explosions. Meanwhile, Mrs Ghandi has died. She had been an implacable opponent of the NPT, seeing in it a vehicle for continuing domination of the rest of the world by the white races, as in colonial days. Her son continued her opposition during his time as Prime Minister.

The Indian explosion, coming on top of anxieties regarding the supply of reprocessing and enrichment technology to Pakistan, South Korea, and Brazil, led at American insistence to the strengthening of international constraints on the supply of materials and equipment needed for the development of nuclear weapons. A *Nuclear Suppliers Group* (informally known as the London Suppliers Group) was set up in 1975 with secretarial assistance provided by the British Foreign Office. It has continued to expand beyond the original membership of seven countries, until today it includes twenty-three of the main industrial nations. Notably its membership includes both OECD and the Soviet Union and other Eastern European countries. The original members drew up a set of guidelines, and on 11 January 1978 communicated them to the IAEA. They cover exports of materials and equipment to any non-nuclear-weapons state, and also technology transfers. Under these guidelines supply is made dependent on assurances of peaceful use, IAEA safeguards, physical protection, and undertakings regarding downstream use or further transfers. Restraint is called for in the export of specially sensitive technologies, enrichment and reprocessing. For instance, when Pakistan built a uranium-enrichment plant using information purloined from a URENCO plant in the Netherlands, the Swiss government was embarrassed to learn that some components had come from Swiss companies; it tightened its export rules in 1987. The German government has had a similar experience, again on account of Pakistan and some other countries. The guidelines retain a strong element of pragmatism, and full-scope safeguards over all nuclear installations operated by a recipient country are not called for.

There was already another set of guidelines in existence, on which the Nuclear Suppliers Group could build. It arose from the coming into force on 5 March 1970 of the NPT, and the very general wording of the Treaty's Articles. As a matter of practicality it was necessary to spell out for the benefit of manufacturing states exactly what kind of exports would be in contravention of Articles I, II, and III(2). As a result the *Non-Proliferation Treaty Exporters Committee*, known informally as the Zangger Committee after its first Swiss Chairman, was set up to consider the implications for exports of the commitments made under the NPT. By July 1974 the

Committee had produced a 'trigger list' of items for which safeguards should apply (IAEA information circular 209), and this list is regularly updated. The UK provides the secretariat for the Committee from its IAEA Mission in Vienna. There are twenty-one members of the Committee, from Europe, Eastern Europe and the USSR, USA, Australia, and Japan. On 22 August 1974 ten countries individually communicated to the Director-General of the IAEA their intentions regarding controls to be placed on the supply of nuclear plant, equipment, and material[92].

The Zangger 'trigger list' and the guidelines of the Nuclear Suppliers Group have caused some resentment amongst the signatories of the NPT who are not themselves weapons states, since they can be represented as conflicting with the spirit of Article IV of that Treaty. However, those who apply them hold them to be completely consonant with Article III(2), which obliges all parties not to provide to NNWS 'source or special fissionable material, or equipment or material especially designed' for its processing, use, or production, except under safeguards. It is true that the Nuclear Suppliers Group asks for assurances (see IAEA information circular 254) which go beyond anything stated specifically in the Treaty; but those assurances are not at odds with the Treaty, and should pose no difficulty to an importer who has no interest in proliferation.

These are evidently not matters capable of tidy solution: pragmatism is the only way forward. The industrial nations have not given way, deeming the possible embarrassment over Article IV ('inalienable right . . . to use nuclear energy for peaceful purposes without discrimination') to be of less significance than the task of preventing the further spread of nuclear weapons. There are signs that understanding and acceptance of their position is now more widespread, and this might account for the satisfactory outcome of the 1985 NPT Review. The UN Conference on the Promotion of International Co-operation in the Peaceful Uses of Nuclear Energy—UNCPICPUNE—which met in 1987 after ten years of preparation, focused on the issue of the principles which should govern the assurances of continuing supply of nuclear materials and technology. It failed to create a consensus, but led to few difficulties for the supplier countries—perhaps because the general slow-down in the nuclear industry had reduced any sense of unfairness which might otherwise have been felt.

Unilateral reactions to the 1974 explosion

There were national as well as multilateral reactions to the Indian 'peaceful explosion'. Canada's sense of aggrievance, as a supplier who had been let down, led to a political resolve to use the leverage available from being a substantial exporter of uranium to secure binding agreements from recipient countries, requiring that all downstream use, including reprocessing, should be subject to Canadian approval; and that materials, equipment, or technology supplied by Canada should not be used to produce a nuclear explosive device, whether or not this was stated to be for 'peaceful' purposes. The new policy was announced on 20 December 1974, seven months after the Indian explosion. It was strengthened twenty-four months later by making the export of reactors and uranium conditional on acceptance of international safeguards by recipients over their entire nuclear programme.

Arising out of this policy a curious difficulty emerged for the best part of a year during 1977, regarding uranium supply to the Federal German Republic. Germany is a signatory of the NPT; but she is also a partner in Euratom, whose members have the right to move nuclear fuel freely within the Euratom Community under the Treaty of Rome. Indeed, the Euratom Supply Agency has as one of its duties the monitoring of contracts to ensure that this right of free movement is not infringed by supply contract provisions. However, two of the Euratom countries—the United Kingdom and France—possess nuclear weapons, and this was held to open up the possibility, in principle, that through the Euratom route Canadian uranium might find its way into weapons. The Federal German Republic is not a nuclear-weapons power and—arising from the 1954 revision of the Brussels Treaty, which opened the way to becoming a member of NATO—had voted in the Bundestag to accept an undertaking 'not to manufacture in its territory any atomic weapons'. Nevertheless the Canadian government was unwilling to concede what might have been regarded as a precedent restricting her freedom to press forward vigorously with non-proliferation measures. The result was a supply embargo from which Germany suffered from January 1977 and throughout that year, despite her 1954 undertaking. The problem was resolved first by an interim agreement, and then more permanently.

The Canadian policy encouraged Australia to follow a broadly similar course. However, Australia was able to profit from the Canadian difficulties with Euratom, and her 1979 agreement with the United Kingdom took care to include references to Euratom ('uranium supplied by Australia will not be retransferred to any other country other than another member of Euratom'). Later Australia negotiated an understanding directly with Euratom.

The Canadian determination to ensure that non-proliferation controls were effective was matched by that of the Carter administration in the US. Prior to his taking office in January 1977 a distinguished group had completed a major study on nuclear proliferation (the 'Ford-Mitre' report[97]). They had concluded that the key to combating proliferation lay in the ready availability of uranium. The argument ran that if uranium supplies were abundant there should be little incentive to go in for all the complications of plutonium recycling in existing types of reactor, and so incur the dangers of proliferation; still less to develop the fast reactor as a means of using separated plutonium; and that market forces would ensure the supply of uranium for many years into the future. So the way was open to outlawing plutonium, and with it chemical reprocessing.

The force to be accorded to the argument depends on one's time horizon. Nearly a decade and a half later we can see that the period of serious uranium supply tightness is still half a century away, though there could well be a price rise in the early 1990s. This buyer's market did not exist in the mid-seventies, in the aftermath of the jolt which OPEC had administered to the world's views on energy security. The uranium price was sky-high, and only broke sharply downwards in 1980, three years after the Ford-Mitre report was published. Had it appeared then it is conceivable that its conclusions might have carried more weight.

What happened was that the rest of the world decided that at a time of tightening uranium markets it was not prepared to forgo the plutonium option, on which so much effort had already been expended. Preparing for the era when uranium was no longer easily obtainable, and when the energy-efficient fast reactor might be needed, was something which could not be hurried. The accumulation of the necessary experience in fast-reactor technology, fuel reprocessing, and plutonium recycling could easily take a further three decades of steady work. Strong opposition developed to the Ford-Mitre arguments.

These doubts did not deter the US Congress from enacting, or President Carter from approving, the *Nuclear Non-Proliferation Act of 1978*, drafted along Ford-Mitre lines. Politically the NNPA was bipartisan in origin, much of the groundwork having been done during the life of the previous administration. It had received unanimous support in the House of Representatives, and attracted only three contrary votes in the Senate. It was an immensely complex Act, which sought to exploit the leverage then possessed by the USA as the leading exporter of both enriched uranium and reactors. Whatever happened downstream was to require prior approval by one or more US government agencies, working on a case-by-case basis. Furthermore, the Act required all earlier US agreements to be renegotiated within a limited time period: after March 1980 exports would be permitted only to non-weapons countries accepting full-scope safeguards. The Act may be regarded as extending the concept of proliferation to include *capability* as well as actual achievement.

These provisions took no account of the operational difficulties they would cause for a country like Sweden, where the 'Stipulation Act' of 1977 required that there should be agreement about what was to be done with the waste from a reactor *before authorization for start-up could be given*. The German Basic Atomic Energy Act similarly requires reactor operators to define their proposals for spent-fuel management six years ahead of fuel discharge. Under the US legislation this would be the subject of a case-by-case decision at some future time, by persons as yet unappointed. Euratom too found difficulties with the NNPA, because an agreement had been concluded with the USA in 1958 waiving any requirement for prior agreement over reprocessing. Euratom refused to renegotiate the agreement. In the Far East Japan's spent-fuel shipments to the European plants of United Reprocessors were held up in 1978 for some months while a policy decision was reached by the Carter administration. There was an evident mismatch here, as with Sweden, between operational and administrative time-horizons, and inconsistencies on such issues between the laws of the various jurisdictions. Japan's determination to provide herself with a complete range of fuel-cycle facilities must owe something to this experience.

Although greater understanding has been shown subsequently, reflected in the arrangement with Japan for 'generic' rather than case-by-case approvals, the lesson was taken by more than one country that it would be as well to minimize dependence on the USA. Most countries could not agree that a significant part of their own laboriously worked-out energy policies should be constrained in this way by a foreign country. The paradoxical result of the NNPA's stringent controls, designed to allow the US to police non-proliferation world-wide, has been to set in train events which have eroded that possibility, and incidentally created strong commercial competition for the US nuclear fuel industry. The assurances built into the Act—that the US would continue to be a reliable supplier to states agreeing to its conditions—have had no noticeable effect on subsequent events.

Because of the turmoil created by the Nuclear Non-Proliferation Act the US government convened an international technical 'evaluation' of nuclear fuel-cycle options, to be conducted at Vienna using the IAEA's facilities. It was known as the International Nuclear Fuel Cycle Evaluation, and the US clearly hoped that it would create support for a policy of abandoning plutonium. It was not to be. When INFCE reported in 1980, after two and a half years work, plutonium was rather more firmly entrenched than before as an intended future option. The fact that more use is not made of plutonium today owes more to technical difficulties, and the inevitably slow build-up of plutonium recycling, than to any political or regulatory obstacles. This same slowness and inability to hurry appears to the industry as a strong argument for not delaying unnecessarily over acquiring fuel-recycling technology.

Many lessons have been learned from this period of a decade ago. Non-proliferation policies, however well intentioned, are unlikely to work unless they are based on a realistic appreciation of the operational problems of the industry. The industry is sympathetic to what is being sought in terms of non-proliferation, as shown by the Uranium Institute's initiative at the time of the 1985 NPT Review Conference. The industry remains anxious to work with governments to find a satisfactory balance between effectiveness of proliferation control and the efficiency of its own operations. What continues to function with reasonable smoothness are the 'flags on atoms' policies of the various nuclear supplier governments (see Chapter 2). Such controls have become part of the everyday life of nuclear-fuel managers throughout the world. They add to administrative burdens, but are accepted because, as the industry sees so clearly, without them democratic governments would be unable to face their electorates with effective assurances that 'their' nuclear exports were not being put to non-peaceful uses. They are an essential underpinning for nuclear trade.

The issue of staff probity

In the gradual elaboration of the armoury of controls against proliferation it is probably fair to say that, on the whole, good faith on the part of the operators has been implicitly assumed, in the absence of evidence to the contrary. This is entirely natural. Nuclear energy began as the preserve of a select priesthood, close to government and accorded a high degree of trust. But steady growth, and competition for staff from other advanced industries, mean that this is no longer as true as it was; perhaps it is no longer sufficiently true to provide a basis for policy[98]. Certainly this unwelcome thought must now be entertained as a result of the 1987 Transnuklear scandal (Chapter 4), even though no diversion that was in any way significant from a proliferation viewpoint took place[99].

It is inconceivable that this incident should be allowed to undo the work of the past thirty years. What are needed are condign penalties for tampering with nuclear records and deliberately giving false information about nuclear movements—because we are concerned with matters affecting international confidence. This would still leave us far from the 'police state' which nuclear opponents have claimed would necessarily accompany a plutonium-based economy. But the critics do have a point when they imply that regard must be paid to the sheer malevolence of some human beings. The inevitable transition from a priesthood to an ordinary mix of staff should be a trigger for a further review, and where necessary tightening of the regulations.

In conclusion

There can be no guarantee that the pursuit of civil nuclear power will not aid proliferation in some states; but equally its abandonment would not remove the danger of proliferation. While most civil reactor designs, fortunately, are not ideal starting-points for clandestine weapons production, there are no absolute 'technical fixes' that can sanitize the key civil nuclear materials to make them unusable by would-be proliferators. The INFCE conference confirmed this view in 1980 after two years of study. Barriers to the unauthorized use of nuclear materials must therefore be political even more than technical. It is clearly in the interests of world stability, and not least of the superpowers themselves, that those barriers should be as strong as possible.

Looking back over the history of the past forty years we are left with the impression that the barriers to proliferation, though imperfect, have proved stronger than they were expected to be in 1963, when President Kennedy looked forward to a world which might, in short order, contain fifteen to twenty-five nuclear-weapons states. As opportunities have presented themselves non-proliferation constraints have been progressively tightened. In 1960 we could rely only on very weak IAEA safeguards, with just three inspectors carrying out a few largely symbolic inspections. By 1970 the NPT was in place, and has since attracted the support of the overwhelming majority of nations; by then the IAEA inspection team had grown to twenty-seven. By 1980 international inspection had become a regular feature of the day-to-day life of the nuclear industry. We had also learned not to place reliance on the word of governments, but to judge them on their actions, constraining them if necessary through the political limitations on nuclear trade applied by their intended suppliers, according to internationally agreed guidelines. By 1988 there were 168 safeguards agreements with 99 states, and the Agency's 185 inspectors carried out more than 2,100 inspections in the course of the year. By the early 1990s the Transnuklear lessons should be making their way into freshly tightened regulations. In no way was that incident as serious as the Indian explosion of 1974. That did not slow the development of nuclear power, nor will Transnuklear. But the regulations will need to be periodically reviewed, so that they keep step with the world's broad perception of the proliferation risk in the light of the ever-changing political context, and the development of new technologies which might increase unauthorized access to materials usable in weapons[100].

The revision conferences of the NPT will be the debating ground for the political issues which are at present only imperfectly resolved: how the nuclear aspirations of the developing countries which Article IV supports are to be squared with the policing of anti-proliferation; how much weight should be accorded to that Article, given that only three developing countries that are parties to the Treaty have nuclear programmes; who should pay for safeguards, particularly if their scale is extended; and whether disarmament negotiations are being conducted between the nuclear-weapons states, as required by Article VI, with sufficient 'good faith'. The encouraging historical record of developing non-proliferation policy gives confidence that answers will eventually be found. Meanwhile there is still much for the foreign offices of the world to do. The best help industry can give, to them and to itself, is to run a 'tight ship'.

8 Risk and Radiation

THREE Mile Island and Chernobyl sharply altered the focus of public concern over nuclear power. From the political anxiety over possible future proliferation that had been the main preoccupation in the 1970s it switched to more immediate issues of safety: the biological effects of radiation on the living and on those still to be born; the safety of reactors; the dangers of contaminating the environment, should an accident occur; and the problem of managing nuclear waste. This and the two following chapters deal with these issues, beginning with the biological effects of radiation.

All human activity involves some risk, and the risks of normal living provide a rough measure of what it is reasonable to ask for as regards protection from damage by radiation. Each year one in a million people are killed by domestic gas explosions in their own homes. Even in the safest industries the chance of a fatal accident is one in 100,000 annually, while the most dangerous may be twenty times, even a hundred times, worse. A mother-to-be has one chance in 13,000 of dying in childbirth, even given good medical attention. When it comes to amusing ourselves we are quite prodigal with our lives. A skier has a chance of killing himself once in a million hours—or perhaps a one in a thousand chance of death in a skiing lifetime. A rock climber accepts an hourly risk forty times higher still[101]. A heavy smoker exposes himself to rather more than a one in a million chance of contracting lung cancer every time he lights a cigarette: that is a statistical description of the effects of smoking twenty or more a day, for thirty or forty years.

All these risks are accepted because they are part of the normal pattern of life; because the risk-bearing activities bring with them some kind of advantage or pleasure, which we are prepared to balance against the risk; and because, almost without exception, the risks are perceived by individuals, rightly or wrongly, as acceptably low. (Even with the appallingly risky business of long-term smoking the *marginal* risk of lighting another cigarette is all but negligible.) But perhaps most importantly the reason why rational people tolerate such risks is because they believe them to be largely under their own control.

Table 8.1 One in a Million Risks

400 miles air travel
100 kilometres car travel
10 days of typical UK factory work
4 days of agricultural employment
3 days of underground coal mining in UK
2 ½ hours of being a man aged 50
Use of oral contraceptive pills during 2½ weeks
Being vaccinated once
90 seconds of rock climbing
¾ of a cigarette
½ bottle wine
1 to 10 days of living in an energy-efficient house with reduced ventilation
  (radon-induced cancer risk)
2 to 10 days of average work at a UK nuclear power station (on basis of
  recently proposed upwards revision of inferred risk—see text)

Sources: References 101–4.

There is another class of risks, those which are *not* under our own control, and over these we undeniably show far more anxiety. A classic case concerned motorway central barriers. Occasionally, on dual-track roads without such barriers, a car travelling at high speed leaves one carriageway and causes a fatal accident to someone going in the other direction. In vain did British transport experts demonstrate in the 1960s that the frequency of such accidents was so low that money could be better spent on safety measures in cities, where traffic deaths were far more frequent. The public felt instinctively, if not always correctly, that they were perfectly capable of judging when it was safe to dash across a busy road. But a fast car crossing a central reservation was something against which even the most alert driver was defenceless. The public got its barriers.

Radiation risks have this in common with such motorway accidents: in many cases they are outside the control of the individual. Not only that, radiation is undetectable by any of our senses. Some radioactivity persists for far longer than the human life-span. It may be absorbed into our bodies, making us unwilling victims of a game of Russian roulette, depending on whether its reaction with our body cells happens to produce carcinogenic mutations. Two-thirds of women interviewed in a Swedish poll[34] feared radiation because they could not tell whether they had already suffered injury. Even more—76 per cent—feared genetic damage to their descendants. Such fears, though exaggerated, add to the picture which ordinary people have in their minds when they think of radiation: a lesser Hiroshima. And the public quite certainly doubts whether the decision-makers fully understand what they are doing.

In fact much of the anxiety is unjustified. There is by now a great depth of knowledge, accumulated from a wide variety of sources over the past ninety years: industrial exposure in the early days of the radium industry, when nothing was known of the dangers and safety practices were almost non-existent; mining experience; professional exposure to X-radiation by radiologists, in the days before instrument sensitivity was vastly improved; medical exposures generally; animal experiments; occupational health and follow-up surveys over the past forty years of the atomic energy work-force; and the great tragedies of Hiroshima and Nagasaki. The importance of the war experience cannot be exaggerated, because of its scale, and because it covered such a wide range of dose. Over the next decade Chernobyl will add its own contribution to this already extensive data bank, particularly as regards effects on the thyroid, and the incidence of leukaemias amongst the hundreds of thousands who were exposed to varying quantities of radiation[173].

The main problem when interpreting the mass of older historical information is in knowing just how much radiation the early workers received, and the still greater difficulties of assessing the exact exposures of bomb victims. Much careful work has been concentrated on this problem of calibration. Indeed, a recent review of Japanese wartime radiation casualties[105,106] has had the effect of reducing the amount of exposure that can be regarded as acceptable.

The number of different organizations which independently monitor the effects of radiation, and their high standing, should satisfy the public that no efforts are spared to learn everything possible about the effects of radiation on the human body and on our environment. There is no cover-up; nor is there good reason for thinking that our present knowledge is likely to have many serious gaps.

The learning process began to be systematized in 1928, when the Second International Congress of Radiology, held in London, set up the committee from which grew the International Commission on Radiological Protection (ICRP). The original task was to study ways of mitigating the damage which the medical profession in particular was suffering through the increasing use of X-rays and radium; but with the coming of nuclear energy the remit became much wider. The members of ICRP hold office in a personal capacity, as internationally recognized experts. The twelve members, plus their chairman, continue to be appointed for terms of four years by the International Society of Radiology. Although the Commission has no official status, governments have been willing to follow its recommendations, which remain the basis of national and international regulations.

A few nuclear objectors have made the ridiculous suggestion, which hardly gives credit to the Commission's medical origins, that because its members have a detailed knowledge of radiation they cannot be relied on to speak objectively. Governments clearly do not share this view. Like most of us, they prefer to rely in a difficult field on experts rather than amateurs. A criticism which may have slightly more substance is that the choice of exposure limits involves an arbitrary value-judgement, which a professional body should arguably leave to politicians. But again governments seem generally unconcerned, and are prepared to leave matters in what experience has shown to be safe hands. The ICRP has its small headquarters at the Medical Research Council's Radiobiology Unit at Harwell, England.

The United Nations Scientific Committee on the Effects of Atomic Radiation (UNSCEAR) uses the resources of member governments to collect and extend the data base—the extent of radiation exposure, and its effects—on which the ICRP and the national organizations need to draw. UNSCEAR has recently re-evaluated Japanese bomb-casualty data to take account of the delayed cancers which have appeared since its 1977 assessment, and which are still appearing amongst the two-thirds of the exposed population who are still alive. In addition, it has been realized that the humidity of the air at the time would have had the effect of cutting down the numbers of fast neutrons, relative to those observed in the much drier air of the Nevada testing site. The effect is that the observed effects must now be attributed to somewhat lower radiation levels, and to a higher relative proportion of gamma radiation. For these reasons one unit of radiation is somewhat more damaging than previously thought, and a revision seems likely to the current ICRP recommendations, which also date back[107] to 1977. Further follow-up of exposed populations, and revised models for the projection of lifetime risk, reinforce the case for tighter controls. A revision of the ICRP recommendations is expected in 1990. Meanwhile the UK has taken informal action to lower the nationally recommended exposure maxima[108]. This is a good example of the way international co-operation works in this field, and of the alertness of the authorities to any significant extensions of knowledge.

Several other international bodies also play a part. The World Health Organization, the International Atomic Energy Agency, the Nuclear Energy Agency of the Organization for Economic Co-operation and Development, the International Maritime Organization, the International Labour Office, and the Food and Agriculture Organization all monitor various aspects of the problem. The Commission of the European Communities has a statutory obligation under Article 30 of the Euratom Treaty to develop radiation exposure standards within the Community[109].

At the national level most governments have regulatory bodies dealing with radiation. In the case of the United Kingdom these efforts are backed up by a major professional research effort operated by the independent National Radiological . Protection Board, which has financial support from the Department of Health. Under the 1974 Health and Safety at Work etc. Act the NRPB, although not a government department, must be consulted by the British Health and Safety Executive on safety matters involving radiation. In its turn the NRPB has an obligation to seek advice from the Medical Research Council on the biological basis of radiation standards. France has the Institute for Protection and Nuclear Safety (IPSN). In the United States the National Research Council's Committee on the Biological Effects of Ionizing Radiations (BEIR) maintains a similar watching brief. This extensive worldwide professional network is the public's best safeguard against industrial or political laxity in matters of radiological protection.

Measuring radiation exposure

Although radiation is invisible it is easily detected and measured, using the *ionization* phenomenon described in the Technical Appendix, plus a simple application of electronics. Ionization—the temporary liberation of electric charges on a microsopic (literally atomic) scale—is the way energy is transferred from radiation to the human body. This energy can lead to biochemical changes in our bodies in ways that nature never intended; so it also provides a natural unit of biological damage. The internationally recognized unit is the *gray*, named after a British physicist, equal to one joule of energy per kilogram of target matter—in this case the body. (A joule, while very significant in the context of radiation protection, is not a large energy unit in everyday terms: it is the amount of energy which a small domestic electric fire would use in a thousandth of a second.) The gray replaces a previously used unit, the *rad*, which was one hundred times smaller. Although the gray fits logically into the international scheme of physical units, it is inconveniently large for radiation-protection purposes: a whole body dose of only 10 grays would lead to death in a few weeks, and would be far above anything encountered in normal industrial operations. Consequently in radiological protection it is usual to work with smaller units— the milligray (mGy, one thousandth) or the microgray (μGy, one millionth).

The three main kinds of nuclear radiation—alpha, beta, and gamma (see Technical Appendix)—have different capacities for creating ionization when passing through materials, including the human body. Radiation which produces a particularly high density of ionization (which is what happens with alpha radiation, or fast-moving helium nuclei) provides additional opportunities for unwanted biochemical reactions to take place. The amount of damage per unit of energy deposited by alpha particles is about twenty times greater than with gamma rays or beta particles (which are fast electrons), and the units measuring biological effects have to take these differences into account. A unit called the *sievert*, after a distinguished Swedish physicist, is equal to the energy deposition, measured in grays, multiplied by a *quality factor* which roughly takes account of the *relative biological effectiveness* in causing damage of the particular kind of radiation. For beta and gamma radiation this factor is taken as one; for alpha radiation it is twenty.

Like the gray from which it is derived, the sievert is also a very large unit in terms of damage to tissue; so here again we often have to work with millisieverts (mSv) or microsieverts(μSv). One sievert equals 100 *rems*, the older unit. When dealing with collective populations rather than individuals, the dose unit is the *man-*

sievert, the total of all the individual already-experienced and unavoidably committed doses. When studying genetic risk the period of interest is the average reproductive phase, up to thirty or forty years of age.

The natural radiation background

The radiation produced by reactors is not the only source to which we are exposed. By far the largest contribution to the radiation received by the general population is the naturally occurring 'background', arising from a variety of causes. Weak gamma radiation and fast electrons stream in from outer space—the 'cosmic' radiation. One hundred thousand cosmic ray neutrons penetrate our bodies every hour, and four times as many particles of other kinds. The intensity increases the higher we are in the atmosphere: long-distance flights (at 0.005 mSv per hour), or a skiing holiday at a high resort, both slightly increase our exposure. Then there are radioactive materials commonly occurring in the soil and in some building materials. The average uranium content in the earth's crust is four parts per million; but its concentration is often much higher in, for instance, granite—which is used as a house-building material in some parts of the world, including Cornwall in the UK. The daughter-products of uranium include radon–222, a short half-life (3.8 days) radioactive gas with a short-lived solid alpha-emitting daughter-product of its own, polonium–218. This can be deposited inside the lung after radon-containing air has been inhaled, and is known to contribute to lung cancers of miners in many different kinds of mine. People living in poorly ventilated houses with inadequate floors in granite areas are also at risk: their individual dose levels can exceed those permitted in the UK for radiation workers[110,111]. Potassium, an abundant element making up 2.4 per cent of the earth's crust, also has a naturally radioactive isotope, potassium–40. It is a constituent of our own bodies, responsible for about two-thirds of the 300–400 micro-sieverts each of us receives internally in the course of a year, over and above the contribution from radon[112,113].

These naturally occurring radiations provide some kind of natural yardstick of radiation risk. In the United Kingdom they add up on average to about 2.5 millisieverts per year per person (Table 8.2), though the total can be considerably higher, depending on

Table 8.2 Sources of Radiation in the United Kingdom
(millisieverts per year per person, 1988 (average of whole population))

Cosmic rays at sea-level	0.25
Cosmic rays at 9,000 feet	0.7
Terrestrial gamma rays	0.35
Internal from food and drink	0.3
Natural radon and thoron emissions	1.3*
Medical uses of radiation	0.3
Past nuclear weapons testing	0.01
Nuclear power	0.001
TOTAL AT SEA-LEVEL	2.5
Compare: occupational exposure of work-force in UK atomic energy industry (average)	2

* In extreme cases of poor ventilation can be ten to fifty times higher.
Sources: References 112, 113.

where one lives. To this must be added man-made radiation—
nearly another third of a millisievert annually on average, mainly
from medical uses. For instance, a single chest X-ray contributes
about 0.05 millisieverts. In normal operational conditions the
average exposure of radiation workers in the atomic energy
industry in the United Kingdom is comparable with the natural
background at sea level.

Types of damage

The effects of radiation on the human body fall into two main
categories. There are those, such as cataracts and skin ulcerations,
which do not occur below a certain threshold dose; they are known
as *deterministic* (or non-stochastic) effects, and are what matters if
a serious nuclear accident gives rise to acute high-intensity
irradiation, as happened to the fire-fighters at Chernobyl. Secondly
there are effects which apparently do not have any threshold level,
which depend on the statistical probability of suffering cellular
damage which can then propagate through the normal processes of
life, and for which the amount of damage is assumed to be
proportional to the amount of radiation received. These are the
stochastic effects, which can lead to fatal or non-fatal cancers, or
possibly to genetic damage in later generations.

Short-term effects. Radiation can kill body-cells. This is indeed the basis for radiotherapy, where large doses—tens of sieverts—may be directed locally into tumours (which fortunately tend to be more radiosensitive than healthy tissue). A dose of 6 sieverts delivered to most of the body in a short burst is in most cases fatal. There is a 50 per cent chance of survival, provided medical attention is available, with a single rapid dose of 2.5 to 4 sieverts. For doses around 1 Sv the likelihood of early death is practically zero[114]. The cell-killing effects become much less serious if the dose is delivered over a long period, because of the body's self-healing abilities. At the low doses experienced in normal occupational exposure these healing processes make it impossible to observe any effects due to cell killing.

Delayed cancers and leukaemias. The deterministic effects have importance only in accident conditions. What matters for everyday exposure, whether from ordinary living or from one's occupation, are the delayed stochastic effects. Carcinogenic effects take a long time to express themselves: five to twenty-five years for leukaemias and up to thirty years or more for solid cancers. The public's anxiety about this 'sword of Damocles' explains a large part of its concern over radiation. But exposure to radiation does *not* mean an automatic sentence to cancer. The chance of inducing a fatal cancer is reasonably well established: it is now thought to be a few per cent for each sievert of radiation[108]. One prime objective of radiation protection, therefore, is to make any such additional long-term risk from radiation small compared with the inescapable other risks of living, taking care to include the *total detriment* incurred over the whole period of exposure.

From the statistical nature of the damage it is probably logical and certainly prudent to assume that the same chance, of a few per cent per sievert, will continue to apply however low the actual intensity of the radiation. This is the so-called 'linear hypothesis', which can be demonstrated by an examination of medical statistics only down to doses of about 200 millisieverts, or around eighty times the average annual contribution in the UK from background radiation. Below that the effects that are being studied are lost in the 'noise' of other sources of cancer. Attempts have been made to compare cancer risks in areas of different natural backgrounds—for instance, by choosing sample populations from the high cities of South America, where the intensity of cosmic radiation is several times that at sea-level. The results have been inconclusive, which is to be expected, given the large and variable background of cancers from other causes.

The linear basis for extrapolating the probability of stochastic effects to very low doses is almost certainly conservative. If it is incorrect it can only be in the direction of providing an overestimate of the risk, because of some degree of self-healing. There are no reasons for thinking that it could lead to a dangerous underestimate of damage.

Assuming that damage is proportional to dose, with the likelihood of cancer induction per millisievert being the same at low doses as at high doses, then in the UK, with a population of fifty-seven million, we might expect up to 5,000 deaths per year from the cancer effects of background radiation. This is completely swamped by the 140,000 deaths from cancer annually from all causes. Nevertheless, a statement that 'the radiation (from all sources) to which the general British population is exposed may cause 5,000 deaths a year' could cause an outcry. It could well be true; but no one will be able unambiguously to assign cause and effect, still less for the far smaller inferred number of deaths from atomic energy activities. Nor does the statement say anything about the reduction in life expectancy, given the thirty-year period or longer for the expression of many cancers. Moreover, there is almost nothing that can be done about the great majority of these cases, because they derive either from natural causes over which we have no control; or in a minority of cases from medical irradiation, where doctors have had to balance the immediate and certain needs of patients against the low individual probability of inducing long-delayed cancers. On this same linear hypothesis no more than about three fatal cancers per year, plus about one genetic defect per year in the first or second generation, are likely to result from the small public exposure due to the UK's atomic energy activities, short of some major disaster. It is therefore hardly surprising that the British Office of Population Census and Surveys was able to demonstrate[119] that there was no general increase in cancer mortality in the vicinity of nuclear installations over the twenty-two year period 1959–80. Similar expectations apply for other countries with properly controlled nuclear power programmes.

Such low figures may surprise many who read in newspapers of vastly greater numbers of inferred future cancer deaths attributable to the hypothetical accidents that are postulated in reactor safety studies. They are derived by estimating the size of the population likely to be affected, the likely levels of radiation fall-out, and the known facts about radiation damage. The extent to which the results can be moved around, depending on assumptions, is enormous: almost any desired result can be produced.

The experience following the Chernobyl accident provides a more certain basis for discussion. During the following year, even in the most contaminated areas in the European Community countries, the radiation dose from the accident was still only about 10 per cent of that due to the natural background; while the dose in later years was smaller still. The total collective dose from the fall-out summed over the whole of the European Community and over all time is estimated to be about 78,000 man-sieverts, of which about two-thirds were received in the first year[116]. Using the risk factors derived by UNSCEAR the total number of extra deaths arising over the next half-century in the Community as a result of Chernobyl will be of the order of 2,000. In the same period the numbers dying from cancer due to other causes will be around 30 million, or 15,000 times greater. Thus there will be no possibility of correlating individual deaths in Europe with Chernobyl rather than some other cause. In the world as a whole the collective dose of 620,000 man-sieverts (as estimated by UNSCEAR) is predicted to result in 12,400 deaths over the next half-century, against 500 million 'normal' cancers in the affected population of 4.3 billion. Even amongst the 135,000 evacuees from the immediate vicinity of Chernobyl the expectation of disaster-induced cancers is still only about 1 per cent of the normal cancer expectancy of about 27,000, mostly (apart from a minority of leukaemias) after delays of several decades. Presenting the facts in this way is not an incitement to callous disregard of human life, simply an invitation to see the Chernobyl statistics in perspective[117].

Childhood leukaemias. In recent years there have been follow-up studies[118,119] to test a suggestion that a small excess of childhood leukaemias observed near Sellafield in the north-west of England might be related to the activities of the local nuclear fuel reprocessing plant. Five cases were observed over the period 1950 to 1986 in a population of 1,068 children. Applying the normal rates observed in the rest of the British population the expected incidence should have been roughly ten times lower. Attempts to correlate the observed discrepancy with any previously known radiological effect attributable to the plant failed—the calculated radiation doses were too low by a factor of about 300. Moreover, 'clusters' of leukaemia cases occur all over England in numbers which, though low, appear to be statistically significant[28]. However, the search for an explanation was given added urgency by the existence of a similar cluster near the Dounreay nuclear plant, in Scotland. The committee which investigated that occurence also failed to find any convincing explanation, but concluded that ' . . . if the findings are not a consequence of chance . . . there must be a mechanism, potentially discoverable and remediable'[120].

A suggestion was made, though it has not yet been rigorously tested, that populations which have recently received an influx of people from outside the area—which was certainly true of Sellafield—are in some way more susceptible to childhood leukaemias: a similar cluster was observed at a Scottish new town, Glenrothes, which has no nuclear involvement[121]. There is a further possibility that a contributory factor could in some way be the chemicals to which workers at Sellafield are exposed. In the same area children of fathers in other occupations which use chemicals—including farm workers and iron and steel workers—also appear to have an increased susceptibility to childhood leukaemias.

Possible genetic effects. A report[122] which appeared early in 1990 suggested that the Sellafield childhood leukaemias might be due to genetic affects of radiation on the sperm of fathers working at the Sellafield plant. An exposure of 100 mSv or more appeared to be associated with a sixfold to eightfold increased risk of leukaemia in the offspring. Statistically there did appear to be this association, though genetic damage was not the only possible explanation. The British Medical Journal commented in an editorial: 'If workers were internally contaminated with a radionuclide which was concentrated in the urogenital organs or the semen, the doses to the germ cell or foetus could be greater than those recorded on the worker's film badges . . . Some radionuclides may be concentrated in the prostate.' The Sellafield experience appears to differ from that in the neighbourhood of the La Hague plant in France, where a preliminary assessment[123] found no evidence of excess childhood leukaemias.

The suggestion that genetic effects might underlie the Sellafield cases conflicts confusingly with the other evidence, which is one reason for looking for other possibly associated explanations, like contamination of the prostate. It has been known for fifty years that radiation can cause mutations; but fortunately these are passed through the sieve of natural selection and are unlikely to survive as well as those that have evolved over thousands or millions of years. Experimental mice have been exposed to 2 grays per generation for more than one hundred generations with no visible effects on fertility or viability[102], though it is known that genetic effects can be induced by sufficiently high doses of radiation. Unfortunately, extrapolation to human rates of risk is not easy. So far as direct human experience is concerned, no excess leukaemias, solid cancers, or other genetic effects have been observed in the 7,400 progeny of the male Hiroshima and Nagasaki survivors, whose average irradiation was four times that of the Sellafield workers. All measures of congenital defects have shown no differences between the nearly 15,000 children of irradiated parents and those of control groups[114,124]. This observation enables an upper limit to be placed on genetic damage in the human species. Moreover the Japanese data refer to single large exposures; but animal experiments show that the same dose spread out in time produces about three times less genetic damage.

It is believed that there is about a one in fifty risk of genetic damage per sievert of exposure of either parent, spread over all subsequent generations. Since a majority of any population—at least in Europe—that is exposed to radiation will have passed the time of producing children, it is judged permissible to use a figure of one 1 in 125 per sievert to describe the possible genetic effects of exposure of a large population. With an annual additional dose to each member of the general population due to atomic energy activities of around 0.001 mSv (the average figure currently applying in the United Kingdom) the extra individual risk is tiny— less than one genetic defect per year of nuclear operation. Side effects of medical irradiation could be ten to one hundred times higher, which is one reason why doctors are enjoined to minimize radiation dosages where possible.

Regulatory aspects

The recommendations of the ICRP, on which all governments have based their regulations, are centred[107,125,126] on three general principles. First, no practice involving exposure to radiation should be adopted unless it produces a positive 'net benefit', as determined by some appropriate kind of cost-benefit analysis. Secondly, all radiation exposures should be kept as low as reasonably achievable—the ALARA principle—using sensible economic and social considerations when deciding what 'reasonable' means in this context. Thirdly, the maximum dose that an individual or a population can receive must be clearly specified and must not exceed the permitted limits.

Logically the first principle—the one requiring justification of a practice—should apply to the use of nuclear reactors to produce electricity. It might be thought that nuclear power would fall at this first fence. That is not in fact self-evident, since the alternatives also have their costs. 'Black lung' was a notorious cause of deaths amongst American coal-miners, just as silicosis used to be in the Welsh pits. Moreover, coal contains traces of uranium, which leads to radon hazards in coal-mines and to a small increase in radiological exposure of the whole population from chimney fly-ash. Coal contributes to acid rain and certainly to the 'greenhouse effect'. Striking an overall balance would rationally involve examining the whole context; though so many assumptions would have to be made that we should not be much further forward than we are at present, by leaving decisions on energy to politicians and their advisers.

The second principle—ALARA—replaces the old pre-1960 idea of there being a 'tolerable' level of radiation, below which one was supposed to be absolutely safe. We now believe that all unnecessary exposure to radiation should if possible be avoided, even though the regulations will ensure that any additional risk is extremely small. It is really not so very different from prudent behaviour in regard to smoking tobacco.

The third principle leads to national regulations which define the maximum radiation doses to which any worker or member of the public can be legally subjected. The ICRP is at pains to stress that the policy should be to limit the risk *committed* by each year of operation, with no credit being taken for lower doses in earlier or later years.

The British legal limits[127] are typical of those in other countries. The legal *maximum* exposure (1990) for any member of the general public in a single year is 5 millisieverts; though the National Radiological Protection Board[108], in line with recent

ICRP thinking[128,129], recommends that the long-term exposure of the population as a whole to man-made non-medical radiation should not on average exceed 1 millisievert per year, which is less than the natural background (Table 8.2). Such whole-population dose maxima are directed towards avoiding fatal cancers, but they also effectively deal with the genetic problem. This regulatory concern with the health of the whole population is unique to nuclear power, and is an indication both of the knowledge that has been acquired and of the technical possibility of control. No other industry is subject to such precise controls with such a broad sweep.

For the relatively small number of workers who have to deal with radiation the permitted maximum is 50 millisieverts of whole-body radiation per year, from all sources other than medical uses (which themselves should be minimized where possible). Allowing a worker to exceed this permitted maximum dose in the United Kingdom is a criminal offence. On the most recent evidence, following the reappraisal of Japanese wartime casualties, the figure corresponds to a maximum single-year risk rate for an individual of around one in 700 of being killed by his or her occupation through cancer formation. That is far from trivial, and in the view of the NRPB[101,108] is verging on the unacceptable for the 2,000 people in the UK who work near the dose limit. To bring risks down to a figure more in line with normal industrial risks NRPB recommends that the average annual dose for radiation workers should not exceed 15 millisieverts, an annual risk of about one in 2000. This is not operationally impossible: the Central Electricity Generating Board has already applied an even lower limit of 10 millisieverts per year. At such levels the radiation risk would be well below the total risks to which all of us are exposed in normal life, which are as high as one in 300 annually for a man of fifty (see Table 8.1). The ICRP is also considering the Japanese wartime data. It held a preliminary discussion at Como[129] in 1987. Its considered response, due in 1990, will be the signal for national authorities everywhere to review their regulations.

Accidents

We have so far been discussing normal operations. Accidents pose different and unique problems, which cannot be legislated for in any detail in advance. We may find ourselves taken well beyond our intended dose limits. We then need to know in broad terms what levels of dose should act as triggers for particular kinds of action. In the UK if it is expected that the whole-body dose to members of the public is likely to exceed 30 millisieverts evacuation would need to be considered. Below that level it would be sufficient to take normal sensible precautions like staying indoors, closing doors and windows, and blocking off chimneys. This can provide a useful degree of protection, by perhaps as much as a factor of five. Taking potassium iodate tablets would also be useful, to inhibit the take-up by the thyroid of radioactive iodine (which is one of the fission products) when it arrives in the fall-out. Above a level of 300 millisieverts evacuation should be carried out unless there are overwhelming reasons to the contrary. In between these two levels is an area where judgement reached at the time is likely to be the best guide[130].

The doses from whole-body external radiation in the United Kingdom following Chernobyl were far below these levels. During the first year after the emergency they were between 0.02 millisieverts in areas which remained dry, and 0.2 millisieverts in wet areas where rain washed contamination out of the air. The average for the whole country was about 0.05 millisieverts, about one-fiftieth of a year's background radiation, or one-third of the European average. In sharp contrast, some of the Russian firemen who fought the Chernobyl fire received acute doses of 4 sieverts or more, which were rapidly fatal.

Regulating foodstuffs following an accident

Choosing limits up to which slightly contaminated food can still be regarded as fit for human consumption following a nuclear accident is a more complicated matter, both scientifically and politically—as the confusion within Europe in the days and weeks immediately after Chernobyl made abundantly clear to an anxious public. Chernobyl provided the much-needed trigger for rethinking the position. It released something like 2×10^{18} becquerels of activity—of which iodine–131, which is easily taken up by the thyroid, represented about 10 per cent, and caesium–137, with a thirty-year half-life, a further 2 per cent. The cloud reached Scandinavia on 28 April 1986, two days after the accident, and the UK by 2 May. In the following days the whole of Europe was affected. Each country, and sometimes different regions within the same country, used different trigger levels for controls over food distribution. Milk sold in Switzerland would have been banned in Germany; and even within Germany milk sold in Bavaria would not have been used in Hessen.

In choosing an intervention level for public health control which is consistent with the ICRP guidelines there are many variables to consider: the great mixture of fission-product radionuclides in the fall-out, each with their own half-life (see Technical Appendix for definitions); how they diffuse through the soil and are picked up by growing crops, or absorbed by cattle or sheep (or, in the case of the Lapps, reindeer); how quickly each kind of food gets to market, who buys it and in what quantities; and how the various radionuclides are absorbed or eliminated by the human body.

The controls needed after a once-in-a-lifetime accident whose effects will diminish with time are not necessarily the same as those needed in normal circumstances, where lower levels of radiation need to be controlled on the basis that they are a permanent feature of the environment. But the complexity of the calculations needed to reach *derived intervention levels* means that reaching an international consensus is bound to be difficult, unless very conservative figures are chosen. We quickly see that two levels may be needed—one for administration within a country, where a government can decide for its own good reasons on levels which it regards as acceptable in all the circumstances, but which minimize disruption of the normal patterns of life; and another, almost certainly lower set of levels, below which there should be no problems over international trade in foodstuffs, or arguments with foreign administrations whose views might differ in detail.

The ICRP has provided guidance which proposes controls over the distribution of foodstuffs if the dose to individual consumers could otherwise exceed 5 millisieverts as a result of contamination during the first year following an accident. This is equivalent to limiting the additional risk to each individual to about one in 5,000. The World Health Organization, as a guide to public health officials, prepared consumer-related derived intervention levels for various kinds of foodstuffs which were consistent with the ICRP guidelines. Table 8.3 gives illustrative figures for a variety of foodstuffs for non-plutonium contamination (i.e. caesium–134 and –137, strontium–90, and iodine–131).

Table 8.3. Examples of World Health Organization-Derived
Intervention Levels in Foodstuffs
(becquerels per kilogram)

Cereals	3,500
Roots and tubers	5,000
Vegetables	8,000
Fruit	7,000
Meat	10,000
Milk	4,500
Fish	35,000
Drinking-water	700

Sources: References 131, 132.

The fact that the figures are different for different foodstuffs implies a degree of administrative complexity as the price for minimizing the disruption of people's ordinary eating habits. The smooth operation of cross-border trade requires a simpler set of more conservative limits, to avoid argument at frontiers. The Food and Agriculture Organization, working with the World Health Organisation, produced such a simplified scheme for the Codex Alimentarius Commission to consider during 1989 (the Commission is the competent international body for developing harmonized food standards). In this simplified scheme controls over all radio-contaminants, other than strontium–90 and plutonium, are exercised under the global requirement that the total gamma activity should not exceed 1,000 becquerels per kilogram. This is roughly ten times greater than the radioactivity occurring naturally in most foods in the absence of a reactor accident—though some instant coffees and nuts approach this figure. These FAO recommended levels are lower—in some cases considerably lower—than strictly necessary, but their conservative nature should ensure that disruption of trade would be minimized. They involve a good deal of political judgement, which governments will doubtless keep under review. But should a future accident occur a basis has now been established which should avoid a repetition of the confusion which took place in Europe in the summer of 1986.

Radiation protection in uranium mining

The exposure of uranium miners to radiation—external gamma rays, and internal exposure to the daughter-products of ore dust and of the radioactive gas radon–222—has frequently been used by nuclear objectors as a moral argument against nuclear power. Usually no comparisons are made with the hazards inseparable from other forms of mineral extraction, including coal and oil. The reality is that at least since the sixteenth century lung cancer has been a fairly common mining hazard, almost irrespective of the mineral being mined, because of the widespread occurrence of uranium, and therefore radon, in the earth's crust. Before the risks of radon exposure were properly understood the situation was certainly serious. A paper published in 1879 stated that half of all deceased silver miners in the Joachimstahl region of what is now Czechoslovakia had malignant changes in their respiratory tracts. They were clearly suffering from the same 'Schneeberg disease' that was recorded in the Middle Ages amongst miners of the same area. Today the need for a proper level of ventilation in mines with high concentrations of uranium is a basic safety requirement. Moreover, the arrival of uranium mining *per se* has undoubtedly contributed to a far higher awareness within the mining community as a whole of the need for dealing with the radon hazard—even in mines that have nothing to do with uranium.

Canada is the world's largest uranium producer, and the history of its mines[133] illustrates the improving trend. Underground mining for radium (a daughter-product of uranium which was sought for medical purposes) started at the Port Radium mine in the North-West Territories in 1933. Within a decade the focus of interest had become uranium itself, sources of radiation vastly greater than any obtainable from radium having become available with the invention of reactors. Port Radium continued as a uranium mine until 1960.

Studies made forty years later estimated the radon concentration in that mine in the mid-1940s to be many times greater than would nowadays be permitted. No forced ventilation was installed before 1947, after which the position progressively improved. By then the centre of Canadian uranium mining was moving to the province of Ontario, which in 1957 issued regulations limiting the amount of airborne radioactivity that would be permitted. However, excess lung cancers continued to develop, as they also did in the USA, and the limit was progressively lowered to the current standard. It was, however, not until 1978 that Canada designated uranium miners as 'atomic radiation workers', bringing them under the umbrella of the Atomic Energy Control Board. Further regulatory refinements, introduced five years later, were intended to take into account the totality of hazards from radiation exposure and ingestion: daughter-products of radon and thoron (another radioactive gas), radioactive dust, and gamma radiation coming from the uranium in the ore-body still to be mined.

In France the domestic uranium mining industry has been a state-owned enterprise, under the direct surveillance of the Commissariat à l'Énergie Atomique, whose developmental resources few private companies could match. The first tonne of uranium was produced in 1949; but it was another four years before the importance of radon–222 was fully appreciated. By 1956 a system of individual dosimetry for uranium miners had been established. However, monitoring alpha radiation presents some difficulties, and the early attempts at instrumentation were rather inaccurate. It took until the early 1980s before a reliable and more precise individual monitor was available, capable of measuring an individual worker's monthly internal irradiation from alpha particles and inhaled dust. Miners likely to experience more than 30 per cent of the annual exposure limit of 50 millisieverts are provided with these individual dosimeters. Their availability and relative accuracy have allowed mine managements for the first time to optimize operations and mine conditions—such as the quantity of ventilating air—so that individual monitoring and protection can go hand in hand with operational efficiency.

The basis for control in both Canada and France is the amount of airborne radioactivity in the air of the mine, defined in terms of the potential release of alpha particle energy during the chain of disintegrations leading from radon–222 to lead–210. Canada, like the USA, uses a practical engineers' unit, the 'Working Level Month' (WLM). The term originated at a conference in Salt Lake City in 1955, and was originally believed to be consistent with the intentions of the ICRP, in the sense that an exposure of 12 WLMs per year was expected to be safe. (One WLM is equivalent[133] to an exposure to one 'Working Level' of 3.7 becquerels of radon and its daughters, in equilibrium, per litre for a working month of 170 hours.) It is now believed that 12 WLM per year is too high to be an acceptable working limit. As further medical statistics became available, it became clear that in order to avoid excess lung cancers amongst miners a substantial reduction in the annual exposure to around 4 WLM per year was necessary (i.e. a concentration of radon daughters of one-third of a Working Level—which unfortunately makes the present terminology somewhat confusing). The reduction took place in Canada over the period 1973–5. The level of 4 WLM per year is regarded as a maximum: there is an overriding requirement that radiation exposure should be kept as low as reasonably achievable—the ALARA principle. The difference between today's uranium mining and what happened in earlier years is striking: at Port Radium it is estimated that the radon daughter concentrations in 1945 (before ventilation was fitted) totalled about 77 Working Levels, 38 WL in 1952, and were still as high as 10 WL in 1956.

France[134] keeps the average annual individual dose equivalent below—in most cases well below—a limit of 50 millisieverts, which corresponds roughly to the 4 WLM limit in North America. Consideration has been given in the USA to a further reduction in permitted levels.

Given this very encouraging improvement in the awareness of the need for protection since the late 1950s there can now be some confidence that lung cancer as a serious occupational hazard for today's miners is no longer a serious worry. No statistically significant excess, over the normal number of lung cancers, has been reported for either US or Czech workers with cumulative exposures below 100 WLM—which at the current permitted level would correspond to a twenty-five-year working life in the mines even at the maximum rate of 4 WLM per year. The record is in fact better than this: average annual exposures at the big underground Elliot Lake mines in Ontario have fallen from over 4 WLM per year in 1971 to a little over one in 1984. The average in France is around 2 WLM per year.

At such exposure levels the additional risk of dying from lung cancer in Canadian mines is less than that of dying from a fatal mining accident[133]. A miner who completes forty years work underground (few in fact come anywhere near to this) in the average conditions which have now been established in the Elliot Lake area would have an additional risk of dying from lung cancer of less than 1 per cent. Further protection for the worker has also come from the opening of surface mines like Key Lake in Saskatchewan—now the world's biggest uranium producer—where ventilation is not a problem.

There is, however, one factor which is working in the other

direction. Better basic knowledge about how uranium deposits were formed, and therefore where they are likely to be found, has resulted in the discovery of a few ore-bodies with astonishingly high uranium content. One such mine is Cigar Lake in Northern Saskatchewan, where the average mineralization[135] is 12 per cent uranium, and where it can be as high in some places as 60 per cent (compare this with the Rössing mine in Namibia, where the average grade is a mere 0.03 per cent). Some uranium daughter-products give off penetrating gamma radiation, which in such high-grade mines poses an additional hazard which must be circumvented by a suitable mining plan, and by remote-handling techniques.

Three other comparisons may be of general interest. Firstly, the limit of 4 WLM per year means that there is a sharp cut-off in occupational exposure at this level, or at a little below it. But one does not have to be a miner to experience such conditions: in Cornwall and Devon, in the south-west of England, there are estimated to be more than 20,000 houses whose inhabitants are exposed to radiation doses of more than 20 millisieverts (roughly 2 WLM) per year[110,111,113,136]. In these houses, therefore, radon levels are broadly similar to those found in a uranium mine. Energy-efficient houses elsewhere, where natural ventilation has been cut down to avoid wasting heat, can also reach one WLM per year, while a few are several times worse[14]—at which level they become a public health problem. In the UK, radon in houses may be responsible for 2,500 cases of lung cancer a year, in the USA[103,137] perhaps as many as 20,000. These are levels of risk a hundred times higher than those to the general population from nuclear energy. It is an extraordinary inconsistency for the same public that shows so much anxiety over industrial nuclear activities to remain so unconcerned over radon. In terms of public health policy some of the lavish expenditure of funds on nuclear waste facilities might arguably show better returns if devoted to a campaign of domestic radon reduction.

Secondly, some of the concern that has been expressed by anti-nuclear activists has been based on a belief that uranium miners are at much greater risk than coal-miners, and that it would therefore be more moral from this viewpoint to generate electricity by coal-burning. Whatever happened in the past—and both uranium and coal-mining were then more dangerous—this proposition is no longer true. An interesting comparison shows that if we compare risks on the basis of what happens *per gigawatt-year of electricity generated*, UK coal is about eight times more dangerous for the mine worker than underground uranium mines in Ontario or France, and nearly 300 times worse than the open-pit Key Lake uranium operation[14]. In terms of the risk of ordinary mining fatalities during a working lifetime uranium mining compares well with other types of mine[133]—and, unlike coal, uranium does not generally suffer from the hazards of explosive gases.

Thirdly, this concern over radon has benefited other kinds of miners. Most badly ventilated mines have radon problems, regardless of the mineral. In tin mines in the UK, for instance, miners were being exposed in some cases to 20 WLM every year, because of radon arising from the uranium content of the ore-bodies. This was put right after the mid-1970s by installing better ventilation. The porosity of the rock plays a part, because it allows radon to diffuse for considerable distances. This was also a problem in gypsum mines in the English Midlands which had gone for years unsuspected of harbouring a radon hazard.

This short chapter can only hint at the vast efforts that have gone into understanding the effects of radiation on the human body, and regulating the extent to which people can be allowed to be exposed. Perhaps only the aviation industry shows a comparable concern over safety, and for a very similar reason: the highly trained practitioners, and in some cases their families, are themselves in the front line. The result is that risks from the normal operation of atomic energy installations are today well under control. If any new fact emerges which is prima-facie surprising—like the reported and so far unexplained 'clusters' of childhood leukaemias in the neighbourhood of the Sellafield reprocessing plant—it is likely to be concerned with small-scale effects, and will in any case immediately be made the subject of a public inquiry or research study. Apart from such research, the emphasis need no longer be on further protection at any price, but on how much it is worth spending—resources always being limited—for what, given the existence of the natural radiation background, can often at best be only marginal improvements.

Accidents are of course another matter; even so, a philosophy has been evolved about how the public should be protected. But the best protection is avoidance of major reactor accidents. That is the subject of the next chapter.

9   Reactor Safety and Nuclear Insurance

A GOOD deal of modern engineering involves a Faustian bargain between the public and the technologists: an acceptance of benefits here and now, but a discounting of future dangers—which, while theoretically possible, 'will never happen here'. This was indisputably true of nuclear power at the outset. The problem is that despite all the professional assurances of scrupulous care in design, manufacture, and operation, two major accidents have indeed 'happened here'; and moreover in quick succession, at Three Mile Island and Chernobyl. Inevitably, the public is uneasy about the bargain.

The Technical Appendix deals with the basic physics of reactors, and what could go wrong. In simple terms a reactor is a machine for making steam or hot gas, which then powers a turbine, which turns an electric generator. The special problem of reactor engineering is not that the reactor might explode like a nuclear weapon: the most that could happen, even with catastrophically inept operation, is an explosion equivalent to that from a few hundred kilograms of TNT. While substantial, this is 50,000 times smaller than even the 'small' Hiroshima bomb, and the direct explosive effects would be limited to the immediate vicinity. The problem is rather that, unlike other machines, once a reactor has been running for any appreciable time the heat it produces cannot be completely turned off. Moreover the core is intensely radioactive and cannot be approached directly; safety inspections are far from straightforward; and if a serious failure occurs some of the radioactivity might be released to the environment.

When a shut-down is ordered the heat production falls immediately to about 6 per cent of normal power—which for a modern one GWe reactor is 200,000 kilowatts. A day later it is about ten times less; but this is still a large quantity of heat. This residual heat is generated by the radioactivity of the fission products, which falls away very slowly (see Technical Appendix). Unless we can guarantee that the reactor core will be kept cool, either passively because of the intrinsic properties of the design, or actively through cooling arrangements of guaranteed reliability (the 'emergency core-cooling system'), it will eventually overheat and, if left long enough, melt. Part of the radioactivity will then escape into the surrounding 'containment' building—the large pressure-vessel completely enclosing the reactor—which is provided on almost every Western reactor, but which, significantly, was not a feature of the Chernobyl design. If the containment fails; or if it has to be vented (which would be done through filters) to avoid a dangerous build-up of pressure; or if it is bypassed in some way—then some of the radioactivity could reach the external environment. What would happen thereafter would depend very much on the scale of the release. At the uncontained Chernobyl reactor thirty-two people were killed by radiation as a result of the early stages of making the reactor safe, and 135,000 had to be evacuated. At the far better protected Three Mile Island the hazards to anyone outside the reactor compound, despite the accompanying near-panic, were insignificant.

The public, being uncertain what might happen should anything go wrong with one of its local reactors, is keeping an open mind. The industry, knowing that any further major accidents in the near-term future could have the gravest policy consequences, has taken the lessons to heart. If to err is human, it is also human to learn from others' mistakes. Reactor safety philosophy, details of reactor design, the efforts made to prevent operators from making mistakes, the regulatory framework, the regime of international conventions which come into force should another serious accident occur, compulsory insurance—all have all changed, and are still changing for the better in the light of experience and deeper understanding of the problems. The position is far from static, and risk predictions made on the basis of the position today are almost bound to be over-pessimistic. But anxieties will remain—if not for ever, then certainly for decades—and will inevitably colour the public's attitude.

The approach to safety

Everything touching on safety must be systematically and meticu-lously planned[138]. Operating responsibilities must be scrupulously observed, from the owners of the plant down to the operators. The limits to permissible action must be understood and adhered to. Safety must be built into every aspect of the design. A first safeguard is redundancy: a deliberate excess of protection systems. A second is diversity: a variety of different systems, operating in different ways, so that one systemic fault cannot put all of them out of service simultaneously. A third is rigorous use of the 'fail-safe' principle—so that if a failure occurs the system automatically places itself in a condition that is more secure, not less. A fourth precaution is the physical separation of vital functions—so that, for instance, a local fire cannot destroy the whole safety system. Everything possible is done to prevent incidents starting; but if they do, operator training and protection systems come into play to mitigate their effects. The philosophy is summed-up in the phrase: 'if it matters it must not happen; if it happens it must not matter'.

Whenever possible reactors are designed to incorporate inherent nuclear safety features, such as a negative temperature-coefficient of reactivity (see Technical Appendix), to damp down the nuclear chain reaction automatically should the temperature rise (the Chernobyl reactor had a positive coefficient, which made it dangerous in a power runaway); or neutron-absorbing safety systems which drop automatically under gravity into the core in the event of a sufficiently strong warning signal. Shut-down systems should remove large amounts of reactivity (see Appendix) very quickly (at Chernobyl they were disastrously slow-acting). The steel of the primary pressure-vessel must not be liable to brittle fracture, and must have the necessary toughness and crack-resistance. Quality assurance everywhere is essential. Safety margins are carefully considered, components rigorously tested. Core cooling is divided between a number of parallel circuits, or 'loops', to allow for regular maintenance and pump replacement. Emergency core cooling systems guarantee that cooling will continue after an emergency shut-down, even if the main coolant-pumps are out of action.

For further protection the reactor is given a substantial measure of passive safety, by being enclosed in a large 'containment' pressure-vessel. The containment is only the last of several successive barriers to the escape of radioactivity into the environment. The first is the ceramic temperature-resistant nuclear fuel that is now used almost universally; the second its leak-tight and corrosion-resistant cladding; the third the integrity of the primary coolant circuit. Unlike the other barriers to the prevention of escape of fission products, the containment does not itself take part in the operation of the reactor, being there only as a final line of defence in the event of failure elsewhere.

When the TMI accident occurred an unexpectedly small proportion of the fission products (the 'source term') which escaped from the reactor found their way into the outside environment. This led to an extended research programme, which confirmed[139] that a 'plating-out' process had occurred, with the overwhelming majority of the fission products being deposited on the interior surfaces of the containment. The proportion of fission-product species escaping into the atmosphere was reduced in some cases by several orders of magnitude. The only fission products which did escape at TMI in approximately the anticipated amounts were those, like krypton and iodine, which exist in gaseous or vapour form. This previously unforeseen ability of containment buildings to trap the bulk of the fission products so effectively, even if there is some leakage, is of enormous importance to the safety of all who live in the vicinity of contained nuclear reactors, provided the containment has not been seriously breached in the course of an accident.

To reduce that likelihood containment vessels for pressurized and boiling-water reactors are typically designed to stand a few atmospheres pressure with a good margin of safety. To prevent a larger pressure build-up a spray system operates to condense any steam, while mitigation systems deal with the potentially explosive hydrogen which can be produced by the action of radiation on water, and by the chemical reaction between steam and zirconium fuel cladding (at Three Mile Island a hydrogen reaction produced a pressure-pulse of two atmospheres, without damaging the containment). With graphite reactors the need is to avoid entry of air, and to keep the graphite sufficiently cool to avoid any chemical reaction. In some reactors controlled venting of the containment is allowed as a precaution against a dangerous pressure rise. This would be done via filters which would remove at least 90 per cent of any aerosols.

Container integrity depends to some extent on safe design and operation. The Chernobyl accident released about the same amount of energy as a quarter of a ton of high explosive, according to a French estimate. That could not have been dealt with by existing containment vessels. But such an unstable design as Chernobyl should not have been allowed in the first place. Safety has to be judged as a whole.

Safety analysis

With this degree of built-in safety the probability of a severe accident is very low indeed, though unfortunately not as low as the first risk assessments suggested. The first serious attempt, in 1975, to estimate the probability of a major accident[46] concluded that the chance of a major accident, on something like the scale of what happened eleven years later at Chernobyl, was one in a billion years of reactor operation. With the experience of two major accidents in less than a decade, this clearly cannot be right, even allowing for the serious deficiencies in the Chernobyl safety arrangements. The analytical error lay partly in the failure to explore all the possible modes by which a number of simultaneous smaller and more likely failures could combine to produce an accident-provoking situation, and partly in the difficulties of modelling human error. The analysis had in fact been rejected as unreliable by the American Nuclear Regulatory Commission even before the 1979 Three Mile Island accident. Nevertheless, risk analysis is an essential part of the safety armoury. It provides a disciplined framework for working through the large number of factors (Table 9.1) that are relevant to safety. It may not reveal the whole truth, but what it does help to identify is extremely important.

Table 9.1 Factors Relevant to Reactor-Hazard Evaluation

Basic reactor features:
   Design, structures, fuel, moderator
   Resistance to design-base accidents (DBAs)
   Stability of reactor throughout the power range
   Speed and effectiveness of control system
   On/off load refuelling
   Number of independent core-cooling circuits ('loops')
   Post-shut-down heating and heat-removal system
   Quality assurance in manufacture
Support and safety systems:
   Inherent safety, redundancy, diversity, autarky
   Quality standards
   Passive safety systems (e.g. barriers, filters)
   Active safety systems (e.g. cooling, emergency feedwater)
   Guaranteed emergency power supplies
   Man–machine control interface

Containment:
  Materials (steel, concrete), and how they age
  Design pressure, free volume, energy release in design-basis accidents
  Pressure suppression, controlled ventilation, bypassing
  Hydrogen control
  Melt-through resistance of floor
  Tests against plane crash, earthquake, etc.
Overall safety:
  Previous experience of systems under accident conditions
  Complexity of system
  Have all possible event chains been identified?
  Is the reactor easy to inspect?
  How sensitive to sabotage or war?
  What steps have been taken to avoid operator confusion?
  Consequences of worst-possible scenario
  How reliable are existing safety reviews?
  Have independent safety reviews been made?
  What accidents have already occurred with this type?
  Are there known weak points?
  Manufacturing country's attitude to reactor safety
  Vigilance of user-country's regulatory authorities
  Secondary hazards: adjacent reactors or used-fuel storage
  Difficulties of decommissioning

A basic tool in safety analysis is a series of hypothetical 'design-basis accidents' (DBAs). They are accidents which could conceivably happen, and whose consequences must therefore be made tolerable. Accidents worse than DBAs could have unacceptable consequences, and must therefore be made inconceivable on any reasonable judgement. The operator is provided with detailed procedures for managing faults within the range of DBAs, and is responsible for seeing that the plant does not operate outside its design limits.

Fault analysis can be either 'deterministic' or 'probabilistic'. With the former, postulated causes are assumed to lead to deduced effects—a conceptually straightforward approach which leads to a choice of safety systems. Probabilistic analysis is based on fault and event trees, which trace out the possible sequences in which events could occur. On the basis of past experience this approach can be used to quantify risk from known mechanical and electrical faults and failures, though it is not easily applied to human error.

For example: in the case of a pressurized-water reactor a DBA may specify a certain size of rupture which could conceivably occur in the primary circuit. This would then define the volume of containment space needed to handle the resulting pressure rise, and the emergency arrangements for holding it down by condensing the steam. Or, against loss of the main coolant-pumps, separate emergency core-cooling systems would be provided to deal with shut-down heating for a specified time, consistent with the nature of the relevant DBA.

This analytical approach in principle allows probabilities to be assigned to the various danger levels, which helps in judging whether sufficient safety protection has been provided. A judgement of what is 'sufficient' is necessarily subjective. The target in the UK is to ensure that the risk to individuals from accidents is less than one in a million per year. On the basis of DBAs a lower figure of one in one hundred million per year can be deduced for the new pressurized water reactor at Sizewell B. Smaller incidents could happen more frequently; so it is essential that their consequences should be less serious. In this way a picture is built up of the potential risk to the reactor and its surroundings, which must be kept at a level which will not interfere with the life of the community. For Western-style reactors with containment, the calculated risks to the population are negligible.

It is of course always possible to invent a theoretically feasible, if extremely unlikely, chain of events which might leave the reactor unprotected. Objectors will therefore always be able to criticize almost any chosen safety arrangement (e.g. reference 140); but equally those responsible for the design and its licensing can defend their choices in good faith, as good practical engineering solutions.

It is worth remarking that a safety debate would go on even if there were no anti-nuclear pressure groups, partly for the normal reasons of professional curiosity, but also because electrical utilities have a variety of reactor types to choose from, with many possible configurations, from several possible suppliers. In their own interests the utilities need to maximize reliability and safety, and therefore cross-check the solutions that are on offer. They are also linked with other utilities by a variety of professional networks, including the Institute of Nuclear Power Operations that was set up after Three Mile Island, and the extremely important World Association of Nuclear Operators (WANO) that came into existence as a direct result of Chernobyl[141]. As experience is accumulated the small residual dangers from unforeseen failure modes and operator errors will steadily diminish. A reasonable initial safety target would be no major reactor accident anywhere in the world for the next hundred years. Allowing for growth, that is ten or twenty times better than the record so far. However, given what we now know about the causes of TMI and Chernobyl, and the many steps that have since been taken to improve safety, that kind of improvement does not seem out of reach. Comparable progress is taken for granted in aviation safety. But for nuclear power only long experience can provide actual proof.

The free information-flow and peer-group appraisal that underlie this confident expectation are part of Western culture; but for years there was nothing comparable in the East. Truly free professional discussion was impossible in the secretive USSR of the pre-Gorbachev era. The inherent instability of the Chernobyl RBMK reactor design when operating at low power had long been known in the West; but there was no forum where a proper safety debate could be effectively mounted, no readiness to listen, and certainly no willingness to depart from an established reactor policy which had developed such momentum. The Chernobyl disaster was a watershed. The Soviet Union's new and apparently sincere commitment to *glasnost*, and its enthusiastic sponsorship of WANO, are grounds—one cultural, one professional—for believing that this blindness to the need for peer-group criticism is a thing of the past in the Soviet Union.

Human factors

To assume a perfectly rational operator reaction to every failure would be to ignore the lessons of experience. Operators get tired; they get confused. It was operator confusion, created by a misleading signal in the control room, which turned a single mechanical failure at Three Mile Island into a full-scale accident (page 110). Reactors must as far as possible be made 'operator-proof'. Unfortunately irrational or confused behaviour is not the stuff of which good statistics are made, and risk analysis stops short of assigning probabilities to particular kinds of operator error.

We cannot do without the operator, who must be there to monitor that nothing is going wrong; but there is no need to rely on him as much as at Chernobyl. The difficulty was that the safety of the Soviet RBMK reactors depended far more on implicit obedience by the operating crew to rigorous, predetermined, and on the whole sensible procedures than on built-in safety. Of the reactor's 211 neutron absorbing rods, no less than 163 were manually operated. It was absolutely forbidden to operate the reactor with less than 30 rods in the core, for reasons of control effectiveness; but when the accident happened calculations suggest that the operators had withdrawn all but 6 to 8 rods—a scandalous case of disobedience. Their actions showed a complete lack of awareness of the dangerously unstable characteristics of the reactor they were supposed to be controlling. In flouting the operating regulations they destroyed the whole basis of Chernobyl's pitifully weak margin of safety[142–4]. The primary design error at Chernobyl lay in relying on the operator as the primary protection for a complex system.

Far more of the safety protection in a modern Western nuclear power-station is automatic, and it comes into action much faster. The operator is there primarily as a system manager, to monitor the safe operation of the plant. The plant process computers are there to relieve him of much of the load, and to give him time to think should conditions require his intervention. The operator therefore needs to be kept informed of the functioning of all safety systems, so that decisions can be taken in good time, and correctly. The information is needed in a form in which it can be easily assimilated under what might be conditions of stress. This may be more easily said than done: at Three Mile Island the operators' misreading of a situation which had already been partly brought under control by the automatic safety systems contributed to the seriousness of the accident. Afterwards an intensive re-examination took place of the 'man–machine interface', to avoid a repetition of the confusing instrumental indications that had led to the accident.

Operating a nuclear plant has something in common with piloting an aeroplane when cruising at high altitude on a long-distance flight. In both cases the minute-by-minute operation is largely automated; but the human controllers must understand the various systems, how to respond to deviations from normal, and how to restore correct operating conditions. In both cases boredom and fatigue are potential dangers. But there the resemblance ends. A nuclear operator does not have the stimulus of constant changes of scene, or of the landings, every one different, and accompanied by a guiding sense of self-preservation. Other ways must be found or invented of retaining his attention during the period on watch, where the ideal outcome is that nothing abnormal should disturb the smoothly running routine. Operators need to be deliberately 'sensitized' so that they are fully aware that their machine, which normally behaves with such docility, could show a very different face if badly handled.

Operator comprehension is the central issue. A reactor's automatic monitoring and safety systems handle more data than any human mind can easily assimilate. The operator needs an appropriate résumé of the most relevant information, with the rest available to be called on only if necessary. The development of modern colour-graphic television-type interactive display systems has made this entirely possible. Should a reactor fault occur the key information can be displayed automatically. In older stations information is displayed in logical order on carefully designed control panels, with easily understood symbols denoting the current state of each piece of equipment.

There remains the problem of how to ensure a correct operator response should an abnormal situation develop—as is possible with any piece of equipment. It is obviously necessary to start with people of the right background and temperament. The task is akin to engineering watch-keeping at sea, and indeed many of the early reactors were manned by ex-naval watchkeepers. Training through simulation is important. Modern simulators can exactly duplicate the control panels used in actual nuclear stations, and can reproduce possible system faults. Just as with airline pilots, periodical refresher courses maintain an operator's diagnostic competence. If he moves to a different type of reactor, he can become familiar with the equipment's handling characteristics before taking charge.

In addition to good training, properly thought-out operating procedures lie at the heart of reactor safety. They were missing at Chernobyl, where the team not only had little idea of the safety implications of the experiment they were attempting, but had made no effort to secure approval from a competent authority. The Chernobyl example stands as a permanent warning to operating teams everywhere. An Italian delegate pointed out to a surprised Academician Legasov at the international post-mortem held at Vienna in August 1986, that in some Western countries such flagrant disregard of safety procedures would be a criminal offence.

Properly thought-out procedures should identify, in advance, the expected consequences of any plant changes which might be contemplated; the steps which might be critical from a safety viewpoint; the measurements which would indicate that everything is going as expected; and the deviations which could represent potential danger signals, and so require corrective action.

Proper procedures are especially necessary when the operating crew is under stress, if things have started to go wrong. For that type of situation Électricité de France[144] has introduced special 'ultimate procedures':

We do not ask the operator to try to understand what has happened in his reactor; we just want him to look at a few very simple things. Is at least one steam generator available? Is safety injection in service or not? Then a glance at a few parameters. What is the temperature of the coolant compared with the saturation temperature (to see if the water is going to boil)? What is the temperature, and rate of increase of temperature with time? With a few such parameters . . . we can give the operator precise instructions with the objective of saving the reactor core.

Électricité de France has gone still further, by providing an additional degree of peer-group consultation on site—in effect deliberate human redundancy—in the event of abnormal conditions arising. A special safety officer is present on watch, as supernumary. He monitors what is happening, but intervenes only if a significant abnormality arises, when he takes charge. After encouraging results when this approach was tried out on a simulator EdF recruited 160 engineers to fill such positions, which they hold for about three years.

Since the unexpected may always happen, despite every care, each nuclear power-station maintains an 'event reporting system', to record and investigate any abnormal functioning of equipment or operator error. The log is reviewed by independent safety experts. If the consequences go beyond certain pre-defined safety thresholds they must be reported to the regulatory authorities. The details may also be passed to the International Atomic Energy Agency's Incident Reporting System, which provides a world-wide information service which alerts management and operators everywhere to incidents which could shed light on the safety of their own operations. The World Association of Nuclear Operators provides an independent industry-level reporting and assessment organization for the 130 or so electrical utilities which operate nuclear reactors, or plan to do so. If this regular exchange had existed in 1979 the Three Mile Island accident might never have taken place, since a mechanical failure like the one which set off the accident sequence had occurred a few months earlier at the very similar Davis-Besse reactor, near Toledo.

Despite the most careful organization occasional cases are reported where operator complacency and poor supervision allow slack and potentially dangerous operation to continue. The case of the Peach Bottom reactor in the USA reached the newspapers in the spring of 1987, with stories of operating crews asleep on duty or absent from the control room, or at other times reading, while the reactor (which was fortunately very reliable) was under the sole control of the automatic systems. The fact that no disaster occurred was, rightly, not allowed to mitigate the severity of the punishment that was meted out by the regulatory authorities. Reactor 'safety culture', like peace, must be indivisible—and must be seen to be so (see also page 111).

The sharp reaction of the US Nuclear Regulatory Commission was a world away from the complacency it had shown over operating problems prior to Three Mile Island. Requirements for training were then minimal, and there were no established criteria for certifying the instructors' competence. Although the NRC routinely collected reports on reactor operation, there was no systematic attempt to distil lessons regarding best practice. The US administration's General Accounting Office pointed out these deficiencies in a critique of the NRC in 1978, but no effective action had been taken by the time the TMI accident occurred in the following year. Since then the National Academy for Nuclear Training has been created. These criticisms would not apply in the USA today.

Emergency planning

Since it would be unrealistic and irresponsible to assume that no accident could ever take place, emergency planning is a vital part of 'defence-in-depth'. In a sense it begins before the first concrete is poured, with the choice of site, which should minimize as far as possible any risk to the population. In practice, particularly in small and crowded industrial countries like Belgium, Switzerland, or the UK, siting choices are restricted. So we have the Doel reactor only

15 kilometres from Antwerp, Muhleberg 15 kilometres from Berne, and Hinkley Point 30 kilometres from Cardiff. The safety of the local area then depends in the last resort on the safety systems and the integrity of the containment.

Emergency planning involves establishing a system for informing the safety authorities what is happening; for warning the public at large to stay indoors, as the first (and really quite useful) protective action; setting up a system for radiation monitoring; arranging for restrictions to be placed when necessary on the consumption of foodstuffs if contaminated; distributing iodine tablets (to mitigate the effects of radio-iodine escape, by swamping any radio-iodine that might otherwise be taken up by the thyroid with stable, non-radioactive iodine); and, if the release of radioactivity exceeds a pre-determined level, arranging for evacuation and follow-up actions like restrictions on the consumption of water and food, medical surveillance of any exposed members of the population, and in due course decontamination of the ground. All this was made familiar through the unfolding of events at Chernobyl.

A crucial factor in these emergency plans is the distance from the reactor within which special measures might be needed to safeguard the safety of the general population, on the assumption that the containment will provide a substantial measure of emergency protection. In France the 'reference distances' for emergency planning are a radius of 5 kilometres for evacuation and 10 kilometres for confinement of the population indoors. It is believed that the built-in safety features of French reactors are consistent with these figures, since they virtually guarantee that any release of radioactivity would be less than 1 per cent of that at Chernobyl, where evacuation out to 30 kilometres was necessary. If this guarantee could not be given it is obvious that in the crowded countries of Western Europe there would be real difficulties over reactor siting. In the UK there are predetermined emergency plans within a radius of 1.5 miles, and arrangements for a flexible response outside that zone. These should ensure that for at least the Reference Accident—the worst design-basis accident—the population could be evacuated quickly enough to avoid contamination from the passing radioactive plume. Evacuation of larger areas would only be necessary for severe beyond-design-basis accidents. In the USA the radius within which emergency planning is mandatory is 10 miles—it is this which caused the problem with the local authorities in the adjoining State of Massachusetts at the Seabrook reactor in New Hampshire (Chapter 5). Some Americans have expressed anxiety at this figure, pointing out that at Chernobyl the population was evacuated out to a radius nearly twice as great; but unlike Chernobyl Seabrook is contained.

Anxieties

Challenges to reactor safety assessments continue to be mounted by anti-nuclear pressure groups. They are of two kinds. One cites the potential implications of actual incidents, where things went unexpectedly wrong, but where a serious accident was averted by a combination of favourable circumstances. The other seeks to expose weaknesses in the technical arguments on which safety analyses are based.

The incident at the Brown's Ferry power station, Alabama, on 22 March 1975 was in the first category[145]. Reactors 1 and 2, which shared a common control room, were at full power, and a third reactor was under construction. The control room was outside the reactor building, which was normally sealed and under slight negative pressure, as a design precaution against emission of radioactivity into the atmosphere. An air leak was however discovered at the point where the cable trays passed through the reactor building wall on their way to the control room. The leak was difficult to pinpoint because of the mass of cabling, and to track it down a workman used a candle as a simple test to locate the draught. In doing so he set fire to the polyurethane sealing, and the draught caused the flames to spread to places which were not easily accessible. The damage to the cabling launched a chain of electrical faults. After about twenty minutes the operator on reactor 1 noticed a succession of anomalous indications, and ten minutes later shut down the reactor. Because of damaged circuitry there were difficulties in ensuring the removal of radioactive shut-down heating, and the redundancy normally available as a 'belt and braces' safety precaution was seriously reduced, though the problems were successfully overcome. Reactor 2 was shut down about ten minutes after reactor 1, and was less affected.

At St-Laurent-des-Eaux in France the morning of 12 January 1987 was very cold. An accumulation of ice in the inlet taking cooling-water from the River Loire blocked the flow, causing an automatic shut-down of the No. 1 graphite-gas reactor and the main generators. At the same time the small auxiliary generators, intended to provide electrical services for the station, also tripped. Services were restored by temporary connection to the grid, and an hour later the auxiliary generators were restarted. A few hours later that same morning, also due to the cold weather, a large coal-fired station at Cordemais, near Nantes, tripped off-line, causing such a drop in the national grid voltage that four 1.3 MWe PWRs, two 0.9 GWe PWRs, and the other gas-cooled reactor at St-Laurent-des-Eaux also tripped. One-third of France was without power for one or two hours. The solution to avoiding that multiple-tripping problem proved to be a simple readjustment of the voltage-trip levels. While neither incident led to particularly serious consequences, critics were quick to point out that if St-Laurent had been unable to rely on the grid while its auxiliary generators were out of service there might have been an emergency core-cooling problem.

These are only two out of a dozen or so potentially serious incidents that have occurred over the past couple of decades, all of them arising from some combination of circumstances which could not possibly have been foreseen in detail. More serious consequences were avoided by a combination of defence in depth, equipment duplication, operator action and a sprinkling of good luck. Critics complain, first, that this is not an adequate basis for assuring the safety of the thousands of people who live close to the affected reactors; and secondly that if such incidents can occur, they call into question the validity of predictions of a very low incidence of serious accidents, even though the reactors were protected by redundancy and diversity.

There is no way, other than long-term experience, of finally resolving the argument. Meanwhile such incidents, through their impact on design and safety philosophy, provide important stepping-stones towards reactors that are more comprehensively safe. It is this learning process which tends to be omitted from the sometimes technically excellent critiques produced by the anti-nuclear pressure-groups (e.g. reference 140).

A second kind of criticism challenges the technical assumptions lying behind current assessments of reactor safety. A crucial issue concerns the integrity of the reactor pressure-vessels used to house the reactor core, and in the process contain the gas or water coolant, which is at very high pressure. The vessels are of course built from materials with the necessary toughness, and their design ensures that the material is not overstressed, provided it is free from defects. The practical problem is that structural materials are rarely perfect: pressure vessels commonly include small cracks, which if large enough might propagate and lead to catastrophic failure—as in the cases of a small number of aircaft whose pressure-cabins have exploded after long service. With pressure-tube reactors (see Technical Appendix), this would not be catastrophic, because a crack would reach the outside of the material, causing a leak, before complete failure occurred: this is 'leak-before-break'. The concrete pressure-vessels for gas-cooled reactors are also free from crack propagation, because the material is not itself homogeneous.

The worry has been over the large pressure-vessels needed for pressurized and boiling-water reactors. These are 3 or 4 metres in internal diameter, and may be 13 metres high. The walls are about 20 centimetres thick, and even more at the lid-seating and flanges. Here there is no possibility of 'leak-before-break': a crack large enough to reach the outside of the vessel would also lead to its rapid failure in a fraction of a second. It is therefore essential to prevent the existence of cracks greater than the critical size at which they could propagate. This is normally around 10 centimetres in the tough crack-resistant steels used for pressure-vessels; but in some circumstances it could be as little as 2–3 centimetres, which is not far above the size that can be reliably identified by ultrasonic crack-detection methods.

A prolonged debate, which continued in the United Kingdom for more than a decade in the 1970s and 1980s, eventually led to the conclusion that modern crack-detection methods can indeed provide adequate defences[146,147]. A vessel failure-rate of between one in a million, and one in one hundred million vessel-years has been estimated as being attainable—subject to the important proviso that all necessary precautions have been taken. These include adopting a design which avoids stress concentrations as far as possible; using properly specified materials of the right strength and fracture toughness, including a limitation on impurities like copper which could lead to radiation embrittlement; insisting on competent quality control during manufacture; and thorough inspection subsequently, preferably by more than one independent team. The need for care continues after the vessel enters reactor service, because crack propagation could occur if a hot vessel were subjected to fatigue by temperature cycling; or, in an extreme case, by thermal shock due to the injection of cold cooling water. The pressure vessel's integrity depends on the control system's ability to prevent such shocks, and on well thought-out and reliable operating procedures.

The integrity of the reactor pressure-vessel in PWRs and BWRs underpins that of the containment building. Should a vessel fail it may be impossible to guarantee that the containment would remain intact. The possibility of a release of fission products on the same scale as at Chernobyl would then have to be considered. While such an accident is very highly improbable, it cannot in principle be totally excluded. This raises a problem over safety clearance. France resolves the difficulty by accepting that certain kinds of accident are so improbable that in practice they can be ignored. Other countries prefer to retain a conscious acknowledgement in public discussion of a finite though very small probability that a serious containment failure cannot be wholly excluded. Provided the probabilities are indeed very small—and there is no reason to think otherwise—there is little between the two positions from a practical standpoint. Nevertheless, the anti-nuclear pressure groups are unlikely to let such points drop, until accumulated experience has shown their fears to be of no practical consequence; and that will take many decades.

'Inherently safe' reactors

Only a few years ago reactor technology seemed to be on the point of becoming 'mature'—in the sense that few radically new concepts were on the horizon. But a combination of factors, including notably the consequences of the Chernobyl disaster, led to a radical rethinking of how reactor design should evolve. The consideration in everyone's mind was that, with existing reactor designs, it is impossible to give an absolute guarantee that mechanical failure or operator error will not have disastrous consequences. Sophisticated, and therefore usually expensive, engineering reduces the chances of disaster to a very low figure; but that is not the same as offering a guarantee based on fundamental laws of physics having the same reliability as, for instance, the force of gravity. An exploration was begun of designs offering a high degree of passive safety, which would allow the operators a far longer period than they had at

TMI—many hours or days instead of twenty or thirty minutes—in which to think out how to respond to an emergency.

A second consideration was the urgent need to simplify the licensing process by introducing standard reactor designs which could be replicated exactly. As already emphasized, standardization has so far been the exception rather than the rule. Almost every reactor has been different, and as licensing necessarily depends on the meticulous working-out of the consequences of design *details*, the clearance process has been an administrative nightmare. If licensing approval, for all aspects except site characteristics, could be taken as available at the time of ordering—as it is for commercial aircraft—a major stumbling-block would disappear.

A third point concerns the size of today's large reactors—up to 1.4 GWe in a single unit. This has resulted from a search for economies of scale, in an effort to better the economics of coal-fired generation: within a given reactor family doubling the size reduces the cost per installed kilowatt by roughly 30 per cent. However, such large outputs bring with them the problem of dealing with decay heating after shut-down with absolute certainty in an emergency. Moreover the market for these large reactors is limited by the inability of many electricity grids, especially in small countries or the Third World, to accept such large additional amounts of electrical power; while the engineering complexity requires a degree of operator competence not always available in non-industrial countries. It had long been assumed that smaller reactors better suited to the Third World's electricity grids would necessarily be 'uneconomic': that assumption too has come to be questioned.

These considerations were brought together in 1986 in a design initiative which was given strong support by the US electrical utilities, through the Electric Power Research Institute. The design targets included: building on existing technology where possible; achieving certainty of licensing; speeding up assembly; maintaining good economics; improving safety margins for the reactor pressure vessel; assuring a core-melt frequency of less than one in 100,000 years, which would offer high protection for the owners' investment (TMI was a financial disaster, even though the public was protected by the containment); improving seismic resistance, which should be made easier by having smaller buildings; and, most importantly, incorporating passive safety features which would allow up to three days in which to work out a plan for dealing with an emergency, during which time the reactor could safely be left to its own devices. Sweden had already been thinking independently on such lines, with its PIUS reactor; but the new US interest, born out of what was fast becoming a licensing policy impasse, provided a major impetus. The work of EPRI is being pursued with the active support of several countries, including France and Japan.

There is now some confidence that these targets can be met, and in a variety of ways; though until full safety assessments have been completed it would be prudent to avoid an excess of optimism. The Westinghouse Advanced Passive 600 MWe design offers decay heat removal by natural circulation, with 60 per cent fewer valves than a normal PWR, 60 per cent less pipework, and 80 per cent less cabling. General Electric's Safe Boiling-Water reactor aims to go further, by being able to operate at full power without pumps, using only natural circulation. Like the AP600, it too aims to offer three days of passive safety in the event of a fault. These two reactors were given the support of the US Department of Energy in the summer of 1989. Licensing by the US Nuclear Regulatory Commission should be greatly simplified because the designs build on established light-water reactor technology.

In Britain the Atomic Energy Authority and Rolls Royce have designed the Safe Integral Reactor, of 320 MWe, which packs the entire primary circuit and core into a single pressure-vessel of the same diameter as that for Sizewell, enabling the whole to be fabricated prior to assembly. It too offers passive shut-down cooling. The 600 MWe Swedish PIUS (process inherent ultimate safety) reactor design goes further still, by dispensing with any need for conventional control rods. It has been described as a reactor in a swimming-pool, which exploits the inherent thermo-hydraulic safety of an ingenious interfacing of the reactor cooling-water with a lower and cooler pool of borated water. If a fault develops, the borated water—boron is a strong neutron absorber—floods the reactor core automatically without any need for mechanical or human intervention, and closes down the reactor.

Apart from these light-water reactor projects there are further lines of development, making use of the high-temperature safety of helium-cooled ceramic fuel elements containing dispersed grains of uranium, or the excellent heat-removal characteristics of liquid metals.

Admiral Rickover, the creator of the US nuclear Navy, liked to distinguish between 'academic reactors', which existed only on paper, and practical reactors—those which had been built and shown to work as intended. While the implied warning against over-optimism is as salutary as ever, the momentum behind the drive for reactor safety is such that several of these reactor designs will undoubtedly be taken to completion. Moreover, as three of them build on the experience drawn from thousands of light-water reactor-years of service, they can reasonably be expected to operate as predicted. Their economics are also expected to match those of today's far larger reactors (Table 6.1). If these expectations are fulfilled this could transform the outlook for nuclear power, as regards both public acceptability and financing.

National safety regulation and its international implications

Every country with a nuclear power programme has established its own regulatory body as policeman and surrogate for the public interest. In the United States the Nuclear Regulatory Commission has a high degree of independence from political control. It grew in 1975 out of the former Atomic Energy Commission, after the view had developed, and been enshrined in law, that practitioners of this difficult art should not also be its regulators. In the United Kingdom there is a similar divorce of the regulatory function from any responsibility for promoting atomic energy. The main legislation is the Health and Safety at Work etc., Act 1974, and the relevant provisions of the Nuclear Installations Act 1965. The independent Nuclear Installations Inspectorate is part of the Health and Safety Executive. In Parliament nuclear safety and licensing questions are dealt with not by the energy minister but by the employment minister.

These national regulatory bodies provide the front line of defence on matters of reactor safety, and technically strong industrialized countries have traditionally been reluctant to derogate from their responsibility by accepting international guidance. Even Euratom safety inspection has been opposed by some EEC members. However, the Chernobyl accident called into question the view that nuclear safety should be regarded as an exclusively national prerogative, it being self-evident that radioactive clouds are no respecters of frontiers. It led to the formulation of 'basic safety principles for existing and future reactor types, with special attention given to those principles which emerge from post-accident analyses'. The work was entrusted to the International Nuclear Safety Group (INSAG) of the International Atomic Energy Agency in Vienna.

Chernobyl also added emphasis to the IAEA's programme of visits to reactor sites by expert Operational Safety Review Teams (OSARTs). They were originally planned with the developing countries in mind, and prior to the disaster the technically advanced countries showed little enthusiasm for such visits, which are by invitation of the host country. Post-Chernobyl, OSART visits came to be viewed as providing a useful check on national perceptions of reactor safety; and perhaps, in addition, as a useful device to which governments and regulatory authorities could point, should their absolute commitment to public safety be questioned. Since the first mission in 1983 their frequency has increased to about eight or ten a year, and of these about half have been to European countries.

The European Community provides a further mechanism for applying international influence to what had previously been purely national decisions. A relevant case concerns the French four-reactor Cattenom station, construction of which began in 1979. It lies in the Moselle valley, only 10 kilometres from Germany and a dozen kilometres from Luxembourg. France refused to give binding assurances about the level of emissions from the plant, and the issue was debated in the European Parliament. EEC Council Directive 85/337, which came into effect on 3 July 1988, has since established an obligation on member states to provide environmental information to other members 'likely to be significantly affected'. According to both the text and the general spirit of the directive, this should happen before another project with similar political implications to Cattenom gets under way in future[148].

Yet another consequence of Chernobyl was a new international agreement on cross-border radiological effects. A *Convention on Early Notification in the Event of a Nuclear Accident* was negotiated under the aegis of the IAEA in September 1986, only five months after the disaster. It had been drafted during the summer by delegates from sixty-two countries and ten international organizations. By 1 February 1988 there were seventy-two signatories. In terms of international diplomacy such speed and coverage is wholly exceptional, and underlines the extreme political urgency at the time of reassuring the world's population, and of seizing the opportunity afforded by Chernobyl to tackle a problem which had previously met with political apathy.

The rapid agreement was also a gesture on the part of the Soviets, whose silence in the days immediately following Chernobyl had been such an affront to the international community. Their delay in providing information, until after Sweden and Finland had made the story public, was from a strictly legal viewpoint consonant with the doctrine that safety policy is a national prerogative. However, it was gravely damaging to the country's reputation generally, and specifically to the new and more open regime which Mikhail Gorbachev had introduced only a few weeks earlier. The Soviets provided further evidence of goodwill only a week after signing, by issuing information on an accident to a Soviet nuclear submarine in international waters, even though the Convention specifically excluded military installations.

The Convention can be faulted, since it leaves individual states free to decide for themselves whether an incident is sufficiently serious to warrant invoking its provisions. However, it provided a beginning, and a much-needed change of atmosphere. The rapid strides that have since been made towards building a truly international reactor information network encourage the hope that the Convention's drafting deficiencies are now more of academic than practical interest.

At the same IAEA conference a further *Convention on Assistance in the Case of a Nuclear Accident or Radiological Emergency* was adopted by unanimous resolution. The parties are to co-operate to 'facilitate prompt assistance in the event of . . . an accident, to minimize its consequences and to protect life, property, and the environment . . . '. Assistance may be sought by states other than the state in which the emergency originated, if they are affected by its consequences. The Convention provides a basis for the machinery that would be needed, and deals with the issue of liability for actions undertaken by those responding to the call for assistance. The IAEA must be informed about the availability of experts and equipment, and may be invited by the state requesting assistance to assume a co-ordinating role.

The Convention was first called into service not for a reactor failure, but following a serious and quite extraordinary incident involving a disused caesium–137 medical gamma-ray source in Goiania, Brazil, in which four persons died from radiation sickness, and more than 200 were seriously contaminated. The source had been picked up from a scrap-heap by children, taken home and opened, and found to contain an attractive yellow compound, which the children used as carnival make-up. Once it was realized that their subsequent illness was radiation-induced, six countries responded with equipment and expertise.

While the two Vienna 1986 Conventions offer a beginning, they do not place powerful tools in the hands of the IAEA or anyone else; indeed, in view of the gravity of what happened at Chernobyl they might be considered as *de minimis* measures. However, they have established detailed rules of procedure where before there were only the vaguest principles; and perhaps more importantly they mark a change of atmosphere. A number of bilateral agreements covering similar ground have followed. Europe has become involved at the Community level, under the rules allowing international bodies to participate. The IAEA has established the communication system needed for rapid notification of emergencies: the first trials were held at the beginning of 1988. The Goiania experience showed the importance of even the smallest details: an initial request for assistance was not understood because it was in Portuguese. English is now the standard language for communication.

Insurance in the event of accident

Reactor accident insurance is a classic example of the problem of arranging third-party financial protection against an unlikely contingency which, should it occur, could have consequences going far beyond the ability of any single utility or any insurance pool to pay. Some kind of state assistance is therefore unavoidable. It should not weaken the prudent and primary requirement that responsibility should rest squarely on the operating organization. It should also strike a fair balance between providing fair protection for third parties, while protecting an essential public service from potentially ruinous claims.

So far as 14 European countries are concerned the *Paris Convention* (of 29 July 1960) *on Third-Party Liability in the Field of Nuclear Energy*[148] established the principles that financial responsibility would be exclusively channelled to the corporate operator of a nuclear installation (not to individual employees), and that insurance would be compulsory. The strict liability of the operator results from the existence of risk, irrespective of any fault. The Convention was negotiated in the light of contemporary assessments, such as that in the 1957 Brookhaven Report[45], that in a 'worst-case' accident there might be from zero to over 3,000 lethal casualties, up to 40,000 non-lethal injuries, and property damage of up to $7 billion. The Chernobyl experience, as reassessed at the time of the fourth anniversary in April 1990, was broadly consistent with this solemn warning.

The Paris Convention was supplemented by the *Brussels Supplementary Convention* of 31 January 1963, through which eleven of the Paris signatories set up a system of state compensation should the damage exceed a relatively small amount of operator liability. As revised in 1982 300 million Special Drawing Rights would be available, to be paid as to 5 million by the operator (a minimum which could be varied by the state concerned), up to 175 million by the state itself, and the remainder, up to 300 million in all, by subscription by the contracting states, according to a formula depending on the country's GDP and installed nuclear capacity. As one SDR is a little over one US dollar ($1.30 in March 1990) the sums available under the Paris-Brussels arrangements bear little relation to the vast cost of Chernobyl. The amendment to the Brussels Convention was not yet universally in force at the beginning of 1990.

Individual countries have continued to review, and where necessary revise, their nuclear insurance arrangements. For instance, on grounds of legal principle Germany in 1985 decided to opt for unlimited liability—as Switzerland had done in the previous year, and as is the case with Japan—but with a limitation on the amount of insurance required by law. In practice the sum of one billion DM is available, contributed partly by the operator concerned, partly from industry, and the bulk if required from the government.

In the UK, under the Nuclear Installations Act of 1965 and the 1983 Energy Act, the operator is liable for £20 million per station, to cover third-party personal injury and damage, though not economic loss resulting from an accident. The government will make good compensation claims up to 300 million SDRs. If claims were to exceed this limit they would be met 'to such extent . . . as Parliament may determine'. The UK prefers this cautious and pragmatic case-by-case approach to the alternative of offering very large sums, such as those available in the US under the Price-Anderson arrangement (see below).

The Paris and Brussels Conventions are agreements between highly industrialized countries. A few countries from the developing world took a similar step on 21 May 1963, through the *Vienna Convention on Civil Liability for Nuclear Damage*. The position by February 1990 was that the Convention still had only thirteen members, and of these only about half were seriously interested as operators or potential operators of nuclear power-plants. Work is in hand to bring up to date and extend the Convention's provisions.

Important though these conventions are, they cover less than half of the world's reactors, neither the USA nor Canada nor the USSR being signatories. However, the United States Congress has given close and prolonged attention to the issue of civil nuclear liability, in the light of the lessons of Three Mile Island and Chernobyl. Revised legislation was passed in September 1988, in the closing months of the Reagan administration. The basic legislation was the *Price-Anderson Act* of 1957, which pre-dated and partly inspired the Paris Convention. As most recently extended in 1988 it provides[149] a mechanism for dealing with liabilities of up to $7 billion, with the liability of the individual operating company supplemented by retrospective contributions by all other US reactor operators (the main provisions are summarized on page 112).

The prospect

Nuclear engineers and operators, like all human beings, learn from their mistakes. Both the financial disaster of Three Mile Island and the tragedy of Chernobyl had far-reaching effects, sharpening the industry's awareness of what could happen yet again if it did not immediately improve its design and operating standards. The statistics bear witness that the message has been taken. Unplanned automatic shut-downs in the USA dropped by more than 50 per cent between 1980 and 1987. Radiation exposure of the work-force—a rough measure of operational planning efficiency—showed a similar fall. High-quality simulators for operator training have been developed, and world-wide communication networks established for the exchange of experience. Efforts are being devoted to creating a new generation of reactors with improved passive safety features. While it is beyond anyone's power to offer a future wholly free of nuclear risk, what is being done is making that risk vastly smaller than it was even as recently as 1986. The industry has been jolted into realizing that one more serious accident anywhere in the world could call its future everywhere into question. That, as Dr Johnson might have said, 'concentrates the mind wonderfully'.

10   Managing Radioactive Waste

'THE problem of nuclear waste has proved insoluble'. 'The nuclear waste disposal problem has become the Achilles' heel of the nuclear industry'. The public's view has been conditioned by such disturbing messages[28,150] for the past decade. But the first is being steadily outdated by the efforts made around the world since governments were roused to action in the late 1970s by the environmental movement, which deserves proper credit for having 'blown the whistle'. Progress, though patchy, is taking place.

The second comment may be nearer the mark, though in a political rather than a technological sense. There is no disputing that—if judged by actual results—the performance in the field of waste-management of the United Kingdom, where these views were published in 1987, had fallen short of what might be expected from a country which had taken such a leading role in the development of civil nuclear power, and which had additionally pioneered the difficult technology of nuclear reprocessing. The long-term systematic approach needed for the necessary engineering developments had suffered at the hands of political expediency. The industry must also take its share of the blame: technical failures and human errors at the Sellafield reprocessing plant had been too frequent, leading to a disturbing number of well-publicized leaks of radioactivity that had worried the politicians. It is some consolation that the publication of these comments coincided with a change for the better. The story in the United States is similar, though the more explicit debate fostered by that country's separation of political powers eventually led rather more systematically towards agreement on the main lines of nuclear waste policy.

When judging the long-term potential of nuclear energy we are entitled to put short-term politics aside, and start from what is now technically possible. The encouraging fact is that waste-management has leapt ahead since 1980. The first fully-engineered underground handling facilities have been completed. Some of the smaller countries, Sweden in particular, lead the field. Given the right policy framework, dealing with nuclear waste proves to be simpler than many of the other activities routinely undertaken by the human race. There is little risk of ecological disaster, none at a racial suicide.

Waste with low levels of radioactivity comes from a wide vaɪ of sources and in many forms: slightly contaminated solids and liquids, air filters, laboratory clothing and equipment, or ash from the burning of combustible materials. Some comes from places having nothing to do with the nuclear industry, particularly radioisotopes used for diagnosis in hospitals, or for industrial radiography or well-logging. Disposal of such *low-level waste* poses, at least in principle, no great difficulty. Britain, with about forty reactors, produces about 40,000 cubic metres each year. The USA, with about one hundred civil power reactors, has considerably reduced the volume of waste in recent years through appropriate financial incentives, and in 1988 produced only 42,000 cubic metres.

Some countries recognize a separate category of more radioactive *intermediate-level wastes*—things like ion exchange resins and fuel cladding. These need shielding, but can otherwise be safely stored until permanent disposal facilities are available. They are ten times smaller in volume than the low-level wastes. There is beginning to be an additional contribution to this category from the dismantling of reactor structures, as the first generation of reactors reach the ends of their useful lives.

Overwhelmingly the most significant part of the radioactivity in the waste—95 per cent—comes from about thirty important fission products which are either still in the spent fuel elements where they were created, or which have been chemically separated in plants like Sellafield in the UK or Cap de la Hague in France. These are the *high-level (or heat-generating) wastes*. Handling and storing them is simplified by their small volume: the first thirty years of Britain's nuclear programme produced only 1,100 cubic metres of such waste, about the size of a medium-sized house. In a fuel-reprocessing plant close to 100 per cent of the radioactivity is concentrated in the high-level effluent stream. It can be stored for periods of years in stainless steel tanks in liquid form; but in the long term the fission products must be virtually immobilized by conversion into some solid form for easier handling prior to ultimate burial. The radioactivity of the waste is such that this necessarily involves the remote handling that only a specially equipped facility can provide.

The existence of the waste problem was obvious from the earliest

days of atomic energy. It is implicit in the elaborate precautions—
from glove-boxes to frogmen's suits—needed in plutonium laboratories to prevent ingestion of that very toxic material. But little was
done to develop satisfactory engineered permanent solutions. For
public relations that was a regrettable oversight. A third of a
century ago 'atomic' was a fashionable and glamorous word, which
helped marketing managers to sell consumer products as diverse as
skis and parquet flooring. The nuclear industry could have made a
demonstration then of successful fission product immobilization,
and been assured of public support. It did not do so, and the
opportunity was lost.

The reasons for this inaction included competition for scarce
professional resources within the still infant industry from the more
immediate business of developing working reactors; a dearth of the
chemical engineers needed to produce practical results; and not
least the perception of many atomic energy scientists (mostly
physicists) that the subject of waste lacked glamour. There was also
the industry's conscious judgement that the normal 'cooling' period
of fifty to one hundred years (to allow both the heat and the
radioactive emissions from used fuel elements to die away, and so
make them easier to deal with on a permanent basis) would give
ample time to develop satisfactory engineered solutions: until then
temporary storage would suffice.

What was not foreseen was the eruption of the new mood of
public questioning (the subject of the next chapter) that began in
the 1960s in America, and quickly spread around the world. It was
symbolized by the 1972 UN Conference on the Human Environment
in Stockholm. Four years later it was reflected in the UK in the Sixth
Report of the Royal Commission on Environmental Pollution[151],
which had a great impact when it appeared because its chairman,
later Lord Flowers, had been one of the earliest recruits to atomic
energy. The Commission criticized the industry for not deploying
sufficient resources on the development of permanent storage of
radioactive wastes:

There should be no commitment to a large programme of nuclear fission
power until it has been demonstrated beyond reasonable doubt that a
method exists to ensure the safe containment of long-lived highly
radioactive waste for the indefinite future.

The Commission added that they were 'confident that an acceptable
solution will be found'; but this small piece of optimism was lost in

the generally negative impact of their conclusions. The British public took away a picture of an industry which had come close to reneging on one of its implied social commitments.

Before long the world-wide shift of public opinion towards environmentalism led to new laws, which forced the industry to take action. Sweden passed the Stipulation Act of 1977, which made firm plans for providing a 'completely safe method' of handling future nuclear wastes a legal requirement for nuclear operations. Swiss legislation of 1979 also made a firm programme of action for dealing with radioactive wastes a condition for licensing power reactors[152,153]. By the early 1980s almost all countries with nuclear power programmes had recognized the political urgency of tackling the nuclear waste issue.

The technical requirements

At first sight the problem seems dauntingly difficult. The longevity and toxicity of some fission products, and of the heavy alpha-active elements like plutonium, mean that when they are 'finally' disposed of there must be certainty, amounting to a virtual guarantee, that they cannot reappear and contaminate food, water, or air to any significant degree. This must remain true not simply for a few years or decades, but (if we take our duties to our descendants seriously) for times long-compared with the longest half-lives of the more toxic radioactive species. Plutonium has a half-life of 24,000 years, which implies that if we choose not to separate and 'burn' it as a reactor fuel, but instead to leave it unseparated from the rest of the fuel-elements, we must ideally plan for their disposal in a way which can be presumed to be safe for a period even longer than that which separates us from Neanderthal man of 50,000 years ago.

Despite this, finding good solutions is not in fact particularly difficult by the standards of modern technology—far easier than sending a man to the moon, or building a Boeing 747. It is simply a matter of careful engineering in the light of chemical and geological knowledge, plus the provision of adequate resources. The real difficulties are political: agreeing targets, and then maintaining consistency of purpose and strategy over many years, in democratic societies where arguments about nuclear policy offer convenient bludgeons for oppositions wishing to attack governments.

For high-level waste the first step is to take advantage of the natural decay of the radioactivity, time in this sense being on our side; the second to package the radioactive material in some chemically stable solid form; the third to provide as many further man-made barriers to the dispersal of the radioactivity as the facts require; and the fourth to utilize the additional natural barrier of geological immobility by burying the packaged waste deep underground in a stable and impervious rock formation. For low-level wastes of relatively short half-life these precautions can be relaxed, even to the point of using shallow disposal, provided there can be certainty that this will not contaminate the water or food chains. In Britain radioactive waste disposal requires government authorization under the 1960 Radioactive Substances Act; other countries have comparable laws.

With proper management the risk to health of the general public is very small. In Britain nearly 88 per cent of the radiation received by the population is from natural sources (Table 8.2), the variation in this natural background from place to place being far greater than the contribution to radiation from the nuclear industry. A further 12 per cent of the radiation experienced by the general public comes from medical uses. Less than 0.1 per cent comes from radioactive discharges to the environment[154,155].

Nevertheless, there are real political difficulties. Despite the minimal risk, the public has been sensitized by years of anti-nuclear campaigning, and anxiety can surface during planning inquiries for waste-disposal sites. It is reflected in political reluctance, particularly when a general election is in the offing (and in Western democracies one is never far away), to authorize even the exploratory drilling needed prior to choosing a site for an underground repository. The non-intrusive nature of a well-planned disposal facility, most of it underground, is something which the public finds hard to accept. The gut issue of 'not in my backyard' operates powerfully and communicates itself to the politicians, to the frustration of those trying to find effective solutions to this final step in the nuclear fuel cycle. And yet nuclear power is by no means the only industry producing hazardous wastes, some of which are stable, *never* decaying, and for ever highly toxic: lead, mercury, and dioxin are examples. It is simply more politically 'visible'—and for that reason it is judged by criteria far stricter than those applying to other industries.

For nuclear waste disposal the public has been led to believe that the target should be zero risk—a target set in no other aspect of life. Reducing the emissions into the Irish Sea from the British Sellafield reprocessing plant, in pursuit of the ALARA principle (p. 216), involved an investment of £250 million. Health-modelling studies suggest that up to two lives (only!) may thereby be saved over the next 10,000 years—thus putting an implied value on a life saved of over £100 million. (The cost should perhaps also be escalated over the mean delay of 5,000 years!). As a rational allocation of resources, set alongside all the other health and safety improvements that the same money could buy, the expenditure is clearly difficult to justify. But there is little doubt that it was needed politically to create confidence and buy peace.

Initial storage

With hindsight, it seems that the industry everywhere failed to seize the initiative while it could still count on public sympathy. However, no very serious loss of time has yet occurred, at least with high-level waste, for an intrinsic technical reason which is explained more fully in the Technical Appendix. Because of the energy of the radiations they emit, the fission products in the used fuel bundles continue to give off a good deal of heat even after they are taken out of a reactor. They must not be allowed to melt— which could happen if no precautions were taken. A week after a 1,000 MWe pressurized-water reactor is shut down the used fuel in the core—all the fuel bundles taken together—still produces 12 MW of low-grade heat, or about 60 kilowatts per fuel assembly. After a month these levels have fallen by only 50 per cent. Even a year later each individual assembly is emitting several kilowatts, which is still uncomfortably large for permanent storage. But over the next thirty years, which is not an unreasonable period of storage, the heat production falls to below one kilowatt per fuel assembly—less than is emitted by a small domestic electric fire. Thereafter it drops away more slowly, as the thirty-year half-life of caesium–137 starts to dominate the decay pattern. This is the basis for considering fifty to one hundred years as a natural waiting time prior to disposal. By then the fuel assemblies could be reclassified as intermediate-level waste. The timing of the transfer from an initial storage site to a place of permanent disposal is not particularly critical.

Initial storage of spent fuel elements can be under water, or in dry conditions, the choice depending on corrosion considerations. If the fuel bundle comes from a pressurized-water reactor underwater storage presents no difficulty, because the cladding material has been chosen for its corrosion resistance under the far more testing conditions encountered in a reactor. Fuel bundles have been stored in this way without difficulty for twenty-five years. Wet storage is a particularly simple method, because the depth of several metres of water over the bundles acts as a conveniently transparent radiation shield, moreover one which offers no obstruction when moving the fuel elements from one part of the store to another. But with the Magnox fuel elements from the early British gas-cooled reactors there is a definite limit to the time for which they can be kept under water, without an undesirable degree of corrosion of the cladding and risk of contamination of the water.

The alternative is dry storage, in casks, vaults, or silos, engineered to allow cooling by forced circulation or, where the heat production is sufficiently low, natural convection. Both wet and dry casks are commonly used for transporting used fuel elements between reactor sites and reprocessing or disposal plants. They weigh many tonnes, because of the gamma-ray shielding needed; and must also satisfy stringent national and international safety standards as regards leak-tightness and resistance to collision damage and fire. Their engineering integrity was spectacularly demonstrated by the British Central Electricity Generating Board in July 1984, when a high-speed train was deliberately crashed into a cask, with negligible damage to the latter. This, however, is less surprising than it might appear, since even the peak forces experienced during the impact were well below those which occur in the extremely stringent standard IAEA regulatory tests for such casks[156].

Reprocessing

Following initial storage, the fuel bundles may go to a reprocessing plant for recovery of the unused uranium and by-product plutonium. The commercial services offered by France and the UK are used by a number of other countries, including Germany—now that the Wackersdorf project has been abandoned—and Japan, which plans to build its own reprocessing plant. Reprocessing also opens up the option of concentrating the highly radioactive fission products ready for incorporation into a 'host' material, where they can be immobilized; but not everyone regards this as essential. Alternatively the reprocessing stage can be omitted, and the fuel elements kept in initial or intermediate storage until ready for permanent disposal. The choice between the two routes is partly economic, partly strategic. Reprocessing costs money, and whether it can be justified or not in terms of short-run economics depends on the balance of advantage compared to starting with a fresh batch of fuel: the very low uranium prices of recent years have reduced its immediate economic attraction. However, reprocessing will gradually become more important as uranium supplies become tighter, since it avoids throwing away the uranium and plutonium that remain at the end of the first pass of the fuel elements through the reactor.

Immobilization

No one can provide a complete guarantee that a depository for radioactive materials will remain undamaged for all time; so a further precaution is needed. The radioactive material must be 'immobilized', so that even if ground water enters the depository there will be no danger of contaminating the food-chain. The most widely accepted solution is to encapsulate the high-level radioactive wastes in glass blocks ('vitrification'): being chemically inert, the glass forms a first barrier against dispersal. France has gone further than any other country with vitrification technology, and operates plants at Marcoule in the Rhône Valley, and at Cap de la Hague near Cherbourg. Britain has taken up the technology again after a gap of nearly two decades, and is building a plant at Sellafield, based on French experience, for operation by 1990.

An alternative approach is the Australian Synroc process[157,158]. As the name suggests, the aim is to bond fission product radionuclides inside a synthetic rock, chosen to have a crystal structure which can accept nearly all the high-level radioactive species; and to do this in a material with outstanding resistance to heat and leaching by ground water. The materials selected (an assembly of titanite minerals) are known to have survived in geological environments for hundreds of millions of years.

Given these competing approaches to the technology of immo-bilization, some confusion has been caused by the vigour with which the advocates of Synroc, in defending their own solution, have attacked the alternative of vitrification. One debatable issue is the extent to which it is necessary to take account of the hypothetical risk of vulcanism, or at least the possibility of unusual increases in geological heating in the locality of an underground storage site. Depending on the view taken about the maximum temperatures to be expected, different conclusions can be reached about the acceptability of immobilizing the fission products in glass blocks, or whether some higher melting-point material like Synroc is needed. Fortunately sufficient is known about geology and the earth's tectonic-plate structure to enable most countries to choose sites and design systems for which vitrification in glass should be adequate. However, the work on Synroc still attracts interest on account of its greater safety margin, even at the cost of a significantly more difficult production process.

Ultimate long-term disposal

Disposing of low-level waste presents few technical problems. The low concentration of radioactivity means that shallow repositories should be adequate, provided proper precautions are taken to minimize contamination of ground water by the use of properly designed and constructed clay or concrete linings. Typically the waste, which takes a wide variety of forms, is sorted according to its radioactivity, and packed into standard drums and containers, which can later be sealed by concreting and grouting after transfer to their final resting place. Britain has been using a factory site at Drigg in the north-west of the country where waste is deposited in concrete-lined trenches 10–20 metres deep, arranged so that the bottom of the trench rests on an impermeable layer of clay. Any water which enters is drained off and led to the sea[159].

The much greater radioactivity of intermediate and high-level wastes, and the greater concentration of long-lived alpha-emitters like plutonium, require a more elaborate system exploiting not only man-made but also additional geological barriers. Burial is typically at depths of a hundred metres or more below the surface, to prevent contamination of drinking-water or of the food-chain through any foreseeable process of migration, including convection and geyser action. An ideal disposal site, therefore, is one where there is good evidence that the geological formations have been stable for millions of years; and where the rocks are dry, or failing that where ground-water movement is known to be slow. The clay-like deposits of Belgium, crystalline rocks such as the granites of Canada, Sweden, and Switzerland, and the basalts and tuffs of the USA are all potentially suitable. So are the salt deposits of Germany and the USA, provided the natural exclusion of water has not been seriously compromised by past exploratory drilling, for instance for oil. Clay can additionally be used as a lining for silos where maximum protection from water seepage is needed; its flexibility provides an additional degree of insurance against any small rock movements.

To be acceptable, a permanent disposal repository for high-level waste should be designed to retain radioactivity over the course of many thousands of years. When the inevitable degradation of the engineered barriers occurs, allowing the radioactive material to come into contact with ground water, there should be no chance of any significant degree of contamination reappearing one day at the surface. We are helped by the highly alkaline chemical conditions which are known to exist at the depths likely to be used in practice. Under these conditions the majority of the important radioactive species, including plutonium, are virtually insoluble—which limits the capacity of any ground water which may be present to dissolve and transport the waste, even if the containers were no longer intact. For instance, half of the thirty or so kinds of fission product produced in the prehistoric natural nuclear reactors which operated in a rich uranium deposit at Oklo in Gabon—at a time when uranium contained a very much greater proportion of the fissile isotope uranium–235—are still identifiable: they have hardly moved in 1800 million years[160].

Much research has been carried out to study ways of preventing migration via underground water. Fortunately alkaline conditions can be created and maintained very simply, by including enough concrete in the design of a repository. Concrete is a durable material, whose history goes back well beyond the Romans. However, two important fission products, caesium–137 and strontium–90, both with half-lives of about thirty years, are not strongly adsorbed onto concrete, and are readily soluble in water. They need to be isolated in containers that will remain reasonably leak-tight for long enough to allow their radioactivity to become insignificant: 300 years, or ten half-lives (representing a thousand-fold reduction in the radioactivity) would be a reasonable design target. At a well-chosen site the chance of ground water from around the depository reaching the surface in this time would be virtually zero.

As a further precaution, accelerated corrosion tests of the container materials can be carried out. One centimetre of titanium, or ordinary carbon steel of considerably greater thickness, can be made to last for a thousand years. Sweden has studied very thick copper cylinders: in alkaline chemical conditions virtually no corrosion takes place, giving them an almost infinite useful life—a million years does not seem impossible[161].

The waste problem is made less daunting by the fact that nuclear engineering does not start from a blank page: it has a powerful ally in the accumulated scientific knowledge of the human race, particularly in chemistry and geology. The searches that have already been undertaken for many minerals provide a huge corpus of information about the rock structure underlying most developed countries. Altogether there are strong grounds for believing that deep underground disposal in well-chosen sites should be entirely satisfactory. That said, it is of course self-evident that no *physical* demonstration can ever be given that a chosen disposal system will in fact perform as expected. All that is possible is *intellectual* proof, based on experimental evidence, of the ability of the various barriers to continue to perform their functions for the required times far into the future. Assembling evidence in this way unfortunately cannot have the same public impact as being able to point to a storage plant that has, historically, performed well for hundreds or thousands of years; so the arguments are likely to rumble on.

The industry can nevertheless have confidence in the relatively simple and well-proven nature of the steps involved in disposal of high-level waste; in the solid, leach-resistant materials chosen for immobilization; and in the multiple barriers, all of which must be breached before radioactivity can escape. The technical case is convincing, the costs quite reasonable. Because of the relatively small volumes involved even such elaborate precautions should add only about 2 per cent to the total cost of energy, an amount which a number of countries already include in their electricity charges.

National waste-management policies

While the media give the impression that the waste issue is everywhere in limbo the facts are more encouraging. All the twenty or so countries using nuclear energy for electricity production on more than a pilot scale have formulated (or are in the process of formulating) plans for intermediate storage and ultimate disposal; many have active research programmes; and a few have already gone to the stage of actual hardware[152]. Some examples are given in what follows.

A national waste-management organization should not only be able to call on the necessary technical skills; it should also be adequately funded through a levy on nuclear electricity production. With some variations in administrative detail, this is already the case in (for instance) Belgium, Canada, the Federal Republic of Germany, Spain, Sweden, the United Kingdom, and the United States[153]. In France part of the cost is shared between the Commissariat à l'Énergie Atomique and COGEMA, the nationalized fuel-cycle company.

Belgium

The management of used fuel in Belgium is entrusted to Synatom, a company whose ownership is shared between the private utility industry and the government. A new agency, ONDRAF/NIRAS, was set up in 1982 to look after the transport and disposal of radioactive waste. Operations are conducted under the overall control of the Ministries of Health and Labour. Intermediate storage vaults are designed to be adequate for periods of fifty years or more. A site at Mol in the north-east of the country has been chosen for ultimate disposal of high-level waste in an area which has a deep clay layer, which is believed to be suitable. An experimental laboratory was constructed in 1984 at a depth of 220 metres, where *in situ* experiments can be conducted on soil mechanics, hydrology, heat transfer, etc. Confirmation of Mol as the chosen disposal site for high-level waste awaits the results of this experimental work.

Canada

Canadian reactors use low-cost natural uranium fuel, of which the country is the world's largest producer. Consequently reprocessing and plutonium extraction do not at present have a high priority. Storage of used fuel elements takes place in water-filled 'lagoons' on reactor sites. Existing and planned facilities will be adequate to handle all fuel until the year 2025, and there will be no need to construct repositories for ultimate disposal for many years. In case a decision on disposal is postponed even further, the electrical utility Ontario Hydro (which in spite of its name has twenty reactors operating or under construction) is studying a number of alternative long-term storage methods. Research and development is directed towards the possibilities of ultimate disposal in sites at depths of 500 metres or more in hard rock. An underground laboratory has been built in Manitoba at a depth of 250 metres to obtain a better understanding of the processes by which radionuclides move through the biosphere: for instance, how radioactive material escaping from a waste-disposal vault might be carried by ground water to the surface. Depending on progress, a demonstration disposal vault might be constructed in the first few years of the next century, to be followed by a commercial facility.

France

In 1979 France set up a new national agency for the disposal of radioactive waste, ANDRA, as part of the Commissariat à l'Énergie Atomique. Its work is overseen and regulated by the national nuclear safety inspectorate, SCSIN, under the Ministry of Industry. ANDRA took over responsibility for the near-surface waste repository for short-lived wastes on the Cherbourg peninsula. Another facility at Soulaines in the Aube, 200 km east of Paris, is scheduled to be ready by 1991.

It is also intended to construct a deep repository for long-lived high-level waste; but plans have been delayed more than once by fierce public opposition. The plan was to carry out exploratory drilling at four candidate sites spread throughout the country; but after the march by 15,000 people at Angers on 20 January 1990 the Prime Minister, Michel Rocard, imposed at least a twelve-months moratorium on further drilling, to give time for all concerned to talk to each other and understand the implications, both social and technical, of what is intended. The protesters were particularly concerned that any waste disposal should not be irreversible—this being a point made in a 1983 report on waste disposal by the Castaing Commission. ANDRA points out that if the repository is opened in 2010, as seems possible, and if as intended it is designed to handle waste material over fifty to sixty years of nuclear operations, the waste would remain recoverable—albeit at an additional cost—for the best part of a century. There would thus be ample time for second thoughts should better technologies become available.

Federal Republic of Germany

Under the German Nuclear Law of 1976 used fuel management is the responsibility of the owners of nuclear power-plants. They have a legal requirement to demonstrate how the spent fuel will be managed six years before it is discharged from a reactor. The companies concerned joined together in 1977 to create a new organization, DWK, to be responsible for the handling and management of used fuels, from their removal from a reactor to the final conditioning of the waste. However, the plans for a reprocessing plant, to be built by DWK at Wackersdorf in Bavaria, were cancelled in 1989 because of cost and public opposition. The spent fuel will now go to France and Britain for reprocessing; but should German policy change so as to eliminate the reprocessing option at any time before 2005, the new contracts could be cancelled without penalty. The change of plans led DWK to abandon most of its activities at the beginning of 1990.

Intermediate storage and final geological disposal are responsibilities of the Federal government, but users have to meet the administrative and running costs of such facilities from their electricity sales. The organization to which the day-to-day responsibility has been delegated is DBE (the German Company for the Construction and Operation of Final Repositories). High-level wastes will be vitrified; lower-level wastes will be immobilized in bitumen or concrete.

A first intermediate storage facility has existed at the Gorleben salt-dome in Lower Saxony since 1983; but due to a pending court action DWK had not been allowed to use it by 1989. A similar plant at Ahaus in Nordrhein-Westfalen suffered the same fate. Gorleben is intended for high-level permanent disposal from around 2010. Boring and exploration should be complete by the end of the century, but detailed project planning and licensing could take nearly another decade. Another salt-mine at Asse was used for some lower-level waste disposal until 1978; it has since been used as a research facility.

Sweden

Following the 1977 Stipulation Act[162] and other legislation effective from 1984, Sweden has gone further than most countries in providing engineered solutions to the waste-disposal problem. Responsibility is placed squarely on the electrical utilities, whose subsidiary SKB is responsible for developing and operating systems for the 'back end' of the fuel cycle. The work is monitored by the National Board for Spent Fuel (SKN), the Nuclear Power Inspectorate (SKI), and the National Institute of Radiological Protection (SSI)— all reporting to the Ministry of Environment and Energy.

Since all the Swedish reactors are sited on the coast, transport to the central storage and disposal facilities is in a specially built ship, the 2,000 ton *Sigyn*, named after a heroine of Norse mythology who protected her husband Loki from death by snake venom, after he had incurred the displeasure of the Gods. The ship makes about twenty trips a year between the Swedish reactors and the central storage sites, plus half a dozen to France (for fuel reprocessing at La Hague, near Cherbourg).

Two underground facilities have already been built—SFR for the final disposal of low-level and intermediate-level waste in tunnels at Forsmark, 100 kilometres north of Stockholm; and CLAB, an intermediate storage facility for highly radioactive used fuel elements, at Oskarshamn in the south-east. The SFR tunnels are under the sea, offshore, as an additional protection against disturbance from surface drilling at some time in the remote future. A third facility, SFL, about 500 metres underground, will start construction about 2010. It will be used for the final disposal of fuel elements after thirty to forty years cooling at CLAB.

Used fuel elements are initially stored at the various reactor sites. After cooling for four or five years the ship takes them to CLAB. Inaugurated in April 1986, this facility takes the form of four large storage pools, in a cavern about 120 metres long located about 30 metres below the surface. It will eventually have the capacity to provide intermediate storage under water for all the fuel elements used in their operating lifetimes by all twelve Swedish reactors. Although not intended as the final repository, it is capable of safely handling the spent fuel for several decades. The underground location means that environmental intrusion is surprisingly small: all that is visible on the surface is a medium-sized building typical of those used by light industry or for offices.

As regards the cost of the waste management operation, which will keep 100 persons permanently employed, Swedish public policy is that the burden placed on future generations should be limited as far as possible, and with this in mind the 1981 Finance Act established a levy on current electricity sales, set each year to cover outgoings. The long-term cost of operating the final repository is estimated to be around 2 per cent of total electricity costs—similar to the Swiss estimate.

Switzerland

Swiss legislation passed in 1978 placed responsibility for waste-management on the electrical utilities operating nuclear stations, and called for a 'warranty' of satisfactory plans for disposing of radioactive wastes as a condition for licensing those stations. The utilities joined with the government to form a new organization, NAGRA, whose task is to prepare plans for final disposal, with particular emphasis on deep disposal of wastes. The Federal Office of Health has a department dealing with waste disposal.

NAGRA has two major projects under active development. Four locations have been selected as possible sites for a medium- and low-level depository, which it is hoped to have in service by the year 2000. Although a high-level repository will not be needed before 2020, drilling has been in progress since 1982 to explore the crystalline rock under the lowlands in the north of the country. Following a report on this programme, the Swiss government has asked for the exploration to be extended to include sedimentary deposits.

United Kingdom

The history of waste-disposal in the UK has been confused by political vacillation. The work began well enough: the first White Paper on the subject[163] appeared in 1959, and laid down a policy which resulted in the 1960 Radioactive Substances Act, governing amongst other things the disposal of waste. Research was started, and by 1967 the 'Fingal' pilot plant at Harwell had succeeded in producing metre-long glass cylinders containing waste from Windscale. There was then a pause, and a conscious—and in retrospect unfortunate—decision not to proceed to the industrial stage, on the grounds that there was no obvious urgency. Some low-level waste continued to be disposed of in the English Channel off Alderney, after careful assessment of the safety implications, though in apparent contradiction of a 1958 United Nations declaration against pollution of the seas from the dumping of radioactive waste.

The criticisms already quoted from the Flowers Royal Commission report of 1976 provided a fresh stimulus. The government responded in a White Paper[164] which defended sea-dumping, when properly controlled, but also promised fresh action. A Radioactive Waste Management Advisory Committee was set up in 1978. Preparations for geological investigations of possible sites for disposing of high-level waste were begun jointly by the UK Atomic Energy Authority and the Institute of Geological Sciences (now the British Geological Survey). Several sites were proposed, including both hard rock and clay-like formations; but before deep drilling could begin, even for preliminary investigations, the work was held to be 'development' requiring planning permission. A broad alliance of objectors strongly opposed the proposed investigations and created political difficulties. In two cases public inquiries were held, and despite objections the Inspectors reported favourably. However, against the advice of its Advisory Committee, the Conservative government cancelled the work in 1981 on the face-saving grounds that other countries had established the validity of deep disposal of high-level waste, and that in any case the issue could safely be left for several decades (it was envisaged that vitrified high-level wastes would be stored on the surface for at least fifty years).

A fresh White Paper which appeared the following year[154] noted the abandonment of the deep-drilling programme. Neverthe-less it contained the statement that 'the lack of suitable disposal facilities for intermediate-level wastes is the major current gap in waste management'—apparently overlooking the fact that this too would require geological exploration, since the requirements are not dissimilar to those for high-level waste.

Meanwhile, low-level wastes were being dumped, often untidily, in shallow trenches at Drigg, in the north-west, near Sellafield. Dilute low-level liquid waste continued to be discharged into the sea from nuclear establishments, with the largest amount flowing into the Irish Sea from Sellafield—the latter however under more tightly controlled conditions than previously. Some packaged low-level wastes were disposed of in the deep Atlantic Ocean about 500 miles south-west of Land's End until 1982. That year's White Paper contemplated that the practice would continue, at least for a time. The quantities involved, and the method of packaging, presented no significant hazard to anyone, in the opinion of the assessments then available to the government—a view which was subsequently reinforced in 1984 by further independent expert examination[165]. But soon after the publication of that report the government came under pressure from Greenpeace and British and foreign seamen's unions. At the International Maritime Organization a halt was forced by some of the other signatories of the Convention on the Prevention of Marine Pollution by Dumping of Wastes and Other Matter (the 'London Dumping Convention'), which Britain had ratified in 1975.

The 1982 White Paper announced the formation of a Nuclear Industry Radioactive Waste Executive, NIREX, to provide a focus for the industry's efforts for disposal of low- and intermediate-level wastes. Its legal status was altered to that of a limited company in 1985 to facilitate operations, and the staff was considerably expanded. NIREX soon had to face the political difficulties which arose towards the end of 1983 following allegations of a causal connection between a small 'cluster' of childhood leukaemias and reports of leaks of radioactive materials at Sellafield. This coincided with confirmation by the government that, to relieve Drigg, two further potential sites for the disposal of low-level waste were being studied, one at an old anhydrite mine at Billingham in the north-east, with a capacity for storing 275,000 cubic metres; the other, with a considerably larger capacity, in shallow clay in a brick-making area at Elstow, about 50 kilometres from the northern edge of the London conurbation. Public opposition developed, and was supported by remarkably expert criticism of the criteria on which the choices had been made. The Billingham proposal was abandoned. In 1985 the government requested NIREX to find other sites.

Exactly one year later the Environment Committee of the House of Commons commented that the nuclear industry still had no coherent waste policy[166]. This was hardly fair to the industry. The line to be followed had been clear since 1977; but, in the words of the Advisory Committee[167]:

consideration of political expediency and action—or inaction—specifically at the Parliamentary level has been responsible for the disastrous stop–go policy of bold announcement followed by abject withdrawal.

In 1985 Parliament had approved exploratory drilling on four clay sites, to study their suitability for low-level waste in deep trenches as a preliminary to a public inquiry; but once again the plans were abruptly cancelled on 1 May 1987, significantly without consulting the Radioactive Waste Management Advisory Committee. The timing of the announcement bears witness to the political visibility of the waste issue: the cancellation must have been part of the deck-clearing operations prior to the general election which took place on 11 June. The government's decision was a serious set-back for NIREX, which had already invested £14 million in drilling 300 bore-holes to explore the site geologies. With cancellation costs the sum rose to £20 million. Constitutionalists may care to ponder a waste of resources on this scale for what appears to have been party-political convenience.

NIREX wrote off the money and turned its attention to planning a deep repository at what might be thought the most obvious sites: either Sellafield, close to the existing reprocessing plant; or Dounreay, the fast-reactor site in the north of Scotland. The former was operationally the more suitable choice, since so much of the waste had its origin at Sellafield; but the geology was more complex. Dounreay's geology was excellent, but the site had major implications for the long-distance transport of radioactive materials. Once again the choice was not a simple matter of technology and economics: at both sites the local authorities opposed even the preliminary stage of drilling. In both cases NIREX had to appeal to the government before work could proceed.

The 1987 upset had left NIREX with a determination to make its case more effectively, to ensure that it was not lost through default. Well-produced and authoritative brochures were prepared and widely distributed[168]. Politicans were informed, and NIREX made a point of always having experts available during party political conferences, to answer questions and report on progress. By 1989 this groundwork was beginning to show results. Voices could be heard in Parliament praising NIREX for its professionalism, even from members who had been opponents as recently as 1987. Thirteen years after the Flowers Report there were at last grounds for looking forward with more confidence to the construction of adequate British waste disposal facilities. But the fundamental nature of the changes resulting from electricity privatization only became apparent in November 1989 (p. 136). Until they work their way through the system the future of British waste policy will be subject to this further uncertainty.

The United States

America, a continental-sized country, has by far the largest number of power reactors, as well as the largest nuclear-weapons programme. Its nuclear-waste production consequently outstrips that of other countries. This was beginning to be a matter of concern even by the mid-1970s. By then the weapons programme had generated 200 million gallons of high-level waste—nearly one million tonnes—from plutonium production[97]. Storing it safely presented problems: at the Hanford production site near Richland in the state of Washington in the north-west of the country, where three-quarters of this high-level waste was stored, almost half a million gallons had escaped in a series of leaks, averaging one per year from 1958 to 1974. The steel tanks were only single-skinned; some were without automatic leak-detection systems. Some plutonium solution had been dumped in sub-surface trenches, not properly isolated from the surrounding environment. As much as 100 kilograms of plutonium were involved. By the 1970s the short cuts of the wartime Manhattan Project, and the subsequent drive to produce large quantities of new weapons, had led to substantial contamination. It became doubtful whether the 5 square miles of the site could ever be cleaned up. But at the Savannah River site in South Carolina, where most of the rest of the high-level waste was stored at that time, extra design precautions had produced conspicuously better results.

There were also problems with waste from the small commercial reprocessing plant at West Valley, New York State, which had been closed in 1971 because of difficulties in meeting changing effluent-control standards. Some contamination of local streams had been observed.

For the ultimate disposal of low-level reactor wastes there were six licensed commercial and five federal burial sites in the mid-1970s, some of which had begun to release radioactivity into the environment. The site at Maxey Flats, near Moorhead, Kentucky, is in an area of heavy rainfall, and was known to be leaking. At Oak Ridge in Tennessee some material had been leached into the Clinch River. In neither case were the levels of contamination serious, but the fact that leaks and transportation by ground water could occur created worries for the future.

These early problems led to many Congressional debates over the next dozen years on institutional methods of controlling nuclear waste. The mid-1980s saw only slow progress. In 1988 an experienced political observer described nuclear waste as still amongst the most contentious issues, even though he judged that only a dozen or so out of the 535 US Congressmen took a strong personal interest.

Reactor operators are responsible for managing all the wastes while stored on reactor sites, and for meeting the requirements of the Nuclear Regulatory Commission (NRC). Once the Department of Energy's (USDOE) national high-level waste repository is open, this federal department will take over the custody and ultimate disposal of high-level waste. Low-level wastes will go to regional centres established under inter-state 'compacts' (see below), subject to federal regulation by the Environmental Protection Agency, the NRC, and some state regulatory boards. (Some US low-level wastes would be categorized as 'intermediate-level' in the UK.)

Although in the civil field this broad division of responsibilities is clear enough, there have been problems over the extent of the responsibility of the NRC and the Environmental Protection Agency (EPA) for what happens over the clean-up of federally-owned weapons-facility sites like Hanford. This is not just an empty wrangle between competing government agencies: it concerns employer liability, and therefore the willingness of the work-force to engage in lengthy and in some cases potentially hazardous clean-up operations.

The present legal basis for high-level waste management is the Nuclear Waste Policy Act of 1982, as amended in 1987. An environmental impact report, completed by the USDOE in 1980, had considered a spectrum of eight disposal options, including storage under the seabed, ice-sheet disposal, rock melt, transmutation, disposal in outer space, and deep underground 'geologic' repositories. The option of dumping at sea had been foreclosed by the Ocean Dumping Act of 1972. Congress decided that geologic repositories should be the approved choice, and the 1982 Act gave the USDOE authority to construct one such repository. It will be a major undertaking, with an operational work-force of more than a thousand and an even larger construction work-force.

Nine potential sites were considered and three were selected in 1986 for 'site characterization' (or evaluation): Deaf Smith County, Texas (a salt formation), in an agricultural community where there was strong opposition from the farmers and their Congressional representatives; Richland (basalt), in an area in the State of Washington long used to nuclear operations; and Yucca Mountain, Nevada (tuff). Because of very effective political opposition in all three states Congress again became embroiled in the selection controversy. It provided new directions in an Amendment to the Nuclear Waste Policy Act in December 1987, which specifically designated the Yucca Mountain site as the only one to be considered for a potential repository. (It may be relevant that Nevada not only has a very small population, but also the smallest number of Congressional votes—four—of any state of the Union).

The choice was not final: Yucca Mountain has yet to be evaluated to determine if it is satisfactory, a task expected to take about seven years. Nevada has continued to oppose this activity, and from the time of USDOE's application early in 1988 has refused to issue the necessary state environmental permits to allow access to the site. The normal time for processing such applications is seventy-five days; but these were returned to the DOE unprocessed in December 1989. The Energy Department announced that it would take Nevada to court to settle the issue, at the same time admitting that the facility could not be completed before 2010, seven years later than previously expected, and twelve years behind the original plan. The action began at Las Vegas on 25 January 1990.

Yucca Mountain is far from the main producers of radioactive waste in the east of the country. As a site it has the advantage of a low water-table, 1,800 feet below the ridge. However, the area is mildly seismic, and also experiences underground shocks from the nearby Yucca Flats weapons-testing site. The acceptability of the site will be decided only after the site characterization report is available, and the NRC has conducted a licensing review. The costs of the engineered facility at Yucca, at least for the first hundred years after the opening, will be met from a levy imposed under the 1982 Act on nuclear-generated electricity. The current rate of one dollar per megawatt-hour is worth a total of $500 million annually. What is to happen a century from now is not dealt with in the legislation; nor would it be reasonable to try to do so, given the rapidity with which the technology could change. The 1987 legislation postponed until 2007 any attempt to consider alternative sites or build a second high-level repository east of the Mississippi, pending final clearance of Yucca as a suitable site.

The 1982 Act also directed that a study should be carried out and a site recommended for an interim Monitored Retrievable Storage Center, where waste could be temporarily stored and consolidated. The recommendation of the Department of Energy was for a MRS facility in the vicinity of Oak Ridge, Tennessee. While the community of Oak Ridge, which has a long history of association with nuclear power, was willing to host such a facility, the Governor of Tennessee objected strongly. Congress, in the 1987 Amendment, provided new guidance by authorizing a MRS, linking it rigidly to progress on the main waste repository (a political device intended to prevent the MRS from becoming a *de facto* substitute for Yucca Mountain), withdrawing the earlier Oak Ridge recommendation, and establishing a MRS Commission to evaluate the issue. The Commission reported on 1 November 1989 in somewhat inconclusive terms, though questioning the mandatory linkage between the MRS and progress on the delayed high-level waste-repository. Their report also recommended the construction of two further emergency/interim storage facilities. This proposal did not find favour with Congress, which invited the Commission to look further into the reality of the need, and the likely cost in comparison with on-site storage. The nuclear industry also saw little point in building two additional facilities, and pointed out that if the legislative linkage could be broken a MRS could be operational by 1998. That would 'hasten the day the nation begins to dispose of spent nuclear fuel'. The industry was conscious that US electricity ratepayers had by 1990 already contributed $4 billion to the Department of Energy's nuclear-waste fund—about twice what had been spent by the DOE—and that by 1998 the figure would be nearer $10 billion. If a MRS was not available by 1998, the utilities themselves might have to make additional interim storage provision.

Low-level waste is dealt with under separate legislation, the Low-level Radioactive Waste Policy Act[169] of 1980, as amended in 1985. This encourages states to form groupings, or 'compacts', to deal with the much larger volume of low-level wastes produced within their geographical regions; and offers financial incentives to begin operations by the end of 1992, after which the three existing sites in Nevada, Washington, and South Carolina will no longer be available for wastes generated outside their local compact regions. Nationwide, the volume of such wastes ran to nearly 42,000 cubic metres in 1988. By the end of that year nine compacts had been formed, though siting, jurisdictional, and public acceptance issues were still presenting difficulties. Texas and New York State decided to continue on their own, without forming a compact. Financing is on the basis of a fee depending on radioactivity and volume of the material being dumped, the volume provision offering a strong incentive for volume reduction prior to disposal. That, and the regional basis of the policy, should help to simplify transport problems.

The early low-level disposal sites were fairly primitive. Of the six that had been used three—Maxey Flats, West Valley, and Sheffield, Illinois—had been closed by the mid-1980s because of limited capacity or operating difficulties, mainly due to water ingress. At Maxey Flats the trenches were on a site lying above a tributary of the Ohio River, which is used as a source of drinking water. They were unlined, and when closed down their capping was permeable. In 1975 an Environmental Protection Agency investigation found that some of the 64 kilograms of plutonium which had been dumped there had begun to migrate. Simple remedial action was undertaken in 1981: polythene covers were placed over most of the trenches to minimize entry of rain-water, though some water continued to enter. At Sheffield, Illinois, one trench intersected the water-table, and contamination of ground water was observed. The trench caps placed over the site when it was closed in 1979 deteriorated and required constant maintenance. In contrast, relatively few problems were experienced at the semi-desert Beatty site north-west of Las Vegas, near Death Valley; or at Richland, which is in an area of low rainfall[28]. But the inference that low-level waste repositories might usefully be confined to areas of low rainfall encounters two problems: one is their great distances from the major waste-producing regions in the north-east; the other is the recommendation of the 1980 Act that waste should be disposed of locally, within the producing region.

The unsatisfactory experience with some of the early sites inevitably led to far stricter Nuclear Regulatory Commission rules. Future 'compact' sites will have to meet tighter specifications for containers, extra barriers, and buffer zones, and for the relation of the site excavations and method of isolation to the water-table and ground-water movement. Even though these NRC requirements should be more acceptable to the public they have been challenged by environmental groups such as the Sierra Club. The existence of such well-funded groups, with their ability to engage expert professional advisers, provides a virtual guarantee that a detailed debate will continue.

Meanwhile, the state governments responsible for the 'compacts' were becoming nervous, and anxious to lay off their potential financial obligations if possible through the insurance market. But the insurers were also cautious, and once litigation over Maxey Flats began they imposed a temporary suspension of new insurance for waste sites in January 1987. They had in mind both the increasing frequency of litigation for alleged bodily injury (2000 claims were filed following the Three Mile Island accident, even though no one was obviously hurt), and the tendency of the US courts to award enormous sums for damages. Additionally there was anxiety over the possible costs of cleaning up a site, should this become necessary. Insurers understand normal third-party claims, which are part of their everyday business; but in this case the costs which might be involved in site decontamination are both outside their experience, and also potentially huge in relation to their capital resources. A significant concern is whether insurance coverage includes on-site clean-up, or whether it is limited to off-site liability. Discussions were begun in 1988 to find ways of permitting the very necessary business of insurance to proceed.

There is one further point of legislative interest in the US context. 'Nuclear' waste is in many cases industrial waste, possessing the normal non-nuclear characteristics of whatever materials might be involved. Some could be hazardous in a non-nuclear sense. Some details of the US Resource Conservation and Recovery Act as amended in 1984, which governs normal hazardous waste, are not necessarily consistent with the nuclear provisions. So far as low-level wastes are concerned the chemical hazards could well be of more consequence to public health than the easily-monitored radionuclides. Difficulties could occur when designing storage and disposal facilities for these so-called 'mixed wastes', because of discrepancies between the regulations of the Nuclear Regulatory Commission and those of the Environmental Protection Agency.

Reactor decommissioning

The 'problem of decommissioning', about which many warnings have been voiced by the nuclear opposition, appears less daunting in the light of the practical experience that has already been accumulated. The first stage of decommissioning involves de-fuelling the reactor prior to the routine, if expensive, task of dealing with the highly radioactive and heat-producing final charge of used fuel elements, along the lines already described. At the same time the radioactive sludges, resins, and other wastes that accumulate during operation would be prepared for disposal. All this could take a few years. During a second stage the non-radioactive buildings would be dismantled, leaving the reactor itself undisturbed in its radiation ('biological') shield. This would take a further two or three years, and require a work-force of perhaps 200 people.

At this point there is a choice. One option is for the reactor to be prepared for disposal as a package, either by burying it on site to a depth of 5 metres or more under a well-engineered mound, provided with its own ground-water barriers; or by transporting it on a tractor to a special burial site. A second option would be to cut the reactor into sections for disposal as intermediate-level waste, piece by piece. Remote-controlled machinery would be used when sectioning the reactor structure to minimize the exposure of the staff; such techniques are already available. The sectioning operation would be made easier, and therefore cheaper, by allowing for an initial delay of some decades: the major radio isotope in irradiated steel has a five-year half-life, so that over a century the intensity of this radiation falls by one millionfold. Such a delay would present no safety problems; but keeping a reactor mothballed costs money, so a financial judgement about the best timing would be needed in each particular case. All this, of course, is in the context of a reactor which has not suffered damage. If an accident like Three Mile Island had taken place there could well be abnormal problems of dealing with the much longer-lived and toxic heavy elements; engineering solutions would have to be found *ad hoc*.

In practice the complete return of a site to unrestricted use is unlikely to be the norm, because generating stations will still be required. It is therefore more likely that existing sites will be 'replanted' with new stations, in which case leaving part or all of a reactor installation untouched for a period of some decades would cause only slight aesthetic damage or operational inconvenience.

Experience of decommissioning is accumulating, as more and more reactors reach the ends of their useful lives. Nearly fifty reactors have already been taken out of service world-wide, and are at various stages of decommissioning. By the year 2000 the number will be over 100; by 2030, around 400. Progress is marked by the international conferences that are now regularly held on the subject. The International Atomic Energy Agency has an expert decommissioning group; so has the Nuclear Energy Agency of the OECD.

The USA's prototype power-station, Shippingport (72 MWe), was shut down in 1982, and the site is being returned to its original condition—it being a requirement of the 1955 lease that the land must be available for unrestricted use by 1994. The packaged reactor will be placed on a barge, floated down the Ohio and Mississippi rivers, through the Panama Canal, and brought to a final disposal site in Washington state, at an estimated cost of just on $100m. Prior to this operation the US decommissioned the 58 MW(thermal) Elk River reactor in the early 1970s, and also the Sodium Reactor Experiment of 30 MWe. In the UK work has been done on decommissioning the early Windscale AGR prototype. In Japan the 12 MW prototype BWR is due to be completely dismantled by 1992.

The experience gained from such exercises is enabling firmer estimates to be made of the extra man-days needed on account of precautions against radiation hazards: typically they add about 25 per cent. With 'know-how' being important for such operations, specialist decommissioning operations contractors (DOCs) are becoming part of the nuclear industry in the USA. The early cases are also driving home the lesson that decommissioning will be easier if the associated engineering problems can be considered years earlier, at the reactor design stage—a point which was explicitly addressed during the British Sizewell B reactor inquiry (p. 132).

It is still too early for decommissioning costs to be accurately known, but the evidence seems to be that for stages 2 and 3 (to green-field site) they are likely to be between $200m and $400m per reactor[71], the sum depending to some extent on the delay selected before stage 3 is begun. There could be a minimum of eight years or a maximum of a century before the final stage of expenditure is incurred. Most electrical utilities already make provision for decommissioning in their accounts. In the USA the Nuclear Regulatory Commission requires utility licensees to begin assembling, by 1990, a decommissioning fund of $75–135m (1986 dollars) per unit. The US utilities' own estimates of the sums needed are somewhat higher, at \$150–350m; that is, very roughly, 10 per cent of the original construction cost, at constant money values. However, the US Federal Energy Regulatory Commission has argued[170] that the utilities are overestimating the cost, because decommissioning techniques can already be refined in the light of experience. If this is right, it is further encouragement for the view that decommissioning is far from being the make-or-break element in nuclear-power economics that it has been represented to be: it seems likely to add only about 0.5 per cent to the cost of nuclear electricity.

International collaboration

The commonality of both the problems and the solutions for nuclear waste disposal, and the virtual absence of conflicts of commercial interest, make this a quintessentially apt field for international collaboration. The International Atomic Energy Agency has prepared a schedule of agreed criteria for high-level waste disposal. Its Director-General draws a comparison between the modest volumes of nuclear waste and the vast volumes of waste produced by the other energy industries, a great deal of it invisible 'greenhouse'-promoting carbon dioxide. Non-energy industries are also major producers of hazardous waste on a far greater scale than the nuclear industry—perhaps 40 million tonnes a year emanate from the European Community alone.

The Nuclear Energy Agency of OECD has a Radioactive Waste Management Committee, which provides a meeting-place for the world's experts. It reviews scientific data on such matters as the migration of radioactive species, under-the-seabed disposal, and the problems of decommissioning reactors.

International collaboration of a quite different nature has also been proposed: the offering of a commercial service by countries with suitable sites in areas of low population for storing or disposing of wastes from other countries with less suitable geology. The idea was given some support during the General Conference of the IAEA in 1985. The main anxiety in Western countries over such a development relates to a possible risk of nuclear proliferation: waste dumps for unreprocessed spent fuel are potential 'plutonium mines', which would need to be monitored and kept permanently under IAEA safeguards. Physically there are certainly large parts of the world that are potentially suitable, in countries (like Canada) with stable political frameworks and impeccable non-proliferation credentials. Alternatively the recipient could be a country which is already a weapons state. Russia regularly receives spent fuel from its neighbours, and this has caused the West no anxiety. But the overtures made since 1984 by the Peoples' Republic of China, to the effect that it would welcome a chance of earning foreign currency by offering this kind of waste-storage service, have lacked credibility, given the country's chronic political instability. The reported Chinese reluctance to import packaged (vitrified) waste, and their apparent preference for untreated spent fuel, pose difficulties for Western democracies, whose electorates would find it hard to accept the implication that further unspecified use might be made of their nuclear waste. The terrible events in Tiananmen Square in June 1989 reinforced such doubts, and for the majority of potential users effectively destroyed the Chinese option for the foreseeable future.

Conclusions

This brief review shows, first, a striking degree of common ground regarding the best technical approaches to be followed. What should be done is well understood. With current technology, and proper attention to detail, high-level waste can be disposed of with risks of exposure so minor that they should be entirely acceptable.

Secondly, the early attempts fell far short of what would now be regarded as necessary. It was not until the end of the 1970s that the nuclear industry in most countries began to get to grips seriously with the waste issue. The results are only now (1990) beginning to flow through. We can look forward within a few years to a rapid change in the readiness of the industry to deal with this problem.

Thirdly, this is a long-haul matter, where consistency of purpose maintained for many years is paramount, despite the very real political difficulties. Vacillation is unfortunately more common. As a former head of NIREX observed[159] in the British context: 'the publication of two reports from Royal Commissions, seven from Advisory Committees, and many White Papers have not been sufficient to achieve a consensus'. In the absence of an effective parliamentary mechanism providing a policy 'flywheel' to maintain momentum, or otherwise legitimize a proposed approach, the nuclear industry faces an uphill task in convincing the public. Determination and immaculate professionalism are both needed. Sweden has shown what can be done even when domestic political circumstances are not propitious.

Lastly, it is a matter for regret that the environmental protest organizations devote such efforts to obstructing a technology whose sole purpose is to protect public health, and which is likely to involve a residual radiation risk to the community far smaller than the other risks to which we are all exposed—including the use of radiation in medicine. It is difficult to avoid the conclusion that radioactive waste is not the ultimate target, merely the convenient Achilles' heel of an industry which the opposition still hopes to see proscribed *in toto*. This brings us to the crucial issue of public acceptance, which is the subject of the next chapter.

11   Public Acceptance or Public Reluctance?

THE previous chapters bear witness to the universality of public concern about nuclear power, despite vastly different political circumstances. Every country with a nuclear-power programme has experienced the consequences of:

- public reactions to specific major accidents
- more generalized public fears about nuclear power
- a lack of confidence in nuclear policy and its execution
- difficulties of public access to reliable information
- conflicting personal value-systems
- the activities of the environmental organizations
- direct self-interest—'not in my backyard'
- institutional opportunities for dissent
- political opportunism and bias

This list, rooted as it is in human nature, forms a permanent agenda for the nuclear industry: in the time-frame of current managerial interest the problem of public acceptance will not go away.

The electricity industry should have something to say on all these points. Moreover, the evidence shows that it can exert an influence, providing it is scrupulously fair in dealing with the public. There is of course a price to be paid in managerial resources; but there comes a point where lack of public support can wreck carefully prepared investment plans—as in Italy. The industry's duty to communicate with the public is part of its duty to itself.

The list is a reminder that the potential audience is far from homogeneous. Ecologists who oppose the encroachment of industry on the countryside as a matter of principle are bound to be strongly anti-nuclear. The only conceivable way of persuading them towards even lukewarm acceptance would be to demonstrate that in the long run nuclear power is less undesirable than some other energy sources. (This clumsy 'double negative' formulation is probably the best the nuclear industry can hope for—though the 'greenhouse effect' could yet modify attitudes.) Others with political objections may also be difficult to persuade, not least those for whom the cause of nuclear disarmament is a cornerstone of belief. There are some whose amenities will be directly and adversely affected by a new nuclear project. And finally there is the silent majority of uncommitted pragmatic lay citizens, who need information and, where possible, reassurance about nuclear issues, which in most cases lie far outside their personal or professional experience. They will be judging, accepting or rejecting information, and deciding by their own private calculus whether the provider deserves their trust. These different groups may need different approaches; but the messages given to all must be convincing, consistent, and correct.

Reactions to recent accidents

It has been said, with some justification, that the nuclear industry's public relations problems arise, paradoxically, from the very *small* number of serious accidents that have so far occurred. Its position is not in the least like that of the aircraft industry in the 1950s, when there was a grim succession of accidents which gradually led, at great cost in human lives, to the far safer flying we enjoy today. The public has had mercifully little to draw on when making its own judgements about nuclear safety. We now have the experiences of Three Mile Island and Chernobyl. The first was a financial disaster for the owners, but it showed how containment can prevent serious consequences to the surroundings despite operator misunderstanding and error, even when a substantial part of the reactor is destroyed. The second, not far short of the worst-imaginable accident, was a devastating reminder of what can happen to an uncontained reactor which is dynamically unstable and operated with criminal disregard for correct practices. What is striking is that, despite Chernobyl's catastrophic nature, the peak of anxiety in Europe lasted for less than twelve months; after which public confidence returned to a level not far short of what had applied prior to the accident.

What happened in Sweden is particularly instructive, because of the fortunate accident that a public opinion survey had already been in progress for four days in the neighbourhood of the Forsmark nuclear station, on the Baltic coast north of Stockholm. By a further chance this was where the first public warnings of the

Chernobyl disaster originated. At around 0700 on Monday 28 April 1986, two days after the accident, but before the USSR had made any announcement, the Forsmark operators noticed abnormally high levels of radiation. By 1015 hours the authorities had been informed, the plant closed to non-essential traffic, and a search begun for a leak from one of the local reactors. A quarter of an hour later the first news was sent over the local radio. Preparations were made to cut exports of electricity to Norway, and evacuation began. But by 1330 it was known that the true cause was not local; and by 1450 it had been traced to a source outside Sweden. An hour later the people who had been evacuated were allowed to return home. The emergency arrangements had successfully passed the test. This contributed to a mood in the local population during the immediate post-accident period that was noticeably different from that elsewhere in Sweden.

The Swedish Institute for Opinion Research (SIFO) expanded its opinion poll to cover the immediate consequences. The proportion of people who were 'somewhat afraid' of the Forsmark plant increased—from 35 per cent before the accident to 42 per cent afterwards. Nevertheless, the accident had the result of noticeably increasing confidence within the district about the way that Sweden handles and regulates its nuclear-power programme. After the accident three-quarters of the local inhabitants felt[171] that Sweden did this better than other countries, a sharp increase of 18 per cent.

Although the pre-arranged emergency measures which applied in the Forsmark area did not have a national counterpart, the government took swift action. The aircraft which had once been used to identify uranium deposits now measured radioactive fall-out. The National Institute of Radiation Protection decided on a policy of complete openness, which was undoubtedly the right decision, though its impact was somewhat blunted by the inability of most journalists to judge the significance of the various published measurements. Meanwhile the Lapps in the far north were hard hit by the deposition of radio-caesium, and within a few weeks reindeer meat was contaminated with unacceptably high concentrations: 'filth comes from nuclear plants and poisons the land which is our home'. To complicate matters, the radioactive fall-out was very uneven, depending on the local rainfall in the days after the accident.

There was a sharp decrease of Swedish public confidence in nuclear power. Nationally the response was strikingly more adverse than at Forsmark. Nevertheless, when SIFO carried out another survey of public opinion a year and a half after Chernobyl, in October 1987, they found a return to something approaching pre-Chernobyl levels of confidence (Table 11.1), despite government

Table 11.1. Changes in Swedish Public Attitudes

	Pre-Chernobyl	Post-Chernobyl		
	Apr. 86	Sept. 86	Oct. 87	May 89
Anxious about nuclear power	26	42	29	27
Is Swedish investment in nuclear power:				
good?	55	40	50	55
bad?	28	43	34	30
Close all nuclear stations by 2010?	24	45	39	—
Continue to operate nuclear power	51	42	48	decision already taken

Sources: References 36, 37.

attitudes generally in the other direction. Another poll in May 1989 showed confidence still growing; but, as we saw in Chapter 4, by an ironical twist of fate the decision had by then been taken to phase out nuclear power.

A similar recovery of public confidence after about a year was noticed elsewhere in Europe. In the UK only 41 per cent of the population supported the nuclear programme immediately after Chernobyl; eighteen months later the figure had risen[172] to 56 per cent. Out of sight, out of mind, applies to nuclear energy as to much else. But this works both ways: in some places confidence received a second, though smaller, knock following newspaper articles published on the anniversary of the disaster; and a third when books appeared. Interestingly, in Japan, where the initial reaction was muted by distance, the long-term effects took longer to make themselves felt, but were apparently more persistent.

The nuclear industry can take some comfort from the fact that public confidence is capable of recovering so quickly even after so serious an accident; and also that the unusually well-informed inhabitants of Forsmark reacted in a balanced way—which is an encouragement for those planning information campaigns. But as Chernobyl undoubtedly sensitized the public, the industry's first duty to itself is clear: to ensure that no more serious accidents occur.

The effects of Chernobyl within the USSR

No country suffered more from Chernobyl than the USSR itself. None experienced a more traumatic awakening to a horrified awareness of the real dangers of a badly run nuclear programme. The early reports spoke of thirty-one people dead from the acute effects of radiation; 135,000 evacuated from within a 30 kilometres radius of the plant; 600,000 to be kept under long-term observation. Time showed the damage to be even greater. Reportedly by the fourth anniversary 300 workers had died. The numbers to be kept under observation had risen to 1.5 million. Byelorussia had effectively lost 20 per cent of its farmland. Cost estimates had shot up from 8 billion roubles to approaching 200 billion roubles for a ten-year monitoring and rehabilitation programme[173].

The effect on public opinion was dramatic: Suddenly all the reactions that had long been apparent in the West became manifest, to such an extent that some in the medical profession spoke of a new pyschological illness—'radiophobia'. Of 260,000 people examined since the disaster nearly 40 per cent were found to be in need of help for pyschological and social problems.

Politically the effects were profound. Gorbachev's economic restructuring, *perestroika*, was less than nine weeks old. The accident served to confirm its urgent necessity, by exposing the old paternalism—'the State knows best and will provide'—as a hollow sham. The lack of official information for several days, until after the Swedes and the Finns had deduced, with striking precision, what had happened from their own analyses of the radioactive fallout, showed how novel and uncongenial the Moscow bureaucracy still found the new doctrine of openness, *glasnost*.

It must be said that once the specially appointed State Commission—led on the political side by Boris Shcherbina, deputy-chairman of the USSR Council of Ministers, and on the technical side by Valerii Legasov—had taken the measure of the disaster, the damage-containment operations and the evacuation were handled with spectacular efficiency. The violently radioactive remains of the No. 4 reactor were successfully entombed in a concrete 'sarcophagus'. An accident investigation was put in hand, and Legasov's resulting report to an international conference of experts arranged by the International Atomic Energy Agency in Vienna in August 1986 was a model of clarity. The gross violations of operating procedures were not glossed over, nor the fundamental instability of the RBMK family of reactors—whereby a runaway, once initiated, could feed on itself as more and more steam was generated, through a 'positive void coefficient of reactivity' (see Technical Appendix). This was a particular danger when operating at reduced power, as immediately prior to the disaster.

Abandoning the RBMKs immediately was hardly an economic option: the Soviets would have been dangerously short of electric power. Modifying them to reduce their instability was possible, and the Soviet nuclear authorities set about the task, while making clear their intention to phase out this reactor family in due course. The time for insertion of the control rods was cut from 18–20 seconds to 10–12 seconds. A still faster shut-down mechanism, operating in just over 2 seconds, was designed. The fuel enrichment was increased from 2.0 to 2.4 per cent uranium–235, to eliminate the positive void coefficient at the cost of a small economic penalty. Steps were taken to improve the standards of reactor management and operator training, which the Soviets admitted had been 'amateurish': simulator training was far behind that in the West. The other main Soviet family of pressurized-water reactors (VVER) was provided with additional protection against brittle fracture of the large pressure vessels. German advice on control systems was sought. The need for proper international peer-group discussion on safety matters was admitted: symbolically, it was in Moscow that the World Association of Nuclear Operators was formally inaugurated in May 1989. IAEA safety reviews were arranged for a PWR reactor at Rovno in the Ukraine and at a nuclear district-heating plant still under construction at Gorkiy. The authorities put in hand a root-and-branch overhaul of reactor safety policy. Siting requirements were made far more stringent. A safety research programme was started[174].

None of this provided an effective prophylaxis against extreme public anxiety, which was kept alive by the new freedom of the press to write as it saw and judged. On the second anniversary in April 1988 *Pravda* wrote scathingly of the large Kombinat organization, with 8,000 employees, which was set up to decontaminate the affected zone: there were sloppy repairs, drunkenness, and nepotism 'as though there hadn't been an accident'. On the following day Legasov committed suicide in a state of deep depression, but not before writing a personal memoir[175] which flayed the establishment for its complacency and sins of omission: Chernobyl was 'the apotheosis and peak of the economic mismanagement in our country over decades . . . we knew the safety system was inadequate. . . . collective responsibility is an incorrect approach.' Since the disaster he had been in and out of hospital, which may have led to his being passed over in the spring of 1987, though nominally next in line, for the directorship of the Kurchatov Institute of Atomic Energy. An additional cause of his final despair[176] was the rejection of a plan which he had worked out for rejuvenating Soviet chemistry, on the grounds that 'we won't let a mere lad lead us' (Legasov was 52). The depth of his professional disquiet became clear to the Soviet public when his memoir was published in *Pravda* on 20 May 1988. The impact was all the greater because, prior to Chernobyl, criticism of the nuclear industry had been almost unheard of.

The Soviet decision to give nuclear energy a high priority had been a central feature of economic planning. Amongst its other effects it alleviated strain on the railways, which would otherwise have had to carry coal over long distances. But the result was overhasty implementation, poor quality assurance, and a decision to forgo containment as an economy measure. Since the Three Mile Island accident in the USA this last decision had been reversed, so far as PWRs were concerned; but containment of the RBMK type was all but impossible. All this was exposed in the post-Chernobyl self-examination.

It was a central argument of Legasov that open critical analysis was in decline. In the USSR there had been nothing like the Rasmussen safety report[46] and the subsequent sustained professional argument which the West regarded as the most reliable means of making progress. The cry was taken up by others, even those far removed from science. *Literaturnaya Gazeta* wrote that over the doors of all nuclear power institutes the phrase 'dissenting opinions required' should be inscribed[177]. But the Communist Party establishment became concerned at the effects of too open a discussion on public confidence in the nuclear industry, which was still vital to the economy. On the third anniversary of Chernobyl a ban was imposed on press coverage of all accidents and break-downs at nuclear plants falling short of outright catastrophe. *Izvestia* asked: 'For how long will public offices worried over their secrets be able to define the limits of *glasnost*?'

The authorities had reason to be worried. Prior to Chernobyl there were plans—wildly unrealistic, but indicative of the general mood of complacent optimism—for 150 GWe of nuclear power by around the year 2000. But by the beginning of 1989 there were only 34 GWe actually installed, and at a meeting with Gorbachev early in 1988 28 GWe were stripped from the plans for new construc-tion[178]. The reasons were a combination of new and more stringent siting and licensing restrictions, particularly for district-heating reactors, and the need to win public agreement for projects which in earlier years would have been dealt with unopposed, by administrative fiat.

As in the West, nuclear opposition became interlinked with more widespread dissent, notably the 'nationalities issue', which was to shake the USSR to its foundations as the 1990s began. There was widespread hostility in the Ukraine, where Chernobyl is located. Construction of units 5 and 6 at that station was abandoned. Plans for expanding the Ignalina station in Lithuania were shelved. A two-reactor station in Armenia was closed early in 1989 owing to public anxiety following the great earthquake. In the Crimea too there was anxiety about siting nuclear reactors in earthquake regions: an undertaking was given that US and Japanese advice would be sought, but in October 1989 work on a half-built reactor was abandoned. A station at Minsk in Byelorussia, a republic which suffered severely due to fall-out from Chernobyl (which is only a few miles away over its southern border) was stopped. Twenty-one thousand Byelorussians had been allowed back after the disaster, but as late as February 1989 twenty villages had to be evacuated for a second time, after the discovery of some 'hot spots'. The people of this Soviet republic, it was said, didn't want any kind of nuclear power—even safe nuclear power!

In an effort to stem the tide of nuclear dissent a Nuclear Energy

Public Information Centre was set up at the beginning of 1989, with branches at each reactor site. Direct meetings were arranged with ecologists and other opponents. The anxieties of the public were found to be very similar to those discussed elsewhere in this chapter: the possible weapons link, doubts over the quality of nuclear plant construction, the opposition to large modern technology generally. They had become distrustful of the same Soviet technologists who had been acclaimed only three years earlier, but were still willing to listen to foreign experts. Indeed the Director-General of the International Atomic Energy Agency, Hans Blix, had become something of a folk hero; and foreign technical participation was seen as a much-needed contribution to safety. Russian experts visited Western countries to discuss their experience of communicating a balanced view to the public. In July 1989 they attended the British Hinkley Point inquiry.

Paradoxically, the task of the Information Centre was made more difficult by *glasnost*, which had the effect of alerting the Soviet public to negative aspects of foreign events, such as the planned phase-out of nuclear power in Sweden and Italy. The USSR was being forced to learn the lesson that the vastly less serious Three Mile Island accident had taught the West a decade earlier: that in societies blessed with even a moderately free press nuclear power cannot be insulated from the rest of the world. Alexander Lapshin, a vice-minister, spoke of the huge moral and political harm which Chernobyl had caused. He had no illusions about the ability of information alone to restore public confidence: only a long period of continued safe operation could do that.

Three and a half years after Chernobyl the countries of Eastern Europe erupted in political turmoil as they struggled to escape from Communist influence. The reactors which the USSR had exported to her former satellites became symbols of the wider discontent, and a wave of anti-nuclear sentiment developed.

More generalized fears regarding nuclear power

For many members of the public any nuclear reactor is a potential Chernobyl or TMI. The important point made in Chapter 9, that safety is a matter of detail—so that, just as with aircraft, one reactor's faults do not necessarily carry implications for other designs—has yet to be generally understood. In addition, there is little public awareness of the depth of knowledge now available on the effects of radiation on man; or of the generally very low levels of risk that accompany nuclear power—the result of careful regulation backed up by a professional work-force that is unusually well qualified, professionally involved and, should anything go wrong, personally at risk. What hits the headlines is the need to avoid radiation of any kind, the limits on irradiation in pregnancy, and possible genetic effects. The opposition gives the impression that these are new worries; but in fact all these points have for years been explicitly dealt with in radiation safety regulations (Chapter 8). They nevertheless provide a ready-made springboard for campaigns against nuclear power, particularly those based on overt appeals by women to other women.

The Japanese began to experience the consequences in May 1987, when large numbers of a pamphlet[179] called 'Is it too late?' started to circulate. Within a year a third of a million copies had been issued. Subtitled 'The longest letter I've ever written', it is a sustained and emotional attack, clothed in words of deceptive simplicity, on the view that Japan needs nuclear power. Even before it appeared the Japanese people were understandably ambivalent about the nuclear power which supplies nearly a third of their electricity. A majority accepted that it would be the main alternative source of electricity in future; but 70 per cent were worried by the prospect.

Taeko Kansho's 'letter' created some institutional anxiety in Japan's tightly-organized man's world. As one nuclear engineer put it: 'there are no official channels through which we can influence what is happening'! The industry's difficulties were compounded when a novel, *Boys of Chernobyl*, revived wartime memories of the evacuations from Hiroshima and Nagasaki, and led to an upsurge of anti-nuclear sentiment considerably more striking than at the time of Chernobyl itself. Older women, who still remembered the chaos of the wartime evacuations, led the campaign. One consequence was a strong protest in 1988 following an announcement that the Ikata nuclear plant was to conduct a load-following test, made necessary because nuclear power was growing beyond the base-load requirement. The public felt—wrongly—that there was a close analogy with the Chernobyl experiment which had led to the disaster.

Japan is of course a special case, even apart from its wartime experience. The traditional non-involvement of womenfolk in activities outside the home must imply almost no personal contact with industry—nuclear or any other—except as sufferers from the pollution and frenetic activity that have accompanied the Japanese economic miracle. Such traditional and major differences of training and experience can hardly be without their effects in shaping different attitudes. A 1987 poll, which asked respondents whether they knew how nuclear power was generated, received affirmative answers from 61 per cent of men, but from only 21 per cent of women. In such circumstances Taeko Kansho's propagandist 'letter' found a ready audience amongst her own sex.

A massive targeted information campaign designed to bring Japanese women out of the home and closer to the world of twentieth-century technology might be an appropriate response for the Japanese nuclear industry—though one, if successful, that might induce changes in more than nuclear attitudes alone! Change is in the air anyway, symbolized by the political upheaval of the 1989 elections for half the seats in the upper house of the Diet. The Japan Socialist Party scored a startling success, under its charismatic woman leader, Miss Takako Doi. She had been chosen in 1986 after her party's worst-ever election results. Her reversal of its fortunes brought into question the future of the Liberal Democratic Party, which since it was founded in 1955 had held power and—until 1989—control of the upper house. However, the LDP had been gravely weakened in the 1980s by a spate of highly-publicized financial and personal scandals. Once the result of the upper house elections was clear, and in the awareness that a general election for the more powerful lower house would be held within a year, an immediate defensive reaction of the LDP was to appoint two women to cabinet posts (there had been only three such appointments in previous Japanese history). In the world of business that bastion of arch-conservatism, the Keidanren employers' organization, offered to hold policy talks with the JSP. When the election came in February 1990 Miss Doi's party substantially increased its representation in the lower house. This steady strengthening of women's position in politics could well exert some long-term influence on the future of Japan's nuclear programme.

It is not only in Japan that women tend to be generally more anti-nuclear than men. In Sweden SIFO polls showed from 1979 to the time of Chernobyl, throughout the period of immediate alarm, and for eighteen months thereafter, a consistent difference of 20 to 25 per cent between the percentages of men and women expressing anxiety about nuclear power. Until Chernobyl anxiety amongst men was low—around 15 per cent (the poll questions were: 'Are you afraid when you think of nuclear power? How deep is this fear?'). For women it was more than twice as great. In the USA a similar difference between the sexes—around 20 per cent—was measured[180] in 1982. In the area around the British Hinkley Point station during the 1988/9 planning inquiry one poll failed to record a single woman who was in favour of nuclear power. The interesting question is whether such differences between the sexes represent anything more fundamental than differences of training, knowledge, and employment.

The suspicion that training and knowledge might have something to do with it received some support from an interesting experiment organized[181] at the request of the German government by the Jülich nuclear research centre in 1982–4. Twenty-four 'planning cells', each of twenty-five ordinary citizens chosen at random and paid as 'consultants' for a few days of study and inquiry, were given a good deal of information about nuclear energy in the context of four possible energy scenarios, two of which used and two avoided nuclear power. It was a considerable justification for the procedure that all shades of opinion found no difficulty in agreeing on a 'value-tree' (the basic analytical device used to present the multidimensional nature of the problem). The participants' attitudes were monitored over four days, during which some movement was noticed towards greater sympathy with the nuclear viewpoint. Interestingly, there were no significant male–female differences, once the participating ladies had become as familiar with the subject as the men. What differentiated the Jülich study from others involving women is that good information was available to all the participants, time was available to absorb it, both sexes participated equally in the discussions, and the consequences of possible policy choices were explicitly recognized as part of the exercise.

The evidence on the influence of technical knowledge is unfortunately inconclusive. There is some evidence that between men and women of comparable scientific training there are no significant differences in attitudes to nuclear power; though in any population scientifically trained persons are of course in a minority. Other investigators reach a somewhat contradictory conclusion—

that women's opposition does not stem from lack of knowledge about nuclear power, but rather from a perceived lack of safety, and a feeling that it leads to the wrong sort of economic growth. The confusing state of the evidence on the influence of acquired knowledge over intuitive judgement is sufficiently interesting to warrant pursuit. But until women's training, and the experience they gain through employment, are closer to those of men, differences in the attitudes of the two sexes to nuclear power seem likely to persist.

Lack of confidence in nuclear policy and its execution

Opinion polls show consistently that while a majority of the public is anxious about the potential hazards, it accepts the need for a nuclear contribution to energy supplies. It would be easier to win more wholehearted support if the managerial reputation of the industry stood higher. The appalling construction records in the US and the UK cannot be overlooked. The policy failures in too many countries to develop waste-management technology in step with the reactors that create the waste, have escalated public anxieties to a point at which many believe, incorrectly, that no effective waste management is possible. Such managerial blunders offset the impact on public opinion of the astonishing achievements of the French nuclear programme; and of the evident nuclear competence of smaller countries like Belgium, Finland, South Korea, Sweden, and Taiwan as well.

With 70 per cent of electricity now of nuclear origin the French programme is a clear technical success. This poses a problem for the objectors. They therefore attack it on the economic grounds that the French have 'over-invested'; that by incurring such large levels of debt to pay for their nuclear programme they have starved other industries of much-needed investment capital, and held back the economic development of the country. In fact the French programme has been funded since 1982 entirely from the money markets, without support from the government. The foreign-currency proportion of debt peaked in 1984 at 44 per cent.

The frequently voiced objection that nuclear power is 'uneconomic' is meant to imply that the whole direction of policy has been mistaken; and that governments and electrical utilities alike have been infected with a kind of technological megalomania, for essentially frivolous reasons. Constant repetition leads the public to question the judgement, if not the sanity, of the decision-makers. Argued responses can be heard during public inquiries like that for Sizewell B in the UK; but the attacks have a cumulative impact which a clinical dismissal in an Inspector's report published many months later cannot undo.

As we saw earlier, the economic arguments are complex and essentially long-term. An electrical utility wishing to build a nuclear station is in effect making an economic judgement about the future cost of alternative fuels over the next three decades. There is really no way of knowing for certain in advance whether the judgement is right; but opting for a nuclear station, for reasons already discussed, carries a promise of stability in generating costs. For Japan and France, both with poor indigenous energy resources, this long-term prospect is one of nuclear power's main economic attractions. Nevertheless, to maintain good relations with the public it is as well not to appear too dogmatic about the best solution. Électricité de France wisely pursues—and makes sure that it is seen to pursue—a variety of other forms of electricity production, including the 'renewables'—even though, as we shall see in the next chapter, on present knowledge most of the novel options have severe practical limitations.

By the end of the 1980s a new anti-nuclear line was appearing, attacking the underpinning for nuclear power provided by the steady growth in demand for electricity. Some interesting and unexpected facts were unearthed—like the insight that switching to more efficient designs of fluorescent lighting could save 7 GWe of peak demand in the USA alone[182], so avoiding the necessity for half a dozen large new generating stations. The conservationists are right to point out the possibilities generally of a 30–50 per cent improvement in energy efficiency; but only time will tell whether a cutback in demand will actually occur. That will depend on millions of micro-economic decisions made by each and every consumer, at the same time as human ingenuity is constantly working in the other direction of finding new uses for electricity. Meanwhile the utilities have to plan on the only basis they know: assessing demand in the light of current trends and available forecasts.

Other issues regularly used to cast doubt on the validity of nuclear policies include all those discussed in earlier chapters. As we have seen, they are far from straightforward. But neither is nuclear engineering. We are invited to believe that the human race, though clever enough to develop the physics, chemistry, and engineering necessary for this new form of energy, somehow remains ignorant of its side-effects. The nuclear industry may be faulted for delay in some essential but unexciting areas of the supporting technology; but there is no industry where there has been wider circulation and fuller exchange of technical information (at least in the non-Communist world); none where the participation of highly knowledgeable scientists provides a stronger built-in guarantee that the professional staff themselves form the first line of defence.

Although the attacks are made on a broad front, the main underlying issue is that of safety. Confidence will take many years to establish, just as it did with aviation. Aviation's safety record has shown an extraordinary improvement, because of the constant circulation of safety bulletins, and the reliance on check-lists and fail-safe design, maintenance and operation which is drummed into every recruit to the industry. Nuclear power is now taking a similar path. One of the lasting benefits of the Three Mile Island accident is that it quickly led to the creation of the Institute of Nuclear Power Operations (INPO), which a decade later has become an influential body having its own staff of 400. Chernobyl was soon followed by the first steps towards a World Association of Nuclear Operators, an association of electrical utilities, which was brought into existence[141] in May 1989. Both these organizations exist to facilitate the exchange of operating experience. Of course they came twenty years too late. But, to be realistic, the creation of a truly global safety exchange needed the jolt which Chernobyl administered. 'In this world nothing is done[183] until everyone is convinced that it ought to be done.' WANO's creation is a guarantee that a progressive improvement in reactor safety will occur as a result of international peer-group scrutiny.

The problem of public access to reliable information

Many opinion polls record the public's difficulties and frustrations in trying to understand where the truth about nuclear power lies. In these days, when the idealized image of science has been lost, and when trained scientists do not always agree even on matters of fact, the public turns perforce to the news media. They do not have an easy task if they take their responsibilities seriously, as anyone who has attempted to explain nuclear power to a lay audience will understand. Unfortunately in the nuclear controversy the media are not always neutral. Surveys have shown that their attitudes are considerably more negative than those of the general public. This is understandable, quite apart from the possibility that many journalists were influenced by the left-wing movements of the 1960s and 1970s during their student days. The uncomfortable fact is that all too often it is in their commercial and career interests to fan the flames. The media form an important interest group in their own right.

Nuclear power taxes journalistic professionalism. There is little that is newsworthy about a power-station which operates safely and quietly day after day. It may produce very large amounts of electricity, but it does not have the visual glamour of an airliner or high-speed train. Moreover, nuclear power is an increasingly mature industry: there are few new technical surprises to report, simply steady consolidation and incremental development.

Real 'news' occurs only when things go wrong. And then the journalist's troubles begin. Information in official statements may use unfamiliar jargon, with levels of risk indicated by unfamiliar physical units and obscure nomenclature. A busy journalist has little incentive to spend time on the subject in advance of an emergency; if one occurs it is then too late to do the background reading. Under pressure journalists turn *faute de mieux* to the sources most readily available for colourful on-the-record comment: Greenpeace, Friends of the Earth, or the multitudinous minor protest groups—of which a count taken in 1978 showed there were already nearly thirty in the UK alone[184]. If industry is not geared to help it will simply be bypassed. Moreover, 'les absents ont toujours tort'.

There are many reasons why the nuclear industry has not done well in expounding its views. There is the problem of finding good popularizers, people knowing the subject well, capable of explaining the issues in terms the public can understand, and able to hold their own in live radio and TV discussions. (These, it will be noticed, are also the qualities of managerial high-flyers, of whom there are never enough.) Then there is the fundamental difficulty mentioned in Chapter 1—that the anti-nuclear critic can ply his trade without overrunning his poster space, air time, or ration of column-inches, by using the shortest and most telling catch-phrases, like

'*Nuclear power is dangerous to life*' (the slogan used in the Swedish referendum of 1980). But an honest nuclear spokesman has to complicate his case with a welter of conditions and caveats; if not, he risks over-simplifying. Even if he is successful in his own terms, ninety per cent of the population may fail to follow the debate in detail, and will in the end be looking simply for signs of credibility in the protagonists—something no more technical, perhaps, than the body language visible on the television screen. What the industry spokesman must not do is cheat. It is not that he is intrinsically more honest than the rest of us, simply that to be caught cheating would spell the end of credibility for the organization he represents.

The media, particularly television, are less inhibited. It is salutary to recall the British politician Richard Crossman's words of advice to a colleague who was about to appear on television: 'Remember, you are there not to instruct, but to entertain.' One French film made in 1976 for an anti-nuclear trade union purported to have been taken in the La Hague reprocessing plant near Cherbourg, when in fact it was partly shot in a dairy-products factory. Coverage of the Three Mile Island accident was fleshed out by a story about some cows which were in trouble for totally unrelated reasons. Hypothetical questions can be used to elicit answers which may give the opposite impression to that intended by the person being interviewed. Leading experts are asked to record statements which are then force-fitted into an already-written framework, which they have not been shown, to support a producer's view with which they may disagree. The principle of 'balance' can allow a plausible but poorly informed objector as much time on subjects where real expertise is needed as someone who has spent a lifetime in its study.

The medical profession protects the public by the standards it sets for itself: there are no amateur surgeons. There is no comparable protection provided by television journalists' professional organizations. Quality and accuracy are very variable. Some specialist programmes are quite excellent, valuable sources even for professional scientists. Some of the worst problems come from current affairs programmes. Cutting of pre-recorded visual material can so distort the message which an expert is trying to put over— whether by design or ignorance on the part of the producer is not always clear—that some people in positions of responsibility agree to interviews only when the transmission is going out 'live', when the responsibility for what is said, and where it fits into the discussion, is entirely on their own shoulders.

A salutary example of the influence of television editing occurred in the USA in November 1979, during the period of hysteria induced by the Three Mile Island accident[185]. A small US electrical utility, Illinois Power, succeeded in scoring a modest victory over the Columbia Broadcasting System, which had asked permission to make a fourteen-minute documentary on construction problems at one of its nuclear stations. The utility agreed, providing it could have its own cameramen also present at the same time. They were instructed to film everything that was filmed by CBS. The programme duly appeared in the *60 Minutes* series, beginning with the statement:

The American Nuclear programme is in trouble, and not only because of Three Mile Island and the Presidential Commission's Report on Hazards. It's in trouble because the cost of building the plants has gone crazy. A *China Syndrome* of costs.

The remark about construction costs was justified; but the reference to Jane Fonda's propagandist film about a nuclear disaster hardly falls into the category of dispassionate reporting. The CBS film gave a poor impression of the utility's management record. However, because of its foresight the utility was able to make its own response. Within a week it had produced a videotaped rebuttal entitled *60 Minutes: Our Reply*, using the same basic material, but with altered cutting giving a totally different impression of its own competence. Illinois Power's motivation was the modest one of protecting industrial relations with its own staff; but as word got around that this David had produced an effective riposte to the CBS Goliath the video was widely shown. For those who saw it, it provided an effective answer to trial by television.

This story carries a lesson for nuclear proponents. Wringing hands and staying silent in the face of organized opposition or media bias is no policy: that merely ensures that only one side is heard. And since a wrong statement repeated half a dozen times becomes a received 'truth', silence is a disservice to that substantial proportion of the public which is prepared to listen and judge for itself. In Britain, as elsewhere, something like half the population is neither strongly for nor strongly against nuclear power. That half is the industry's audience.

The record shows that efforts to communicate directly with this silent constituency can indeed be effective. Obviously there is no simple and effortless way of refuting a poster campaign announcing bluntly that 'Nuclear Power Kills'. What the industry has to do is less direct and far more labour-intensive. An invitation to the public to ask for information led to Électricité de France despatching two million brochures over a period of five years from 1977 (Chapter 3). During that same period French public opinion moved from having a majority opposed to nuclear power, to being two-thirds in favour, despite the Three Mile Island disaster in 1979.

A similar policy of going out to meet the public was adopted by British Nuclear Fuels Limited in 1983. The company's reputation had reached a dangerously low level, after an unauthorized release of radioactivity from Sellafield into the Irish Sea, and an almost simultaneous TV programme asserting that a 'cluster' of childhood leukaemias existed amongst the families at Sellafield (Chapter 8). The plant processes 99 per cent of British radioactive waste, and was a prime target. Calls for closure were heard, and its continued existence seemed at one time to be threatened.

Inquiries by BNFL revealed that the management was regarded as secretive, and the plant as a danger to health. The company decided that in addition to tightening supervision and improving maintenance, rewinning public approval should head the list of corporate objectives. This was more than mere public relations: it was necessary if skilled staff were to be retained, and kept sufficiently confident to act as ambassadors to the local population. By a lucky stroke of timing a policy of full disclosure got under way three weeks before Chernobyl, and almost certainly helped to protect the company's reputation during the dark days which followed.

Sellafield was opened to public visits. Eight million invitation cards were printed and distributed with the Sunday newspapers. A press-advertising campaign audaciously invited the public to write to Greenpeace—address supplied—for information on nuclear power; and then, 'if you do have queries', to get in touch with BNFL. An imaginative television-advertising campaign was launched, with fifty-second 'spots'—a great deal can be shown in that time. Special steam-trains were run to the local station, adding their touch of enjoyment and nostalgia to a day out for the family. A permanent exhibition was opened seven days a week throughout the year—Christmas Day only excepted. Despite the remote location the annual intake of visitors rose steadily to 160,000 by 1988. Sellafield staff gave over 400 talks to local interest groups annually. Invitations to debate nuclear issues were willingly accepted, on the one entirely reasonable precondition that there should be a neutral chairman.

Journalists, both as a profession and as individuals, were given an especially warm welcome. Easy access to authentic information reduced the incentive to turn to self-appointed outside experts: the Press could glean more information directly from those at the work-face. The mere fact of seeing things for themselves changed previously held impressions. Électricité de France had earlier adopted a similar policy of 'open house' to journalists. Permanent 'press rooms' were set up both in Paris and at all power-stations, where journalists could find the basic documentation they needed. This paid off in long-term improvements in the factual accuracy of reporting—which is all that the industry has any right to expect.

EdF's experience confirms the need for a speedy response. Early in 1988 the Transnuklear affair (page 91) led the German magazine *Stern* to question the propriety of certain French fuel transactions; EdF's fuel department arranged a meeting with journalists the following day. When the French newspaper *Libération* published a four-page article questioning the leak-tightness of reactor containment in the event of an accident a press meeting was arranged the same afternoon. In both cases the opportunity of direct discussion with those responsible, and the precision of the answers, impressed the journalists who were present. EdF offers a night-and-day service to the media, so that they can be given authentic information at the earliest possible moment on any event likely to be of public interest. Information held in the 'Magnuc' database is also available to the public on the Minitel service of small cable-linked visual display units, four million of which are installed in French homes. The number of Minitel calls for information made by the public is not in practice large. What matters is the confidence-building aspect of knowing that the information is freely available. The Bavarian Ministry of the Environment and Development decided at the end of 1989 to offer a similar videotext service, based in part on the French experience.

EdF also makes special efforts to inform medical doctors, in view of their role as informal advisers on safety at the family level[186]. It organizes a National Committee for Medical Information which includes independent medical radiation experts.

The Swedish referendum of 1980 provided a laboratory test of the impact of information on public opinion. It was monitored in great detail by SIFO, the Swedish Institute for Opinion Research[34]. When an anti-nuclear poster was displayed all over the country in February 1980—'Nuclear power is dangerous to life'—SIFO observed an immediate increase of several per cent in public anxiety. The industry's response was the slogan: 'Dare to ask!' The polls shed light on the response time for the absorption of new knowledge. Even with a vigorous campaign the soaking-in process can take two or three months, which is incidentally longer than it takes to mount a parliamentary debate. Moreover, the constant renewal of individuals in society means that the job, like the proverbial painting of the Forth Bridge, can never be finished: there are always young people just emerging into political consciousness. From their school-days onwards they need the industry's attention, being the decision-makers and opinion-formers of twenty years on.

The choice of ground on which to fight a public information campaign is crucial. Safety is a particularly difficult issue—not because nuclear power is especially dangerous by industrial standards, but because defensive arguments are unavoidably lengthy. It is not enough to point out that the average exposure of the population to radiation created by the nuclear industry is far less than that from medical exposure plus the unavoidable natural radioactivity (Table 8.2). The public will reflect that while this may be true of normal operation, accidents are what matter. That leads to a debating morass. Nuclear professionals have to pick their way through it in their own pursuit of improvements in safety, but it is hardly the stuff of effective advocacy or easy reading for the public. What the industry can do is to offer journalists a helping hand, through direct discussion of the kind of technical points which the press found so confusing at the time of Chernobyl—becquerels and sieverts, alpha and beta radiation, radio-caesium and iodine, the confusing and sometimes contradictory regulations on contaminated food.

Economic arguments are easier to present. Everyone knows something about money, and the public is well able to understand the economic forces that are in play. It is not difficult to point out what happens if nuclear power is *not* used: the downwards effect it had on the oil price after 1979 is something which everyone can appreciate, just as all can understand that abandoning nuclear energy would lead ineluctably to upward pressures on the prices of other fuels. The implausibility of some environmentalist goals in the real world of devolved micro-economic decisions can also be emphasized. The inclusion of sufficient detail is important: a public which earns its living through commerce is likely to be sceptical about woolly generalizations, and grateful for anything helping it to form views which are solidly based.

As the anti-nuclear campaigners essentially seek to exploit human feelings, the industry can reasonably take a leaf out of their book by also looking for human interest, which is always a staple diet of the media. There is nothing immoral in actively searching out positive stories. And even the simplest and most basic facts need constant reiteration. Not so long ago, when 85 reactors had been built in the USA (the number has since passed 110), two-thirds of those polled thought the figure was less than 20. One poll recorded, as late as May 1988, that 59 per cent of the inhabitants of Ontario did not know that nuclear power, not hydro, was the main source of electricity in the province[187].

There is a big job of general education to be done. In all these ways the nuclear industry can defend its purpose and reputation, and win a fairer hearing. But the constant proviso is that further major accidents must be avoided.

Conflicting personal value-systems

The attempted correlation of personal value-systems with nuclear attitudes became a growth industry amongst psychologists in the 1970s. A questioning mood, sparked off by the Vietnam War, had spread outwards from the USA. The young found themselves increasingly out of sympathy with consumerist society, with its emphasis on 'growth'—including growth of electricity demand—and ever more complex technologies that seemed completely outside the control of the general populace. It became a case of 'the good little people versus the bad top people'. There was also understandable concern about the dangers of nuclear proliferation. Nuclear power, after its initial brief period of stardom, became both a specific target for the crusading Left, and a convenient general symbol for wider discontent. As the British Royal Commission on Environmental Pollution noted[151] in 1976, nuclear power had become a 'whipping-boy for technological development as a whole'.

Ralph Nader brought together a number of anti-nuclear groups in his 'Critical Mass' in 1973, which had a noticeable effect on national American politics. President Carter came to office in January 1977 after a period of study by his Democratic colleagues which emphasized the connection between nuclear energy and future nuclear proliferation—Alfvén's 'Siamese twins'. Carter dubbed nuclear power 'the energy of last resort', and in so doing conferred on its opponents his Presidential authority. But the very long time horizons of nuclear construction meant that, however strong the protests, plans could not easily be altered. Seeing that debate was achieving very little the protesters turned to violence. This reached a climax in 1977 with one dead and several seriously injured at the Creys-Malville fast reactor site in France, after a demonstration by a highly organized crowd of 30,000, of whom an estimated 20 per cent were foreigners brought into France for the purpose. Academic commentators issued the gravest warnings of what would happen if governments did not treat people's anxieties over nuclear power with greater understanding[184].

In fact what happened at Creys-Malville had little effect on the course of events, apart from harming the cause of the protesters, and more than a decade later things look rather different. True, the anxiety has not gone away, having been fuelled by two major accidents. But those who cry out for the world to stop, so that they can get off, no longer automatically rank with the Old Testament prophets. In escaping at least temporarily from a serious energy shortage the world has concentrated on cutting waste and improving energy efficiency, ironically moving by different means towards one of the main objectives of the protesters. In the process it has also moved politically to the right. It is entirely possible that new sources of future disaffection have been created thereby. But in a growing number of countries the prime test has become less one of admirable but ill-defined environmentalist morality, than of whether a given energy policy is likely to work in practice.

The reluctance—or inability—of the campaigners of the seventies to spell out, convincingly and quantitatively, what kind of a world they were seeking did not go unnoticed. It may be true that if consumerism were halted energy problems could be largely solved; but how to bring that about has not been demonstrated, only asserted. More people are now willing to recognize the inconsistency of enlightened middle-class leaders who profess willingness to forgo the benefits of energy consumption, while continuing to invest personally in electrical devices of all kinds, thereby helping to compel the electricity generating companies to meet their demands. Even Mrs Dahl, then Swedish energy minister and an opponent of nuclear power, admitted in August 1988 in London that the environmentalists of the 1970s had been unrealistic in their campaign for zero growth. Few members of the public are willing to believe that 'centralization of power'—in the sense of a national grid—could possibly have the political implication of a police state, as was asserted more than once in the 1970s. There is scepticism about an argument which implies that not to build Sizewell B in the UK would in some way help the cause of non-proliferation.

The old values have not disappeared: they are, as before, such things as: safety for oneself and one's descendants, personal control over hazards where safety cannot be guaranteed (the fact that our senses do not respond to radiation will always remain a tremendous hurdle), freedom from pollution, care for the environment, husbanding of the earth's resources, etc., etc. Any lessening of the former critical stridency stems from one thought: how? Awareness has grown that the future is a great deal more difficult than the protesters of the 1970s were willing to admit. Their device of broadening a single issue such as safety into a much wider attack on societal values—even on democratic structures—cuts less ice in an industrial world where unemployment seems endemic, and where feeding the teeming billions of the Third World remains a problem without a satisfactory solution. 'Greenhouse' issues and acid rain are reminders that some of the alternatives to nuclear power are far from environmentally benign.

It remains as true as ever that purely institutional procedures cannot resolve conflicts that are based on different value-systems. There the psychologists of the 1970s were right: these are matters of feeling rather than rationality. Where they were wrong was in overweighting the point, in suggesting (as some did) that there is something almost unconstitutional in not giving way to protest. That is a mis-reading of democracy. It is, and always will be, the task of government to make choices between conflicting value-judgements—for the obvious reason that if contentious issues could be more easily resolved they would be settled at a lower level. The energy crises of 1973 and 1979 meant that governments could not avoid taking a view of what would be in the interests of their peoples. To seek by violent means and in the name of democracy to deny their right to do so—as at Creys-Malville—is in the last analysis deeply anti-democratic. The right way is that of Sweden, via the ballot-box. The Swedish decision to phase out nuclear power may be ill-judged; but that is Sweden's affair. That country has the right to take any quixotic decisions it may choose. It also has the democratic machinery to correct them later.

What can and will eventually resolve the conflict between personal values is time. Bacon's short essay *Of Innovations*[188], published at the end of the sixteenth century, says it all:

. . . those things which have long gone together are, as it were, confederate within themselves; whereas new things piece not so well . . . time itself . . . indeed innovateth greatly, but quietly, and by degrees scarce to be perceived; for otherwise, whatsoever is new is unlooked for; and ever it mends some and injures others; and he that is holpen takes it for a fortune, and thanks the time; and he that is hurt, for a wrong, and imputeth it to the author.

The underlying problem is that the pace of innovation generally has become so great, changing the world dramatically even within a single generation, that attitudes and personal values have not had time to adjust. In the specifically nuclear field the problem is compounded by the difficulties of assessing an industry which has been heard to claim that serious accidents will occur only once in some astronomical number of years, but which has nevertheless managed to produce two within a decade. It may be true that a high level of safety is indeed attainable, but it will take decades for the public to be persuaded.

Meanwhile individuals are still completing those private and intuitive cost-benefit calculations which determine whether they can accept that nuclear technology's good points outweigh the bad. They have been hampered by the complexity of the knowledge needed to understand what is happening, and by the missionary spreading of half-truths like: *there is no solution to the waste problem*; or *environmentally benign 'soft energy paths'* (meaning the 'renewable' resources) *can provide adequate supplies of energy for our needs*—a point taken up in the next chapter. For failing to discharge their educational duty to the public, and exposing the unattainability—and therefore in a sense the falsity—of some of the environmentalists' stated goals the media, particularly television, must take a considerable share of responsibility. It is no service to the public to pretend that policy choices are easier than they really are.

The activities of the environmental organizations

The many environmental organizations that intervene in the nuclear debate are largely products of the United States of the late 1960s and early 1970s. They have become an important political influence, with a serious message which deserves attention despite the often deliberate distortions and frequent gimmickry. We shall take as examples two of the major organizations, whose considerable differences serve as a reminder of the breadth and variety of the environmental movement.

The Natural Resources Defense Council was started in 1970 by a group of lawyers from Harvard and Yale, their aim being to force the Executive branch of the US government to implement the environmental laws which Congress had passed. They were concerned about weapons testing in the atmosphere, the space programme, and pollution generally. Under US law individual citizens had the right to intervene if they were likely to be affected by the decisions of the Nuclear Regulatory Commission; but government legal aid was not available to assist them in presenting their case. That was to be NRDC's role. Very early in its existence a successful battle was fought with the Internal Revenue Service on the issue of whether such interventions could be regarded as a charitable activity. The victory opened the way to private support on a tax-deductible basis. By 1988 NRDC enjoyed an annual income of ten million dollars, half from private contributions, half from funding by some of the USA's nearly 5,000 private charitable foundations.

During the 1970s the NRDC began to campaign actively against the use of plutonium recycling in PWRs and against the whole breeder programme, the driving force being fear of terrorism and proliferation. The campaign was conducted at the level of public policy; more technical issues such as reactor safety were left to bodies like the Union of Concerned Scientists, or to Ralph Nader's organization Public Citizen. In 1976—two years after the Indian explosion—an intervention was made before the Nuclear Regulatory Agency over the export of reactor hardware for the Tarapur reactor.

In 1981 NRDC became concerned over military reactors used for the production of plutonium and tritium (a bomb component). The operators, by then the Department of Energy, wanted to restart production at Savannah River, using a reactor which was uncontained. As a result of NRDC's intervention the DOE was forced to carry out an environmental threat assessment, which NRDC criticized as being founded on incorrect information. Since then the military production facilities have remained in NRDC's sights, including the numerous hazardous waste-dumps at Hanford (Chapter 10). Chernobyl reinforced NRDC's determination to oppose the uncontained US military production reactors, which are of a somewhat similar design, though more stable and better controlled. By comparison the civil nuclear-power debate has occupied relatively little of NRDC's time.

The great heatwave of 1988 found NRDC beginning to express concerns about global warming and the 'greenhouse effect' (the subject of Chapter 13). Nuclear power is not a contributor to the warming, and NRDC's staff profess to have open minds as to whether this recently recognized hazard should lead them to modify their opposition. They say they would be prepared to do so if unbiased energy economics ('a level playing-field') pointed in the direction of nuclear power as a preferred option.

Greenpeace has grown from a group which was also formed in 1970 to protest at US weapons testing. Today it exemplifies the enormous sums that are at the disposal of the major pressure groups. It had a world-wide income in 1988 of $75 million, of which $30 million came from the USA. The organization functions as a benevolent paternalistic autocracy, answerable to no one but itself. It publishes widely, but issues no formal Annual Report. The bulk of the money is subscribed by the public for 'soft' issues, like the conservation of whales or dolphins; but the governing body—a top management group of four, and an eighteen-member international council, elected by a small number of voting members (sixty-five members in the case of the USA)—allocate the money to a wider range of issues, on the basis of their collective judgement of the dangers facing the human race. The funds were allocated in 1988 in roughly the ratio 7 : 4: 4 between protection of the oceans, the fight against the discharge of toxic or environmentally damaging wastes, and nuclear issues, both civil and military. The sums available allow highly professional studies to be funded on matters such as nuclear safety (e.g. reference 140).

In recent years Greenpeace's stance has been vigorously anti-nuclear. Some senior members of the management profess to believe that nuclear power will be phased out, at least in the United States, by the year 2020. Greenpeace also claims that it is unrealistic to attempt to build a wall between civil nuclear power and weapons production; in other words, that proliferation is inevitable if the nuclear-power industry is allowed to remain: 'Nuclear power has never had a peaceful purpose[189]. Truly peaceful nuclear power is a myth.'

Such views, which might be received with surprise in Belgium, Finland, or Switzerland, offer little incentive to the nuclear industry to open a dialogue. But ironically Greenpeace's very success in attracting financial support is creating a need for a more constructive approach—one that is, in their own words, prescriptive rather than proscriptive. The rate at which the organization's income has been rising—at 40 per cent annually through most of the 1980s—has placed considerable strains on the central management. With around $15 million devoted (1988) to nuclear issues, a point has been reached where the market for protest is becoming saturated, particularly as Greenpeace is not the only voice. And yet the momentum of civil nuclear power persists. Some more constructive use for the available funds is now needed.

An awareness is developing that the end-objectives of the electrical utility industry cannot be so very different from their own. It remains to be seen whether Greenpeace and the other main protest organizations will accept the challenge of engaging in direct debate with those who believe that the potential benefits from nuclear power are too valuable to be thrown away, despite technical difficulties and two serious accidents. The nearest Greenpeace has so far (1989) come to the nuclear industry, apart from direct confrontation in public inquiries, is in meetings with international organizations like the International Atomic Energy Agency, and the Nuclear Energy Agency of the OECD. These are

310 Public acceptance or reluctance

310 Public acceptance or reluctance

important contacts; but the officials of such bodies are not commercial decision-makers in the same sense as the chairmen and chief executives of electrical utilities, and do not have to face up to the difficulties of making choices in the same direct way.

It is the people at the point of action with whom the pressure groups should seek to debate. Without such direct contact the environmentalists will be limited to working on historical data, pointing to mistakes as they occur, forever a little out of date. The nuclear industry is a large one, and no one can deny that many things have happened which are capable of improvement, as in any major industry. What really matters for the future is not past slips and failures, but the extent to which the industry has learned from its mistakes.

To illustrate: a Greenpeace handout, dated July 1988, states that:

uranium mining is amongst the world's most hazardous mining operations . . . in the USA the occupational mortality is higher than for virtually any other occupation, including coal-mining.

As we saw at the end of Chapter 8, that is quite simply not true. It may have been nearer the truth in the 1950s and early 1960s, before the full effects of radon and the need for adequate ventilation had been properly understood, and before surface and *in-situ* leach mining had started to challenge conventional deep mines; but we are dealing with an industry which is well capable of learning, and it is not true today. Moreover, there are no reasons to believe that normal mining hazards, such as rock falls, are worse than in any other kind of mining; and unlike coal-mining, there are only rarely dangers of explosion or fire. Again:

. . . the most recent studies of 'atom bomb survivor' populations show that exposure to certain kinds of radiation may be considerably more dangerous than is assumed in . . . current official models.

Intentionally or otherwise, this passage gives the impression of an industry moving forward in ignorance, while the environmentalist 'good guys' in the white Stetsons point out the truth. The reality is the existence of a world-wide network of epidemiologists, health physicists, national regulatory authorities, and safety officials from the industry, who are constantly in touch with each other, working together to improve their understanding of radiation effects. The interests of the nuclear industry are far from being the only driving force. Such studies began sixty years ago as a result of injury to medical radiologists, and that is still a guarantee that the medical profession, both in its own interests and out of scientific curiosity, will insist on pursuing the truth until there is complete assurance that our understanding is adequate. It is a travesty of the truth to imply that the nuclear industry is even in a position to conduct its business in defiance of medical knowledge on radiation effects: the law is there to ensure compliance with national regulations.

And yet, irritating and unfair though some of what is written by the pressure groups may be, they have an important role. Without them it is possible, even probable, that corrective action would take longer. In the noisy world of democratic politics, where politicians lose votes if they are not seen to keep potentially hazardous industries under control, the upraised voices of the Friends of the Earth and Greenpeace, and the more measured activities of NRDC, provide some assurance that nuclear issues will remain exposed to the scrutiny of public opinion.

Direct self-interest: 'not in my backyard'

Wherever any large or visually intrusive industrial complex is sited some inhabitants will oppose the coming changes to the character of their district. Many will fear new hazards; some will resent the inflow of outsiders. In a conservation area there will be worries about driving away the tourists who come for peaceful enjoyment of unspoiled countryside (nuclear stations unfortunately often have to be sited on the coast or by large rivers, in lightly populated and often beautiful areas). Professional fishermen may worry about the effect of heat pollution from the cooling-water on fish stocks, or about controlled low-level discharges of radioactivity. The people of Cornwall in Britain, and of Brittany in France, have both successfully opposed the construction of nuclear stations, despite their vulnerability to grid breakdowns through having no large power-stations nearby. On the other hand some in commerce will give a guarded welcome to a new nuclear station, because of the benefits it brings to the local economy.

All this is entirely to be expected, and by no means all of it relates to the special physical nature of nuclear power. An equal degree of passion was evident throughout 1989 in Kent, the beautiful south-east corner of England, over the planning of the high-speed rail-link to the Channel Tunnel.

If a substantial part of local opinion is adverse, but if a nuclear project is nevertheless driven through by government authority, the host locality may feel that it is being asked to pay a price so that other more populous areas can benefit from the electricity generated. If so, some cash transfer via government grants and subsidies seems a reasonable way of helping to redress the balance. The justice may be rather rough—who is to make an exact valuation of an uncluttered landscape?—but it is some recognition that the locals have a claim to be treated sympathetically.

Where this approach has been tried it seems to work, at least in countries where nuclear power is otherwise tolerated. In France the host communities benefit from substantial cash inflows from local taxes paid by the power-stations: a power-plant with four units generating a total of nearly 4 GWe may pay around 100 million francs a year. Such arrangements are so much appreciated that at times there has actually been a surplus of potential sites, as community leaders pressed EdF to select their areas. One mayor told EdF's chief construction engineer in 1985, after the Paluel station on the north coast was finished, that he had been able in a mere ten years to provide amenities for his constituents that otherwise he could not have dreamed of in fifty. At Creys-Malville in 1988 the local community pressed for the shut-down fast reactor to be restarted, to restore the cash flow of levies to the local administration.

In Japan local fishermen are compensated for the heat pollution and other effects a nuclear station may have on their livelihood, while the local community receives a special grant under the 1974 legislation known as the *Three Laws Pertaining to Sources of Electricity*[31]. Such financial compensation is regarded as 'bribery' by some whose reasons for taking an anti-nuclear stance may be as much national-political as personal, and many of whom live elsewhere. The vigour of their protests suggests that the method must have some validity as a way of assuaging local feelings.

A nuclear utility's responsibilities go further than providing additional local revenue. It has a social duty to keep in touch with the local population through bulletins and personal contacts, and in particular to instruct them about emergency arrangements. These may never be needed, but are as essential as fire-drill in large office-blocks or lifeboat drill at sea. The people of Forsmark were well looked after in this respect; those living near Three Mile Island were not.

There are also broader social responsibilities, stemming from the implantation of a large industrial unit in what may previously have been a rural farming community. At the early Trino Vercellese reactor in Piedmont the Italian utility ENEL carried out socio-economic studies jointly with the commune, trying to forecast and plan for as many as possible of the local economic effects the station would bring in its train. The district is a rice-growing area, and the water-management procedures needed for the nuclear-plant might have interfered with irrigation. The problem seemed intractable until ENEL realized that it could adjust the management of its hydro stations further up the Po river to fit in with local needs, so as to minimize any inconvenience from the nuclear station. Possibilities for local investment, work, and training, and the utilization of waste heat were also explored[39]. In the UK British Nuclear Fuels Limited have helped to improve the road network round Sellafield, and organized a conservation programme for local architecture in the neighbouring town of Whitehaven. Such good neighbourliness helps to explain the support BNFL has received from the local community.

Planning inquiries and other quasi-judicial investigations

In an ideal democracy the appointed government, counselled by wise and experienced advisers, would consider facts, reach decisions in the public interest, and receive the thanks of a grateful electorate. France, in its paternalistic post-war constitutional manifestation, has come closer to this model than most other democracies. But in countries with more Anglo-Saxon attitudes to administration paternalism is seen as inappropriate when dealing with technologies which lie at the limit of engineering knowledge; and which, if that knowledge were to prove faulty, could bring trouble to those living nearby. In Britain and the USA the public simply does not believe that the closed processes of government are any substitute for open argument. The less its own grasp of the technologies in question the more it wants its spokesmen to have a chance of taking part in the decision-making process, and putting questions and arguments to an independent arbiter in terms understandable to laymen. For their part successive British governments have been ready to share some of their prerogatives with independent tribunals. They provide a useful excuse should things go wrong, and a convenient way of deferring an awkward decision during a run-up to an election. Moreover, a well-chosen Inspector of independent mind provides a check on bureaucratic complacency, exposes cracks that have been papered over, and may identify hazards that some would prefer to leave undiscussed. For a government an inquiry serves the multiple functions of umbrella, safety-valve, and lightning-conductor.

From the nuclear industry's viewpoint it has disadvantages. It is enormously expensive in terms of managerial effort, the more so the wider an inquiry's terms of reference. Its unpredictable timetable interrupts the normal rhythm of production and construction, and is certainly not the way to create a competitive industry. And it reacts adversely on the issue of public acceptance, by dredging up problems and opinions which the industry must carefully examine and where necessary rebut. The industry is in an awkward position. If the opponents' points are found to have substance, it must make an appropriate admission. Even if its own arguments in rebuttal are sound, it may still not be believed. But this is democracy at work. Such inquiries at least have the benefit of honing the 'pro' arguments as much as the 'anti'. If they identify points of real substance which the industry has overlooked, that can hardly be regretted. And in principle they should make the acceptance of similar proposals easier in future.

The difficulty is that this is not always so. In Canada the report of the exhaustive inquiry into the Cluff Lake mining project, which took eighteen months, was attacked immediately it was published. What even the meticulous four-year-long investigation into every aspect of the British Sizewell B reactor and related policy issues did not do was to convince those who did not wish to be convinced. The report of the Inspector, Sir Frank Layfield, appeared in January 1987, and a site licence was granted in the following June. The Central Electricity Generating Board soon asked for permission to build a second almost identical reactor at Hinkley Point on the Bristol Channel. In August 1988 twenty-one local authorities condemned the proposed reactor as 'unsafe, uneconomic, and unwanted'. At the statutory inquiry which began a few weeks later, they queried not only local environmental and planning matters, but also the need for the new reactor, the economics of nuclear power, the safety of PWRs, and the management of radioactive waste. It was as though Layfield's exhaustive inquisition had never taken place. The strength of the public protest may have contributed to the Thatcher government's decision on 9 November 1989 to halt further PWR construction for several years —which would take the country well past the next general election.

Such constant questioning may be a democratic right; but it is also destructive of that other common good—economic progress—not only because of wasted time, but more insidiously through a loss of confidence in the national ability to manage big engineering projects. In France policy once made is broadly accepted, and the purpose of local inquiries is the more limited and complementary task of making the adjustments that are always necessary in the cause of equity. Even two authors generally sympathetic to the anti-nuclear movement were moved to comment[190], when comparing France and the UK:

faced with the luxury of choice the decision-making process slows down to the point of meandering, and energy planning wallows in incoherence . . . precipitate action on a major scale is checked, but the price of these checks may be slackening technical impetus and loss of commercial advantage.

At an earlier British inquiry into an extension of the Windscale (now renamed Sellafield) nuclear fuel reprocessing plant in 1977, the objectors advanced seventeen points, every one of which was considered and dismissed by the Inspector, the Hon. Mr Justice Parker, who did, however, accept thirteen of British Nuclear Fuels submissions. Shortly after his report was published a letter in *The Times* expressed astonishment that the Inspector could find no merit in any of the objections. An American lawyer[192] could not resist expressing in turn his own surprise at the implied logical theorem that, provided sufficient points of contention were put forward, 'the truth must necessarily lie somewhere between the positions advanced by the parties'! The opposition remained unconvinced, and continued to maintain[184] that the Windscale report was 'highly selective'.

There is a further interesting aspect of major planning inquiries: they are international in their effects. Modern communications, supplemented by the world-wide personal links of the anti-nuclear lobbyists, ensure that every argument deployed in an inquiry in one country is quickly adapted for use in another. There is a travelling circus of witnesses waiting to appear, provided the inquiry will accept their evidence. Weakness in the arguments put forward by the industry of one country can therefore be damaging everywhere. The nuclear industry cannot escape the duty to itself and to its foreign colleagues of thinking through its arguments, and deploying them with maximum effectiveness when offering testimony.

The anti-nuclear campaign at the political level

No one who has read the histories in Chapters 4 and 5 can harbour the illusion that all attacks by politicians on nuclear power are motivated by the purest concern for truth: electoral advantage has more to do with what happens. Why else should the local government administration in the London borough of Hounslow (to give one specific example from many) make the meaningless declaration, on road-signs erected at public expense, that its area is a 'nuclear-free zone'? Hounslow is not, nor is ever likely to be, the site of a nuclear reactor; but it is host to hospitals with well-developed radio-therapy units, dental surgeries with X-ray facilities, industrial radiography units at London's Heathrow airport, and thousands of smoke detectors in houses and offices which rely on the artificially produced radioactive element americium–241. Hounslow receives its fair share of nuclear-generated electricity. The bodies of its inhabitants are, like everyone else's, radioactive from naturally occurring potassium and carbon. Its gardens and subsoil no doubt contain the usual traces of uranium, which no municipal clean-up campaign could ever remove. Hounslow adds the comforting slogan: 'Working for a Safer Future'—a gloss with the self-evidently false implication that conclusive assessments have been made of the risks and benefits of nuclear power relative to coal, oil, and gas, including (one may be forgiven for assuming) the consequences of climatic change from the 'greenhouse effect' as a result of fossil-fuel burning—i.e. most of the subject-matter of Part Two of this book, and possibly more—and that nuclear power comes out worst. The only possible purpose for such transparently tendentious propaganda is party-political.

But sometimes the wheels of politics, in turning, bring into office avowed critics who then have to decide what should be done. Not all follow the Swedish example of preferring to retain the policy on which they were elected, despite subsequently identified costs. The British politician Richard Crossman once commented that 'the tragedy of politics is not promises that are broken but promises that are kept'. Sweden may yet be fortunate in being able to look for protection to the little-publicized escape clauses which hedge the official policy of reactor closure.

Spain provides an example of a different kind. At the beginning of the 1980s the Socialists, then in opposition, could hardly have been more opposed to nuclear power. *The nuclear crisis*[193,194], which they published in 1981, was a virulent attack:

Nuclear energy is a minor and short-term means of supplying energy . . . it will last no more than 30–40 years . , . nuclear power-stations are the best way of supplying plutonium for nuclear weapons.

None of these statements is factually correct. The paper goes on:

. . . nuclear energy will be as negative for the world as oil energy has been; the costs have reached unbelievable levels. The price of uranium has risen eightfold since the energy crisis of 1973 . . .

This is a particularly clear case of unfamiliarity with the subject. Uranium accounts for one-tenth or less of the total cost of nuclear power, so electricity costs are insensitive to what is happening on that commodity market; moreover, the price of uranium was falling sharply as the article appeared, and within two years was back in constant-money terms to the pre-1973 level. However, what matters more is that the Socialists shortly afterwards became Spain's government, and settled down with a commendable degree of pragmatism to administer the nuclear industry.

There was an initial nuclear moratorium in 1984, for unassailable reasons: lower than anticipated energy growth, plus continued Basque separatist opposition, which had already resulted in the murders, in 1981 and 1982, of two senior nuclear engineers connected with the Lemoniz reactors. A political compromise was reached, which included placing the reactors then under construction on 'hold'. But by 1989 energy growth—at 6.5 per cent a year—was fast outstripping the predictions (based on 3.3 per cent) of the 1983 energy plan. A more favourable attitude was being taken by the government towards the nuclear programme, which was already producing nearly 40 per cent of Spain's electricity. Publicity about the greenhouse effect, and a favourable stock-market rating for Spanish utilities, may have played a part.

It was therefore particularly unfortunate that on 19 October 1989 a mechanical blade failure and turbine fire occurred at the usually reliable seventeen-year-old French-designed graphite-gas-cooled reactor at Vandellos in the north-east of Spain. This was not a nuclear accident, and the reactor core was unaffected; but public anxiety was aroused because part of the reactor cooling arrangements were disabled—the turbine and reactor buildings were not sufficiently separated, and the fire damaged some safety-related cables. However, the reactor was shut down normally. Subsequent inquiries also revealed that the management had failed to implement an earlier recommendation that fire-fighting standards should be improved. This is yet another example of how a single incident, even when non-nuclear, can sour the atmosphere for the whole industry, and jeopardize years of excellent work. But it does not invalidate the prior point—that politicians who hold power behave differently from those in opposition, as regards nuclear power as in so much else.

A similar evolution in government attitudes was observable in the Carter administration's nuclear policies in the USA. The initially doctrinaire stance and unrealistic wish to act as the world's policeman over proliferation altered in direct relationship to the administration's increasing involvement with the practicalities of nuclear policy.

These examples provide some kind of answer to pessimists who fear that better information is unlikely to sway attitudes. For those who carry no responsibility that may be true. For those who cannot avoid doing so reliable information is the raw material for future decisions.

In conclusion

The nuclear opposition is the nuclear industry's unsought companion. For years the policy was to keep silent, hoping it would go away. But there is no shaking it off; nor can the opposition ever be finally defeated because, as Hans Zetterberg, head of the Swedish Institute of Opinion Research (SIFO) has percipiently observed, it has no leader with whom to reach agreement. In only one country has it been possible for the nuclear industry to overwhelm its opponents by sheer speed—which on the admission of the opposition itself is what happened in France as, over a period of six years, one reactor was completed on average every eleven weeks. In other countries with less ambitious programmes the best the industry can hope for is to promote a degree of balance in the views of the public, which will permit nuclear power to make its proper contribution to energy supplies. The sudden alarm which developed during 1988 over the potentially disastrous environmental consequences of burning fossil fuels underlines the importance of retaining this freedom of choice in the years ahead—as we shall see in the two remaining chapters.

12   The Energy Alternatives

THE charge is frequently made that nuclear power is unnecessary. However, only one government, that of Sweden, has so far shown itself willing to accept the consequences of abandoning an already established—and in this case highly successful—nuclear-energy strategy. Sweden happens to be a rich country, able to pay the cost if it wishes of premature replacement of expensive generating equipment. Nevertheless, from the time of the first firm closure announcement in March 1988—planned to take effect in 1995 and 1996—the cost in financial and employment terms has fuelled a continuing political debate. More than a dozen other governments take a different view, and continue with their nuclear programmes, despite the problems, despite Chernobyl. They are sceptical about 'easy' alternative solutions, do not pin excessive hopes on energy conservation, see positive advantages in diversity, look to the long-term, and prefer a bird in the hand to one in the bush.

In this chapter we make a quick *tour d'horizon* of the alternative energy sources, so that the reader can place the nuclear option in the global energy context. This will take us a long way from nuclear electricity, and in the process underline the close connection between energy availability and life-style. The details are not only interesting for their own sake, but also as a warning against expecting tidy solutions for a sector of the world economy which accounts for over 3 per cent of GDP in the European Community, 4–6 per cent in the USSR, and often 30 per cent or more of public investment.

Inevitabilities

Any such global survey is an essay in forecasting. One has only to look back to the dramatic changes since the 1973 oil crisis to be conscious of the pitfalls. Anyone trying to peer into the future would therefore be well advised to heed Professor Russell Ackoff's evergreen advice—that predictions should preferably be made on the basis of what is inevitable: they are then more likely to be right!

Even in the uncertain world of energy forecasting inevitabilities help to give shape to the discussion.

The first is the *importance of cost* to the consumer, unless there are overwhelming policy reasons to the contrary. This is not encouraging for those who wish on environmental or even ideological grounds to make greater use of renewable energy sources irrespective of the economics. If fusion energy ever becomes possible, it will have to march to the same drum. To see what happens when the price of energy rises we need look back no further than 1973. The impact of the OPEC oil-price shock was swift and dramatic. In France in 1973 oil and gas accounted for 46 per cent of her electricity production; seven years later[1] the figure was down to 21 per cent, and for 1990 the planned oil figure is a mere 1–2 per cent. Oil formed 77 per cent of Japan's total primary energy supply in 1973, 72 per cent in 1979, 58 per cent in 1989, and is planned to fall further. Conservation also received a boost. After the oil shock it became not merely desirable but economically necessary. Most industrial countries reduced their energy consumption per unit of GDP by 25 per cent. France, through a combination of public education and government regulation, reduced the energy requirements of new buildings by more than half over the period 1974–90. In the same period the French dairy industry reduced its energy consumption by one-third, the sugar industry by nearly half; newly registered cars achieved a 25 per cent improvement in petrol consumption[195]. Other industrial countries showed similar progress. However, on a global scale the reduction seemed by 1988 to have run its course for the time being: for the first time in fifteen years consumption per unit of world economic activity ceased falling[191].

A second inevitability will be the continued *search for security of supply*, including protection from disruptions of a political nature, such as those associated in the world's mind with the two oil-price shocks. The problem is not confined to oil. The prolonged coal-miners' strike in the UK in 1984–5 was defeated only because of a well-run electricity grid, which enabled oil-fired stations to be used on a massive scale, despite their expense, while nuclear power-stations also made a full contribution. Diversity proved on this occasion an essential defence for the country against the monopoly power of the miners' union.

A third inevitability will be *continuing and growing concern over environmental issues.* But this touches conventional fuels at least as much as nuclear power. The death of forests in Europe is a real political issue, associated as it is with the emission of oxides of sulphur and nitrogen from vehicles and coal-burning central power-stations, in roughly equal measure. Compulsory addition of scrubbers to power-station exhaust stacks, to extract sulphur and solid particles, represents a considerable extra capital investment, adding 10 per cent to the cost of generating electricity. Environmental considerations will continue to grow in importance as the implications of the potentially catastrophic increase in world population for the management of the planet become more evident over the next three decades. At the same time the enhancement of the greenhouse effect, caused mainly by the production of carbon dioxide from fossil fuel, will become more evident. Almost every form of energy production will feel its influence—which could indeed become 'an overwhelming policy reason' for not necessarily choosing the cheapest fossil-fuel solution.

A fourth inevitability is that the *inertia built into energy markets will continue to stabilize patterns of energy consumption, and hold back change.* It is rarely a simple matter to substitute one form or use of energy by another. Take transport: constantly growing reliance on the car over the past forty years has by now led to radically altered home-to-work geographical relationships, which make it much more difficult to run our lives without one. Again, the use for district-heating of waste heat from power-stations—65 per cent of the total energy is usually wasted—is capable of making huge inroads into energy demand; but first an urban distribution network is needed. The time-scale for that is set by the pace of urban renewal—decades rather than years—and by the political acceptability of comprehensive planning rather than piecemeal market-led development. These examples highlight the limitations of conventional market forces in encouraging progress towards solutions that would be more optimal from an energy viewpoint. The 'market' can only choose between the options open to it, and then usually on a short time-horizon. The structural changes needed for energy efficiency are matters needing government help. If government stands aside, the result can only be continuing inertia. In the twenty-first century the countries which will be accounted fortunate in energy matters will be those whose governments systematically tackled the problems twenty or thirty years earlier, not those whose energy policy remained simply the sum of the parts.

And a fifth near-inevitability will be the *progressive enhancement of the role of electricity*, because of its versatility, convenience, and ability to be 'focused' at the point of use. Lenin foresaw its importance when he wrote: 'Communism equals the power of the Soviets plus electricity'. In OECD electricity has a major share of primary energy consumption: 30 per cent in 1978; nearly 37 per cent in 1988. Its use is increasing by 3.8 per cent annually, faster than total energy demand. The long-term stability of electricity prices is clearly of major and growing economic significance.

World energy consumption

Figures are at the heart of the energy argument. We should be ill-advised to follow the example of the senior British civil servant who, faced with statistics that were crucial to the meeting he was chairing, left the task to his deputy, remarking that 'there is nothing here to detain a gentleman'.

The four sources on which the world mainly relies for its energy are oil, coal, natural gas, and hydroelectricity. Although nuclear power has been expanding in percentage terms more rapidly than these other sources, it is not yet in the first four, and is unlikely to overtake hydroelectricity before the end of the century. Its long-term potential is, however, considerably greater than that of hydropower, once the issues discussed earler have been satisfactorily resolved.

The world's consumption of these energy sources is shown in Table 12.1. Such global figures conceal a huge disparity between the industrialized countries of OECD and the less-developed countries (LDCs). OECD accounts at present for almost exactly half of the world's energy consumption. The vastly more populous LDCs, including China, use only about 30 per cent of world energy. But their populations are still growing rapidly, and many are reaching the industrial phase. Their energy requirements are shooting ahead: 4 per cent or more annually, against half that figure in the industrialized world. Indeed, the recently industrialized countries of South East Asia used 11 per cent more energy in 1988 than in the previous year, and twice as much as in 1978. The combined effect is that world energy consumption is rising at

Table 12.1. World Primary Energy Consumption
(gigatonnes oil equivalent)

	1975	1979	1988	2020
Oil	2.7	3.1	3.0	3.2 – 3.6
Coal	1.7	2.0	2.2	3.2 – 4.0
Natural gas	1.1	1.3	1.6	2.5 – 3.3
Hydro	0.35	0.42	0.52	0.8 – 0.9
Nuclear	0.15	0.20	0.43	0.8 – 1.5
New energies	minor contribution			0.15– 0.4
Biomass	0.7	0.85	1.2	1.3 – 1.1
TOTAL	6.7	7.9	9.0	12.0–14.8

Notes: (1) For ease of comparison between the various energy sources in this Table and in the text the common unit of gigatonnes of oil equivalent (Gtoe) has been used, based on heat content. The prefix 'giga' indicates one thousand million. Nuclear and hydropower have been evaluated on the basis of the oil that would otherwise be burnt to produce the same amount of electricity, at 35 per cent efficiency. One gigawatt (1 GWe) of electrical capacity at 70 per cent load factor is equivalent to 1.5 million tonnes of oil equivalent (Mtoe) per year; 1.5 tonnes of coal are equivalent to 1.0 tonne of oil; 1,100 cubic metres of natural gas are equivalent to 1 tonne of oil. (2) The biomass sources referred to in the Table are the dung, agricultural wastes, wood, etc. used for heating and cooking in many developing countries; also (as bio-ethanol) for motor fuel. The figures are very approximate. Availability is limited by depletion. Note that if there is low energy growth (implying that commercial sources are expensive), non-commercial energy will be more used. (3) World-wide, total primary energy consumption grew[191] by 3.0 per cent between 1984 and 1988. Even the upper figure given in the Table for 2020 assumes considerably slower average energy growth, of under 2 per cent a year; i.e. an 'energy efficiency' scenario, particularly given the expected growth in world population (p. 346).(4) The larger nuclear figure for 2020 (equivalent to 1,000 GWe) assumes an average rate of reactor completions, world-wide, about double that of the past twenty years, with future station sizes averaging 1 GWe. It includes an allowance for the replacement of stations ending their useful lives. This rate is certainly feasible.

Sources: References 15, 191, 196–8.

around 3 per cent a year—it doubled in the twenty-five years to 1988. This trend shows no sign of ending, which is perhaps a sixth 'inevitability'. A further near-doubling of energy consumption by the beginning of the second quarter of the twenty-first century cannot be ruled out, despite a growing awareness of the need for greater efficiency in energy use.

Oil

Immediately after the second shock in 1979 oil lost a little of the energy market, and other energy sources gained, through a process of substitution where this was technically possible—notably through the change to nuclear electricity. The arrival of nuclear power on a significant scale has taken the equivalent of several million barrels a day out of an electricity market which, prior to 1973, was becoming dominated by oil. Had it not been for this, oil supplies would have been much tighter in the 1980s.

The relatively slow change in the overall position of oil conceals significant shifts in the geographical distribution of oil production. The Middle East fell from being the leading producer in 1975, with 36 per cent, to only 19 per cent in 1985; it partially recovered to 26 per cent in 1989. These changes reflected the political reactions of consumers to the two oil shocks, and their subsequent conscious policy of diversifying supply sources, and where possible increasing indigenous production; and also the effects of the Iraq–Iran war. In the long run the dominant fact is that the Middle East's reserves are much larger than those elsewhere (Table 12.2). This is bound to influence future market shares—and political relationships.

The figure of 'proved reserves' given in Table 12.2 is a snapshot taken at a particular moment. It and the reserves-to-production ratio could vary for a number of reasons: changes in market price, exhaustion, exploration. Exploration was highly successful in the 1960s; but this ceased to be true about 1970, which led by 1973 to a fall in reserves, which must have been a factor lying behind the first oil shock. The market reactions to that event led with surprising speed to a marked, albeit probably temporary, excess of oil production. As always with mineral commodities, the associated fall in prices resulted in a failure to maintain some oilfields properly, and a reduction in exploration. As a result proved reserves remained almost static until 1986. Since then there has been a move towards increased exploration in the Middle East, which has had some success. This is just as well, because as reserves elsewhere are exhausted, it will inevitably fall to that region to

Table 12.2. Oil Production and Proved Reserves[a] (1 Jan. 1989)

	Reserves (Gt)	Production (Gt/year)	R/P (years)
Middle East	77	0.74	over 100[b]
Latin America	17.1	0.34	50
USSR	8.0	0.62	13
Africa	7.5	0.26	30
North America	5.5	0.55	10
Asia and Australasia	2.7	0.16	17
Western Europe	2.4	0.20	12
World TOTAL	124	3.03	40
of which OPEC	92	1.03	90[b]

[a] Proved oil reserves are those which can be recovered with reasonable certainty from known reservoirs under existing economic and operating conditions. See reference 191.

[b] But see text below.

supply more to the market. Without further exploration successes the regional reserves-to-production ratio could fall sharply below the figure of over one hundred years quoted in Table 12.2— possibly to only fifty years.

An important question, therefore, is how much oil remains to be discovered. The answer is necessarily speculative; but estimates of 'undiscovered recoverable resources' lie in the range 50 to 200 gigatonnes, with a most probable figure around 80 gigatonnes. What is significant is that this is comparable with what has already been produced (86 Gt to 1 January 1989), and also with the level of already-demonstrated reserves (124 Gt in 1989). Given that oil usage is still increasing, these estimates point to one of the world's central political considerations: what remains of the age of abundant oil will be measured in decades rather than centuries.

Oil will not suddenly 'run out'; but it will gradually become more expensive, which will induce economies in use and a progressive switch to other forms of energy. Exploration will be reinvigorated, but will be increasingly difficult and costly, much of it off-shore. Total world oil production seems likely to show only minor growth until about the year 2020, and thereafter fall by about half over the following half century. Given the inertia of energy markets, all that

326 The energy alternatives

time and all the available alternatives will be needed if the consequences of this fall are to be handled without threat to world economic stability.

Coal

As oil declines early in the next century coal will become the leading energy source. Coal resources are relatively large compared to current production levels, and even on present knowledge we can look forward to secure supplies until well into the twenty-second century, and probably for a considerable time thereafter (see Table 12.3). As coal takes over from oil production will need to rise; so the reserve-to-production ratios given in the Table may present a somewhat optimistic view. But the conclusion remains: there are very large coal resources waiting to be used.

A major use for coal—*the* major use in some countries, including the UK—is for electricity generation. By reversing a tendency in the sixties to displacement by oil, coal rebuilt its market share in the OECD countries[191,196] to 42 per cent of electricity in 1988, compared with 36 per cent in 1973. As we saw in Chapter 6, in many countries coal's economics are broadly comparable with those of nuclear energy, with the latter able to compete effectively far from the main coalfields, and with coal able to hold its own near a source of supply, where transport costs are low. There are, however,

Table 12.3. Coal Production 1988 and Reserves (Gtoe) at 1 Jan. 1989

	Reserves	Production	R/P (years)
USA	116	0.52	220
PR China	105	0.58	180
USSR	102	0.39	260
Australia	29	0.09	320
Poland	22	0.14	160
India	8	0.12	65
United Kingdom	6	0.06	100
World TOTAL	484	2.44	200

Note: See reference 191. The conversion to Gtoe allows for the difference in calorific content between hard coal and lignite.

reasons other than economics why electrical utilities might prefer coal, notably the relative absence of public objection to new coal-fired stations, particularly after Chernobyl, and the perceived uncertainties of nuclear waste and decommissioning costs.

A 50 per cent increase of coal production, to around 3.5 Gtoe, seems well within the bounds of possibility—though because energy consumption generally would be expanding at the same time coal's share of the world primary-energy market would be little changed, at around 27 per cent (Table 12.1). Such an increase would, however, be in direct conflict with the 'greenhouse' considerations discussed in the concluding chapter.

From the mid–1980s onwards developments in the world trade in coal began to call into question the relative economics of nuclear power. Previously only relatively small quantities of coal had been traded internationally, and the economics of electricity generation from coal had been largely determined by the cost of the indigenously-mined product in each of the principal user countries. In that context nuclear power was often able to compete. However, bulk imports of coal from Australia, Colombia, South Africa, and Venezuela became available in Europe in the 1980s at very low prices, swinging the balance—for coastal power-stations at least—in favour of coal. What was not clear was whether the low prices could be sustained for large long-term contracts, once the new producers had ceased waging a price war between themselves, in their efforts to recoup the capital costs of their under-utilized new mines. Moreover the World Energy Conference commented[198] in 1989 that 'today's low-cost suppliers are moving into less propitious geological conditions'. Sea-borne traded-prices rose 30 per cent between 1988 and 1989, and long-term prices of $50 dollars a tonne began to seem more realistic than the $30 dollars quoted earlier in the decade.

Coal electricity generation has its own environmental problems. It creates atmospheric pollution by the emission of sulphur and nitrogen oxides, which are expensive and technically difficult to eliminate completely—though some improvements are possible by using fluidized-bed combustion, and by the injection of natural gas. There are also political problems over persuading countries to accept an addition to capital costs of 10 per cent or more for flue-gas clean-up: once again the 'inevitable' search for minimum cost is evident.

Natural gas

The third most important energy resource is natural gas, representing nearly one-fifth of the world's energy market. Proved reserves are around 100 gigatonnes of oil equivalent[191], giving a R/P ratio of about sixty years. However, this figure does not include the vast quantities of gas locked up in solid gas hydrates, formed under high pressure below the ocean floor; or theoretical suggestions that there may be an additional deep resource deriving from the origins of the earth. Even without these supplements the known or inferred natural gas resources are similar in scale to those of oil. Gas can therefore provide a useful extension of the hydrocabon era, certainly for decades, and possibly for centuries.

Gas supplies, like coal, are at present mainly used in or near the country of origin. This is a reflection of the need for extensive infrastructure before a new export trade can commence. Pipelines carry gas long distances—across the Mediterranean from Algeria, or from the USSR to Western Europe as far as Italy (exports which represent a substantial part of Soviet foreign currency earnings). Alternatively the trade can use special refrigerator-ships and refrigerated onshore-storage for liquefied natural gas. Given this degree of prior investment, economic considerations strongly influence the timing of new projects. Liquefied natural gas projects have long lead-times; and returns are not always easy to estimate, since the price at which the natural gas can be sold into a new market is significantly affected by the future prices of competing fuels. These factors limit the rate at which new markets for natural gas can be opened up.

Table 12.4. Natural Gas Production 1988 (Mtoe)

USSR	694	could show strong growth
USA	425	prospect of slow decline
Western Europe	150	no rapid change expected
Middle East	65	could double by 2000
World TOTAL	1,738	growing at 2.3 per cent annually
Internationally traded	205	

Note: although only 4 per cent of production is at present from the Middle East, it has 30 per cent of world reserves.

Sources: References 191, 198.

Nevertheless, gas-fired electricity generating plants, with their low capital cost, are growing in numbers rapidly, partly as a result of coal's problems with sulphur dioxide air pollution. Some gas is also being used in some places directly for transport applications: Russia has filling stations able to replenish vehicles' fuel tanks with gas under pressure in about 10 minutes.

Other hydrocarbons

Potentially usable hydrocarbons also occur in the form of 'unconventional' deposits—extra-heavy oils, deposits in oil sands which are almost solid, solid kerogen (the fossilized remains of micro-algae) in oil-shales, high-pressure gas in very deep formations, or frozen gaseous hydrates in Siberia. Large energy resources are known to be in such deposits, though extractable only at costs which at present usually preclude production. The price rises of the 1970s permitted a start to be made on small-scale exploitation.

Biomass

Oil, coal, and natural gas are non-renewable energy resources. In contrast 'biomass' (the jargon word covering wood, charcoal, animal dung, and agricultural waste) is commonly regarded as a renewable resource—subject to the important and by no means universally valid proviso that the scale of use should not destroy its ecological basis. Biomass is the main choice for many developing countries. It provides 84 per cent of the energy used by China's rural population of 800 million, and half of India's energy supply[198]. These rural populations pose energy problems quite different from those of the industrialized and largely urbanized world. But the two worlds come together in competition for oil—and in this contest the developing countries are poorly placed. In 1984 some spent more than 30 per cent of their export revenues on energy purchases, seven more than 50 per cent. A good part of the international debt crisis still afflicting the banking world arose from the inability of Third World debtor countries to maintain interest payments, over and above their purchases of essential energy imports. Against such a background it would be idle to expect any easy abandonment of the traditional dependence on biomass as a main source of energy, despite the often dire environmental consequences of deforestation.

The quantities involved are large—globally about one gigatonne of oil equivalent[191,196]. India produces 160 Mt of fuel-wood annually [198]; some peasant women in India spend four hours a day collecting firewood. In Chile each household uses 10 tonnes of wood per year—with very low efficiency; it has been estimated that no trees will be left in the Coquimbo region by the year 2000, unless the Chilean government enforces a drastic change of habit. In some Chinese districts two-thirds of the forests have been lost in the past thirty years—though conversion of land-use to agriculture has played its part. Whole regions of the world are in imminent danger of becoming deserts because of over-cropping, which is what happened in historical times in the previously fertile North Africa coastal strip under the Romans. Half the world's population suffers from a deficit of firewood, and wood is in danger of being the first of the renewable resources to be depleted. But some responses are possible. One is an active policy of reafforestation; another is encouraging people to switch from traditional open fires, whose efficiencies may be as low as 7 per cent, to enclosed stoves which use fuel five times more effectively. By the end of the century India will have a hundred million such stoves.

In developed countries the biomass methane produced from municipal waste is coming into use as a fuel for electricity generation. This has the further beneficial effect of converting the methane to carbon dioxide, which creates a smaller greenhouse effect (see Chapter 13). The biological processes involved are quite complex, and research programmes on both sides of the Atlantic are aimed at improving the yield of useful gas[199]. There is a strong economic incentive: the value of the energy potentially extractable from US municipal wastes is measured in billions of dollars. On a smaller scale in developing countries 'digesters' are used to convert animal and agricultural waste into synthetic gas for cooking and lighting; fertilizer is a useful byproduct. India plans to install twelve million such domestic bio-gas plants by the year 2000.

Hydroelectricity

Oil, coal, natural gas, and biomass need oxygen for their combustion. The resulting carbon dioxide is becoming a major political problem because of the greenhouse effect. Of the energy sources which function independently of the atmosphere, other than nuclear power, far and away the most important is hydro-electricity, currently fourth in rank of the 'classical' energy resources.

Hydropower was responsible for 6 per cent of world primary energy production in 1988, and there is potential for further growth within the OECD to about twice the present operating capacity[196]. In the developing countries progress is likely to be delayed because of a shortage of capital, combined with the generally undeveloped state of national grids—particularly in remoter regions where hydroelectric possibilities exist. For instance, Indonesia has a large potential, amounting to 31 GWe, but most of it is scattered over several islands, far from the main population centres in Java. Although an upward change in the level of energy prices would theoretically help to justify new schemes, the world's experience at the time of the oil-price shocks was that rising energy prices eroded the capital base, and made such schemes less, rather than more, likely.

For reasons of capital availability the expansion of hydropower is unlikely to be rapid; but a twofold expansion beyond anything yet available seems within the bounds of technical possibility. How far it is everywhere politically possible remains to be seen: in the richer countries hydro schemes are no more immune from the attentions of environmentalists than nuclear power itself. In the developing world the necessity for finding new resources is likely to take precedence over such appeals to aesthetics, provided the necessary capital can be found.

Other inexhaustible sources of energy

The search for other possible replacements for hydrocarbon fuels leads naturally to a closer look at the newer forms of inexhaustible, or 'renewable', energy sources—those derived directly or indirectly from the heat energy of the sun (solar heat, direct conversion to electricity, wind, and waves); from the energy of the tides, which is gravitational in origin; and from geothermal heat, a manifestation of the energy constantly being created in the core of the earth through the radioactive disintegrations of uranium and thorium [200,201].

All these sources, which are inexhaustible in the sense that they will exist for as long as the human race survives, can provide energy that can be harnessed in some degree. But, like nuclear power, they must also meet the normal economic tests of cost and reliability. When advocates speak optimistically of 'renewables' having already achieved a contribution, for instance, of around 7–8 per cent to US electricity supplies, it would be wrong to assume that a sea-change has occurred in the energy world. The bulk is old-fashioned hydroelectricity (4 per cent) and wood-burning (3 per cent). Less than 1 per cent comes (1988) from new technology: 0.3 per cent from geothermal, 0.25 per cent from wind, and 0.025 per cent from solar. While these resources could be more important in future, their present contribution is marginal. A recital of what they involve may explain why. The popular view that they provide an immediate and effective substitute for large-scale central generating stations—including nuclear power—is not borne out by the facts.

Solar energy

Although the total energy reaching the earth from the sun is enormous, exceeding by 10,000 times what man himself produces, the amount falling on a given area is inconveniently low for large-scale applications. The raw energy per square kilometre at midday on a clear day in the tropics is comparable with the 1 GWe power output of a large modern nuclear power-station; but by the time allowance is made for daily and seasonal variations, and for realistic efficiencies for conversion of sunlight to electricity, collection areas at least ten times greater still would be needed for an equivalent solar station. Even in the megawatt power range, ten or a hundred times smaller, schemes for solar electricity generation require engineering on a scale which verges on the heroic. Not surprisingly, the costs are not competitive with fossil fuels or nuclear power for base-load electricity generation.

Conceptually the simplest approach is to use an array of parabolic mirrors to concentrate the sun's direct beams on a long pipe through which a liquid heat-transfer agent is pumped. Sufficiently high temperatures can be achieved to enable steam to be raised and electricity generated. In the Mojave Desert, in the USA, there are three large arrays, with a total output of 0.6 GWe[202]. The power produced is not competitive for base-load operation, but is viable if it can be sold to utilities at their 'avoided costs' at times of power peaks—as is encouraged by US legislation (p. 341).

The 15 per cent or more of scattered radiation coming from the sky cannot be exploited in this way.

A technically more interesting approach is direct photo-voltaic conversion of sunlight energy into electricity. Considerable progress has been made in recent years: a factor of twenty reduction in the cost per peak-watt output was achieved during the 1980s, and the conversion efficiencies of silicon solar modules have increased to 18 per cent. But there is still a long way to go: currently solar photo-voltaic electricity is still several times more expensive than coal or nuclear generation. Even though further cost reductions are probable, central power-station use in developed countries seems inherently unlikely.

Even at the current cost per installed peak-watt there are many places around the world where small amounts of solar electricity already provide a convenient alternative to diesel generators—or going without—for such diverse applications as satellite communications, tunnel- and road-lighting, beacons and lighthouses, and water-pumping. There is also scope for giving electricity to the 10 million small villages with populations under 1,000 in the developing world, or to the 100,000 homes still without electricity in southern Europe[196]. There are applications in the leisure markets for yachts and mobile homes. However, despite the undoubted technical interest of direct conversion, and in some locations its social significance, in terms of supplementing worldwide energy resources it has only a very minor contribution to offer.

The distributed nature of solar energy strongly suggests that it is intrinsically most suitable for applications which are also distributed. Houses which exploit natural solar heating—with well-located windows, appropriate thermal insulation, and roof-mounted systems for water, domestic heating, and possibly air-conditioning (which needs a source of *heat* if it is to operate)—may sound technically trivial, but are potentially of first-order importance in terms of the energy savings that are possible, in some cases by as much as three-quarters[203]. It may seem at first sight surprising that so few householders attempt to harvest these potential benefits. The causes begin with the lack of public awareness of what is possible, plus the physical problems of converting houses built in the days of cheaper energy. But the biggest difficulty is the long pay-back time for conversion costs. In the cloudy northern climate of the UK, and in the absence of a subsidy, this could be decades. Even in the sunnier USA, the loss in 1986 of a federal tax credit for residential solar installations caused an immediate threefold fall in annual sales. Individuals' economic criteria are not identical with those of energy policy-makers, unless fiscal levers are used to bring them into line.

Wind energy

It is easier to use solar heat indirectly, by harnessing the wind energy created by solar heating of the atmosphere. The potential resource is large and available world-wide; but once again it is inconveniently 'dilute'. A large modern horizontal-axis windmill— or wind turbine—may have slim aerofoil blades measuring 60 metres from tip to tip, with the top blade reaching to a height of 90 metres; but it generates only about 3 MWe even when the wind is blowing strongly, at about 50 kilometres an hour, and on average about one-quarter of that. This peak power is only 1/300th of the energy from a modern 1 GWe power-station. Moreover, to avoid aerodynamic interference the individual windmills must be separated. The result is that, in contrast to the very compact and visually non-intrusive nature of nuclear power, a 1 GWe windmill farm would be huge, covering 10 square kilometres or more. There is also some acoustic intrusion owing to the high tip speed of the blades (up to 90 metres a second), and a separation of 200 metres from dwellings is desirable. Nevertheless there are many windy sites in remote areas or offshore where large arrays could be built. In these days of television, remote siting would also minimize the effects of picture interference from the rotating arms.

Progress in exploiting this form of energy in recent years has been encouraging, particularly since the 1973 oil crisis applied a spur. By 1989 about 15,000 wind turbines, with a total capacity of 1.5 GWe, were operating as grid-connected machines throughout the world. Three-quarters were in California and Denmark, the reason in both cases being strong government support, backed by financial incentives. Denmark took a political initiative in 1985, which led to 100 MWe of wind power being connected to the grid five years later, with individual capacities of 0.3 to 0.7 MWe being favoured as operationally most suitable[204]. The Netherlands and the UK both aim to install 1 GWe of wind power by the early years of the twenty-first century.

There were problems of reliability with the first-generation windmills. However, Danish experience was that the failure rate fell more than tenfold within the first few years of operation. The indications are that with further development wind generation should be competitive with nuclear power at a discount rate of 10 per cent, which makes wind energy probably the most attractive of the renewable resources. The power generated is of course intermittent, which means that the invested capital will frequently lie idle, and that wind energy can only be part of a larger system. Nevertheless the inherent attraction of an energy source with zero 'fuel' cost, and the possibilities of future capital cost savings through mass production, mean that wind is certain to make a significant contribution to world energy within the next twenty years.

Apart from this high-technology application of wind energy it continues to be widely used in the traditional smaller sizes for water pumping and power in remote regions.

Wave energy

For countries with exposed coastlines it is tempting to look to wave energy as another inexhaustible resource. The waves can be made to pump air in and out of fixed or floating structures, in the process driving Wells turbines—which ingeniously turn the same way whatever the direction of air-flow—and so powering electrical generators.

The power of the waves in the open sea flowing across an imaginary line is certainly large, and can reach 1 MW per metre in a storm; but the mean annual usable-power density in the North Atlantic is ten to twenty times lower. This implies that a 1 GWe station would require the total conversion to electricity of the energy passing a line some kilometres long, which is clearly a formidable problem. The difficulties increase when the practical engineering considerations of working in a hostile marine environment and the attainable conversion efficiencies are taken into account. The potential mean annual wave power reaching the 1,000 kilometres long Atlantic coastline of the United Kingdom is around 36 GW, which appears significant when compared with the size of the British national electricity grid. However, the 'available resource', after taking account of practical constraints of geography, is only half that amount; and the 'achievable resource', taking conversion efficiencies into account, is estimated to be a factor of five lower still—around 6 GWe[205].

This would nevertheless still be worth pursuing if the power obtained were economic. The United Kingdom government therefore spent nearly ten years (1975–84) studying wave energy. Over three hundred ideas were examined in wave-tanks. Nine devices were taken to a stage at which reference designs for 2 GWe (peak) stations were produced and costed. Unfortunately the cost of power produced seemed likely to be at least three times that from nuclear stations. The conclusion was that, even in the geographically favourable circumstances of the United Kingdom, wave energy involving off-shore systems was not likely to be an attractive option for large-scale power production.

There is, however, more promise for smaller on-shore systems, exploiting coastal features such as rock gullies which can produce a natural amplification of the surface motion. Several countries are pursuing such an approach. A small (200 Kwe) station to supply the electricity requirements of the island of Islay, off the west coast of Scotland, is scheduled for completion in 1990.

Tidal energy

The tides are another potential source of energy, which can be extracted by using barrages where there is a large tidal range between high and low water. The 'fuel' is free, but capital costs are high and construction and pay-off times long. Moreover, because of the phasing of the tides the average power availability is much less than the total installed turbine capacity: the projected 16-kilometres-long Severn barrage in the UK could produce a peak output of 8.6 GWe—equivalent to seven or more nuclear stations; but for planning purposes it can be credited[68,206] with a load factor of only 22 per cent. Estimated generating costs are about 50 per cent more than from nuclear power.

The energy potential for countries with suitable geography is nevertheless considerable: in the United Kingdom, for instance, tidal energy could potentially displace up to 4 GWe (average)—equivalent to four nuclear stations or 8 million tonnes annually of oil equivalent of primary energy, which is certainly of economic interest. This, however, is still only 5 per cent of the national grid; so tidal power can make only a minor contribution even in a country which is an island with strong tides. It is of no interest to inland countries, or to those with tideless seas like the Mediterranean. Clearly its contribution to world power supplies, in percentage terms, will be very small.

Geothermal energy

In places where the earth's molten core comes close to the surface—notably around the Pacific's 'rim of fire'—the heat constantly flowing outwards can be exploited to provide a source of geothermal energy. Unlike some of the other renewable resources geothermal heat is constant in magnitude, or at worst changes only slowly as the hot rocks are cooled down, and is therefore suitable for base-load operation. The installed geothermal electrical capacity in 1989, world-wide, was 5.1 GWe, with another 2 GWe under construction. The leading user was the USA, with 2.2 GWe—a large part of San Francisco's power is produced in this way—followed by the Philippines with 0.9 GWe and Mexico with 0.7 GWe.

The classical requirements for exploiting geothermal heat are a porous water-bearing rock, or aquifer, at sufficient depth—usually a few kilometres—for high temperatures to occur; and an impermeable rock capping to prevent the high-temperature water escaping upwards. Heat can then be collected over a large area and extracted using the hot underground water (or in some cases steam) as a heat-storage medium. In a geothermal power-station there are typically several production wells, plus a reinjection well which not only maintains the aquifer, but also reinjects as much as possible of any heat that would otherwise be wasted. This prevents unacceptable cooling of the rocks during the operating lifetime, which ideally should be twenty to thirty years. Where temperatures and pressures are too low for electricity generation (below 170° C) geothermal heat can still be used to supplement other energy sources in such applications as agriculture or district household heating: 80 per cent of the homes in Iceland are heated in this way, and there are smaller installations in the Paris region. Japan is the main user of direct geothermal heat, with over 4 GW (thermal) used for heating pools and spas[198]. The world total in 1989 for all purposes was 14 GW (thermal).

Not all subterranean formations contain rocks which are capable of acting as aquifers. Work is currently in progress to investigate the possibility of using deep hot dry rocks which are naturally impervious for useful energy production. The development is aimed at exploring ways of fracturing such rocks in a controlled manner at depths of around 5 kilometres, to create the conditions needed for an artificial aquifer. Once this is done water can be injected from the surface and returned after a period in contact with hot rocks at 200° C. Development work has been carried out in France, Germany, Japan, the UK, and the United States, where temperatures as high as 325° C have been encountered.

The use of geothermal heat is a very old technique—the Romans used it for hot baths 2,000 years ago—but recent progress in our understanding of the structure of the earth's crust is giving it a new boost. The 15 GWe of electricity expected to be produced geothermally by the early years of the next century would be the annual equivalent of about 25 million tonnes of oil, or about 0.3 per cent of world total annual energy consumption. While this would still be a minor contribution, it would represent a threefold increase in geothermal electricity in two decades, a rate of expansion holding considerable promise for the next century.

Nuclear fusion

Nuclear fusion—the joining together of light atoms rather than the fissioning of the heavy atoms uranium or plutonium—is the way the energy of the sun and the stars is created. It has this in common with the renewable energy sources: if it proves to be feasible, it would open up a vista of electricity supplies that could last for as long as the human race inhabits the earth.

Fusion is the target for a research programme that has been carried forward with increasing confidence over the past thirty-five years. The striking progress that has been achieved in understanding the physics of the processes leading to the creation of fusion energy in the laboratory has undoubtedly been assisted by the wholly free international interchange of information that has continued since 1958—in sharp contrast to the 'commercial secrecy' with which fission energy was initially shrouded. The European Community (which supports the internationally-funded Joint European Torus (JET) machine at Culham in the UK), the USA, USSR, and Japan have all made major contributions. Over twenty other countries have been working on a smaller scale[207,208]. Already about one billion US dollars a year are committed to this work, world-wide.

The aim is to produce, confine and maintain a state of matter—a *plasma*—at a temperature above 100 million degrees Celsius, for times long compared with one second. Under such conditions atomic nuclei will fuse together, with the emission of energy. If the naturally occurring heavy isotope of hydrogen, deuterium (D), could be used by itself, then the world would have a new source of energy through the 'D–D' reaction. While not strictly speaking renewable, this energy would be for all practical purposes inexhaustible: the sea would be our fuel-tank for millions of years. However, as the D–D reaction needs even higher temperatures, present research is concentrated on the alternative and more easily initiated deuterium–tritium reaction.

Tritium is the still heavier isotope of hydrogen, with a mass of three atomic units. Unfortunately it does not occur naturally, but has to be made from lithium by irradiation with neutrons. It is also radioactive, and working with it involves controlling the radiation risk. Lithium is widely dispersed in the earth's crust, and is present in igneous rocks to the extent of around 30 parts per million on average. Although its minable ores are usually of low concentration, lithium availability is unlikely to constrain the development of commercial fusion energy.

Present knowledge derives from two quite separate approaches. One is magnetic confinement of the extremely hot plasma, so that it is thermally insulated from the walls of the containing-vessel. Five large 'Tokamak' machines using this principle are in operation, and four others are under construction (1990). A second route uses laser-induced compression, where tiny pellets are compressed by laser energy until their density is 100 or more times that of water. Despite steady progress there is still much to be learned about the processes involved in creating and maintaining the hot plasma; but as experience has grown useful rules of thumb have been developed.

However, we are still a long way from the point at which the fusion energy produced exceeds the energy input, which in the best experiments so far completed is still 500 times larger. Even so this is 100 times better than Oliphant achieved with his earliest experiments in 1934. Once we arrive at a self-sustaining state (described as 'ignition'), the next step will be to develop an understanding of the additional physical processes that will then take place. Unfortunately a fusion reactor capable of exploring ignition is inevitably costly. The International Atomic Energy Agency in Vienna is therefore sponsoring a joint design for an International Thermonuclear Experimental Reactor—whose acronym, ITER, means in Latin 'the way'. The target date for completion is 2001. The estimated cost is $5 billion.

As knowledge develops of the underlying physics, the emphasis is beginning to turn to the issue of engineering feasibility. Commercial thermonuclear reactors, when finally created, will be large machines, with electrical outputs probably around 1 GWe, comparable with those of today's large fission reactors. Fusion energy will, however, be intrinsically much safer than fission, and need not be a source of public disquiet.

It is unlikely that fusion will make any significant contribution to world energy supplies for another half century, even if all goes well. One reason is that while it has so far been possible to keep the experimental machines relatively free from radioactive contamination, once ignition is achieved large numbers of neutrons will be generated. There will then be a need to take precautions against the resulting induced radioactivity, which will inevitably slow up the work. It should, however, be possible through a careful choice of materials to exercise much more control over the levels of radioactivity than is possible with fission reactors[209]. There will also be only minor difficulties over waste. Somewhere around 2050 we may hope to see this new energy source up and running.

Reports appeared in March 1989 of an entirely different approach to the problem. Fleischmann and Pons[210] claimed to have induced fusion by the simple device of passing an electric current through heavy water, using a palladium electrode: the fusion was claimed to have occurred within its crystal lattice. The story attracted great attention, and the contrast with the complex processes of classical fusion research was presented by the news media in David and Goliath terms. Unfortunately for the authors there are grave doubts about the validity of their experimental technique, and meticulous attempts[211,212] to reproduce their results have proved fruitless. There is no reason to believe that their report opens a new route to exploitable fusion energy.

Energy efficiency and conservation

The oil shocks produced a new awareness of the need to save energy. Although the subsequent fall in the real price of oil somewhat blunted this perception, it remains central to any rational energy policy. Better conservation is equivalent to, and therefore just as important as, developing new sources of energy; and it may be very much cheaper[203]. Much remains to be done. In industrialized countries about one-fifth of all electric power is used to make domestic living conditions more comfortable; in the USA the summer-demand peak is even larger than in winter because of the air-conditioning load. So clearly there are useful savings to be made not only from solar heating and better house design, but also from the use of reversible heat pumps (using the same principle as the domestic refrigerator) for heating in winter and air-conditioning in summer. Japan has installed over a million such systems. Thirty per cent of new houses in the USA are fitted with heat-pumps[196].

There is also the possibility of using the residual heat from central power-stations for domestic and industrial heating. Unless this is done only 30 to 35 per cent of the energy in the fuel is converted into useful electricity (the proportion is about the same whether the power-station is nuclear or not). The remainder, more often than not, is thrown away. As we saw in Chapter 6, combined heat and power (CHP) stations, in contrast, can provide domestic or industrial users with most of the rest of the available energy in the form of heat—bringing the overall efficiency of energy use up to 80 per cent or even 90 per cent. CHP is well established in northern and central Europe. In the UK it is still a rarity, though the government began to take an interest at the beginning of 1990.

In the USA the Public Utilities Regulatory Policies Act, originally passed in 1978, creates favourable fiscal conditions for combining electricity and heat production. 'Qualifying facilities' under the Act, which meet certain stipulated requirements, can also sell their surplus electricity to a utility at the cost the utility would have had to spend generating the same quantity itself (its 'avoided cost'). The Act requires utilities to purchase power produced by 'qualifying' facilities exploiting renewable energy sources.

There are many other possibilities for energy saving. The energy-intensive industries are obvious targets: sugar production accounts for 2 per cent of the world's consumption of oil; new designs of flash furnaces for aluminium production can save one-third of the energy otherwise needed; in Japan the electricity used per tonne of steel produced has been cut by 21 per cent since the first oil shock. Rail and river transport can be less expensive in energy terms than road transport. As a result of similar economies, the EEC energy demand in 1985 was only 2 per cent above the 1973 level, even though output had gone up[213] by 24 per cent. If energy prices rise as expected in the 1990s many further economies will automatically be made, without any need for intervention by governments.

But while energy conservation may be encouraged through the price mechanism, this is no guarantee in an affluent society and in a totally free market that it will proceed as fast or go as far as would be technically possible. The problem is that some of the biggest savings depend on action taken by millions of consumers at the 'micro' level. Experience shows that the public's actions invariably fall short of what would theoretically be possible. People do not all rush to buy compact fluorescent lights—with five times lower current consumption and much longer lives than incandescent bulbs—partly for lack of information, but more because the advantage of making the change is perceived as *de minimis* in personal terms: people are busy, and there are other things to worry about.

Some US states provide incentives for their electricity generating companies to encourage energy savings, rather than additional consumption, on the part of their customers—a process colloquially known as 'negawatts'. It has been calculated that the enlightened US National Appliance Energy Conservation Act of 1987 could save 22 GWe by the year 2000, simply by encouraging the use of more efficient appliances. This would be equivalent to the output of twenty large conventional or nuclear power-stations. And yet, perversely, changes in fuel efficiency targets for the US automobile industry were made in October 1988 to allow large cars to be marketed more easily.

It is for governments to invent effective fiscal and regulatory devices for modifying free-market price signals, so that rational individual responses can conduce to the community's long-term benefit by saving energy. It is believed that a further 30 per cent cut in energy per unit of economic activity would be realistic within the next twenty to thirty years. But as both economic activity and population are increasing, this is far from implying that *total* energy requirements could be similarly reduced.

Taking stock

For the immediate future there is no shortage of options. Even in the absence of dramatic new developments there could be more than enough energy physically available to meet the foreseeable demand for the next three decades. A decline in oil production will be delayed by further discoveries in previously little-explored areas, including the polar regions. The ascendancy of the Middle East will be re-established in the 1990s. Total world oil production is likely to remain little altered before the second decade of the twenty-first century; and when falling reserves-to-production ratios make a decline inevitable, natural gas and coal will be available as substitutes. Some contribution to energy supplies will come from the renewable energy sources other than hydro, particularly wind power, and although it will remain minor for many years it will grow steadily. The importance of energy conservation, combined heat and power, and district heating will be more widely accepted and expressed in action terms, though probably only to the point of slowing, rather than reversing, the energy growth trends underlying Table 12.1.

This relatively relaxed outlook over the medium-term future does not imply an absence of difficulties. The West will remain anxious about its substantial dependence for oil on the politically unstable Middle East. There will be capital shortages holding back the development of hydropower and natural gas. And the very phrase 'foreseeable demand' implies a judgement about the ability—or rather inability—of the poorest two-thirds of the world's population to afford the energy resources which the West counts as its birthright. Nevertheless, for the next quarter of a century the energy future for the industrialized world at least is reasonably assured.

In this context the critics of nuclear power can argue that fission energy is not, in any absolute and immediate physical sense, 'essential'. But that is to lose sight of the larger picture. Nuclear power exists, and even though it is a comparative newcomer, it has already exerted a profound effect on the whole energy market, which is particularly sensitive to changes in marginal demand. The extended bargaining between OPEC producers in 1988, and the massive oil-price fluctuations during the course of that single year, between a minimum of $10 and a maximum of $18 per barrel, showed how far prices can be moved by changes in the marginal balance of supply and demand of as little as 2 or 3 million barrels per day—even though total world production runs at around 60 million barrels per day. Today's nuclear energy production is the energy equivalent of nearly 9 million barrels of oil per day. Clearly the displacement of oil-fired electricity generation after 1973 by nuclear power must have exerted substantial downward pressure on the oil price, and so helped to curb both OPEC's commercial leverage and inflation.

Internationally traded low-cost coal is a newer market where experience is still being gathered; but there too it seems probable that for the next ten or twenty years nuclear power will help to 'cap' prices, at levels where the economics of the two sources of electricity will run roughly parallel. In the process some of the more expensive sources of coal will lose their economic attraction. Removal of that cap through the general abandonment of the nuclear option—on the Swedish model—could cause a jump in coal prices, when any marginal savings in generating costs might quickly disappear. This illustrates how important it is when discussing the future of energy generally, and of nuclear power in particular, to set the boundaries of the discussion wide enough to encompass the totality of the problem. The importance of nuclear power in promoting diversity and competition can hardly be overestimated.

This balancing role also has a political dimension. As we saw in Chapter 5, it was one of the factors which helped Mrs Thatcher in 1984–5 to break the power of the British miners' trade union, which for years had operated what was in effect a labour cartel. Once nuclear power had taken away 20 per cent of the British domestic coal market, and further nuclear expansion was contemplated, some kind of confrontation became inevitable—with consequences in terms of the efficiency of British coal production that can only be applauded. Such considerations could well justify paying a limited premium to retain the beneficial contribution of nuclear power to energy diversity even during periods when the short-term market may appear to be saying otherwise. Moreover, in the long-term the full development of the fast reactor will offer an almost inexhaustible supply of electrical energy, which is a further argument for actively maintaining the uranium-powered option.

There is yet another factor, which brings an extra dimension to the discussion: the developing greenhouse effect. It casts a shadow over the still abundant supplies of coal and natural gas, and poses the issue of how energy-market mechanisms should be modified to reflect the long-term consequences of global warming. It places the environmental acceptability of nuclear electricity in a new and more favourable light. It is the subject of the concluding chapter.

13 The Global Greenhouse and Energy Policy

THE recital of options in the previous chapter shows how complex the world-wide energy market has become, the stark differences between the rich energy-consuming nations and the Third World, and the longer-term problems of energy supply. But for the immediate future there is no shortage. If the economic structure of the world could stay roughly as at the beginning of the 1990s, and if we closed our eyes to the trouble we might be leaving for our children, the energy picture over the next quarter of a century would be considerably more manageable than most would have thought possible only ten years previously. But history has not stopped: the only certainty is the inevitability of continuing change.

One major factor is the growth in world population, which is accelerating at an alarming pace. It was around one billion in 1800. It had doubled by 1930, and doubled again by the time of the World Population Conference in Bucharest in 1974. Despite all the warnings voiced in the United Nations, the 5.3 billion alive at the beginning of the 1990s are expected to increase to 8.5 billion by the year 2025, and to 10 or 11 billion by 2075. The United Nations Fund for Population Activities regards even 14 billions by the year 2100 as within the bounds of possibility. In one century the world's population will have quadrupled, with a quarter of a million extra mouths to feed each and every day. Ninety-five per cent of the increase is taking place in the Third World[214]. The developing countries, as they enter their industrial phases, are also showing the largest percentage growth in energy consumption—by an average of 4 per cent annually. The result is likely to be an increase in world energy demand by about half in the thirty years to 2020; and of the new total the developing countries would account for nearly one-quarter[196], compared with about one-seventh in 1973.

While the physical resources could be developed to satisfy even a doubled energy demand by 2020, there would be formidable difficulties over financing. Today's Third World debt is largely a product of the energy crises of the 1970s, and the problems will be intensified as fuel reserves-to-production ratios fall and prices rise. Morally the peoples of the developing world have as much right to enjoy the benefits of abundant energy as anyone else. Practically, the combination of high population growth, and the growth in per capita demand, can only add to the world's economic problems. Third World energy aspirations will be met only in part.

Looking ahead to the middle of the twenty-first century in the light of the seemingly unstoppable expansion of population, the long-term outlook is one of accumulating uncertainties. It is disturbing to contemplate a future of burgeoning OECD economies, expanding Third World populations, and ever-increasing energy demand, while having only hazy ideas about how the wheels of the world economy should be powered in the second half of the twenty-first century, during the later years of the lives of some babies already born.

The greenhouse effect

Before the 1980s were out the issue of fossil-fuel wastes also began to stir political awareness: not the spoil dumps which have disfigured mining areas since the beginning of the Industrial Revolution, but the vast quantities of carbon dioxide which are pumped into the atmosphere through the burning of oil, coal, and natural gas, and which now threaten to modify the climate of the whole globe. Quite suddenly, in mid-1988, this 'greenhouse effect' ceased to be merely an interesting scientific curiosity, and became something to be taken seriously at the level of government policy.

Current energy forecasts, even those shown in Table 12.1 which make some allowance for energy-efficiency and conservation, imply a steady increase in the production of carbon dioxide, from the present 5.5 gigatonnes of contained carbon per year, to a figure 25–50 per cent higher by the second quarter of the next century. The greenhouse problem concerns the modifying influence which this carbon dioxide is exerting on the earth's retention of the huge quantity of heat coming from the sun, which is 10,000 times greater than man's own energy production. Much of the sun's heat is re-radiated to cold outer space; but carbon dioxide interferes with this process, resulting in a net warming, in much the same way as the glass of a greenhouse. It is a phenomenon to which nuclear power makes no contribution, except indirectly through the energy used in the manufacture of the necessary hardware.

In one sense the greenhouse effect has always been with us: it is what maintains the average temperature of the earth about 30°C higher than would otherwise be the case, and so provides a climate favourable to life. The new anxieties relate to the probability that industrial, domestic, and transport emissions of carbon dioxide, and agricultural emissions of methane, are about to induce a significant and rapid enhancement of the warming effect, and so upset the present climatic balance. We are in effect progressively returning to the atmosphere and oceans the vast quantities of carbon that were taken out of the biological cycle, and fixed in the form of fossil fuel 300 million years ago, when the climate was warmer and more humid.

The outcome was predicted almost a century ago by Svante Arrhenius, the Swedish physical chemist, in papers written in 1896 and 1908. He estimated that by the time industrialization had doubled the pre-Industrial Revolution atmospheric content of carbon dioxide, which was around 280 parts per million (ppm), the average temperature of the earth would be higher by between 4° and 6°C. For half a century his conclusion was hardly known except to a handful of natural scientists; but in 1957 Roger Revelle and Hans Suess of the Scripps Institute at La Jolla, California, started to question the state of knowledge regarding atmospheric carbon dioxide. In the following year a measurement station was established as part of the International Geophysical Year, high up—11,000 feet—on Mauna Loa in Hawaii, where true atmospheric samples could be taken unperturbed by local industrial waste gases. The record soon revealed a small seasonal variation, plus a systematic increase of about 1.5 ppm per year, which if continued would lead to a doubling of the pre-Industrial Revolution concentration—Arrhenius's yardstick—during the second half of the twenty-first century[214–216].

Thirty or so other kinds of gaseous molecules have similar effects. By far the most important contributor is water vapour, which implies that anything which affects cloud formation could influence and possibly reinforce the total greenhouse contribution. Other products of combustion (carbon monoxide and nitrous oxide) are also important—as are ozone, methane, and the various chlorofluorocarbons (CFCs) which are widely used as refrigerants, solvents, and propellants for spray-cans and fire extinguishers. The CFCs are particularly significant, because molecule for molecule, depending on the type, they are 6,600–23,000 times more effective than carbon dioxide as greenhouse gases[216]. For this reason their contribution to greenhouse warming had by 1985 already reached 20 per cent of the total from all gases, other than water vapour. Fortunately it is possible to envisage a world without CFC-propelled spray-cans and car air-conditioning units. It is far more difficult to replace conventional power-stations or internal-combustion engines (power-stations were responsible in 1988 for 33 per cent of the UK's carbon dioxide emissions, road transport for a further 18 per cent—see Table 13.1). In any case there are few human activities with longer time-horizons and more built-in inertia than the energy industry.

Controlling methane also presents serious problems. Molecule for molecule it is more than twenty times as effective as carbon dioxide as a greenhouse gas, and emissions are growing by about 1 per cent a year. The sources correlate roughly with human activity and therefore with world population: intensive cattle and rice farming to meet the growing demand for food; methane from cellulose-eating termites on forest land that has been cleared for cultivation; wetlands; coal-mining; household waste dumps; and in some cases transport and industry. The total greenhouse contributions from methane and the other gases, apart from water vapour, roughly match that from carbon dioxide. Even if the CFCs could be completely eliminated, methane would remain an important contributor. This means that the warming problem cannot be solved by changes in energy policy alone—though as energy is the largest greenhouse source that is where radical action is most urgently needed.

The development of political interest

By the end of the 1970s some political interest was being shown: the US Congress enacted the 1978 National Climate Program Act, encouraging climatic research. A first World Climate Conference was convened in 1979 by the World Meteorological Organization (WMO). This led to a World Climate Programme (WCP), sponsored jointly by the United Nations Environment Programme (UNEP), the International Council of Scientific Unions, and WMO. The WCP held its own first conference at Villach in Austria in 1980. A second followed in October 1985; its report said that the understanding of the greenhouse effect was sufficiently developed to justify beginning an active international collaboration to explore the effectiveness of alternative energy policies.

In 1983 UNEP set up a twenty-one person World Commission on Environment and Development, headed by the Norwegian Prime Minister, Mrs Gro Harlem Brundtland; a 380 page report[236] was presented to the United Nations in October 1987. Its message was not encouraging for nuclear power, whose generation was held to be 'only justifiable if there are solid solutions to the presently unsolved problems to which it gives rise'. Predictably, the report exhorted governments to manage the world's resources in a 'sustainable' manner.

Public awareness that this might not be easy was aroused, while the Commission was sitting, by confirmation that a 'hole' existed in the ozone layer over the Antarctic, due to the atmospheric effects of man-made pollutants, particularly the CFCs 11 and 12. Since their discovery in 1928 they had found many industrial uses; but besides being greenhouse gases they also attack atmospheric ozone, which is important as a natural shield against the sun's harmful ultra-violet rays which cause skin cancer. This potentially emotive issue is one in which everyone has an interest. Although ozone is itself another of the greenhouse gases, the 'hole' has nothing directly to do with its possible climatic effects or those of carbon dioxide. However, its discovery was important in alerting people to the proposition that human activities are escalating to a point at which the atmosphere can no longer be treated as a convenient 'sink' for any wastes we might wish to put there.

In this case political action followed commendably quickly. The first alarms had been given in the 1970s. The Vienna Convention on the Protection of the Ozone Layer was negotiated in 1985, and a couple of years later, in September 1987, its Montreal Protocol signalled agreement on a 50 per cent cut in CFC production by 1999, relative to the 1986 level. Twenty-four countries signed immediately, though China and India reserved their positions; another 22 signed within the next eighteen months. A follow-up conference of 124 countries, held in London early in 1989, and another a year later, also in London, were both successful in attracting further adherents, bringing the number of ratifications to 59. In addition, China and India promised to join, after developed countries had offered the LDCs financial and technical help over phasing-in less-damaging alternatives. The Protocol's provisions were strengthened to cover the complete phase-out in the developed world of CFCs by the end of the century.

While these moves were taking place public concern was also growing over the slash-and-burn policy which was destroying Brazilian, Indian, and Indonesian rain forests, losing an area more than twice the size of Switzerland every year—and in the process endangering thousands of natural species, ruining part of the world's greatest natural 'factory' for removing carbon dioxide from the atmosphere and replacing it with oxygen, and adding 20 per cent to man-made carbon dioxide emissions. This was taking place at a time of growing certainty that the average temperature of the earth's surface had risen by about 0.5°C over the last century [216,217].

By 1988 the time was ripe for politicians to take the greenhouse effect seriously. In January President Reagan transmitted a report to Congress summarizing the relevant activities of the US government. The Canadian government organized an international conference on the subject in Toronto in June 1988, with delegations from 46 countries. It called, somewhat optimistically, for an initial 20 per cent reduction in carbon dioxide emissions by 2005. Similar views had been expressed twelve months earlier in the US Congress, without raising a ripple in the world's press.

What gave the Toronto message more force was that it fortuitously coincided with a period of extraordinary heat in the United States. A drought lasting three months reduced the country's grain harvest by half. For nineteen days on end in August 1988 the temperature in Washington DC was over 90°F (32°C), and emergency measures were needed to import electricity for air-conditioning from as far away as Manitoba. There was widespread belief that it could be no coincidence that the six hottest years in the twentieth century, world-wide, had all occurred during the 1980s: 1988, 1987, 1983, 1981, 1980, and 1986, in that order. One result had been the near-halving of world grain stocks between 1985 and 1988. The Soviet foreign minister Shevardnadze urged in September that the United Nations should take on a broader role in environmental matters. Both candidates in the US presidential election took up the theme. In September, in a lecture to Britain's scientific academy, the Royal Society, Mrs Thatcher showed a new willingness to recognize the importance of industrial influences on the environment. She commended the environmental virtues of nuclear power, which 'doesn't put up carbon dioxide into the air'. In November the Intergovernmental Panel on Climate Change (IPCC) was set up jointly by the World Meteorological Organization and the United Nations Environment Programme, to prepare for the Second World Climate Conference in 1990. At the close of 1988 President Gorbachev, in his address to the UN General Assembly, drew attention to the importance of paying more attention to the health of the environment: 'humanity is part of the biosphere, and this biosphere is the only one we have'.

The Toronto conference reported[218] that 'humanity is conducting an enormous, unintended, globally pervasive experiment, whose ultimate consequences could be second only to a global war'. This had the desired effect of alerting the press. The magazine *Time* began 1989 with the 'Endangered Earth' on its cover; it was 'planet of the year', taking the place of the traditional personality. But the necessary connections with practical energy choices proved more difficult to forge: a few months after Toronto it was still possible for a professional society of energy economists to meet in London and discuss energy futures without any thought of the policy consequences of the greenhouse effect, until reminded by an intervention on behalf of the nuclear industry; just as two years earlier the triennial World Energy Conference had given it scarcely a mention.

The evidence and the uncertainties

Non-scientists might wonder how far the existence of the effect has been rigorously proved, and whether the great American drought of 1988 might have been a normal climatic fluctuation—like the warming which occurred from 1920 to 1940. Dissenters there certainly were. One American critic called it 'the laugh of the century', attributing the observed temperature rise to recording stations being frequently located in conurbations, and therefore subject to the 'urban heat island effect'. However, climate researchers believe that they have adequately taken this into account in their survey of climatic data over the past century[214,219]. Other sceptics predicted that any greenhouse warming might be balanced by an increase in heat-reflecting clouds. Yet another group attributed climatic fluctuations to the random incidence of major volcanic eruptions[220].

Because of the existence of these natural climatic fluctuations it will be necessary to wait until around 2010 before unequivocal statistical 'proof' of the phenomenon will be available. Meanwhile, the evidence from the neighbouring planets provides its own warning. Venus, with an atmosphere consisting of 97 per cent carbon dioxide, has a surface temperature of about 450°C; while Mars, with little carbon dioxide, has a temperature of −50°C, far below freezing point. And there is the striking constancy of the scientific predictions: despite all the additional knowledge that has accumulated since 1908, today's estimates of the probable effects of doubling the atmosphere's carbon dioxide remain consistent with Arrhenius's calculations.

Other evidence goes back thousands of years. Ice-cores taken by a Franco-Soviet team from the Antarctic ice-cap—they are 2 kilometres long—show a clear correlation[221] between the atmospheric carbon dioxide content and surface temperature over the past 160,000 years (both parameters can be inferred from an analysis of the tiny bubbles of air trapped in the cores). The results are striking and unambiguous. An ice age corresponds to around 190–215 ppm of carbon dioxide in the atmosphere; a warm period to 260–80 ppm, with a peak at nearly 300 ppm. Methane concentrations in the cores also show a somewhat similar correlation with temperature[222,223]. When the Industrial Revolution began the world was nearing the end of a warm interglacial period. Since then carbon dioxide concentrations have risen, as a result of man's activities, from 280 ppm to 315 ppm in 1958, and to 354 ppm in 1990.

The consensus of the available evidence[214–16,224–8,231] is that on 'business as usual' assumptions the additional greenhouse gases will cause an average warming of 0.2 to 0.5°C per decade—leading to an earth 3°C warmer by the year 2100; with appreciably greater rises at the poles. For comparison, a 4°–5°C average difference in the other direction is what separates us from the last ice-age, which terminated abruptly about 14,000–13,000 years ago. We are about to take the earth into a condition which it has not experienced for the past 100,000 years, which is tampering with nature with a vengeance.

Since the last ice-age the sea has risen by about 100 metres—about 10–20 centimetres in the last century—due partly to ice melting, and partly to water expanding as it gets warmer, like mercury in a thermometer[229,230]. However, expansion of the deep oceans depends on the rate at which warming is transmitted downwards, and this is difficult to forecast. Estimates of the likely speed and extent of the rise therefore vary considerably; but the IPCC predict that about 20 centimetres are probable by 2030, and 65 centimetres (just over 2 feet) by the end of the twenty-first century—which would imply a rate of rise three to six times faster than over the past century. To assist in clearing up the uncertainties, a global network of 300 sea-level gauges is being installed under the aegis of the UK's Natural Environment Research Council.

A sea-rise of about 60 centimetres a century from now would be highly significant for many of the world's capital cities, built as they often are at sea-level. Louisiana, Bangladesh, and the Netherlands would all be at risk; the Maldives and Kiribati would face disaster. Apart from the threat of inundation of low-lying land, climatic belts would shift (by 200–300 kilometres per °C of warming), harvests become erratic, once-fertile areas turn into dust-bowls, and some of the world's existing agricultural infrastructure need re-location. Chronic instability in agricultural markets is a real danger—which is a euphemistic way of saying that starvation on a massive scale could also occur. Malthus' fears no longer seem exaggerated.

Extreme heat waves and dry periods are likely to increase substantially in frequency: one model predicts that Dallas in the USA would experience temperatures of over 100°F (38°C), on nearly 80 days a year, compared to the present average of 19; Washington DC would experience 12 such days a year, instead of about one at present in a normal year. Hurricanes would become more damaging, with wind speeds 20 per cent higher. Precipitation would increase. Forests, like agriculture, would migrate towards the poles, extending naturally by 30 kilometres a century, but would be outpaced by the climate shift: the trees could find themselves at odds with their new climatic environment. As we do not yet know enough to construct predictive models giving the necessary detail, we face the possibility that the consequences will be upon us before they can be foreseen with the precision needed for an action programme.

The gradualness with which the oceans will warm will introduce enormous lags—several decades—into the full expression of these changes. Even if we could stop greenhouse pollution today the consequences would continue to develop over the next century.

While this speaks for taking early action, it is bound to complicate the political response. Nor do we yet know precisely how plant life will react to the changing atmosphere or to the coming warming. Experiments suggest that a doubled carbon dioxide content might increase growth by 50 per cent, though this benefit could be offset by the general disturbance to existing agriculture.

Ecological reasons add to the uncertainties over the exact rate at which warming will take place. Quantities of carbon dioxide vastly greater than any produced by man move continually between the atmosphere, the earth's vegetation and the oceans. Photosynthesis by growing plants takes out about 110 billion tonnes of carbon from the atmosphere annually. Plant respiration replaces half of this, soil respiration the other half. The balance in this part of the cycle could be sensitively affected by the warming process[231], creating a destabilizing positive feedback. In addition around 90 billion tonnes of carbon diffuse (as carbon dioxide) into and out of the oceans each year. Man's present fossil fuel output of about 5.5 billion tonnes of carbon annually is arithmetically minor in comparison with these other flows; but it intrudes into what has so far been a delicate and finely adjusted natural balance, and leads to an annual increase of about 3 billion tonnes.

Learning to understand more about this complicated mechanism will be vital for 'greenhouse-avoidance' policy. The role of the oceans is particularly important, since they contain about sixty times more carbon dioxide than the atmosphere. Currently they act as a net 'sink', but a future temperature rise could force some of the carbon dioxide out of solution, thus adding to 'greenhouse' influences (unlike solids such as sugar or salt, the solubility of gases *decreases* as the temperature of the water rises). Again, if the Arctic ice-sheet were removed by melting, there would no longer be a layer separating the relatively warm ocean and the cold polar air. Evaporation would increase, and the extra water-vapour might reinforce climatic warming. There are further little-understood but potentially major effects from the response of marine life to changes in temperature and carbon dioxide concentration.

The deforestation referred to in the previous chapter, arising from the search by Third World peasants for fuel, plus the clearance of new areas for crop planting, can only further upset the natural balance. Planting new forests would certainly help to contain the damage, but only slowly, and huge areas would be needed. An estimate prepared for the IPCC is that replanting with temperate forest of an area half the size of the USA or Australia would result in the annual withdrawal of only one billion (10^9) tonnes of carbon from the atmosphere, or only one-third of the present net rate of carbon dioxide increase; and then only for as long as the trees were still growing. After felling they would need to be preserved from decay and not used for firewood. Clearly reafforestation on its own offers no easy way out.

Consequences for energy policy

The 1988 Toronto overall target of an initial reduction of carbon dioxide emissions by 20 per cent, within the seventeen years to 2005, while not physically impossible given sufficient political determination and the necessary supply of capital, is in terms of real-world politics highly optimistic. The difficulties become apparent if we consider where the carbon dioxide comes from in typical industrial economies.

The figures in Table 13.1 draw attention to three problems. One is the diversity of the sources, and the consequent need to think in terms of a wide spectrum of otherwise unrelated actions, none of which by itself could provide a magic cure-all. A second is the effect of continued growth in economic activity: we are running against a moving staircase. A third is the time taken to modify or replace our stock of carbon-dioxide creating equipment—and the huge cost. Achieving progress will require a continuing world-wide campaign, involving some constraint on growth, and sustained by successive government administrations for as long as we can see into the future. The problem only needs to be stated in such terms for the pitfalls to be immediately apparent.

The self-evident difficulties provide the strongest reason for using every club in the policy bag; and as power-station emissions are the largest single source of greenhouse gases, the case for expanding the use of nuclear power makes itself. This in no way derogates from the urgent necessity of a more serious drive for conservation, wherever it can be obtained. All possible approaches will be needed.

A hotter planet unfortunately does not automatically mean a reduction in energy consumption: a third of the USA's present peak-electricity demand is for air-conditioning in summer. A sharp

Table 13.1. Contributors to Carbon Dioxide Emissions in the UK and the Twelve Nations of the European Community (1988–1989).

Source	Contribution to CO_2 emissions		Average time for major change (years)	Comments
	UK	Europe		
Power-stations	33	30	30–40	Europe–12 places more reliance on nuclear power than UK. The bulk of the French conversion to nuclear was achieved in twenty years.
Industry	23	17	15–20	Energy consumption per unit of output is forecast to fall by 15–20 per cent by 2010. This saving would be offset if industrial growth continued at 1 per cent year.
Road transport	18	22	10–15	UK car population is forecast to grow by 50 per cent (1988 to 2010). An average reduction in CO_2 per car of 20–40 per cent is possible, but the benefit will be offset by growing numbers.
Domestic	15	22		Buildings last for decades, equipment for a few years. Better insulation can be quickly installed as an energy-saving measure.
Other	11	9		

Sources: References 215, 232, with updating from UK Department of the Environment.

reduction in standards of summer comfort in the richer countries may be unavoidable. A wholly new emphasis on 'demand management' will be needed, using fiscal sticks and carrots where necessary to override the normal market behaviour of preferring the cheapest short-run solution. In future 'cheapness' should be measured not only in monetary terms, but also in terms of energy, or volume of carbon dioxide saved. Unfortunately the evidence suggests that any extra taxation will need to be severe—in some cases possibly over 100 per cent—before it begins to bite on long-established habits.

The biggest squanderers of energy are the industrially developed nations. Within that group the USA is prodigally wasteful. With about 4 per cent of the world's population, it is responsible for 22 per cent of carbon dioxide emissions. It shares the unenviable position at the head of the 'rogue's league table' of high carbon dioxide emitters with East Germany: both produce 4.9 tonnes of carbon (as carbon dioxide) per person-year[232], at a time when more economical technologies such as combined-cycle generation, or combined heat and power, are becoming readily available. In contrast five countries in the European Community, with standards of living broadly comparable with those in the USA, produce between 2 and 3 tonnes of carbon per person-year, while in the remaining seven countries the figure is below 2 tonnes. The much higher proportion of nuclear energy in the EEC makes a significant contribution to this better performance. Awareness is stirring in the USA but, as we saw earlier, progress there has been sporadic.

The consequences of greenhouse mitigation will slowly reach into many aspects of our lives, once the policy implications of inaction are fully recognized by governments. It is not only national ministries of energy which will have to deal with the consequences, but also ministries of finance, housing, transport, environment and industry, all of which have a part to play.

However, until people are convinced, action is likely to be slow and inadequate. The history of dealing with acid rain shows the difficulties of agreeing an action agenda when commercial interests are at stake; and the defeat of the Dutch government in May 1989 over its policy of dealing with environmental problems via new taxation illustrates the problems of convincing an electorate. Handling the greenhouse effect will be even more difficult. Nevertheless, progress is being made, because in the end facts are powerful persuaders. It was the fear of commercial loss of competitiveness that initially restrained policy-making regarding the ozone problem, and collective international agreement that eventually provided a way forward via the Montreal protocol. The greenhouse issue raises similar problems, and needs a similar approach.

Conservation and efficiency apart, there is a case for preferring those fossil fuels which minimize the production of carbon dioxide for a given energy output. In this regard natural gas is 25–30 per cent better than oil, and nearly twice as good as coal—always provided that there are no significant leaks of methane into the atmosphere, either in production or in use. Methane being at least twenty times more effective than carbon dioxide as a greenhouse gas, molecule for molecule, a 2–3 per cent leak would undo all the benefit. For a similar reason it would be advantageous to press forward the exploition of methane from rubbish tips as a power source, converting it in the process into the less objectionable carbon dioxide.

Action need not stop at mitigation, since as we saw in the previous chapter energy sources exist which do not produce any carbon dioxide whatsoever. Table 12.1 showed that only one-ninth of the world's primary energy sources—mostly hydro and nuclear—are free from greenhouse consequences. A trebling of installed nuclear capacity, and a 50 per cent increase in hydropower, should both be possible within the first quarter of the twenty-first century. With conservation exerting some restraint on total energy demand, and a contribution from the newer renewable sources—particularly windpower, despite its visual intrusiveness—it would be entirely feasible for the 'non-greenhouse' proportion of primary energy to grow, worldwide, from 11 per cent to 19 per cent by the year 2025, despite a 50 per cent increase in total energy consumption. That would still be only a first step towards dealing with the global problem; but to aim any lower would be to ignore its potential seriousness. Speed in decision-making is important: a thirty years' delay could incur[233] an additional long-term penalty of 0.8°C, which is clearly worth avoiding.

Ensuring that matters do not get worse any faster than they must also clearly implies taking a fresh look at political campaigns directed towards 'phasing-out' nuclear power. Current Swedish policy is not a model to be followed generally. The nuclear industry has every right to ask that future energy choices should take into account the long-term environmental consequences of choosing coal, gas, or oil. Even the crudest approximations would be better than turning a blind eye, and would have the great benefit of making the environmental and social costs of the fossil-fuel alternatives explicit. The effect on perceptions of nuclear power's economic and social acceptability could be dramatic.

Political, jurisdictional, and international issues

The greenhouse effect has already begun to influence political rhetoric, and there can be little doubt that this will lead to some action during the 1990s. Mrs Thatcher addressed the United Nations in November 1989, and undertook to set up a new centre for climate prediction and research. Significantly, she also recognized the need for emission targets. Major conferences on the subject are being held with increasing frequency—including the 72 nation Noordwijk conference, also in November 1989; the 34 nation conference of the Economic Commission for Europe in May 1990, to follow up the Brundtland report; the Second World Climate Conference in November 1990; and the World Conference on Environment and Development in Brazil in 1992.

These very public airings of the issues are leading governments to take seriously the need for new commitments. Mrs Thatcher spelled out her intentions at the opening of the new climate-modelling centre in May 1990. She pledged the UK to work for a return by 2005 to 1990 levels of carbon dioxide emissions, despite hoped-for economic growth in the meantime—but only 'provided others are ready to take their full share'. It was a political judgement in the light of feasibility and, no doubt, electoral reality. She was immediately and variously assailed both for scaremongering and for setting too modest a target. The IPCC scientific panel had pointed out that an immediate reduction in emissions from human activities of 60 per cent would be needed to stabilize temperatures at the 1990 level. Several countries in northern Europe were already considering proposals more radical than Mrs Thatcher's—though none had yet reached the stage of successful implementation.

Even given the political will, tensions will be unavoidable. The countries facing the most difficult choices will be those in the Third World which, up till now, have assumed that they could rely for their long-term energy security and foreign exchange earnings on abundant indigenous reserves of coal, oil, and gas. It is easy to understand the problems that led the governments of China, Saudi Arabia, and the USSR to state bluntly, at an IPCC meeting in Geneva in June 1990, that they could not meet 'early' targets to cut greenhouse emissions. It is also not a happy omen that both China and the second most populous country, India, found difficulties over signing the Montreal Protocol to the Convention on the Protection of the Ozone Layer, which involves far more straightforward issues than the global greenhouse. Environmental anxieties—like the realization that in the early 1980s tropical forest-burning was contributing almost one quarter of man-made carbon dioxide emissions—are more easily entertained by the richer nations. The leverage provided by overseas aid may be needed to cajole recipient countries into adopting more environmentally-aware policies.

There could be tensions between low-lying states and those in regions well above sea-level. How can the Bolivians possibly view the issue in the same light as the Bangladeshis, or for that matter the people of Louisiana? There is no established corpus of international law defining how trans-global pollution should be regulated, and creating instruments appropriate to the problem is a major task for the years ahead[148].

The number of prior legal cases which might be considered relevant is tiny. Arbitration was used in the leading Trail Smelter case of the 1930s between the Canadian and United States governments[234]. A Canadian smelter at Trail, only 10 miles from the US border, had caused trans-boundary pollution for some years within US territory. The Tribunal found that, under the principles of international law, no state had the right to allow injury by fumes to be caused on the territory of another state. This is in line with the Roman law precept of *sic utere tuo*: so to use your own as not to injure your neighbour. In the greenhouse context that provides some encouragement, though the two problems are very different. The basis of *Trail* was the direct effect from a specific and identifiable cause. In contrast, the 'fumes' which contribute to the greenhouse effect come from all across the world, and from ordinary everyday activities in which we all participate.

We are in a realm of inter-governmental conventions still to be formulated, rather than the administration of existing international law. What has happened in the fairly recent past over somewhat analogous problems is that they have been dealt with *ad hoc*. The

June 1988 Toronto conference noted, as partial and encouraging precedents, the Declaration of the UN Conference on the Environment (1972); the Economic Commission for Europe's Convention on Long Range Transboundary Air Pollution and the Helsinki Protocol for Sulphur Reductions (1985); and the Vienna Convention for the Protection of the Ozone Layer (1985), and its Montreal Protocol (1987). But the Toronto conference also noted that there is no overall convention constituting a comprehensive international framework dealing with the problems of the global atmosphere or the issues of climate change. This issue is to be addressed in the negotiations for an international convention on climate which are planned to follow the report of the IPCC and the discussions in the 1990 Second World Climate Conference.

Following Toronto, it did not take long for political differences to emerge about which course to take. A 24-country meeting was held at French initiative in The Hague in March 1989, with the purpose of thinking-through the effects of atmospheric warming on international relations, particularly those between North and South. The Hague Declaration called for a new environmental order, whose central feature would be a new UN body with unprecedented powers to set environmental standards, backed with juridical teeth; while the International Court of Justice in The Hague—the chief judicial organ of the United Nations—would arbitrate in disputes under international environmental law. But herein lies only the first of many serious difficulties, because submission to the Court's jurisdiction has always been voluntary, and few states (Britain being one) have so far chosen to recognize its authority.

The British government did not take part in the meeting at The Hague, and made clear its preference for using existing machinery to deal with greenhouse problems, rather than attempting to create new bodies. However events, and the stately march of international conferences on climatic warming, are leading to a convergence of views on the two sides of the English Channel: it is self-evident that a new international understanding is needed.

There is one possible weakness in the international machinery for studying the consequences for energy policy. Within the United Nations family neither of the two bodies mainly concerned, the UN Environmental Programme and the World Meteorological Organization, are specialists on energy questions. However, the UN already possesses, in the form of the International Atomic Energy Agency in Vienna, a specialized energy agency of competence and standing. It achieved a new significance through its handling of the post-Chernobyl conferences, and has subsequently had a catalytic role in promoting international exchanges on reactor safety. Its remit could be extended to cover the analysis of energy options generally. Prior to 1989 its governing body held back from trying to assume this broader role, fearing charges of special pleading or bias in favour of nuclear power. But if the consequences of the greenhouse effect are truly so all-pervasive, the position changes completely. Instead of being a less-than-welcome competitor, nuclear power suddenly appears as an important component of any future energy scenario. After years of being the *enfant terrible* of the energy world, it deserves to achieve respectability. Broadening the scope of the IAEA would be as quick a way as any of providing the world with the international energy policy-analysis forum which the United Nations now needs.

A further possibility might be to make use of the 'rich man's club', the Paris-based International Energy Agency, which is an off-shoot of OECD rather than the UN. The argument in favour of pressing it into service is that it is a meeting-place for energy policy-makers from the industrialized western world. They are in a position to organize action, since their economies make substantial contributions to atmospheric pollution. The main contrary argument is that the greenhouse creators nowadays also include many countries outside OECD. For instance, whereas in 1950 North America and Western Europe together accounted for 66 per cent of the world's carbon dioxide emissions, and the Third World for only 6 per cent, by 1987 the figures had already changed to 38 per cent and 20 per cent respectively[232,235]—of an expanded total.

In conclusion

Energy production and use are not the only contributors to greenhouse problems—agriculture and the chemical industries are also significant—but they are the main culprits, and must play a major role in mitigating future environmental problems. Choices will inevitably be necessary between a disparate range of benefits and difficulties. Nuclear power offers no greenhouse consequences, readily available technology, energy diversity, security of fuel supply (for centuries, or even millenia, once the fast reactor is fully developed), and—if properly managed—stable energy prices. But it also poses the serious and acknowledged problems of safety, waste disposal, and nuclear proliferation that we have examined. It is to be hoped that the human race will be sufficiently resourceful and politically mature to handle them; but there can be no final answer. These issues must be judged not against some idealized but in practice unattainable environmental concept, but in the light of a steady march towards serious climatic change that is all but irreversible.

Nuclear energy as we now know it cannot be more than one component of a multi-faceted solution to an extraordinarily complex problem. There is no point in complaining, as do some anti-nuclear campaigners, that it cannot do the whole job: there is no single energy source or conservation policy that can do that. What nuclear power can do is to make an indispensable contribution to any long-term solution.

We are fortunate in having the example of France as a reminder of what can be done when the political will is there. In no more than twenty years, starting in 1970, France switched one-third of her primary energy production into nuclear energy and away from fossil fuel—despite a trebling of electricity demand during that same period[1]. The motivation in her case was political security of energy supplies, her indigenous resources being limited.

A similar determination is now needed, in the cause of greenhouse-avoidance, to exploit the benefits of nuclear, hydro, geothermal and wind energies. Henceforth we should rank coal, with its high carbon dioxide emission per unit of energy, below natural gas and oil in the scale of acceptability. We urgently need to promote combined heat and power (CHP), and make energy conservation the accepted creed. We must consciously select the most energy-efficient equipment, starting in the home with low consumption lighting and smaller cars. Better education in Third World countries would help to stabilize the population. While these steps would fall short of eliminating all further warming—there is still the methane problem—they would provide a much-needed breathing-space. The IPCC scientific working group allowed itself to hope for a reduction in warming to just 1°C during the next 100 years, if everything possible was done.

The cost will be enormous, but the stakes are as high as any in human history. Failure to act rapidly and comprehensively risks the creation, within the lifetime of people now living, of catastrophic drought in many tropical and sub-tropical regions, agricultural disruption on a grand scale, mass starvation, and forced migration. As an almost inevitable consequence, there could be new tensions between the resilient North and the weak and vulnerable South; and possibly outbreaks of that most basic type of war—the desperate struggle for resources. Unfortunately, in the short-term world of democratic politics the still considerable uncertainties in the prognosis leave abundant scope for scepticism and inaction. Even such devastating long-term consequences may pose too little of an immediate threat to persuade governments to curb the acquisitive thrust and conspicuous energy consumption of their industrial societies until it is too late. That, in part, is why Table 12.1 predicts a substantial increase (30 to 60 per cent) in energy demand between 1988 and 2020, and an only slightly smaller increase in carbon dioxide. Even to keep the average demand per head the same in both the developed and developing worlds would imply an energy growth of 20 per cent in the same period, because of population increase. It would be a welcome if unexpected triumph of statesmanship over political expediency if events showed the Table's predictions to be overestimates.

The changing level of the sea may offer the most easily comprehended rallying-point; though even here the argument is blurred, the sea having risen 100 metres since the last ice age ended 13,000 years ago, without destroying humanity. The main rise terminated 9,000 years ago, when the population was limited, and there was ample room for migration. Now, if the IPCC climatologists are even roughly right, a crowded globe suddenly faces the prospect of galloping, man-induced, climatic change. The one-third of the world's population which lives within 40 miles of the sea cannot afford the loss of its fertile coastal strips. The vast urban infrastructure at or near sea-level is equally significant, being the repository of so much that is vital to man's cultural and economic heritage. These are compelling reasons for not making things needlessly worse.

If time is wasted in agonizing over difficult choices—not least whether to pursue nuclear energy—and if decades pass without effective action, then the seas will encroach on low-lying land, the people of the Nile Delta and Bangladesh will be the sacrificial victims of other nations' energy choices, and a Venice disappearing before its time will symbolize the human race's lost ability to react to changed and dangerous circumstances.

Technical Appendix: The Basic Physical Principles

IN simple terms power reactors are machines for making steam, which is then used to drive turbines that turn electric generators. The reactor takes the place of the boiler in a conventional coal power-station, using the break-up of uranium—*fission* (see below)—as the source of energy. The size of a *reactor core*—the place from which the energy is extracted by the *coolant*—is not much greater than that of an ordinary boiler, depending of course to some extent on the design and power output. Chernobyl, a 1 GWe reactor, had a core 12 metres in diameter and 7 metres high. The British Sizewell reactor, which will produce about the same amount of power, is more compact, with a core diameter of 3.4 metres and a height of 3.7 metres. Reactor buildings look much larger than this because the core has first to be surrounded with massive shielding about 3 metres thick to protect the operators; then there has to be an operating space with headroom for craneage; and after that the whole must be enclosed in a *containment vessel*, to contain any toxic products in case of an accident, and so protect the environment. The Sizewell containment is over 70 metres high. All power reactors in the non-communist world, except a handful built in the early days and now nearing the ends of their lives, are protected in this way; Chernobyl was without proper containment.

The steam can be made in a variety of ways, depending on the reactor type. In a boiling water reactor (BWR), as the name implies, it comes directly from the reactor core, and is slightly radioactive. Alternatively it can be made indirectly, without risk of radioactive contamination, by heating a secondary water circuit through a *heat-exchanger* or *steam-generator* with hot water that has circulated under very high pressure (to inhibit boiling, as in a domestic pressure-cooker) in a *primary circuit* which includes the core. This is the *pressurized-water reactor*—PWR. Yet another possibility is to remove the heat from the core with high-pressure gas, which is then passed to a heat-exchanger to raise steam; this is the gas-cooled reactor family, which includes the British *advanced gas-cooled reactors* (AGRs). A long-term aim would be to take hot gas from a gas-cooled reactor, and use it to drive a gas-turbine rather than a steam-turbine. This is the target for the *high temperature gas-cooled reactor* (HTR); but development has proceeded slowly, for reasons of technical difficulty and economic competition from PWRs. These are by far the most widely used reactors, followed by BWRs.

Atoms and nuclear particles

To understand in more detail how reactors work it is helpful at this point to introduce a few basic concepts of nuclear physics. The world is made up of 92 chemically different kinds of *atoms*, which were once thought to be indivisible. But in fact they can be split, and it is a particular kind of splitting—fission—that is the source of power for a nuclear reactor.

Atoms are composed of three main constituents: positively charged *protons*, uncharged *neutrons* (which have almost the same weight as protons), and the much lighter negatively-charged *electrons*. The protons and neutrons are joined together in very small *nuclei*, about one-millionth of a millionth of a centimetre across. Around the nuclei fly, like planets round the sun, the orbital electrons, making the whole atom (nucleus plus electrons) electrically neutral. The whole atom, measured to the outside of the outermost electron orbit, is ten thousand times larger than the nucleus, but still only about one hundredth of a millionth of a centimetre across.

The chemical behaviour of an atom—the way it combines with other substances—is determined entirely by the number of orbital electrons, which is what other atoms 'see'. Because each atom is electrically neutral this number is the same as the number of protons in the nucleus. Hydrogen, the lightest chemical *element*, has 1 proton and 1 electron; helium has 2 of each, oxygen 8, uranium (the heaviest naturally-occurring element) 92. It is possible for a given element—that is, a given number of protons in the nucleus and an equal number of orbital electrons—to be associated with several different numbers of neutrons. Thus hydrogen exists both in the common form which has one proton and no neutron, and in the heavier and much rarer form of *deuterium*, or heavy hydrogen, with one proton plus one neutron in the nucleus—but still with only one orbital electron to balance the proton. Hydrogen also has a third form, the radioactive gas *tritium*—with one proton but *two* neutrons.

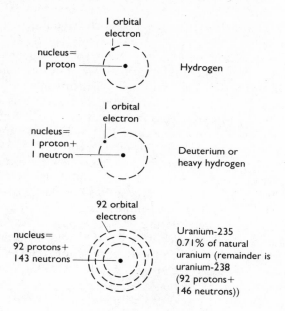

FIG. 1. Atoms and nuclei
(nucleus size $\sim 10^{-12}$ centimetres; atomic size $\sim 10^{-8}$ centimetres)

These different forms are called *isotopes* (meaning the 'same place' in the table of chemical elements). Chemically they behave identically—because they present the same number of electrons to neighbouring atoms; but in their reactions with nuclear particles, which can break through the electron screen and encounter the nucleus itself, they behave quite differently. Thus while hydrogen absorbs neutrons appreciably, in the process turning into its heavier isotope deuterium, deuterium absorbs neutrons hardly at all. This makes it a useful material for reactors, when combined with oxygen in the form of heavy water, because it does not use up the neutrons which, as we shall see, are needed to keep the reactor working (oxygen is also a weak absorber of neutrons). Again, U−235—with 92 protons and 143 neutrons—behaves very differently from the much commoner isotope U−238, which has 146 neutrons. The numbers 235 and 238 are referred to for convenience as the *mass numbers* of the two isotopes. The number 92 is the *atomic number* of both forms of uranium. Ordinary uranium as mined contains 0.71 per cent of U−235 (except at the Oklo site in Gabon, where a prehistoric natural reactor used up much of this isotope). The remainder, 140 times as much, is U−238. It is the rarer form, U−235, which is the main source of heat in an operating reactor.

Ninety-two elements are sufficiently stable to be found in nature, uranium being the heaviest. With light elements like hydrogen or oxygen the ratio of protons to neutrons in the nucleus is about 1 : 1. As the size of the nucleus increases this ratio changes, until with the heaviest elements it is nearer 1 : 1.5. This is important for the subsequent behaviour of the waste products of the fission reaction. For each element (i.e. each given number of protons) there is a narrow range of numbers of neutrons within which the isotope is either absolutely stable or fairly stable. Outside this range the nucleus will not hold together. Isotopes that are unstable break up spontaneously at widely differing rates. U−235 is an example of a very long-lived species, which is so weakly radioactive that it still survives from the time when the earth was formed 4500 million years ago. In contrast, there are many examples of unstable nuclei which survive for mere fractions of a second.

One isotope of an element can be manufactured from another in a variety of ways, but in reactor engineering we are mainly concerned with what happens when we add neutrons, by exposing the nuclei of our chosen materials to the intense concentration (or *flux*) of neutrons which exists within a reactor core. In some cases the product isotope, with a mass number increased by one, but with its chemical properties unaltered, is stable, as in the following example:

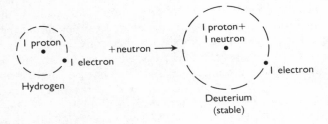

FIG. 2.

But in many cases the resulting nucleus is unstable—it has too many neutrons for stability—and seeks to find that stability by a process called quite arbitrarily, since the early days of nuclear physics, *beta-decay*. One neutron from the nucleus is converted into a proton, thus changing the chemical properties to those of the daughter-product. In the next example sodium is converted into magnesium by a two-step process:

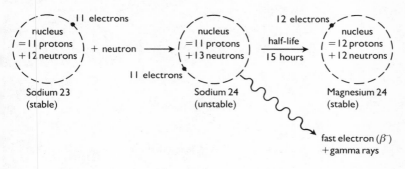

FIG. 3.

The disintegration of the sodium–24 releases a fast-moving electron—a *beta particle*—and also some penetrating electromagnetic radiation. This is called *gamma radiation*: it is similar to but more penetrating than the X-rays used medically for diagnostic purposes, or in airports for baggage checks. The general term for this and other kinds of spontaneous nuclear disintegration is *radioactivity*. With some isotopes more than one beta-decay can occur, giving rise to a chain of daughter-products. As we shall see later, this is what happens when a neutron is added to U−238.

Radioactive decay

If an isotope is radioactive it is a law of nature that the rate of disintegration of a given sample falls over time according to what is known as *exponential decay*, the best known property of which is that the time needed for half the original nuclei to disintegrate is a constant for that particular isotope, known as the *half-life*. After one half-life the number of the original nuclei remaining has dropped to half; after two half-lives it is down to one-quarter; after

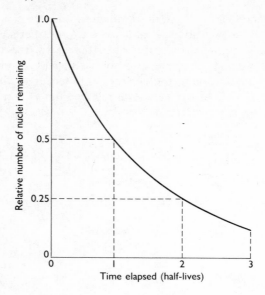

FIG. 4. Radioactive disintegration; the half-life is characteristic of the particular isotope

three half-lives to one-eighth; and so on. The longer the half-life, the smaller is the intensity of the radioactivity—a point sometimes overlooked by people who worry about very long-lived isotopes. In the limit, to describe an isotope as having an infinitely long half-life is another way of saying that it is stable, and therefore by definition emitting no radioactivity whatsoever. The most potentially dangerous isotopes tend to be those with half-lives comparable to the human life-span, and which can also be taken up by the body chemically, by breathing or via the food-chain, and retained without being exhaled or excreted. Caesium–137 is biologically significant because it has a half-life of 30 years. Isotopes with much shorter half-lives may disintegrate before being ingested; those with very much longer half-lives have only a small probability of disintegrating within the body during the lifetime of the person concerned. These considerations are fundamental to assessments of possible damage from the ingestion of fission products, such as those emitted from the damaged Chernobyl reactor.

For experimental and regulatory purposes a unit of radioactive intensity is needed. The unit in use twenty or more years ago was the *curie*, equal to 3.7×10^{10} disintegrations per second. This at first sight curious choice was of practical use when radium was still used in cancer treatment: it is the number of disintegrations taking place in one gram of radium per second. Today the international unit is the *becquerel*, named after the French physicist who shared a Nobel Prize with the Curies for their discovery of radioactivity. It is equal to one disintegration per second in a given sample. The curie was too large a unit for many purposes; the becquerel is inconveniently small.

As we have seen, radioactive disintegration may be accompanied by the emission of beta particles (electrons) or gamma rays. The former are easily stopped by only a few millimetres of solid matter. The latter are much more penetrating, and it takes several centimetres of concrete to cut them down to 10 per cent of the original intensity. It will take the same distance again to cut them down by a further factor of ten to 1 per cent, and so on—a process known as *exponential absorption*.

Biological damage

In the process of being absorbed by matter both beta and gamma radiations knock electrons off the absorbing atoms, leaving them with a net electric charge; they are then said to be *ionized*. Their importance is that ionized atoms are very reactive chemically. If some radioactive material is ingested by the body, the beta and gamma rays which it emits will be absorbed by the body's own atoms, some of which will then become ionized, and possibly join up with other atoms of the body in ways which could lead to cancerous changes. The number of such unwanted biochemical reactions depends, as might be expected, on the total quantity of ionization, and also on the concentration of ionized atoms along the track of the beta or gamma ray before it loses all its original energy. The potential for biological damage by radiation means that reactors have to be surrounded by massive *biological shields*, which are usually of concrete about three metres thick.

Some of the heaviest nuclei disintegrate spontaneously in their search for stability by firing off not an electron, but what is known as an *alpha particle*. This is a clump of two protons and two neutrons—in fact a helium atom minus its orbital electrons. These alpha particles are both far heavier than beta particles (fast-moving electrons), and carry twice the charge. The result is that they cause a much higher density of ionization along their track before they are stopped. In the jargon of the subject they have a high *linear energy transfer* (LET). That is why they are so efficient in causing biological damage—up to twenty times more than beta rays of the same energy.

Fission

When a neutron is added to U−235 a new phenomenon is encountered. Instead of getting U−236 every time, as might be expected, this happens in only about 15 per cent of reactions. Some gamma radiation is emitted at the same time. In the remaining 85 per cent of neutron captures the nucleus splits or *fissions* into two

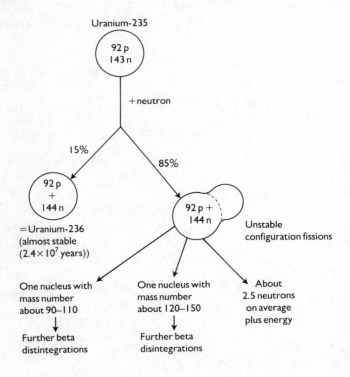

FIG. 5. Fission of uranium−235 (p = proton, n = neutron)

unequal parts, or *fission products*. Energy is released in the process, and appears as heat. In addition, on average about 2.5 neutrons are created. The average is not a whole number because the fission process can take place in a large number of different ways.

The released neutrons can interact with other U−235 nuclei, producing more fissions, more heat and more neutrons, so creating a *chain reaction*. Reactor engineering is concerned with making sure that this process stays stable and controllable under all operating circumstances. There is no problem about finding the first neutron: there are always some about due to the effects of cosmic rays, which are very penetrating electrons and gamma rays coming from outer space. Cosmic rays have so much energy that they can knock neutrons out of the nuclei of the gases of the atmosphere. This also incidentally causes all living matter, including our own bodies, to be slightly radioactive.

The fission products are an important part of the nuclear waste which creates so much controversy. Each fissioning uranium splits into *two* nuclei, each of about half the original size. This statement is equivalent to saying that two new elements, both having different numbers of protons and neutrons from the original uranium, are created in the fission of each U−235 atom. As this is a statistical process of rearranging nuclear particles, after what in nuclear terms is a massive shock—rather like breaking up the triangle of red balls at the beginning of a snooker game—the results can vary. Experimentally we find that the mass numbers of the fission products fall into two groups, one with mass numbers around 96, the other around 136. All are chemically different from uranium: there are as many chemically-distinct species of fission products as there are different numbers of protons in the various fission products. In the lighter group the fission products include strontium and molybdenum; in the heavier group there are iodine, caesium, and many others.

Over twenty fission-product species are important from a health viewpoint, because of their high abundance and their capability of being taken up chemically by the body, if they happen to get into the food-chain. Those that are radioactive can set up damaging reactions in the body's mechanisms. Caesium−137, with a thirty-year half-life, is a particularly important example: it was responsible for controls over sheep-farming continuing in parts of Britain for more than three years after Chernobyl.

Reactor physics

The energy from the fission process starts off mainly as the energy of motion of the fission products, which recoil at high speed as the uranium nucleus breaks up. There is also some extra energy from the beta and gamma rays emitted from the fission products when they disintegrate. After absorption in the material of the reactor all this energy becomes heat, and it is this which is exploited for power purposes. In a 1 GWe reactor, such as a modern PWR, there will be about 10^{20} fissions per second—one hundred million million million—and twice that number of fission products will be formed. The amount of heat energy released in each fission is microscopic, but with such an astronomical number of events taking place every second very large total amounts of heat can be created.

If a neutron-induced chain reaction is to propagate, it is necessary to ensure that for every neutron that causes fission in one neutron generation there is always one available in the next generation to produce another fission. This means using materials which do not absorb neutrons too heavily, otherwise competition will starve the U−235 of neutrons. But the reactor also has to be a sound piece of engineering, constructed so that it will hold together, and indeed if possible be virtually maintenance-free, for periods of thirty to forty years. That means using materials which are also good in an engineering sense—strong, tough, and resistant to the effects of heat, corrosion, and radiation. Unfortunately almost all normal engineering materials absorb neutrons too strongly. It is hardly surprising that the few which do not do so occupy an important place in reactor engineering.

Steel, excellent though it is structurally, is unfortunately not good as regards neutron absorption; so it has to be used sparingly—for instance in the thin tubes used for cladding fuel-elements. We then have to satisfy ourselves by extensive testing that they will not fail—either by fracture from rattling in the coolant stream, or due to pinhole corrosion—otherwise the coolant circuit would become highly radioactive. An alternative engineering material which absorbs fewer neutrons is zirconium. Aluminium is good in a neutron-economy sense, and was used in the earliest British reactors; but it is structurally weak. A magnesium alloy, 'magnox', was later preferred for the next generation of British gas-cooled reactors, to which it gave its name.

By taking great care over neutron economy, and using only low-absorbing materials, it is possible to construct reactors in which the chain reaction can propagate even with the low U–235 concentration of 0.71 per cent found in nature. This was the basis of the first British reactors at Harwell and Windscale. But much greater flexibility and robustness of design are possible if the proportion of U–235 is artificially increased through the *isotopic enrichment* process mentioned in Chapter 2. This allows more structural material to be used, without starving the uranium of neutrons.

Neutrons are most efficiently absorbed by uranium, and also by the other structural materials, when they are travelling slowly in atomic terms: a few kilometres per second. The analogy with catching a ball is irresistible. When originally produced in the fission process the neutrons are travelling much faster than this, and first need to be slowed down until they are in thermal equilibrium with the surroundings (i.e. when they have about the same energy as the individual surrounding atoms). They are then called *thermal* neutrons, a somewhat confusing term which does *not* refer to the heat-producing attributes of reactors. Reactors which rely on fission caused by these slow 'thermal' neutrons are called *thermal reactors*.

The slowing-down is done by including in the reactor core structure materials called *moderators*. They must have light atoms—since in a collision the maximum loss of energy occurs when the neutron collides with an atom of about its own weight (just as with billiard balls). Moderators must not themselves absorb neutrons to any marked extent. There are very few materials with light atoms that can both meet this requirement and still be used in practical designs. Hydrogen (used in the form of ordinary water) absorbs rather more neutrons than is desirable, but because water is such a good heat-transfer medium the engineering neatness of using it as both moderator and coolant makes the additional enrichment that is then required economically acceptable. The alternatives are deuterium or heavy hydrogen (in heavy water, which makes up 0.014 per cent of ordinary naturally occurring water, from which it can be separated by physical means); and specially purified graphite. Beryllium is also a possible moderator, and has been used to a limited extent in some research reactors; but it has difficult mechanical properties. Graphite and heavy water are moderators that are sufficiently free from neutron absorption to allow a working power reactor to be built using natural, unenriched, uranium. Of the two heavy water is better in this respect; and since a reactor can be a source of the military material plutonium (see below) it is one of the sensitive materials in a weapons-proliferation context.

Critical size

We have already seen how the reactor design must ensure that sufficient neutrons are left over from one generation to cause the same number of fissions in the next; and how neutrons can be lost in the structure of the reactor. They can also leak out of the sides. The design of the reactor must allow for this extra loss due to leakage.

If a reactor is too small the leakage over the sides into the surrounding shielding will be excessive—the surface-to-volume ratio being too big—and the chain reaction will not propagate. If the size is increased the relative importance of leakage is reduced—for geometrical reasons—and we eventually reach a point at which sufficient neutrons remain in the core to maintain the chain reaction. This is the *critical size*.

Because of leakage over the edges of the reactor the concentration of neutrons is at a maximum at the centre, and falls away gradually towards the outside. Since it is the neutrons that are the activators of the fission process, and hence the heat generation, the latter also varies both along the length of the fuel rods or plates, and as we go towards the outside of the reactor. This is an engineering nuisance, because it means that the outer fuel elements are not 'pulling their weight' as much as those in the middle of the core. Compensating measures can be taken, both in design—by altering the enrichment across the core, and by surrounding the core with more moderator, which acts as a neutron *reflector*—and also by shuffling the rods according to a predetermined programme during shut-down periods for refuelling.

Plutonium

There is far more U−238 in a thermal power reactor than U−235—from 30 to 140 times as much—and it competes with the U−235 for the neutrons. When a neutron is absorbed by U−238 the resulting nucleus of U−239 is unstable, and changes by beta-decay within an hour or so to a new artificially produced element neptunium−239 (with 93 protons), and within a few days to another new element, *plutonium*−239 (with 94 protons):

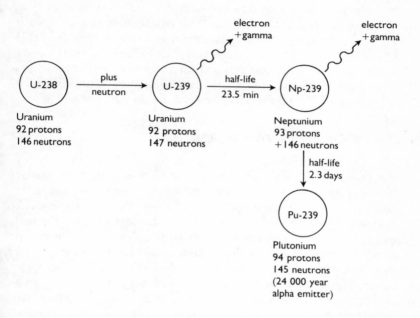

Fɪɢ. 6. Plutonium production

Unlike its grandparent U−238, which is described as a *fertile* material, plutonium is fissile when it collides with slow neutrons, very like U−235. So the neutrons lost to the U−238 are not wasted after all: given a little time the plutonium begins to assist the chain reaction. However, if too many neutrons are absorbed in the U−238 there will not be enough left over to carry on the chain reaction initially—like a man who invests so much that he has no money to pay for his day-to-day expenses. Absorption in the U−238 therefore has to be limited; and for complicated reasons of nuclear physics this drives us towards a regular *lattice* structure. This is also convenient from an engineering viewpoint, since it provides a way of laying out the fuel, moderator, and coolant. In a graphite-moderated reactor the lattice spacing between the parallel fuel elements is about twenty-five centimetres (ten inches). In the more common water-moderated reactors it is a little over one cm.

Pu−239 is not the only important plutonium isotope. If the material stays for a long time in the reactor additional neutrons can attach themselves to the nucleus. With two such neutrons we reach Pu−241, which is yet another fissile material. The intermediate step of adding only one more neutron brings us to Pu−240, which as we saw in Chapter 7 has implications for weapon design because it is spontaneously fissile, and therefore a source of neutrons which might degrade the performance of a plutonium-based bomb.

Radiation structural damage

The fuel rods, plates or bundles cannot stay in the reactor indefinitely, because the constant replacement of uranium atoms by fission products or plutonium within the structure gradually destroys its mechanical properties (*radiation damage*). Much work has been devoted to minimizing this effect; but eventually the fuel has to be taken out, either for disposal or (if the process is cheap enough) refurbishment. In the latter case the plutonium can also be extracted and reused as a secondary fuel. As plutonium is a weapon material, this *reprocessing* stage, like enrichment, is sensitive from a proliferation viewpoint. Radiation damage considerations are important when assessing the safe operating lifetimes of fuel-element cladding, reactor structural materials generally, and not least reactor pressure-vessels.

In a graphite-moderated reactor the intense bombardment of nuclear particles in time displaces some graphite moderator atoms from their regularly arranged places in the normal crystal structure. In early reactors this process led to progressive dimensional deformation—the *Wigner effect*, after its discoverer—which caused engineering problems when refuelling unless dealt with by a process of *annealing*. This involved warming the graphite above its normal operating temperature, when the increased thermal motion of the atoms (which is the physical meaning of temperature) allowed them to jump back into their normal positions. When this happened the energy which had displaced them in the first place reappeared; so the annealing process produced heat, causing a further rise in the graphite temperature. It therefore had to be applied cautiously, to prevent things getting out of hand. That is what happened at Windscale in the UK in 1957, when the operating crew failed to realize from their instrument readings that the graphite temperature was rising to a point at which it would cause failure of the fuel elements. Eventually some of the uranium caught fire; and since the Windscale reactor was cooled by a blast of air which was discharged to the atmosphere via a tall stack, the first major emission of radioactivity to the environment occurred. Fortunately the possibility of a uranium fire had been foreseen at the design stage, and filters had been fitted to the top of the stack; they trapped most of the solid debris, though the gaseous fission products escaped. There are no power reactors today with such crude cooling systems.

More recent reactors which use graphite (such as the Chernobyl design and the British AGRs) are designed to run with it hot enough for the effects of radiation damage to be self-annealing. In other words, the vibrations of the atoms in the crystal structure are large enough to cause them to jump back into their proper average positions automatically even after displacement by an encounter with a nuclear particle.

Reactor families

Our reactor is now beginning to take shape. We need a substantial volume of moderator, within which the uranium fuel must be arranged in some regular way. We must also be able to get the heat away with a coolant; and this must have somewhere to flow. So we are led quite naturally to a lattice pattern of long fuel elements, over which coolant flows, in channels formed in the moderator if it is a solid. The fuel elements contain the fissile material, but an outer cladding of steel, zirconium, or some other material separates the coolant from the uranium fuel, and prevents it from becoming highly radioactive by direct contact. The integrity of the cladding must be preserved as the first protection against an escape of radioactivity. The individual fuel elements can be assembled into bundles to simplify handling.

Reactors can be broadly divided into a number of distinct families, depending on which choices are made for certain key design features. One classification relates to how the coolant is contained. We have already seen how in a water-moderated and cooled reactor core no structural material is needed, apart from the fuel elements and their cladding. The problem is to contain the water under high enough pressure, so that its temperature can rise to a level at which the heat energy is useful in an engineering sense, for power production. This is what happens in both *Pressurized-Water Reactors* (PWR) and *Boiling-Water Reactors* (BWR), where a limited degree of boiling is permitted within the pressure-vessel. The pressure needed for reasonable efficiency is very high—over 2000 pounds per square inch for PWRs, and about half that for BWRs—and this limits the size of pressure-vessel that can safely be used. Some attempts were made in the early days to get round this problem by using special organic liquids as combined coolants and moderators; they would have needed far lower pressures, but were insufficiently resistant to the chemical damage caused by the intense radiation inside a reactor.

If the moderator is solid a pressure-vessel design can still be used, provided the coolant is chemically compatible with the moderator—as in the British AGR design, where it is carbon dioxide; or in the High-Temperature Reactor, which uses helium. At Chernobyl, however, the need for chemical reasons to separate the hot graphite from the water coolant led to the use of a lattice of zirconium *pressure-tubes*—the second basic reactor arrangement. Pressure-tubes have the disadvantage, from a 'neutron economy' viewpoint, of introducing a good deal of structural material.

In the Chernobyl design the moderator was left without direct cooling, even though it was heated by slowing down the neutrons, and also by the radiation it absorbed. About 5 per cent of the total reactor heat output was released in the moderator in this way, amounting to about 150 megawatts. Unlike the AGR design, where the carbon dioxide coolant plays over the graphite, at Chernobyl the graphite ran red-hot, dissipating its heat only indirectly by radiation to the water-cooled zirconium pressure-tubes. Since water reacts chemically with hot graphite, producing an explosive gas, the integrity of the whole reactor depended on the absolute security of these tubes; but when the reactor ran out of control they melted.

Pressure-tubes are also used in the Canadian CANDU reactor design, which uses heavy water as both coolant and moderator; in this case the tubes are of zircaloy-niobium.

There is a further broad classification, into *direct-cycle* reactors, where the coolant passes out of the reactor directly into the turbine, without an intermediate heat exchanger, as was the case at Chernobyl; and *indirect-cycle* systems, where a heat exchanger or steam generator is used to avoid the engineering problems of maintaining a turbine which has been exposed to radioactive steam.

We have now identified a great variety of theoretically possible variants in thermal reactor design. There are three widely-used moderators: hydrogen (in ordinary water), deuterium (in heavy water), or graphite. The coolant can be water, heavy water, helium, or carbon dioxide. Reactors can have pressure vessels or pressure tubes. The primary circuit can feed energy indirectly to the turbines via a heat-exchanger, or the coolant can go directly to the turbine. The fuel can be metallic or ceramic, which is more temperature-resistant. It can be in the form of plates or rods, individually or in bundles. The uranium enrichment can vary. The fuel can use plutonium as an option. Even more variants were explored in the early days of nuclear power; but eventually practical considerations of economics, engineering feasibility, and safety, eliminated all but a very few. We are left today with the light water reactors (pressurized and boiling) which form the overwhelming bulk of the world's reactor stock; the graphite-moderated gas-cooled reactors adopted by the UK and in the early days by France; the deuterium (heavy-water) cooled and moderated CANDU reactors using unenriched uranium; the Soviet Chernobyl RBMK type using graphite and water held in pressure tubes; and a very few others.

Reactivity and control

As a reactor operates it uses up its fissile material. The ability of the chain reaction to propagate falls gradually as time passes, and the reactor would 'go off the boil' unless this were allowed for in the design. Reactors are therefore built so that, when new, rather more neutrons are left over after the slowing-down and capture processes than are needed to propagate the fission chain reaction. These initially surplus neutrons are absorbed in *control rods* inserted in the core. The rods are made of materials which absorb neutrons very readily—such as boron carbide or silver-cadmium alloy. The control system also performs the necessary safety function of absorbing neutrons heavily if for any reason it is necessary to shut down (or *scram*) the reactor. As we shall see in a moment, there are also temperature effects to take care of. So enough *reactivity* needs to be built into the design so that the chain reaction is never starved of neutrons throughout the design lifetime.

In a graphite-moderated reactor like Chernobyl or a British AGR each neutron survives for about one thousandth of a second (the lifetime is even less in water-moderated reactors). If a neutron death were always instantly followed by the creation of the next neutron generation even slight imbalances in neutron availability from generation to generation would lead with astonishing rapidity to enormous control difficulties. If there were only 1 per cent more neutrons in one generation than in the preceding generation—an *excess reactivity* of 0.01—a compound interest sum shows that with a neutron lifetime of one-thousandth of a second the power would rise one hundredfold in only half a second! Such a reactor would be quite uncontrollable. Fortunately for nuclear energy and the world's power supplies another phenomenon dramatically alters the picture in our favour.

This is the existence of *delayed neutrons*. Not all the neutrons which are given off in the fission process emerge instantaneously— within 10^{-14} seconds. A small fraction—about 0.75 per cent in U–235—come from disintegrating neutron-rich fission products, and are delayed by times varying from half a second to 55 seconds for the most-delayed group.

Although the proportion of delayed neutrons seems at first sight to be so small as hardly to matter, the fact is that by limiting the reactivity, so that the chain reaction can propagate only with their aid, the times of response become amply long enough for the control system to handle—many minutes if need be. But nothing must be allowed to bring the reactivity up to a level at which the chain reaction can continue solely on the basis of the 99 per cent or so of undelayed, or *prompt* neutrons; for we should then have lost the benefit of the delayed neutrons, and with it all possibility of control. As Enrico Fermi, the originator of the nuclear reactor, pointed out: the delayed neutrons alone make practical reactor engineering possible.

At Chernobyl the reactor reached, or was very close to, *prompt criticality* in the final moments, with power rising to perhaps a hundred times the design level in as little as four seconds. The effective delayed neutron fraction in the Chernobyl reactor at that time was only about 0.5 per cent, because of the plutonium in the core—plutonium having a smaller delayed neutron fraction than U–235. Moreover, because of the nature of an experiment that was being undertaken the 211 control rods were almost all out of the core, in gross contravention of the local operating rules: six seconds would have elapsed before the reactor could have been shut down, which is exceedingly slow by Western standards. The shut-down button was pressed far too late, and the control system had no chance. Nothing of this kind is remotely possible in Western designs.

There are several ways in which the temperature of a reactor can affect reactivity. In light water reactors the water (which is both coolant and moderator) expands as the temperature rises, leaving fewer hydrogen atoms per unit volume. This reduces unwanted neutron absorption, but at the same time cuts down the moderating effect, leaving the neutrons on average faster. Because the capture probability of neutrons depends on their speed—remember the rough analogy with catching a ball—temperature affects the way the neutrons are captured by the various structural components. This is equally true of the U–235, which is competing with the other reactor materials for the available neutrons. Temperature also affects reactivity through its effect on the speed of oscillation of atoms in the crystal structures of materials. Viewed from the position of an approaching neutron these oscillations alter its relative speed, and hence the probability of capture by the various structural and fuel materials—often in ways that are much more complicated than the simple cricket or baseball analogy would suggest.

Leaving the nuclear physics details aside, the upshot is a variety of *temperature coefficients of reactivity*. At Chernobyl, when operating normally, increasing the fuel temperature tended to reduce the reactivity a little—there was a *negative fuel temperature coefficient*—which would give some help towards shutting the reactor down if it started to get out of control. But the *graphite temperature coefficient* was positive, and therefore reinforced any power changes, either up or down, making control more delicate.

Still more significant in the Chernobyl accident was the way in which the volume of steam in the cooling channels could influence reactivity when the reactor was operating at low power, particularly if the control rods were positioned abnormally, as on the night of the accident. If the steam volume grew so did the reactivity; so that as steam bubbles began to form at the initiation of the accident the reactor tended to 'run away', rather than shut itself down. Chernobyl was designed to operate with about 14 per cent of steam at the top of the reactor tubes. But if the average steam voidage throughout the reactor were for any reason to rise to 25 per cent the reactor would be on the point of going prompt critical.

The RBMK family of reactors, as used at Chernobyl, was thus intrinsically and unacceptably dynamically unstable, which is something that Western reactor designers avoid as far as possible. The Soviet authorities have since made changes to RBMK cores to make them more controllable. But instability by itself was not the only cause of the disaster. Commercial aircraft are also dynamically unstable, and yet they can be controlled, if operated within their 'flight envelopes'. At Chernobyl the instability could also have been controlled by proper attention to operating procedures. But the reactor was being operated in abnormal conditions in order to conduct an experiment which had not been properly thought through. The safety mechanisms had been deliberately deactivated in order to make the experiment possible, something which in other countries would have been illegal. Insufficient attention was paid to the vital nuclear characteristic of steam voidage instability, and an operator error caused the voidage to grow past the danger point.

In the light of the Chernobyl experience it is clear that control and safety systems must not only be able to cope with all normal changes in reactivity, and shut the reactor down if design limits are exceeded; but, as emphasized in Chapter 9, they must also be as far as possible 'operator-proof'.

The broad principles discussed in this Appendix apply to all thermal reactors, just as the basic controls of an aircraft are the same whether it is a Boeing 747 or a tiny Cessna trainer. But a reactor's safety analysis is highly specific, since it turns on the *details* of how these principles are applied. This has important safety implications. It means that an accident to a reactor of one type does not necessarily have any implications whatsoever for reactors of different types. Even within a broad family of reactors, such as the PWRs, a malfunction or accident does not necessarily imply that problems exist in other designs of PWR from different manufacturers. Again the aircraft analogy is helpful: a failure on the brackets securing the ailerons of a 747 may have absolutely no implications whatsoever for the corresponding components of other aircraft. On the other hand it is self-evident that if every individual reactor is different no satisfactory learning process will ever be possible; so the sensible course is to work towards a few standardized designs, using highly conservative judgements when selecting the features chosen for standardization; and then concentrate on making them absolutely reliable.

Post-shut-down fission-product heating

The fission products which are formed in the material of the fuel elements during operation have an important influence on reactor safety. Being radioactive they continue to give off energy after the reactor is shut down. Unlike most machines, therefore, a reactor cannot be completely turned off: immediately after 'scram' it still generates 6.5 per cent of the normal operating heat output, and this residual heat falls only slowly. Remembering that the size of an ordinary domestic electric fire is only about one- or two kilowatts—one- or two-thousandths of a megawatt—the figures in Table A1 speak for themselves. They apply to Chernobyl; but all today's large commercial reactors have shut-down fission product heating of the same order.

Table A1: Fission Product Shut-down Heating in the Chernobyl Reactor

	Megawatts
Electrical energy during operation (gross)	1,000
Heat production during operation	3,140
Heat production at time after shut-down:	
1 minute	115
1 hour	50
1 day	20
1 week	12
1 month	7

The amount of residual heat is sufficient to pose a danger of post-shut-down melting of the core, and possibly a breach of the primary circuit, unless cooling can be guaranteed under all possible fault conditions. The result would be precisely what all the rest of the careful reactor design is intended to avoid: destruction of the reactor, and the escape of toxic fission products. The post-shut-down performance under fault conditions is therefore one of the most vital parts of reactor safety analysis; and ensuring the reliable functioning of the *emergency core cooling system* is a central feature of every power-reactor design.

The fast reactor

There is one further reactor family which will be of growing importance in the twenty-first century and thereafter. This is the *fast reactor*. The purpose of this very different design is to avoid the limitation which exists in thermal reactors on the fraction of uranium that can be fissioned before the reactor runs out of reactivity. In a modern PWR, for every 100 fissile U−235 atoms that are fissioned, only about 60 Pu−239 fissile atoms are formed in the next generation to take their place, following neutron absorption in the fertile U−238. The reactor then gradually runs out of reactivity, and has to be refuelled. Other designs of thermal reactor could increase the figure somewhat, but complete con-version of the U−238 into plutonium in thermal reactors is out of reach.

Clearly if a way existed for the *breeding ratio*—the number of fissile atoms formed per fissile atom destroyed in the previous generation—to surpass 1.00, we should then have a reactor which would actually generate more fissile material than it consumed. We could then use not just 2 per cent or 3 per cent of total uranium atoms, as at present, but something approaching 100 per cent—i.e. thirty to fifty times more. In practice, even in these favourable circumstances, the fuel could not be left in the reactor indefinitely, because long before all the uranium was consumed the mechanical properties of the fuel would begin to give trouble, and some refurbishment would be needed. So in attempting to reach this thirty or fiftyfold advantage it would still be necessary to withdraw the fuel periodically, reprocess it chemically and metallurgically, and replace it in the reactor; that of course would add to the cost of the energy produced.

A breeding ratio well above 1.00 can in fact be achieved if the reactor uses fast neutrons instead of thermal neutrons; i.e. neutrons which still retain most of the energy with which they were born in the fission process. Such fast neutrons also cause fission, but in doing so they administer an even greater shock than thermal neutrons to the fissioning nucleus. The average number of new neutrons released per fission is then a little larger. It also turns out that wasteful capture of neutrons in the structure is reduced, compared with a reactor using thermal neutrons. These factors alter the balance of the various nuclear processes, and can bring the breeding ratio significantly above 1.00—hence the fast reactor's colloquial name of '*breeder*'. Theoretically, breeding ratios can exceed 1.2, and even approach 1.4. In practice the figures are rather lower, but breeding ratios of 1.1–1.2 are attainable.

A reactor exploiting the properties of high speed neutrons uses no slowing-down moderator. But at high speeds the chance of inducing fission through neutron capture is greatly reduced (the cricket-ball analogy again); and to make the chain reaction propagate a much greater critical mass of fissionable material is therefore needed. This could amount to as much as 4 tonnes of plutonium in a 1 GWe reactor—plutonium which would have been manufactured previously in a conventional thermal reactor. Another 2 tonnes of plutonium would be outside the reactor at any given time in the fuel-cycle facilities. Clearly fast reactors will provide a ready use for nuclear warhead plutonium should nuclear disarmament become a reality!

Since the amount of breeding is directly proportional to the heat produced, the heat rating must be high, if the doubling time for the plutonium inventory is to be measured in decades rather than centuries. A typical power-reactor design would produce 400–500 MW of heat per cubic metre of core—about the same amount as would be produced by nearly half a million small domestic electric fires. This is an enormous concentration of energy. The coolant is therefore a liquid metal—sodium—which takes the heat away efficiently. Moreover sodium, because of its atomic weight (twenty-three times heavier than a neutron), introduces only a minor moderating effect. Unlike the water or carbon dioxide used in thermal reactors, the liquid sodium does not require to be under high pressure, which is a valuable safety feature. We finish up with a very compact reactor core, with a surrounding uranium *breeding blanket* to catch the large numbers of neutrons which leak out. This adds an extra 0.4–0.5 to the 'internal' breeding ratio, which for the core alone can be 0.8–0.9. A doubling of the plutonium inventory in a time of thirty to forty years is then well within the bounds of possibility.

The economics that can be achieved with fast reactors, particularly in view of the need for periodical fuel-reprocessing, are still uncertain. Overall they are expected to be somewhat less favourable than for the best of today's thermal reactors, though this should improve with development. There is no urgency, because there will be no shortage of uranium for thermal reactors for at least four decades. But the prize of being able, through this fundamental redesign, to approach 100 per cent usage of the world's uranium is of such potential long-term significance for energy resources that development of the fast reactor will continue on a cost-sharing international basis.

References

Since 1979 the policy review papers given at the conferences of the Uranium Institute, London have been published annually under the title *Uranium and Nuclear Energy*. The abbreviation UNE is used below to denote this series.

1. HANSBERG, M., and MIGNOT, E., *The competitive position of nuclear power in France*, UNE, 1985.
2. International Atomic Energy Agency, Vienna, press release, 18 April 1990.
3. *Nuclear energy data*, Nuclear Energy Agency, OECD, Paris, 1989.
4. Secretary-General's 12th Annual Report to the Organization of Arab Petroleum Exporting Countries, Kuwait, 1985.
5. MIZUMACHI, K., *Nuclear anxieties and their impact on nuclear power programmes*, Uranium supply and demand 1977, Mining Journal Books, London, 1977.
6. MURATO, H., *Japan's nuclear electricity programme*, UNE, 1987.
7. GERHOLM, T. R., *Electrification and social change*, UNE 1985; also *Sweden's energy future*, paper given to Japan Atomic Industrial Forum, April 1989.
8. FERON, J., *The civil uranium market, 1955–1982*, International Conference on Nuclear Power Experience, Vienna, 1982.
9. *Uranium: resources, production and demand*. Published at about two-yearly intervals jointly by OECD, Paris, and the International Atomic Energy Agency, Vienna.
10. CARSON, R., *Silent spring*, Houghton Mifflin, Boston, USA, 1962.
11. EDMONDSON, B., in *Nuclear energy after Chernobyl*, Graham and Trotman, London, 1988.
12. *The accident at the Chernobyl nuclear power-plant and its consequences*, International Atomic Energy Agency, Vienna, August 1986.
13. *Pravda*, quoted in *Nature*, 26 May 1988, Macmillan, London.
14. BROMLEY, J., *A comparison of the hazards of mining coal and uranium*, UNE, 1986.
15. *Uranium market issues 1989–2005*, Uranium Institute, London, 1989.
16. GOLDSCHMIDT, B., *Uranium's scientific history*, UNE, 1989.
17. SPENCE, H. J. M., *Grandfather and the Great Bear*, UNE, 1989.
18. HAHNE, F. J., *Early uranium mining in the USA*, UNE, 1989.
19. GRAY, E., *The great uranium cartel*, McClelland and Stewart, Toronto, 1982.

20. SHENEFIELD, J. H., Evidence to nomination hearing of the US Senate Judiciary Committee, 24 January 1980.
21. McGOLDRICK, F., *Flag swaps*, UNE, 1988.
22. CROCKER, V. S., and ROBERTS, P. F. P., *The policy implications of laser isotope separation in the UK*, UNE, 1986.
23. LONGENECKER, J. R., *Institutional restructuring of the US enrichment enterprise*, UNE, 1986.
24. GOLDSCHMIDT, B., *Le complex atomique*, Fayard, Paris, 1980.
25. *The French nuclear electricity program*, Électricité de France, Paris.
26. CARLE, R., *The French experience*, UNE, 1982.
27. MONTFORT, B., *Nuclear electricity as a key component of French primary energy supply by the year 2000*, UNE, 1983.
28. BLOWERS, A., and PEPPER, D., (eds.), *Nuclear power in crisis*, Nichols Publishing Company, New York, and Croom Helm, London and Sydney, 1987.
29. FAURE, M., *Aspects of the nuclear controversy in France*, UNE, 1978.
30. PHARABOD, J-P., and SCHAPIRA, J-P., *Les jeux de l'atome et du hasard*, Calmann-Lévy, Paris, 1988.
31. TANAKA, Y., *Four nuclear paradoxes which affect Japanese public opinion*, UNE, 1984.
32. *The Annual Register: a record of world events*, Longman, Harlow, UK.
33. SVENKE, E., *Swedish policy for the back end of the nuclear fuel cycle*, UNE, 1981 (see also reference 162).
34. ZETTERBERG, H. L., *The Swedish nuclear referendum 1980*, UNE, 1980.
35. FOGELSTRÖM, L., *Sweden and the energy future*, UNE, 1987.
36. WIKDAHL, C-E., *Public and political attitudes to nuclear power in Sweden*, UNE, 1987; and private communication.
37. WIKDAHL, C-E., paper to Swiss Association for Atomic Energy, quoted in *Nucleonics Week*, 20 October 1988, McGraw-Hill, New York.
38. BELELLI, U., *Italian attitudes and public opinion towards nuclear power stations*, Uranium supply and demand 1978, Mining Journal Books, London, 1978.
39. BELELLI, U., *Public acceptance and the nuclear programme in Italy*, UNE, 1985.
40. RENN, O., *Public response to Chernobyl: lessons for risk management and communication*, UNE, 1987.
41. ROSER, T., *The social and political impact of Chernobyl in the Federal Republic of Germany*, UNE, 1987.
42. STEINBERG, J., *Why Switzerland?*, Cambridge, 1976.
43. *Energy policy*, response by Swiss Federal Council to pending interventions, September 1988.

44. ROWDEN, M. A., *Nuclear acceptance and the regulatory environment*, UNE, 1981.
45. *Possibilities and consequences of accidents in large nuclear power plants (the Brookhaven Report)*, US Atomic Energy Commission, Washingon, DC, USAEC WASH–740, 1957.
46. *Reactor safety study: an assessment of accident risks in US commercial nuclear power plants (the Rasmussen Report)*, US Nuclear Regulatory Commission, Washington, DC, US NRC WASH–1400, 1975.
47. See *Nuclear Law Bulletin*, published at six-monthly intervals by the Nuclear Energy Agency of OECD, Paris.
48. BRAUN, C., *Economics of successful nuclear plant construction*, UNE, 1985.
49. GRAY, J. E., *The United States energy situation: political and institutional issues*, UNE, 1980.
50. DOUB, W. O., *US regulatory and legislative influence on nuclear power*, UNE, 1983.
51. ROWDEN, M. A., *Legislative, regulatory and industry developments in the USA*, UNE, 1986.
52. KEMENY, J. G. (chairman), *The need for change: the legacy of TMI*, the President's Commission on the accident at TMI, Washington, DC, October 1979.
53. WILLRICH, M., *Nuclear power in a changing United States electricity industry*, UNE, 1985.
54. POCOCK, R. F., *Nuclear power: its development in the UK*, Unwin, Woking, 1977.
55. *The development of atomic energy, 1939–1984: a chronology of events*, UK Atomic Energy Authority, 1984.
56. GOWING, M., *Britain and atomic energy 1939–1945*, Macmillan, London, 1964.
57. GOWING, M., *Independence and deterrence—Britain and Atomic Energy 1945–1952*, Macmillan, London, 1974.
58. *A programme of nuclear power*, Cmd. 9389, HMSO, London, 1955.
59. *Second nuclear power programme*, Cmnd. 2335, HMSO, London, 1964.
60. *Fuel policy*, Cmnd. 2798, HMSO, London, 1965.
61. O'RIORDAN, T., KEMP, R., and PURDUE, M., *Sizewell B: an anatomy of the inquiry*, Macmillan, London, 1988.
62. *Sizewell B public inquiry*. Report by Sir Frank Layfield, HMSO, London, 1986.
63. MARSHALL (Lord), 'The future for nuclear power', address to British Nuclear Energy Society, 30 November 1989; and 'Privatization and nuclear power in the UK', address to Edison Electric Institute, January 1990, Phoenix, Arizona.

64. Owen, A. D., *The Australian uranium industry*, University of South Wales, 1987.
65. Fox, R. W., Kelleher, G. G., and Kerr, C. B., *Ranger Uranium Environmental Inquiry: second and final report*, Australian Government Publishing Service, Canberra, 1977.
66. Fisk, B., *Australian mining policy*, UNE, 1984.
67. Lloyd, B., *Socioeconomic aspects of uranium production in Australia*, UNE, 1988.
68. Jenkin, F. P., evidence to Hinkley Point inquiry, CEGB, London, 1988.
69. *Projected costs of generating electricity from nuclear and coal-fired power stations for commissioning in 1995*, Nuclear Energy Agency of OECD, Paris, 1986.
70. Jones, P. M. S., and Crijns, M. J., *International comparison of nuclear fuel cycle and electricity generating costs*, UNE, 1985.
71. *Projected costs of generating electricity from power stations for commissioning in the period 1995–2000*, OECD, Paris, 1989.
72. *Nuclear power reactors in the world*, Reference Data Series No. 2, International Atomic Energy Agency, Vienna, 1989.
73. *An analysis of nuclear power-plant operating costs*, Energy Information Administration, US Department of Energy, DOE/EIA–0511, 1988.
74. *Analysis of generating costs 1983/84*, CEGB, London, 1985.
75. Mortensen, H. C., *The future of CHP and DH systems in Denmark*, paper to District Heating Association Conference, Torquay, UK, 1983.
76. Wilkinson, M., 'The boom in small-scale power', *Financial Times*, 1 July 1988, London.
77. Weyers, L., *Deregulation of electricity supply in the USA*, UNE, 1989.
78. *Financing waste management, decommissioning and site rehabilitation in the nuclear industry*, Uranium Institute, London, 1987.
79. Jones, I., of National Economic Research Associates, letter to *Financial Times*, 9 May 1988, London.
80. Thomas, S. D., *The realities of nuclear power*, Cambridge, 1988.
81. *Why choose coal?*, International Coal Development Institute, London, 1987.
82. Konstantinov, L. V., Char, N. L., and Bennett, L. L., *Nuclear power for the developing world*, UNE, 1986.
83. Ramanna, R., Desai Memorial lecture, 4 March 1985, Hyderabad.
84. Lewis, J. W., and Xue Litai, *China builds the bomb*, Stanford University Press, California, 1988.

85. SPECTOR, L., *The undeclared bomb*, Ballinger, Cambridge, Mass., 1988; also *Nuclear exports: the challenge of control*, Carnegie Endowment for International Peace, Washington, DC, 1990.

86. BLOOM, J. L., *Plutonium up-grade and the risk of nuclear weapons proliferation*, Congressional Research Service Report 85–145S, Washington, DC, 1985.

87. *Nucleonics Week*, 23 October 1986, McGraw-Hill, New York.

88. SCHEINMAN, L., *The International Atomic Energy Agency and world nuclear order*, Resources for the Future, Washington DC, 1987.

89. GOLDSCHMIDT, B., 'A historical survey of non-proliferation policies', in: *International security*, Harvard, Summer 1977.

90. FISCHER, D., and SZASZ, P., *Safeguarding the atom*, Taylor and Francis, London, 1985.

91. MOORE, J. D. L., *South Africa and nuclear proliferation*, MacMillan, London, 1987.

92. MANNING MUNTZING, L. (ed.), *International instruments for nuclear technology transfer*, American Nuclear Society, La Grange Park, Ill., 1978.

93. SIMPSON, J., *The 1990 NPT Review Conference*, UNE, 1989.

94. WALKER, W., 'France and the Non-Proliferation Treaty', in *Économie et Humanisme*, France, March–April 1986.

95. *World armaments and disarmament*, SIPRI year-book, Oxford, 1989.

96. *Non-proliferation and the nuclear industry*, Uranium Institute, London, 1985.

97. *Nuclear power, issues and choices.* Report of the Nuclear Energy Policy Study Group, Ballinger, Cambridge, Mass., 1977.

98. WILLRICH, M., and TAYLOR, T. B., *Nuclear theft: risks and safeguards*, Ballinger, Cambridge, Mass., 1974.

99. *Nucleonics Week*, 7 January 1988, McGraw-Hill, New York.

100. SIMPSON, J., (ed.), *Nuclear non-proliferation: an agenda for the 1990s*, Cambridge, 1987.

101. *The tolerability of risk from nuclear power stations*, UK Health and Safety Executive, HMSO, London, 1987.

102. TUBIANA, M., *Biological bases of radioprotection*, UNE, 1979.

103. Report by US Surgeon-General's Office, quoted in *Nature*, 22 September 1988, Macmillan, London.

104. WARNER, F., *Risk and response*, UNE, 1980; and 'Public and professional attitudes to risk', *Journal of Institute of Actuaries*, Alden Press, Oxford, 1988.

105. *Sources, effects and risks of ionising radiation*, 1986 Report and Annexes by UNSCEAR to UN General Assembly, United Nations, New York (in course of publication).

106. RADFORD, E. P., 'Recent evidence of radiation induced cancer in the Japanese atomic bomb survivors', in *Radiation and Health*, John Wiley and Sons, London, 1987.

107. Publication no. 26, International Commission on Radiological Protection, 26, *Ann. ICRP*, vol. 1, no. 3, Pergamon Press, Oxford, 1977.

108. *Interim guidance on the implications of recent revisions of risk estimates and the ICRP Como statement*, NRPB, Chilton, UK, 1987.

109. Council Directive of 15 July 1980, *Official Journal Euratom Communities*, No. L 246, Euratom, Brussels; also Directives 80/836 and 84/467.

110. *Exposure to radon daughters in dwellings*, Report ASP 10, NRPB, HMSO, London, 1987.

111. FREMLIN, J., 'Safe as houses? The risks of radon', *Nature*, 8 September 1988, Macmillan, London.

112. CLARKE, R. H., and SOUTHWOOD, T. R. E., 'Risks from ionizing radiations', *Nature*, 16 March 1989, Macmillan, London.

113. *Radiation doses—maps and magnitudes;* and *Report NRPB–R227,* National Radiological Protection Board, Harwell, UK, 1989.

114. Gonzalez, A. J., and Anderer, J., *Radiation in the human environment*, UNE, 1989.

115. *Health risks of radon and other internally deposited alpha emitters*, BEIR IV, Committee on the biological effects of ionizing radiation, National Research Council, Washington, DC, 1988.

116. SIMMONDS, J., 'Europe calculates the health risk', in *New Scientist*, 23 April 1987, London.

117. 'Exposures from the Chernobyl accident', report by UNSCEAR to United Nations, Reported in *Nucleonics Week*, 7 July 1988, McGraw-Hill, New York.

118. STATHER, J. W., CLARKE, R. H., and DUNCAN, K. P., *The risk of childhood leukaemia near nuclear establishments*, Report no. 215, NRPB, Chilton, UK, 1988.

119. FORMAN, D., *et al*, 'Cancer near nuclear installations', *Nature*, Macmillan, 8 October 1987, London.

120. *Investigation of the possible increased incidence of leukaemia in young people near the Dounreay nuclear establishment*, Committee on medical aspects of radiation in the environment (COMARE), HMSO, London, 1986.

121. KINLEN, L., 'Evidence for an infective cause of childhood leukaemia: comparison of a Scottish new town with nuclear reprocessing sites in Britain', *The Lancet*, 10 December 1988, London.

122. GARDNER, M. J., *et al.*, 'Results of case-control study of leukaemia and lymphoma among young people near Sellafield nuclear plant in West

Cumbria', *British Medical Journal*, 17 February 1990, London, vol. 300, p. 423.

123. VIEL, J. F., and RICHARDSON, S. T., 'Childhood leukaemia around the La Hague reprocessing plant', *British Medical Journal*, 3 March 1990, London, vol. 300, p. 580.

124. NEEL, J. V., *et al.*, *Genetic effects of the atomic bomb*, paper given to conference on low dose radiation (14th L. H. Gray conference), Oxford, 1988.

125. ROBERTS, G. C., and KELLY, G. N., *Advances in nuclear science and technology*, 16, Plenum Publishing Corp., 1984.

126. BENINSON, D. J., *Current issues in radiation protection philosophy*, UNE, 1984.

127. *The ionizing radiations regulations*, Statutory Instrument 1985, No. 1333, HMSO, London, 1985.

128. International Commission on Radiological Protection, Statement from Paris meeting, *Ann. ICRP*, 15, no. 3, 1985.

129. International Commission on Radiological Protection, Statement from the 1987 Como meeting. *Radiological Protection Bulletin*, no. 85, suppl., 1987.

130. *Living with radiation*, NRPB, HMSO, London, 1989.

131. EMMERSON, B. W., 'Intervening for the protection of the public following a nuclear accident', *IAEA Bulletin*, No. 3, International Atomic Energy Agency, Vienna, 1988.

132. *Derived intervention levels for radionuclides in food*, World Health Organization, Geneva, 1988.

133. CHAMBERS, D. B., *Radiation safety: Canadian experience and policy*, UNE, 1986.

134. ZETTWOOG, P., *Radiation safety: French experience and policy*, UNE, 1986.

135. PEEBLES, G. A., and POTIER, J. M., *Mining the Cigar Lake uranium deposit*, UNE, 1986.

136. *Report NRPB-GS6*, NRPB, Chilton, UK, 1987.

137. *Evaluation of occupational and environmental exposures to radon and radon daughters in the United States*, National Council on Radiation Protection and Measurement Report, No. 78, Bethesda, Md., 1984.

138. *The safety of nuclear power plants*, Uranium Institute, London, 1988.

139. HENNIES, H-H., *New results on ultimate reactor safety*, UNE, 1985.

140. ANDERSON, R., *et al.*, *International nuclear reactor hazard study*, Greenpeace, Hamburg, 1987.

141. ECKERED, T., *International co-operation for reactor safety: the World Association of Nuclear Operators*, UNE, 1988.

142. COLLIER, J. G. and DAVIES, L. M., *Chernobyl*, CEGB, London, 1987.
143. Soviet paper submitted to Chernobyl Post-accident Review Meeting, International Atomic Energy Agency, Vienna, 1986.
144. *Understanding Chernobyl*, Uranium Institute, London, 1986.
145. SCOTT, R. L., 'Brown's Ferry nuclear plant fire', in *Nuclear Safety*, September–October 1976, Office of Science and Technical Information, US Department of Energy, Washington, DC.
146. MARSHALL, W. (chairman), *An assessment of the integrity of PWR pressure vessels*, United Kingdom Atomic Energy Authority, London, 1982; and HIRSCH, P. B. (chairman), *Addendum to 1982 report*, 1987.
147. COTTRELL, A., *How safe is nuclear energy?*, Heinemann, London, 1981.
148. CAMERON P., HANCHER, L., and KÜHN, W., *Nuclear energy law after Chernobyl*, Graham and Trotman, London, 1988.
149. HOLT, M., *Price-Anderson Act renewal issues*, US Congressional Research Service, Washington, DC, 1988.
150. *Nuclear Power*, Information Sheet 16, Ecoropa, Crickhowell, Wales, 1987.
151. Royal Commission on Environmental Pollution, Sixth Report, *Nuclear power and the environment*, Cmnd. 6618, London, HMSO, 1976.
152. *Management and disposal of used nuclear fuel and reprocessing wastes*, Uranium Institute, London, 1989.
153. *Financing waste management, decommissioning and site rehabilitation in the nuclear industry*, Uranium Institute, London, 1987.
154. *Radioactive waste management*, Cmnd. 8607, HMSO, London, 1982.
155. *Report R227*, NRPB, HMSO, London, 1988.
156. MILES, J. C., MOLYNEAUX, T. C. K., and DOWLER, H. J., 'The resistance to impact of spent-fuel management transport flasks', British Nuclear Energy Society Symposium, 30 April 1985.
157. RINGWOOD, A. E., *Safe disposal of high-level nuclear reactor waste: a new strategy*, Australian National University Press, Canberra, 1978; and *Phil. Trans. Roy. Soc.*, Royal Society, London, 1986.
158. REEVE, K. D., and WALKER, D. G., *The Australian Atomic Energy Commission's SYNROC programme*, UNE, 1983.
159. ROBERTS, L. E. J., *Radwaste, spectre or symbol?*, evening discourse at the Royal Society, 20 March 1987, London.
160. *The Oklo phenomenon*, International Atomic Energy Agency, Vienna, 1975.
161. NERETNIEKS, I., *Disposal of used fuel in crystalline rock: technical and natural barriers to migration*, UNE, 1983.

162. CARTER, L. J., *Nuclear imperatives and public trust: dealing with radioactive waste*, Resources for the Future, Washington DC, 1987.

163. *The control of radioactive wastes*, Cmnd. 884, HMSO, London, 1959.

164. *Government response to Flowers Report*, Cmnd. 6820, HMSO, London, 1977.

165. *Review of the continued suitability of the dumping site for radioactive waste in the North-East Atlantic*, Nuclear Energy Agency, Paris, 1984.

166. *First report from the Environment Committee*, paper 191–I, HMSO, London, 1986.

167. *Seventh annual report of the Radioactive Waste Management Committee*, HMSO, London, 1986.

168. *The way forward* (1987); *Responses to The Way Forward* (1988); *Going forward* (1989), United Kingdom NIREX Ltd., Harwell, UK.

169. BURNS, M. E., *Low-level radioactive waste regulation: science, politics and fear*, Lewis Publishers, Chelsea, Mich., 1988.

170. GLICK, T. J., and POSTAR, M. R., 'Nuclear power-plant decommissioning', in *Nuclear News*, November, 1989.

171. ZETTERBERG, H. L., *Public opinion and nuclear energy: Sweden after Chernobyl*, UNE, 1986.

172. HARDING, C. G. F., *A welcoming approach to winning support*, UNE, 1987.

173. Reports in *Nucleonics Week*, 22 March, 12 April, and 3 May, 1990, McGraw-Hill, New York.

174. BOLSHOV, L. A., and PONOMAREV-STEPNOJ, *Nuclear safety in the USSR*, UNE, 1989.

175. Report in *Nucleonics Week*, 3 November 1988, McGraw-Hill, New York.

176. Report in *Nature*, 27 October 1988, Macmillan, London.

177. Report in *Nature*, 4 August 1988, Macmillan, London.

178. Report in *Nucleonics Week*, 16 March 1989, McGraw-Hill, New York.

179. TAEKO KANSHO, *Is it too late?*, Jiyusha, Tokyo, 1987.

180. WALLIS, L. R., *Public knowledge of nuclear power: fact and myth*, UNE, 1982.

181. RENN, O., *Public perception of the future of nuclear energy*, UNE, 1984.

182. Report in *World Watch*, July 1988.

183. CORNFORD, F. M., *Microcosmographia academica*, Bowes and Bowes, Cambridge and London, 1908.

184. PEARCE, D., BEURET, G., and EDWARDS, L., *Opposition to civilian*

nuclear power and the role of the public inquiry, Uranium supply and demand, Mining Journal Books, London, 1978.

185. THEBERGE, L. J., *The role of American media in covering nuclear power*, UNE, 1982.

186. GABOREAU, C., *Developing trust through communication*, UNE, 1988.

187. DIONNE-MARSOLAIS, R., *The challenge of communicating with the Canadian public*, UNE, 1988.

188. BACON, F., *Essays or counsels, civil and moral*, 1597.

189. *Eleven questions and answers on nuclear power*, Greenpeace, Lewes, UK, 1988.

190. BOYLE, M., and ROBINSON, M., *Nuclear energy in France: a foretaste of the future?*, in: *Nuclear power in crisis* (ref. 28 as above).

191. *Statistical review of world energy*, British Petroleum Company, London, 1989.

192. CLARK, R., letter to *The Times*, 6 June 1978.

193. *The nuclear crisis*, Technical Commission of the State Federation of Energy Industries of the General Union of Workers, Madrid, 1981.

194. GARRIDO, G., and VACCHIANO, C., *Structure of public opinion and the nuclear debate in Spain*, UNE, 1986.

195. CHARTIER, P., and MOISAN, F., *Technological progress and improvement in specific consumption*, World Energy Conference, Montreal, 1989.

196. *Energy needs and expectations*, World Energy Conference, Cannes, France, 1986.

197. *Global energy perspectives 2000–2020*, and *World energy horizons 2000–2020*, World Energy Conference, Montreal, 1989.

198. *Survey of energy resources*, World Energy Conference, London, 1989.

199. *Anaerobic digestion and biocatalysis,* Energy Technology Support Unit, Harwell, UK, 1985.

200. SORENSEN, B., *Renewable energy*, Academic Press, London and New York, 1979.

201. *Prospects for the exploitation of renewable energy technologies in the UK*, Energy Technology Support Unit, Harwell, UK, 1985.

202. FRANCOIS, P., PINTO, J., ZILKA, Y., and LIPSKY, L., *A financial model for large-scale solar power systems*, World Energy Conference, Montreal 1989.

203. LOVINS, A. B., *End use/least cost investment strategies*, World Energy Conference, Montreal, 1989.

204. FRANDSEN, S., HASTED, F., JOSEPHSEN, L., and NIELSEN, J. H., *Wind energy development*, World Energy Conference, Montreal, 1989.

205. *Wave energy*, Energy Technology Support Unit, Harwell, UK, 1985.

206. CLARE, R., ODELL, K. M., and WARDLE, D. G., *Recent technological*

aspects of the Severn barrage development project, World Energy Conference, Montreal, 1989.

207. CLARKE, J. F., *World progress toward fusion energy*, World Energy Conference, Montreal, 1989.

208. PEASE, R. S., 'Nuclear fusion comes closer', *Nature*, 11 December 1986, Macmillan, London.

209. HOLDREN, J. P., *et al.*, *Report of the Committee on environmental safety and economic aspects of magnetic fusion energy*, UCRL–53766, Lawrence Livermore National Laboratory, USA, 1989.

210. FLEISCHMANN, M., PONS, S., and HAWKINS, M., *Journal of electroanalytical chemistry*, vol. 261, p. 301, 1989; and *Nature*, Macmillan, 29 June 1989, London.

211. WILLIAMS, D. E., *et al.*, *Upper bounds on "cold fusion" in electrolytic cell*, *Nature*, 23 November 1989, Macmillan, London.

212. Report in *Nature*, 16 November 1989, Macmillan, London.

213. 'What has been happening to energy efficiency?' in *Energy in Europe*, Commission of European Communities, Brussels, July 1987.

214. *Managing planet earth*, special issue of *Scientific American*, September 1989, New York.

215. *Greenhouse effect*, Select Committee on Science and Technology, House of Lords, HMSO, London, 1989.

216. WIGLEY, T. M. L. and CURRIE, K., *Scientific assessment of climate change and its impacts*, Seminar on climate change, Downing Street, Department of the Environment, UK, 1989.

217. SCOTT, M. J., EDMONDS, J. A., KELLOGG, M. A., and SCHULTZ, R. W., *Global energy and the greenhouse issues*, World Energy Conference, Montreal, 1989.

218. Statement by World Conference on The Changing Atmosphere: Implications for Global Security, Toronto, June 1988.

219. JONES, P. D. *et al.*, *Nature*, 28 April 1988, Macmillan, London.

220. IDSO, S. B., 'Carbon dioxide—an alternative view', in *New Scientist*, 12 November 1981, London.

221. BARNOLA, J. M. *et al.*, 'Vostok ice core provides 160,000-year record of atmospheric carbon dioxide', *Nature*, 1 October 1987, Macmillan London.

222. RAYNAUD, D., *et al.*, 'Climatic and methane cycle implications of glacial-interglacial methane change in the Vostok ice-core', *Nature*, 16 June 1988, Macmillan, London.

223. CICERONE, R. J., 'Methane linked to warming', *Nature*, 21 July 1988, Macmillan, London.

224. BOLIN, B., DOOS, B. R., JAGER, J., and WARRICK, R. A., *The greenhouse effect, climatic change and ecosystems*, SCOPE 29, John Wiley, 1986.

225. State-of-the-art series, *Detecting the climatic effects of increasing carbon dioxide*, DOE/ER–0235; *Projecting the climatic effects of increasing carbon dioxide*, DOE/ER–0237; *Direct effects of increasing carbon dioxide in vegetation*, DOE/ER–0238; and *Atmospheric carbon dioxide and the global carbon cycle*, DOE/ER–0239, US Department of Energy, 1985.

226. *Glaciers, ice sheets, and sea-level: effect of a carbon dioxide-induced climate change*; US National Research Council (for US Department of Energy), DOE/ER/60235–1, 1985.

227. GREGORY, S., *Recent climatic change*, Belhaven Press, London, 1989.

228. SMITH, J. B., and TIRPAK, D. A. (eds.), *The potential effects of global climatic change in the United States*, US Environmental Protection Agency, 1989.

229. WIGLEY, T. M. L., and RAPER, S. C. B., 'Thermal expansion of sea-water associated with global warming', *Nature*, 12 November 1987, Macmillan, London.

230. WIGLEY, T. M. L., *European programme on climatic hazards*, Annual Meeting, Cork, Ireland, 3 October 1989.

231. HOUGHTON, R. A., and WOODWELL, G. M., 'Global climatic change', *Scientific American*, April 1989, New York.

232. *Energy in Europe*, Commission of the European Communities, Brussels, September 1989.

233. MINTZER, I. M., *A matter of degree*, World Resources Institute, Washington, DC, 1988.

234. *United Nations Reports of International Arbitral Awards*, United Nations, vol. 3, p. 1905 (1941).

235. TRIVELPEACE, A. W., *Evidence to US Senate Sub-committee on Environmental Protection*, 11 June 1986.

236. *Our common future*, Report by the World Commission on Environment and Development, Oxford, 1987.

Index

Aborigines, and Australian uranium, 143–8
absorption, of radiation, 373
accidents: and radiation risk, 217–20; *see also* Brazil (Goiania); Chernobyl; Three Mile Island (TMI); Windscale
acid rain, 88, 160, 305, 321
Ackoff, Richard, 319
Advanced Gas-cooled Reactor (AGR), 7, 121, 126–33, 136, 141, 367–8; coolant, 382; economics, 137, 156; on-load refuelling, 157; self-annealing of radiation damage, 381
Africa, oil production and reserves, 325
Ailleret, Pierre, 49
ALARA principle, 216, 257
Alfvén, Hannes, 18, 20, 70, 304
Algeria, natural gas exports, 328
Alkem company, 92
alpha radiation, 207, 373
ANDRA, agency for radioactive waste, France, 264
Andreotti, Giulio, 83
Angers, anti-waste demonstration (1990), 59
annealing, of graphite, 380–1
Antarctic ice-cores, evidence for climatic change, 353
anti-nuclear campaign, 12, 20–2, 65, 71–3, 81, 85–90, 92, 97–9, 116–18, 304, 309–11, 316; anxieties over safety, 240; *see also* Campaign for Nuclear Disarmament; public opinion
Arctic ice-sheet, 355
Argentina: and enrichment, 178; Ezeiza reprocessing plant, 181; NPT non-signatory, 188, 190; Tlatelolco non-signatory, 192
Armand, Louis, 49
Arrhenius, Svante, 348
Asia, oil production and reserves, 325
atom, 368
atomic number, 370
Atoms for Peace conferences, 95
Attlee, Clement, 47, 122

Australia: Aborigines and uranium, 143–8; Atomic Energy Commission, 143; coal production, 167, 326–7; Kakadu national park, 145, 147; Northern Land Council, 146; nuclear fuel cycle plant prohibited, 147; and Nuclear Suppliers Group, 195; oil production and reserves, 325; and Pacific nuclear weapons-free zone, 192; and TMI, 146; uranium 'Club', 33; uranium exports and anti-proliferation policy, 145, 147, 197; uranium export ban to France, 146; uranium export interruption, 66, 143, 145; uranium exports and pricing policy, 36, 38, 148; uranium exports and the USA, 35; uranium mining policy, 142–9; Uranium Policy Review Committee, 147; uranium production, 26–8; Ranger inquiry, 144–5; three mines policy, 146–7; and waste treatment, 259
Australia, legislation: Atomic Energy Act (1953), 142; Companies (Foreign Takeovers) Act (1972), 143; Environmental Protection (Impact of Proposals) Act (1974), 143; Aboriginal Land Rights (Northern Territory) Act (1976), 144
AVLIS, *see* enrichment

back end (of fuel cycle), 24, 41–3, 92
Bacon, Francis, 306
Bangladesh, threat from global warming, 15
Baruch Plan (1946), 187
base-load, 154
Bavaria, and public opinion, 301–2
Beatty waste storage site, 275
becquerel, 22, 373
Belgian Congo (now Zaïre), radium industry, 28
Belgium, 13, 294, 309; and Eurodif, 53; and France (joint programme), 50; nuclear economics, 166; nuclear electricity percentage, 4; ONDRAF/

material unaccounted for (MUF), and proliferation, 183–4
Mauna Loa observatory, 348
Maxey Flats waste storage site, 271, 275–6
media attitudes to nuclear power, 21–2, 297–302
Medical Research Council (UK), 207
megawatt, 4
Mendès-France, Pierre, 48
merit order, 154
methane: greenhouse gas, 348–9, 359; from municipal waste, as energy source, 330
Mexico, and geothermal energy, 337
Middle East: natural gas production and reserves, 328; oil exploration, 324; oil production, 324–5, 343
milling, 24, 26
mines, uranium, *see* uranium mines
Mitterand, President François, 53, 57, 58
mixed oxide fuel (MOX), 183
moderator, 122, 177, 377, 383
Mol, waste disposal site, 263
Molin, Rune, 78
Monitored Retrieval Storage, 274; *see also* USA; waste management
Mont Louis, 41
Monte Bello weapons test, 122
Montreal Laboratory, 47
Montreal Protocol (on limitation of CFCs), 350, 359, 361
MUF, *see* material unaccounted for
Mururoa Atoll, French weapons tests, 146

Nader, Ralph, 304, 308
Nagasaki: 16, 175–6, 291; radiation casualty statistics, 205–6, 215
NAGRA, 99, 267; *see also* Switzerland
Nakasone, Yasuhiro, 61
Namibia, uranium production, 26–7, 224; US import ban (to 1990), 36
National Nuclear Corporation (UK), 130, 132
National Power (UK), 138–41
National Radiological Protection Board, 216–17; *see also* UK
natural gas: consumption, 323; production outlook, 328–9
Natural Resources Defense Council, 307–8, 311

naturally occurring radiation, 209–10
Nautilus (submarine), 7
negative fuel temperature coefficient, 385
neptunium–239, 379
Netherlands: government defeat on green issues (1989), 358; and Tlatelolco Treaty, 192; and Urenco consortium, 28, 41; and wind energy, 334
neutron: definition, 368; delayed, 384; lifetime in reactor, 384; neutron reflector, 378; prompt, 384; thermal, 377.
Nevada, and waste disposal, 273–4
New York State, waste storage policy, 275
Niger: uranium production, 26–7; collaboration with France, 53
NIREX, 269–70, 280; *see also* UK
Nixon, President Richard, 10, 85
non-proliferation of nuclear weapons: controls on nuclear fuel, 39–40, 199–200; *see also* proliferation
Non-Proliferation of Nuclear Weapons Treaty (NPT—1968), 179, 186–7; future of, 210; and Japan, 65; NPT Exporters Committee and controls on nuclear trade, 194–5; provisions, 189–90
non-stochastic radiation effects, 210
Noordwijk Conference (1989), 360
North America, contribution to carbon dioxide production, 363
Norway, and heavy water exports, 177
Nuclear Electric, 141
nuclear electricity production, 3–5, 323; oil energy equivalent, 5; *see also* individual countries
Nuclear Energy Agency (OECD), 278, 309; and radiation risk, 207; and waste management, 279
nuclear fuel cycle, 24, 27–8; *see also* conversion; enrichment; reprocessing; uranium; waste
nuclear fuel elements (bundles), 41, 376, 380–1
Nuclear Installations Inspectorate (UK), 129
Nuclear Non-Proliferation Act (NNPA—1978): effect on US and foreign nuclear trade, 198–9
nuclear power's contribution to world energy, 323, 343–4; role in

Reagan, President Ronald, 250, 351
redundancy, and reactor safety, 228
reference accident, 238
reflector, neutron, 378
reforestation, to combat global warming, 356
refuelling on-load of reactors, and proliferation, 182
relative biological effectiveness, 207
rem, definition, 208
renewable energy, 76, 154, 172, 323, 331–8
reprocessing: of spent fuel, 24, 28, 42, 58, 92–3, 135–6, 258–9, 380; by Argentina, 181; and INFCE, 199; and weapons proliferation, 42–3; *see also* Cap de la Hague; Dounreay; Sellafield; West Valley
research reactors, and proliferation risk, 182
Revelle, Roger, 348
Richland waste storage site, 271, 273, 275
Rickover, Admiral Hyman, 7, 175, 245
risk, and radiation, 203–25
risks, of normal living, 203–4
Rocard, Michel, 59, 264
roentgen, 22
Rolls Royce, Safe Integral Reactor, 244
Rome, Treaty of, and nuclear fuel movement, 196
Roosevelt, President Franklin D., 47
Roser, Thomas, 89

safeguards: against proliferation, 28, 181, 185–6, 193; full-scope, 179, 189; inspections, 39–40; in Latin America, 192; progressive strengthening, 201
safety, of nuclear reactors, *see* reactor safety
Saskatchewan, uranium production, 26, 30, 224
Saudia Arabia, 361
Savannah River, waste management, 271
Scargill, Arthur, 133–4
Schmidt, Helmut, 86–8
Schneeberg disease, 221

9, 133, 138, 170; geothermal energy,
338; nuclear fusion, 338; nuclear
power's influence on coal-mining
industry, 133–4; tidal energy, 336;
wave energy, 335–6; wind energy,
334

United Kingdom, non-proliferation
policy: agreement with Australia
(1977), 197; and Canadian uranium
controls, 196; and the NPT, 188; and
safeguards, 189; and Tlatelolco
Treaty, 192

United Kingdom, reactor policy and
engineering: Calder Hall reactor, 7,
123; consortia policy fails, 125–6;
EEC and Euratom (non-member), 49;
fuel policy (1965), 128; history, 120–
42; 'inherently safe' reactors, 244;
and light-water systems, 127; military
plutonium production, 177; miners'
strike (1984–5) and nuclear power,
161, 173, 320, 344; national
economic plan (1965), 128; National
Nuclear Corporation formed, 130,
132; nuclear economics, 163–4, 166;
nuclear electricity percentage, 4;
Nuclear Power Advisory Board, 125,
130; nuclear programme begins
(1955), 123; nuclear programme
continues (1964), 126; privatization
of electricity industry, 19, 136–42,
159, 169; and public opinion, 285,
293, 299–300, 313; PWR adopted,
132–5; Sizewell B inquiry statistics,
173–4; Suez crisis, 124; UK Atomic
Energy Authority formed, 125; Vinter
Committee on reactor policy, 129; *see
also* CEGB

United Kingdom, safety policy: cancer
and nuclear installations, 212;
emergency planning regulations, 238;
Health and Safety Executive, 207,
245; National Radiological
Protection Board (NRPB), 207;
Natural Environment Research
Council, 354; Nuclear Installations
Inspectorate (NII), 129, 131, 136,
245; radiation regulations, 216

United Kingdom, waste management,
252, 254, 258, 260, 267–70, 280;
NIREX, 269–70; Radioactive Waste
Management Advisory Committee,
268–9; Royal Commission on

Environmental Pollution, 254, 267–
8, 304; *see also* Drigg; Sellafield
United Nations Conference on the
Human Environment (1972), 254; *see
also* Brundtland Commission
United Nations Conference on the
Promotion of International Co-
operation in the Peaceful Uses of
Nuclear Energy (UNCPICPUNE),
195
United Nations Environment
Programme, 350, 352, 362
United Nations Scientific Committee on
the Effects of Atomic Radiation
(UNSCEAR), 206, 213
United Reprocessors, and US Nuclear
Non-Proliferation Act, 198
United States of America, legislation:
McMahon Act (1946), 47; Atomic
Energy Act (1954), 105, 115, 118;
Price–Anderson Act (1957), 111–12,
250; Private Ownership of Special
Nuclear Materials Act (1964), 29;
Ocean Dumping Act (1972), 272;
Energy Reorganization Act (1974),
106; National Climate Program Act
(1978), 349; Nuclear Non-
Proliferation Act (1978), 42–3, 66,
198; Public Utilities Regulatory
Policies Act (PURPA—1978), 159–
60, 341; Low-level Radioactive
Waste Policy Act (1980), 274;
Nuclear Waste Policy Act (1982),
114, 272; Resource Conservation and
Recovery Act (1984), 276;
Comprehensive Antiapartheid Act
(1986), 36, 40; National Appliance
Energy Conservation Act (1987), 342
United States of America, non-fission
energy policy and supply: carbon
dioxide emissions, 358; coal
production and reserves, 167, 326;
efficient use of electricity, 341–2;
energy efficiency, 295; fusion
research, 338; geothermal energy,
337–8; methane as energy source,
330; national energy plan (1989–90),
120; natural gas production and
reserves, 328; solar energy and
taxation, 332, 334; wind energy, 334
United States of America, nuclear power
industry: history 103–120; nuclear
economics, 166; nuclear electricity